THE RED EYE

LOVE UNITED HATE GLAZER

LOVE UNITED HATE GLAZER

BY DAVID BLATT

EMPIRE
PUBLICATIONS

First published in 2013

This book is copyright under the Berne Convention. All rights are reserved. Apart from any fair dealing for the purpose of private study, research, criticism or review, as permitted under the Copyright Act, 1956, no part of this publication may be reproduced, stored in a retrieval system, or transmitted, in any form or by any means, electronic, electrical, chemical, mechanical, optical, photocopying, recording or otherwise, without the prior permission of the copyright owner. Enquiries should be sent to the publishers at the undermentioned address:

EMPIRE PUBLICATIONS
1 Newton Street, Manchester M1 1HW
© David Blatt 2013

ISBN: 978-1-909360-15-0

Cover images by Jasmine Blatt.
Printed in Great Britain.

CONTENTS

REDICATION   6

INTRODUCTION   7

INDIA

Mumbai - Feb 10. Aston Villa 1 Manchester United 1 13
Goa - Feb 16. AC Milan 2 Manchester United 3. Champions League 20
Goa - Feb 20. Everton 3 Manchester United 1 23
Goa - Feb 23. Manchester United 3 West Ham United 0 27
Goa - Feb 28. Manchester United 2 Aston Villa 1. Carling Cup Final 27
Gokarna - Mar 6. Wolverhampton Wanderers 0 Manchester United 1 32
Cochin - Mar 10. Manchester United 4 AC Milan 0. Champions League 34
Pondercherry - Mar 14. Manchester United 3 Fulham 0 39
Delhi - Mar 21. Manchester United 2 Liverpool 1 46
Agra - Mar 27. Bolton Wanderers 0 Manchester United 4 55
Udiapur - Bayern Munich 2 Manchester United 1. Champions League 62
Shrinagar - Apr 3. Manchester United 1 Chelsea 2 66
Shrinagar - Apr 7. Manchester United 3 Bayern Munich 2. Champions League. 72

THAILAND

Koh Phi Phi - Apr 11. Blackburn Rovers 0 Manchester United 0 80
Koh Phi Phi - Apr 17. Manchester City 0 Manchester United 1 81
Bangkok - Apr 24. Manchester United 3 Tottenham Hotspur 1 84

LAOS

Louang Phabang - May 2. Sunderland 0 Manchester United 1 93
Viantiene - May 9. Manchester United 4 Stoke City 0 102

VIETNAM   103

CAMBODIA   111

HONG KONG   114

MACAU   118

CHINA   121

JAPAN   142

AUSTRALIA 149

Perth - Jun 23. England 1 Slovenia 0 149
Cairns - Jun 27. Germany 4 England 1 150
Brisbane - Jul 17 Manchester United 3 Glasgow Celtic 1 158
Sydney - Jul 22. Philadelphia Union 0 Manchester United 1 149

NEW ZEALAND 149

Lake Taupo - Jul 26. Kansas City Wizards 2 Manchester United 1 160

COOK ISLANDS 174

Raratonga - Jul 29. MLS All Stars 2 Manchester United 5 175

TAHITI 177

Papeete - Jul 31. Chivas de Guadalajars 3 Manchester United 2 179
Paea - Aug 4. Airtricity League X1 1 Manchester United 7 181
Paea - Aug 8. Manchester United 3 Chelsea 1. Community Shield 182

MOOREA 186

Putea - Aug 18. Manchester United 3 Newcastle United 0 189
Putea - Aug 22. Fulham 2 Manchester United 2 194
Putea - Aug 28. Manchester United 3 West Ham United 0 202

HUAHINE 215

Fare - Sep 11. Everton 3 Manchester United 3 215

EASTER ISLAND 217

Hanga Rua - Sep 14. Manchester United 0 Glasgow Rangers 0. Champions League .. 217

CHILE 220

Santiago - Sep 19. Manchester United 3 Liverpool 2 222
Valpariso - Sep 22. Scunthorpe United 2 Manchester United 5............................. 229
La Serena - Sep 26. Bolton Wanderers 2 Manchester United 2 231
San Pedro de Alcama - Sep 29. Valencia 0 Manchester United 1. Champions League . 235
San Pedro de Alcama - Oct 2. Sunderland 0 Manchester United 0 236

PERU 250

Cusco - Oct 16. Manchester United 2 West Bromwich Albion 2 254
Lima - Oct 20. Manchester United 1 Bursaspor o. Champions League qualifier 260

ECUADOR 263

Quito - Oct 24. Stoke City 1 Manchester United 2 266
Tena - Oct 26. Manchester United 3 Wolverhampton Wanderers 2. Carling Cup 268
Quito - Oct 30. Manchester United 2 Tottenham Hotspur 0 269

ARGENTINA 271

Ushuaia - Nov 2. Bursaspor 0 Manchester United 3 272

CHILE   275
Puerto Natales - Nov 6. Manchester United 2 Wolverhampton Wanderers 1 .... *275*

ARGENTINA   281
Puerto Madryn - Nov 10. Manchester City 0 Manchester United 0 .... *281*
Puerto Madryn - Nov 13. Aston Villa 2 Manchester United 2 .... *285*
Buenos Aires - Nov 16. River Plate 1 Boca Juniors 0 .... *287*
Buenos Aires - Nov 20. Manchester United 2 Wigan Athletic 0 .... *294*

BRAZIL
Puerto Iguazu to Sao Paulo - Nov 24. Glasgow Rangers 0 Manchester United 1. ...... *301*
Sao Paulo to Paraty. Bus - Nov 27. Manchester United 7 Blackburn Rovers 1 .... *301*
Rio de Janeiro - Nov 30. West Ham United 4 Manchester United 0. Carling Cup *306*
Salvador del Bahai - Dec 7.   Manchester United 1 Valancia 1 .... *308*
Caracas-Bogota-San Salvador-Cancun Dec 13. Manchester United 1 Arsenal 0 .... *314*

MEXICO
Tulum - Dec 26. Manchester United 2 Sunderland *321*
Cozumel - Dec 28. Birmingham City 1 Manchester United 1 .... *322*
Tulum - Dec 1. West Bromwich Albion 1 Manchester United 2 .... *324*

COLOMBIA
Cancun-Bogota - Jan 4. Manchester United 2 Stoke City 1 .... *325*
Villa De Leyva - Jan 9. Manchester United 1 Liverpool 0 .... *326*
Isla de Baru - Jan 16. Tottenham Hotspur 0 Manchester United 0 .... *328*
Medelin - Jan 22. Manchester United 5 Birmingham City 0 .... *330*
Cali - Jan 25. Blackpool 2 Manchester United 3 .... *332*

GALAPAGOS ISLANDS
Jan 29. Southampton 1 Manchester United 2. FA Cup 3rd round *337*
Feb 1. Manchester United 3 Aston Villa 1 .... *340*
Feb 5. Wolverhampton Wanderers 2 Manchester United 1 .... *341*

ENGLAND
Manchester - Feb 12. Manchester United 2 Manchester City 1 .... *343*

REDICATION

FIRST AND FOREMOST, to my long suffering wife, Hélène, who's had to put up with my Red rants from the moment we met. If she had known then what she knows now… (let's not go there)

Also to our daughters, Melanie and Jasmine, for accepting, with various degrees of difficulty, that the natural order of things had been knocked on its head, namely that parents stay at home, children play away. Our granddaughter, Lilyella, whose mouth became a teenager long before we set off on our world tour, and continuously delights us with her unique take on the world.

A special thank you must go to planet Earth for producing such wonderful and terrible sights, sounds and smells, people and places.

And no greater reason could there be for leaving behind some of the world's most wondrous sites, than the opportunity to return to M16 0RA. Only Manchester United can do this, because Manchester United reaches parts (of the world) that other teams cannot reach.

And to all those that say it can't be done – yes, it can!

INTRODUCTION

'Travel is a bit like sex. Even when it's bad, it's good.
Manchester United is a bit like sex. Even when it's bad, it's good.'

AS SOON AS THE FOOTBALL SEASON starts I have to get back. Dusky maidens, beautiful beaches, lost civilisations (e.g. 35 years without a trophy Manchester City supporters, 20 years without a league title Liverpool supporters) all pale into insignificance compared to the M1/M6 and the inevitable roadworks between Watford and Luton, meat & potato pies, chips and curry.

Then, a couple of years ago, I had a revelation. I had to get global wanderlust out of my system whilst most of my bits were still in working order. I may be totally obsessed by Manchester United but I retain a semblance of awareness of the outside world, and it was time the outside world and yours truly got it together. There are Reds who go to more matches than me but few can claim to spend more of their waking and sleeping hours living, breathing and shitting United. But now was the time to go cold turkey. A year of voluntary withdrawal. A lot of people wait until retirement, then travel passively absorbing experiences like a sponge. The equivalent of the armchair football fan. OK, it's got its merits, but I'd much rather lose it by totally immersing myself in experiences than having my nose pressed up against the window pane. My motto being, "If something's worth doing, it's worth overdoing!"

For someone whose only qualification when leaving school was 'O' level in "Who Gives a Shit", this is somewhat of a paradox. But I'd like to get one thing straight before we go any further. I'm not one for extreme sports. Bungee jumping, snowboarding off-piste, even synchronized swimming I prefer to leave to others. On the other hand, I'm not one for SAGA style antiseptic, bland, safe, cocooned escorted tours either.

When it comes to football, I'm not a reformed nutter, nor am I an anorak. (Despite what my wife says) Call me an in-betweenee if you must. Like thousands of other football supporters I'm just totally obsessed with my football team.

Manchester United has been a microcosm for everything that has happened to me in my life. They've just happened to have taken me to higher highs and lower lows than anything else on this planet, even sex. A concentration of emotions and experiences so overwhelming that at times I thought I might explode. They've dominated my waking hours (and sleeping hours if the truth be known – which it is now I suppose), a fact that my wife can never come to terms with, hence "Manchester United Ruined My Wife", the title of my first book.

How Hélène has put up with it all I'll never know. Actually that's not quite true. I do know. I have the marks to prove it, although you'll never find them. She's been practising on me for over 40 years and got it down to a fine art. Quentin Tarantino, eat your heart out.

So this book is for us and about us. An account of the most fun two people can have with their clothes both off and on. At no stage did she attempt to stop the world and try to get off, although we did have a number of discussions along the lines of:

"I don't believe it! Look where we are, and all you can think of is +*!**!+ Manchester United!"

She'd have made a good female Victor Meldrew.

I also had a not so secret mission. To catch as many United matches as possible, live, on our travels around the world, and to meet as many of United's 75/330/659 million fans (delete as appropriate) as possible and gauge their level of support.

Could United ever mean to them what United means to me? I doubted it but I vowed to keep an open mind.

So, I hear you ask. Where did we get the money together for this global expedition? Good question. Quite simply, we made ourselves homeless, with all the benefits that can bring. Despite the worst efforts of the banks, the collapse of the sub-prime market in the States, the resulting recession, a two year wait and a £100,000 hit on the value of our property in London, we sold our flat, paid back the naughty bank, bought two Round The World tickets out of the remains and Bob's your auntie.

Basically Hélène and I decided to step off the upwardly mobile conveyor belt. You know...work, career, 2.4 children (well, just two in our case plus one granddaughter) up-grading property, Hi-Fi, car, TV, wives, etc... although regarding the latter I've had the same model I married back in July 1976.

Although I spent the majority of my career in advertising and marketing, for the last twelve years I have been a TEFL (teaching English as a foreign language) Teacher and this has put me in touch with students from all over the world. For most of them, vocabulary and conversation are the most important elements in order to communicate with colleagues, clients and suppliers. So my priority has always been to get them to talk.

And what do you talk about with someone from abroad who wants to learn about British culture?

Why, football and music of course!

And who better to give them a thoroughly Red Eye'd view of this sceptred isle of ours than yours truly.

From time to time I have even taken students of mine with me to Old Trafford as part of their "Red"ucation. All South Korean students wanted to see Ji Sung Park, French students want to see Patrice Evra, Italians want to see Macheda, only this little piggy got too big for his boots and was sent out on loans to reduce the size of his head. And, of course, they all wanted to see Ronaldo in the flesh. (No, playing! Some people!)

However, reverse osmosis came into play as I got more and more fascinated by the origins of my students, especially those from outside of Europe. What would it be like to experience their lifestyles? To be fair, Hélène and I have travelled quite a bit, although it has mainly been two weeks here, occasionally three weeks there, the odd weekend break and my midweek pilgrimages following United in Europe.

You have to know that, apart from sex and football and rock 'n roll, travel is one of my great passions. In September 2000 Hélène and I, together with our younger daughter Jasmine who was only fourteen at the time, decamped to the South of France. Melanie, our eldest, stayed in London as she had her singing career to think of. From our base in Cannes, I literally fell into English teaching by default, and to my surprise I found I rather liked it. The pay is "merde" but it keeps our heads above water rates and other utility bills.

Sun, sea, sand and...satellite TV. Three hundred sunny days a year, and if I booked my Easyjet flights enough in advance, cheap monthly return flights to Luton or Liverpool and on to Eric's own country and Old Trafford. What more could a Red want?

Then in September 2006 we returned to England. This was originally only intended to be a short stay whilst my wife took care of our granddaughter, Lilyella, and Melanie went back in to the recording studio with a reformed All Saints.

Unfortunately, due to the recession, our flat remained unsold for two years. In the end, in December 2009 we finally sold it for £100,000 less than the original asking price set by greedy Hampstead estate agents. At least we could pay back the mortgage, and although we didn't now have enough money to ever buy another property in London, we did have enough equity to buy two Round The World tickets and put the rest into a savings account to act as our spending money for one year.

So, I hear you ask. What about when you come back next year. What will you do? Where will you live?

Who knows? Who cares? We may not even live that long.

However, I don't believe in reincarnation. Unlike James Bond I believe you only live once and you have to give it your best shot. Life is a balance between living for today and planning for tomorrow. We're all different, so what works for me may not work for you. But for all those of you that have a dream, go for it. It's better to try and fail than never try at all. You'll always live with the gnawing regret...if only!

Whether it's travelling round the world, running your own business, going for that boy/girl that everyone says is out of your league...go for it. What's the worst that could happen?

And (think about this) what's the best that could happen?

BEFORE WE BEGIN...

I would like you to picture this. With very few exceptions, throughout the following 365 days I wore a United shirt of one form or another. Not an overpriced Glazer guzzling replica polyester top from the Megastore but a selection of retro 70s gear, politically correct and incorrect United T-shirts and my Green & Gold.

I adopted this one-man fashion statement in an attempt to evoke a response from folk along the way. Positive or negative, it didn't matter. For Hélène, who hates football with the same intensity I adore it, this was a decided negative of course. To the extent that she threatened not to come out with me on a number of occasions if I wore another United top!

It was a delicate balancing act I can tell you, but one I was determined to pursue in the name of research, and love. I've been asked many times, who do you love more, your wife or United? That's the most difficult one for any Red to answer, but put it this way. I have dozens of United shirts but not one with my wife printed on the front. Bet you haven't either so don't have a go at me!

Meanwhile, I have to report one disappointing aspect of my pre-planning. For many years, the start of the season would be heightened with the arrival of my Manchester United membership pack. Glossily produced gumph that I briefly scanned then discarded, but pride of place would be the Year Book. Details of each and every match from the season just passed, every United player from first team squad down through all the reserves and Under this and Under that's, and proudly sitting at the back, page upon page of our official supporters clubs in the UK and Northern Ireland, Ireland and the rest of the world.

We have more supporters than any club on the planet and here was proof. But, disturbingly, in the last few years these pages had begun to diminish. I couldn't work out why until my old Red mate Graham, who had emigrated to Oz about 15 years previously and opened the official Western Australia Manchester United Supporters Club, revealed that a minion from the club had enjoyed an all-expenses paid jaunt around the world, dropping in on each and every "official" supporters club and revoking their official status unless they could prove they had a minimum of 100 paid up members and didn't meet in such squalid places such as "pubs!"

Pubs! Oh, perish the thought...

It transpired the suits at Old Trafford were on a mission to extract as much lolly out of supporters as possible, and any branch that didn't match their strict (dictionary translation = money making) criteria were struck off the list.

"You only form supporters clubs so you can obtain tickets!" he wailed, as though the very thought of distributing tickets around the Empire was akin to slavery or drug trafficking.

How do you answer that?

The end result was that United deleted a significant number of supporters clubs from the official list, thereby making my joint mission that bit harder. What joint mission is that? I hear you yawn. To contact each and every supporters club in those countries around the world we intended to visit, and attempt to meet up and talk, smile, sign language all things United. You know... how did you become a United fan, where do watch the matches, what do you mean you've never heard of the Glazers - that sort of thing.

Now, with an inflated sense of my own importance, I was also aware that in the eyes of the world I was about to enter, I represented United, England, Team GB, the lot. So I was determined to leave a good impression as well as many LUHG stickers as possible.

Hélène wasn't too keen on my master plan, but I tried to convince her that having someone on the ground meant that we could scratch beneath the surface, get to know the place and its people a little better. And we wouldn't only be talking United. I'm sure we'd find time to talk about, well, other things too.

And this was how I intended to use my new United contacts. Meet up with as many as possible and take advantage of their hospitality. I mean, meeting someone like me who had actually been to Old Trafford, surely that was worth one or two brownie points, let alone free food and drink. I'm nothing if not mercenary.

But here's the rub. For those branches with one or more e-mail addresses I e-mailed the addresses. For those with just postal addresses I posted letters. Now I accept that not all branches would have someone who spoke English, but with United being the international language I expected, nay assumed, I would receive a modicum of replies.

Not one.

Yes, you read that right. Not one.

That was bitterly disappointing. Individual excuses I could accept, but not to receive one single response. Hmmm…

OK, we're off.

INDIA

WEDNESDAY 10 FEBRUARY 2010 - LONDON-MUMBAI
ASTON VILLA 1 MANCHESTER UNITED 1

You know how it's so hard to wake up in the morning when you really don't want to, yet it's so easy when there's sex, football or holidays on the menu.

Come in number three. I had set the alarm for 05.15. No need. I was sitting bolt upright with an advertiser's toothpaste smile on my face and it wasn't even five o' clock yet. I leapt out of bed, ran down the stairs without tripping and had the kettle on the boil before you could say, "Malcolm Glazer has United's best interest at heart".

Five minutes later, there were two teas and two slices of toast winging their way back upstairs courtesy of yours truly. (Hélène claims this is the only activity I do voluntarily around the house as she is so much more practical than I am. I'll let you into a secret - it's true. When it comes to doing "manly" things around the house like, you know, fixing things, changing things, putting up things, things..... you know. Well, I'm just not a "things" person.)

Suitably charged for the momentous day ahead, I woke Melanie, Lilyella and Jasmine and we all had breakfast in dribs and drabs. (No, it's not the name of a super cool café in Belsize Park or a slang term for pyjamas.) Tickets, visas, jabs, etc. had been checked and double-checked the night before. I got my umpteenth bollocking off Hélène for not doing enough photocopies of our documents and putting everything in the wrong place, but as this is par for our intercourse. I just gave her my best lapdog impersonation and murmured an apology.

One element took pride of place though, the 100 LUHG stickers I had ordered a couple of weeks back which Hélène knew nothing about. I secreted them about my person and in various compartments of our luggage. A global guerilla campaign was about to be unleashed on an unsuspecting world that Che Guevara himself would have been proud of.

The mini-cab duly arrived at 06.15am. More hugs, though it was hard to kiss the girls goodbye and Hélène found it difficult to find reasons to be cheerful but we left with one of my suitable parting shots.

"See you next year."

We got to Terminal five at Heathrow in no time at all at this hour of the morning, so after the usual check-in and security checks Hélène and I treated ourselves to a full English breakfast. This was my first time inside the much-maligned Terminal Five and fortunately others had suffered so that our passage went rather smoothly.

The morning was bright and sunny from our mezzanine terrace. I had butterflies in my stomach and I could have sworn they were not part of the menu. I made a couple of phone calls to the likes of Barclaycard & Nationwide. informing them we would be away for a year and not to reject any payments from strange places. They demanded to know the list of destinations and dates so I filled them in the best I could, informing them that the system was flexible and not to hold it against me. I then tried to pay my latest Barclaycard credit card bill over the phone only their convoluted and over pedantic security system made this impossible.

I cringed knowing that I might have to try to do this from Mumbai in India.

Brilliant, I thought. I wondered how many of these incidents were to become the norm over the next twelve months.

We then scoured the shops for two cheap waterproof watches. We'd left our Seikos at home as we didn't want to appear affluent. Our policy was to look poorer than those around us, thereby diminishing the likelihood of getting robbed or mugged. That was my master plan and I was sticking to it.

Two cut-price twenty quid 50 metre Sekonda diving watches later we were scouring the vast duty free area looking for any bargains we had space to carry. We thought we'd thought of everything, but as Brian Clough once remarked, "A bargain in the last minute is worth a bargain anytime."

No, nothing. I viewed some United gear in a sports shop but I was torn between lining Glazers' pockets and adding to my already bursting at the seams luggage. I let the moment pass, but not before I had stuck the first of my 100 LUHG stickers in a prominent position within the football section. 1 down, 99 to go.

The British Airways flight was long but uneventful. The headphones in economy were not conducive to intricate speech patterns, so I gave up on the film and listened to the new Muse album instead before attempting a little shut-eye. Sleeping sitting up is not one of my favoured past times and I drifted in and out for the rest of the flight. Hélène claims I fell into a deep sleep, with my eyes wide shut and my mouth wide open. I dispute this. I was aware of sounds and movements throughout. Hélène claims I was dreaming. I dispute all her claims. I was there, right?

We landed around two in the morning, and so did our luggage.

"How long will our luck hold?" I thought to myself, as we pushed our trolleys out into the arrivals concourse. We were met by two smiling gentlemen who led us to their car, and before we knew it we had entered the mad bad world of kamikaze stock car racing that is Mumbai traffic.

Amongst all the usual questions they asked us how we liked the heat.

"We love it", we replied in unison, although I noticed both men were sweating. I thought they'd be used to the heat but then one of them informed us that India was sweltering in an unusually severe heatwave.

It seemed to me we were on a funfair ride as we bumped and grinded our way through the twenty four hour traffic jam without actually bumping or grinding into anything. How, I don't know, as we came within inches of every car we passed. When we commented on this the driver said the equivalent of "A miss is as good as a mile." It soon became apparent there was just one rule when it came to driving in India; there are no rules. People were driving with one arm, the other occupied with speaking on a mobile phone, horns blaring incessantly, spitting out of the window or simply gesticulating to everybody and no-one in particular.

Depending on your point of view, driving in India is both awful and brilliant at the same time. A paradox that we were going to have to come to terms with on everything we were to encounter in India.

After about forty five minutes we arrived at this dark, run down industrial estate. Some uniformed guard opened two large black rusty metal gates and we drove round till we came to this anonymous office block that turned out to be our 2 star hotel I had booked on the internet a couple of weeks back.

Let's just say "nondescript" was a wild exaggeration. Luckily it was dark outside as I emptied our bags from the car, 'cos I didn't want to be in a position to fully evaluate our surroundings. It was now around four in the morning and with sleep and excitement fighting for supremacy and I wanted to keep the illusion in tact.

We were led to our shoe box, sorry, hotel room on the second floor where Hélène and I agreed to go straight to bed and start the adventure proper once it was light. But not before she had examined every nook and cranny before divesting herself of a single element of clothing. The bed and mattress came in for special attention, resulting in us opening one of the large rucksacks and spreading our own double silk sheet over it. Little was I to know this would become a ritual that would continue for the next 364 days, and nights. And with no Wi-Fi on offer I went to bed scoreless, on both accounts.

THURSDAY 11 FEBRUARY. MUMBAI, INDIA

Woke up at a reasonable hour, daylight revealing a dreadful flea-pit of an overpriced 2★ hotel. Opened the filthy curtains to witness the majesty of broken corrugated iron roofs with obligatory pigeons, a dirty courtyard with a few parked cars and little else. Ordered a complimentary breakfast of one vegetable sandwich, one egg sandwich, (spelt 'sandwhitches' on the menu), a bottle of water and one cup of tea with milk, which at 20 rupees was actually 5 rupees cheaper than tea without milk. Doesn't say much for their milk, does it?

By now my brain had woken up and the overriding need to discover the result of the Villa game was omnipresent. Hélène had left me in no doubt as to what would happen to me if she discovered me using my British mobile to access the web and United's results. So I did the only thing left to a man like me. I hid my mobile where the sun don't shine and went for a crap. And crap turned out to be the operative word, as there was no signal in the toilet.

Shit!

Now, although our internal Spicejet flight from Mumbai to Goa wasn't until 16.25 that afternoon, we didn't want to spend a moment longer in the shabby (but without the 'chic') hotel, so we ordered a taxi for 1 o' clock for the half hour ride to the domestic terminal. This gave us two hours to walk around this hot, dusty and characterless Mumbai neighbourhood. Open sewers, broken pavements, mad drivers constantly on the horn, friendly smiling faces and greetings. In fact everything I was expecting India to be.

We encountered our first beggars on the way back to the hotel. Two incredibly beautiful, dark skinned children, no older than 3 and 5 respectively, failed in their attempts to break into my T-Shirt United, anti-Glazer wallet. We arrived back at the hotel at 12.30 only to find the taxi waiting for us already. We must be his big job of the day.

Not very hardcore I know, but Hélène and I decided to acclimatize on this, our first real day in Mumbai, by spending the next three and a half hours in the relative comfort of the air-conditioned departure terminal at the domestic airport. So we bade farewell to the friendly staff at the hotel, only to discover at the airport that they had attempted to open all our luggage in our absence. Luckily we had put locks on most of our bags, but how 'friendly' was that?

By now, not knowing the Villa result was gnawing at my insides. How to escape the other half?

"Ah. Hélène. I just HAVE to go to the loo. Can you wait here with the luggage?"

"Not again. You only went back at the hotel."

"I know. Sorry."

I sneaked off round the corner with Hélène in charge of our two trolleys. I took my trusted Nokia out of my pocket. Phew! I had a signal this time.

www.bbc.co.uk/sport is my home page. The mobile threw up a frustratingly long list of messages, which basically meant I accepted exorbitant charges from a foreign mobile phone provider. Yes, yes, yes, just give me the bloody result. Finally the BBC Sport home page came up. Headline, "Saha winner sinks Chelsea."

Rock on! I wasn't expecting that!. What a bonus. Then I scroll down for the United result.

Villa 1 United 1.

Within this new set of circumstances that seemed all right to me. In fact my last game at Old Trafford had been the 0-1 home defeat to Villa in December. We had laboured against a well organised but nothing special team, with Heskey falling down every time a gust of wind drifted round the ground. I then began to read the first paragraph. Nani sent off in the first half and even Fergie thought it was deserved. Well, would you Adam & Eve it. Fergie agreeing with the referee. Must be all that post Christmas wine.

OK. Just one point behind Chelsea and they still have to come to our place. With the stuttering displays of United this season, that was as good as I could have hoped for. With the pounds stacking up I quickly scanned the rest of the Premiership.

Arsenal 1 Liverpool 0.

OK, you've made my day.

I switched off my mobile, hoping it will be many months before Hélène has to question my parenthood over the bill. I stuck my second LUHG sticker in a prominent position within the men's' toilet (2 down, 98 to go) then returned to the guardian of our luggage with a relieved grin on my face.

"Feel better?"

"Yes dear."

"OK. Let's get something to eat. It's still three hours before our flight and we can't check-in our luggage for another hour."

There was only one restaurant before security and check-in so we had our first proper meal on Indian soil. I had spaghetti with chicken pieces and a cheese sauce whilst Hélène had vegetable lasagne. (I'm sorry. We didn't have a choice. All right?)

After the meal we adjourned to some comfortable chairs. (What?

At an airport! Well, all things are relative, I suppose) I took out my new notebook and attempted to log on to the free airport Wi-Fi. The airport's home page took me on a labyrinth, ending up with a template asking me to text a special number and they would text me back with a special password.

So, with Hélène's approval this time, I used my English mobile to text this Indian number. I tried three times. First with 91, the second with +91 and the third with 00 91.

Nothing. I waited and waited but nothing came through. Muttering genuine Anglo-Saxon under my breath, I gave up and waited for a check-in desk to open.

A simple process and we were finally free of our luggage. Hélène passed immediately though female security whilst I joined a long, slow-moving queue of men. Revenge, I thought, for all those times we men go straight into public toilets whilst women have to queue. Can't complain.

Thirty minutes later and we met up airside. We found two seats together when I spied a magical sign. "Complimentary Internet."

Yippee! Stuff your airport Wi-Fi Mumbai. Victory is mine.

Hélène and I took it in turns to update our Facebook (Me more than her. She hates all this electronic nonsense) and check e-mails. Messages of love and orders to our offspring then it was time to board.

A quick nip to the loo ensured LUHG sticker number 3 found its mark on the hot air hand dryer. Just 97 to go.

Once on board we had to wait almost 45 minutes before we started to taxi. As we did so, we witnessed first hand the slums featured in Slum Dog Millionaire. Row upon row of haphazardly built single story corrugated iron dwellings as far as the eye could see, built on rubbish tips with running children and sewage. Then we were finally airborne, sweeping above Mumbai and the smog, with blue skies above and a grey haze below.

Goa here we come.

FRIDAY 14 FEBRUARY. GOA, INDIA

Valentine's Day. In fact it was 37 years to the day that Hélène and I first went out together. To impress her, I had taken her to see the new super group, 'Sharks' with Chris Spedding on guitar and Cozy Powell on drums at the Imperial College, Kensington. To 'seal the deal' so to speak, a meal at the original Hard Rock Café followed, when the Hard Rock Café was still cool.

I had taken her back to her place for my just desserts, only to encounter "Cheeky", her pesky Yorkshire Terrier, who insisted in settling between us at every opportunity. Thus our first night was spent as a threesome, fully clothed, with only Cheeky sleeping doggy style.

I'd made a pact with myself before we left that I wouldn't constantly compare everything with "back home". Just like New Year resolutions I broke that self-imposed rule within minutes of touching down. Now four days into our global gallivanting a moment of analytical reflection was called for. Everyone says India is a land of contrasts and contradictions. How very true. After just 4 days the following anomalies have become apparent:

We saw many women constantly cleaning clothes, yet the washing hanging to dry looked dull and dirty. Notwithstanding the amount of dust in the air, the vast majority of cars were spotless. There was rubbish everywhere as were half-started building works and demolition.

Most new cars are Suzuki's, followed by Tata, the Indian mark, Honda and Hyundai. We'd seen 2 Ford Mondeos, one BMW and one Mercedes. All cars, motorbikes and mopeds are constantly sounding their horns but hardly anyone signals before turning left or right.

Everyone wants to sell you something, especially if you're white, yet remarkable acts of kindness abound. For example, unknowingly I'd dropped some papers on the ground as I was walking along one day. This old man came up to me and tapped me on the shoulder. I just thought, "What's HE trying to sell?" So I just smiled and shook my head. Thinking no more about it I continued on my way. A few moments later he appeared in front of me and said, "Please sir, I think you dropped these papers". He was right. I smiled sheepishly and thanked him for his unselfish kindness.

MONDAY 15 FEBRUARY GOA, INDIA

My mission today, which has so far ended in unmitigated failure, is to find a bar/pub/restaurant that will be showing the AC Milan v Manchester United Champions League 1/8 final live on TV. You have to understand, for a match kicking off at 19.45 GMT it kicks off at 01.15 Indian time, and so far I haven't found one place that will be open at that time of night.

Our first two nights had been spent in a budget hotel in Colva Beach, the nearest resort to the town of Margoa where I intended to put right 40 years of tooth abuse caused by all things sweet and beautiful. Unfortunately Colva Beach turned out to be a disappointing hotchpotch of characterless buildings and a sewer running right along the back of the dirty beach. However I left my mark with LUHG sticker number 4 in the window of a café near the beach that already had a Liverpool poster on its back wall. That wrong had to be righted, right? OK, just 96 to go. Must remember to pace myself. There are still 11¾ months to go. Yet I reckoned a lot of Europeans come to Goa on holiday so a little concentrated stickeration was justified.

Now we're staying in a shack right on the beach near the village of Benaulim, which is basic but idyllic. Not ideal is the fact we don't have a TV, and nor does the bar/restaurant attached. To compound the problem, I have a dental appointment at 09.00 the following morning, which means I'll miss the ESPN morning repeat. That leaves the afternoon repeat. Now, should I try and stay ignorant of the result and watch it "live" like I did the World Club Championship final in New York at Nevada Smiths (which opened just for us) at 08.00 New York time? Or should I try to find out the result from around 15.00 onwards, knowing full well that some smart Alec in the bar will be shouting the odds and claiming, "Here comes the bit where... etc..."

Plan B allowed me two options:

1) Risk the wrath of the other half as I tune into BBC Sport on my English mobile.

2) Find a way to walk half a kilometre to the village of Benaulim and seek refuge status in the nearest internet café at 30 rupees an hour.

This conundrum had been playing on my mind the whole of the previous night. No, I'm not exaggerating. You see, Hélène and I have been taking malaria tablets since one week before we set off. We were told there might be side affects but I dismissed them as scaremongering.

How wrong could I be?

I was waking up twice every night to go to the loo, and when I got back into bed I had the most vivid and disturbing nightmares which for me is so rare. Even rarer is me remembering them. That's never happened to me before, no matter how hard I've tried. In fact, waking up has come as a blessed relief as soon as I realize it was only a nightmare and I live to fight another day.

WEDNESDAY 16 FEBRUARY. GOA, INDIA
AC MILAN 2 MANCHESTER UNITED 3 - CHAMPIONS LEAGUE LAST SIXTEEN

As luck would have it, I woke up at 06.00 and this time it was a good thing. I crept out of our creaking bamboo base bed, took my mobile and tip-toed to the toilet. Suitably astride the throne I opened the internet connection of the mobile and waited what seemed like an eternity until bbc.co.uk/sport came up.

Scrolled down.

"Rooney header seals United win."

The loudest silent scream ever recorded escaped my lips. Much waving of arms and punching the air later I returned to our marital bed a very happy man.

They'll be no nightmares tonight. I'll make sure of that. I turned off the mobile. I was dying to read the report but at international rates I thought I'd better be captain sensible and wait for our daily visit to one of the laboriously slow internet cafes.

THURSDAY 18 FEBRUARY GOA, INDIA

After just eight days into our round the world trip Hélène and I have agreed to separate. Yup, the next time we visit an internet café we're going to book separate computers. You won't believe the grief I get every time we go on the net. Is it my fault my e-mail account is full of Reds commenting on the latest shenanigans? Is it my fault Reds everywhere want an update on our trip? When are you coming to "Y"? When will you be arriving in "X"? Is it my fault all the bars are closed when United kick off a Champions League match at 01.15 in the early hours of the morning? Is it my fault our beach hut hasn't got a TV and I have to leave Hélène on her tod to watch a lunchtime kick-off at 18.30 or a 16.00 kick-off at 20.30? No, of course not. I have a duty to deal with these matters. So what does Hélène come out with?

You've guessed it, "You love United more than me!" I'm not getting caught with that old chestnut again. "You put United before the welfare of our children!" She's fighting dirty now. I mean, I've followed United long before my children were born, even before I met Hélène. (I'm digging my own grave here, aren't I?)

And the situation is made worse by the fact that internet cafés in India are mind-numbingly slow. Or crash all too frequently. So Hélène takes her frustration out on me. I'm an easy target.

Now, after more than 60 years on this planet consuming an enormous amount of sugar in all its forms, in my tea, on pancakes, chocolate... the end result is that my teeth are in dire need of a major overhaul and I suffer continuously from toothache. With local NHS dentists where we live in London refusing any more NHS patients, my teeth had deteriorated dramatically, so before we left home I had scoured the internet for a reputable dentist that fitted in with our itinerary and I whittled the two finalists down to Goa and Bangkok.

It was a close call but I plumped for the Apollo Victor Hospital in Margoa in Goa, which had some sort of connection with BUPA in the UK. I figured the level of expertise to be acceptable whilst their quote was a fraction of UK prices.

Why am I telling you this? Because for the next month I intended to divide my daylight hours between the beach and the dentist's chair. Yes, voluntarily, and this morning I had my very first appointment.

Did you know that painted on the inside and outside of every tuk-tuk in India is the price of 10 rupees for the first kilometre and 7 rupees for each additional kilometre? Therefore a local would pay 45 rupees from Benaulim to the Apollo Victor hospital in Margoa. We got charged 200 rupees, and that was only after five minutes of good-natured bartering.

This trend is going to rear its ugly head many times over in this coming year, namely one price for locals and one price for tourists.

We arrived at the hospital and I went up to the third floor to wait in this stifling waiting room with no air conditioning and a TV that didn't work.

But it was worth it.

A vision of loveliness came floating towards me and led me down a corridor to her surgery. Wow, she's my dentist! Who needs anaesthetic when all I have to do is gaze into those big beautiful eyes?

She beckoned me to sit in the dentist's chair, then started to explain what lay in store for me. Today she told me she was going to clean my teeth. Then I would be sent away for a blood sample to determine how fit I was to undertake a serious number of procedures.

I looked up and saw a computer screen above my head.

"What's that for?" I thought to myself.

"What's that for?" I asked

"Ah. That's our music system."

She switched on the monitor, and just like on a plane there was a choice of music channels to choose from.

Cool.

"Excuse me, got any heavy metal?"

"Excuse me?"

"Err, any rock music?"

"Oh, I see. Well, let's have a look."

Surprise, surprise…no, just music to calm patients down, so I chose the nearest, country rock, and settled down to this amazing light show before my very eyes.

Very Roger Dean type graphics.

As she cleaned my teeth I started to have naughty thoughts to take my mind off what was happening in my mouth. One shade lighter I was sent downstairs to have X-rays taken. Two student doctors giggled and whispered incomprehensibly between themselves. I was obviously the butt of their jokes, but a bigger joke was that they didn't know how to operate the X-ray machine.

What's Gujarati for wankers?

Three goes and three failures later, a senior doctor dragged himself reluctantly to the X-ray room and explained to the trainees how to operate the machine. Armed with an acceptable set of X-rays I returned to Princess Dentista and once again submitted myself to her spell-binding gaze.

She was obviously impressed with my X-rays as she called her boss in and they both visually dissected them with unbridled enthusiasm. Reluctantly, it seemed, they pulled themselves away and came to stand either side of me.

Then they dropped the bombshell.

My teeth were too far gone and they were going to have to remove ten (yes, 10) teeth before fitting temporary dentures top and bottom. But the good news wasn't finished yet. They would be able to save four of my own teeth (yes, 4) but each of these would need extensive route canal work in order to remove the nerve.

"Ding dang dong for a holiday." "Oh what fun we had…." It took a few seconds for the implications to hit home. So be it. I had been running away for the past fifty years and the dentist profession was adamant it was due its pound of flesh, and, by gum, they were Goa to get it from me. (Sorry)

On the way out I decided against LUHG sticker number 5 as I hadn't seen any tourists coming here for treatment and my wardrobe of United tops would rather give the game away.

Let battle commence.

SATURDAY 20 FEBRUARY. GOA, INDIA
EVERTON 3 MANCHESTER UNITED 1

I'm not saying I believe in ghosts, or UFOs, or poltergeists, or the astral plane, or the occult, or any of that stuff, but just let's say I believe in the POSSIBILITY of that stuff. But this evening was decidedly spooky. You see, earlier on in the week Hélène and I had had a lovely fish meal at a beach shack in Benaulim called Hawaii. And during the meal I could hear an English voice going on about cricket. I turned around and this suntanned stomach was wafting lyrically to any local within earshot about how you should always bowl at the wicket, as the bowler was three times more likely to have the batsman dismissed than if he just bounced the ball in front of the wicket hoping for a catch.

Why was he commenting so? Because a TV screen against the back wall was showing the India v South Africa test match. I was forming my contribution to this one sided debate when he changed tack and asked an elderly English couple on a table at the other end of the room if they knew the FA Cup 4th round scores. For obvious reasons, this year's competition no longer held any interest for me, so I declined to contribute. He actually wanted to know how Portsmouth had got on against the hated Scummers (Southampton). It finally dawned on me that here was a television showing international sport, so I asked what I took to be the owner if they showed Premiership and Champions League games. His answer can only be described as "unsatisfactory". Yes, they showed Premiership games that kick off in England at either 13.00, 15.00 or 16.00. They don't show evening games, be they Premiership or Champions League, as 19.45 GMT equated to 01.15 Indian time and all the bars are closed.

Having suffered the ultimate in withdrawal symptoms on the Tuesday as I was unable to watch United's triumph in Milan, I could at least rest easy knowing that the forthcoming away fixture against Everton due to be broadcast at 18.15 Indian time was well within my grasp. With his permission I planted LUHG sticker number 5 on the wall behind the counter, (95 to go) first explaining the significance of the lettering. He didn't get it, but countless Reds after me would.

I began the morning of the game gazing once again into the large limpet pools of my pretty young dentist's eyes, as she gained a credible score draw with three successful and one unsuccessful root canal procedures. Unfortunately, the toothache I had endured the past three days and nights had yet to subside. This resulted in my continuous use of prescribed antibiotics, one of whose side effects was to diminish the effectiveness of the anaesthetic injections administered by the dentist. Despite impersonating Bill Murray in that hilarious scene with Steve Martin as the demented dentist in "The Little Shop of Horrors", repeated injections failed to numb my lower tooth sufficiently for her to proceed with the procedure. So, with an additional appointment scheduled for the Monday, Hélène and I tuk-tuked our way back to the beach and an afternoon of eating, swimming and sunbathing in 32 degrees of heat. At around ten to six I told Hélène I would make my way along the beach to the "Hawaii" shack to watch the footy. She could follow me there when she was ready. With my green and gold "LOVE UNITED HATE GLAZER" T-shirt in my hand and hope in my heart, I strolled for fifteen minutes along the hard white sand to the bar.

The first sign that something wasn't quite right came the moment I entered the shack. The TV was gone.

""scuse me. Where's your TV?"

"We haven't got a TV."

"But I was here a couple of days ago. My wife and I had a lovely fish meal and you were showing the cricket."

"We haven't got a TV. You must be thinking of the bar a couple down on the right."

I wasn't. But I didn't want to make as scene, so I just mumbled something to myself and left. Spooky. I was SURE I had seen a TV there. In fact I knew I had. Was I living in a parallel universe or something? No time for a philosophical debate. The match was about to start and I had to get my priorities in gear. I strolled briskly back the way I had come and there, two shacks down, was a bar with a TV set. I hadn't set foot in this place before in case that's what you're thinking. The TV was showing some Indian soap opera, so I asked if they would broadcast the United match which was about to start any minute. I told them I believed it to be on ESPN.

"No problem. Have a seat, sir. Would you like something to drink?"

"Fanta, please."

I took out my English mobile with my English sim card and told Hélène, 500 yards away, to meet me in "Leonard's" instead, about 2 shacks nearer, explaining "Hawaii" no longer had a TV.

One of the guys started zapping with the remote control and found Vancouver 2010 on ESPN. My watch must have been a little fast. They were showing the top three skiers in the slalom, so I figured once that was out of the way, the football would begin.

Errr... no.

After the ads, they went to another winter event.

"'Scuse me. Can you see if you can get the United match, please?"

They couldn't do enough for me. On the other hand, they couldn't find the football either, so after another ten minutes I left a half drunk Fanta on the table and strolled briskly out of their bar. Panic was now setting in as I jogged (Me! Jogging! In this heat! That's a first. But needs must) along the beach. Then I spied "Domenic". Or was it "Domenick"? Couldn't tell you. They had tables and chairs outside. At one end was a sign which read, "Domenic". At the other end there was another sign, "Domenick".

But that's not important right now.

I rushed in to see that the score was 0-0 after fifteen minutes.

Phew!

"Have a seat, sir. Would you like a drink?"

Sprite, please."

Thought I'd mix my drinks. I mean, I wasn't driving.

I sat down at the bar, directly in front of the TV. I took out my English mobile with my English sim card and phoned Hélène, 400 yards away, to tell her that the venue had changed yet again. Could she now meet me in "Dominec" or "Domineck". You know, the one with the two different spellings of its name.

OK. We looked to be in control. A few hurried Everton mistakes and Valencia getting in some nice crosses. Nice. Then, with one of his crosses bobbling around the Everton goalmouth, Berbatov pounced and the ball was in the net. 1-0 to the champions and Berba almost smiled. I jumped up with both my arms raised. I was the only one. In fact, I think I was the only one watching. The manager beamed at me.

"United, good".

"United fucking brilliant mate. Sorry, didn't mean to swear."

The game restarted. Both sides pressing. Then two of our lads went up for the same ball with an Everton forward. It bounced right in the path of Bilyaletdinov who rammed the ball home, low inside the post with VDS just looking as it passed by.

Fuck. That only lasted 3 minutes. Everton were coming more into the game as the first half wore on, and the halftime score of 1-1 I had to admit was about right. Hélène hadn't turned up yet, so I pontificated to anyone within earshot what would happen in the second half. Either we'd get stronger as the game wore on, and nick it in the last five minutes, or, and it gives me no pleasure whatsoever in predicting this, our glorious efforts in Milan just two and a half days ago would begin to take their toll. Toll they bloody took. We ran out of "oomph". Both Everton substitutes, Gosling and Rodwell scored good goals but where was our defense?

To make it worse, the manager came over.

"Everton, good?"

"No, United fucking knackered mate."

I tried to explain that life was unfair, and that no way should United have played at Saturday lunchtime when they had played away in Europe on the Wednesday night. We should have played on Sunday afternoon. True, but I knew I was just making excuses. Once again our makeshift defence had been found wanting. In fact, up to this point, Ferdinand and Vidic had only played together in United's defence four times so far this season. Our midfield, led by Fletcher who had risen to such unforeseen heights over the past couple of seasons, failed to impose themselves. Then bringing on Owen as substitute to lead a three-man attack, with the glorious exception of City 4-3 at the beginning of the season, had almost always ended in failure. In the end it was the right result and I knew it. We'd been beaten by the better team on the day. And Everton had beaten Chelsea the week before as I tried to find crumbs of comfort.

I hardly registered the fact that Hélène had entered the bar and was sitting next to me.

"I thought you'd be next door," she said looking slightly confused, "they have a giant screen on the side wall."

TUESDAY 23 FEBRUARY GOA, INDIA
MANCHESTER UNITED 3 WEST HAM UNITED 0

Having discovered the big screen at the weekend, I was hoping to be back for second helpings, only this time hoping United would come first, not second, and erase the memory of that second half capitulation at Goodison Park.

Unfortunately the evening game at Old Trafford kicked off at 01.15am here in Goa, so with no bar to go to I tried streaming on my new Toshiba Notebook for the first time. Everyone had told me about streaming, but I would like to re-christen it 'SCREAMING', as frustration overwhelmed any sense of logical co-ordination I could muster at this hour.

Any site I found demanded registration, a credit card number and an intolerable wait. Fuck it, it's back to bbc.co.uk/sport and 2 minute updates. And so it came to pass, Rooney, so anonymous at his old stomping ground at the weekend, resurrected his form and two ruthless headed finishes put him on 27 goals for the season. It's always a good sign of a radio/internet report when a player or a team is mentioned more than the opposition, such as Valencia's lightening quick crosses which led to Rooney's brace. With Owen adding a third we were now only one point behind Chelsea, albeit having played a game more. OK, now for some sleep.

SUNDAY 28 FEBRUARY. GOA, INDIA
CARLING CUP FINAL. MANCHESTER UNITED 2 ASTON VILLA 1

Since coming off the malaria tablets I've stopped having nightmares but I still wake up around 06.00, just as it's getting light. I creek out of bed (No, not me. You see my wooden bed doesn't half makes a noise when I move) and have a long, slow crap. Nice.

I then slip back into bed without waking the other half. Later on that morning Hélène tells me the shitty tea she drunk the previous day had finally had the desired effect and she had clambered over me a number of times during the night to get to the loo before she let rip with number twos. I hadn't felt a thing.

After a leisurely breakfast in Johncy, the nearest bar/restaurant to the little main square where all the taxis and tuk-tuks ply their trade, a beaming young man came up to me and said,

"Manchester is my favourite team."

Obviously he'd spotted my pre-Glazer United embroidered polo shirt and felt compelled to engage me in conversation. Now, wasn't this the very scenario my not-so-secret mission was on the look-out for? So why was I not best pleased? I'll tell you why. He was only wearing a bloody Leeds United snide football top! WTF! Proof, as if I needed convincing, that "fans" around the world just don't get it. Is it us or is it them?

Just like a politician at election time, I conversed in smiles, then we spotted Pakesh, our regular young smiling super tuk-tuk driver. Having built up a certain rapport I convinced him the addition of one of my LUHG stickers on his dashboard would make him stand out as the tuk-tuk driver of choice amongst locals and tourists alike. He wasn't convinced, but with the amount of fares we were pushing his way he reluctantly agreed. (6 down, 94 to go)

Meanwhile we noticed a number of well-to-do young locals wearing white overalls milling around. Then we noticed the cans of paint and bottles of water and I thought. "Oh, no. They're not getting me."

As they started to chase and spray each other with a rainbow of various colours we gave them a wide berth. Then I felt a cold wet sensation between my shoulder blades.

"Bastards! They've thrown water over me."

"Never mind, it'll soon dry in this heat. Don't make such a fuss." said Hélène as we strolled along the beach but my white polo shirt still felt uncomfortable.

"Stop moaning. Let me have a look. Oh….."

"What?"

"That wasn't water on your back, it's blue paint."

"What! Bastards!"

I was wearing my pre-Glazer white polo shirt with the Manchester United crest embroidered on the left breast. This was my one piece of up-market leisurewear I had allowed myself and now it had been ruined by those childish imbeciles.

I was livid.

"Don't worry. I'll clean it when we get back." said Hélène, trying to calm me down.

Yeah. But what if she can't? My only United polo. Ruined! And still over eleven months to go.

A delightful day was spent down the coast in Palolem and it was still light by the time we arrived back at our hostel in Benaulim. Hélène wouldn't be drawn into accompanying me to the café with the giant screen along the beach for the Carling Cup final between United and

Aston Villa which, in reality, was no bad thing. This way I didn't have to make conversation and I could concentrate on the match.

I may be at odds with many of you here, but in the build up to a match, whether en route or in the pub beforehand, I'll pontificate with the best of them as to who should play, who we should buy/sell and how to dismember one or all of the Glazers without getting caught, but during the match itself I am 100% totally absorbed by the passages of play. Apart from the odd one liner I'm just an animated mass of nerves and basic Anglo-Saxon and not the best company, so Hélène not coming was a blessing without a disguise.

I took my place on a single table with a few minutes to kick-off, ordered my obligatory soft drink which I hoped would last me the whole match and waited for the fun to begin.

I looked around. There were no "proper" football fans there as far as I could tell. Certainly no United fans.

I settled down simply to enjoy the game. With bigger fish to fry and no-one to take the piss, I was shaken out of my nonchalance in the 5th minute when Vidic pulled down Agbonlahor to concede a penalty.

Shit.

Aston Villa 1 United 0

Fortunately for Vidic, and us, there was no red card. The match settled down and we were by far the better team.

"It's only a matter of time" I thought.

It didn't take long. Berbatov, who was having a fine game, dispossesed Richard Dunne, with the ball falling into the path of Michael Owen who levelled with an instant and ruthless finish.

At last, the real Michael Owen. Maybe his arrival was a major coup after all. What a killer that he pulled his hamstring and had to be taken off before the break. We continued to press and should have been leading by half time. Time for another Fanta in the sun.

Valencia, who continues to look a real find, crossed for the winner Rooney, coming off the bench, to head in after 74 minutes. Cue for me to be the only person watching in the bar to stand up and let out a piercing shout. I hadn't meant to. It was only the Carling Cup after all, but it's United and that's the effect they have on me.

Left me in a right good mood though, I can tell you.

TUESDAY 2 MARCH GOA, INDIA

The dastardly deed has been done. Goodbye Shane McGowan, hello George Clooney. Well, in my mind anyway. This morning I had 10 (yes, ten) teeth taken out in the same session and two complete sets of dentures inserted. I'll admit it was not the most pleasant four hours I've ever spent on this planet, and I've yet to control the instinctive reaction to gulp, but all you beautiful ladies out there... form an orderly queue will you please.

I also got Hélène to take some photos, both before and after the ordeal. I don't know which ones are scarier! When I smile now I look like some mad scientist, eyes ablaze and my grey hair blowing in the wind. I also her asked to take pictures with the whole team. They grinned into the camera with their victim (me) sat in the dentist chair in the middle. They then asked if I could Blue-tooth all the photos to their respective mobiles. I duly concurred.

One good thing though, for the next 48 hours I can only eat cold stuff like ice cream and soft fruit. No alcohol, fizzy drinks or anything hot. (Sorry Hélène, you'll have to play by yourself for the next two days.... and nights) So I just had a banana split for lunch.

Nice.

OK, give me a couple of days for me to get use to this foreign invasion of my north and south, then it's off around the north and south of India.

FRIDAY 5 MARCH GOKARMA, INDIA

"What's that coming over the hill? Is it a monster? Is it a monsteeeerrr?"

No, it's a prize wally in the form of yours truly attempting to navigate a treacherous path down the rocky hillside to get to our nirvana below, the beautiful Kudlee beach in Gokarma, carrying the world's needlessly heaviest 80 litre rucksack together with an ordinary army style excessively heavy rucksack on my back and sweat pouring off me like it was going out of fashion.

To add insult to injury, I've inflicted on Hélène the same military style manoeuvre as me. Of course, it's easy for me to accept the blame for this episode, but I would site The Rough Guide to India as a character witness. Beware, when a book or brochure claims a beach hut is ideally situated in paradise, it omits to inform the reader that its very isolation is at the expense of what most people would consider everyday facilities, such as roads, or at least a path down a rocky incline. The Gokarma International Beach Resort has the perfect location on the beach, set back a little by a small garden. However, the taxi that picked us up from Gokarma Road railway station dropped us at the top of a hill overlooking the bay. With temperatures in the upper 30s, Hélène and I had no option but to risk life and limb by descending an invisible path with our oversized luggage.

The British army came to our rescue in the form of Dave, a Geordie who had been on the same train as us from Margoa. Having consumed three Shredded Wheat that morning, he adopted the Indian way of carrying heavy loads by lifting my wife's rucksack on his head and confidently striding downhill where a wimp like me (you know, the sort you'd kick sand in the face of if you met me on the beach) struggled to put one ungainly foot in front of another.

Mind you, once Hélène and I had dragged our infamous rucksacks along the beach to our hotel, it all became worthwhile. You won't find a more idealistic setting than Kudlee Beach in Gokarma. The over commercialisation of Goa has driven the hippies further south, and for some, Gokarma is heaven on earth.

Now, if you like Blackpool, Benidorm and the like, Gokarma is not for you. But if you want to chill, and I mean really chill, meditate, sit cross legged and gaze in awe at incredible sunsets caressed by warm breezes, advance the body and the mind and be spiritually uplifted, this is the place... man.

Lots of hairy and balding hippies, beautiful chicks and intelligent carefree kids. Just observing the joy and happiness on their faces, their stress free lifestyle could teach millions of us that the yuppie philosophy of me me me, money money money, "look at my wad", "loads of money" self-centred superficial existence leaves a lot to be desired.

But here's my dilemma. During the 60s I was what they called a weekend hippy. Semi conventional during the week at work, yet spaced out at the weekend. In fact it's even more complicated than that. We humans are complex creatures. A paradox of conflicting emotions and desires. I yearn for the era of free love that passed me by. Yet my over-riding passion in life is Manchester United, which by definition is a competitive, dog eat dog world of all consuming one-upmanship. Lording it over friends and colleagues who support lesser teams. Feeling I am one of the chosen 75/300/659 million superior people on the planet. A hard-core United fan. A top Red.

The final chapter of my last book was entitled, "United is better than sex". Although a little artistic license allowed me to exaggerate in the pursuit of literary humour, the underlying truth was all too evident. So, as much as I would dearly love to embrace the alternative lifestyle, my raging Red hormones always bring me back to M16 0RA. Having matched and, hopefully, soon to exceed Liverpool's nineteen league championships, and if possible before my ashes are scattered on the pitch at Old Trafford, match then exceed Liverpool's five European Cups.

So my most important mission in this ideal setting is to find an outlet that will broadcast our away fixture tomorrow against Wolves, which will be at 23.00 kick-off Indian time.

SUNDAY 7 MARCH. GOKARNA, INDIA
WOLVERHAMPTON WANDERERS 0 MANCHESTER UNITED 1

This was our first big train day/night. First we arranged with our hotel in Gokarna to have two people help us with our two ginormous rucksacks. We'd learned our lesson the hard way on the way down. They carried them on their heads while Hélène and I struggled for fifteen minutes back up the invisible rocky path to the waiting rickshaw that was to take us back to Gokarna Road railway station. We sweated profusely, then thanked our two helpers profusely. After ten minutes our rickshaw arrived and the driver tried to hide an expression of horror when he realised the size and weight of our luggage. I gave him a hand then off we jiggled and jostled for half an hour over the sort of terrain you used to see in all those "B" movie westerns starring Audi Murphy (one for the oldies there).

Arriving at the station I helped him unload the two extra heavy rucksacks then Hélène and I dragged our luggage up onto the only platform. I asked the man behind the grill where our carriage would stop and he pointed behind him and to the left. I asked him if the train was on time and he said it was.

It arrived half an hour late, which is on time by Indian railway standards. I impressed Hélène with my dexterity at lifting up our two rucksacks into the carriage with the aid of my right knee. We found our two seats and spent the following 45 minute train journey to Karwar chatting to a family opposite.

One of the more positive things about people in India is they love to chat. To friends, family, even complete strangers. A man who later told me he was forty seven, introduced himself as an engineer from Karwar, his wife who was sitting opposite him and their cool looking, long haired son. They asked us where we were from, what we did for a living, was it our first time in India, etc...etc... very pleasant, especially as I knew all the answers.

Then I could see the mother and son whispering to each other and smiling at us. The woman spoke quietly to her husband who then lent forward.

"My wife would like to know how old you are."

"How old do you think I am?"

They huddled together like contestants in Family Fortunes, then the man replied:

"My wife thinks you are about 45"

YES!! A result! All that dentistry had paid off in one fell swoop.

"Actually I'm sixty years old" I said, flashing my new molars at them in the best advertisement cheesy style grin I could manage. Ego enlarging expressions of surprise swept over their faces whilst Hélène tried and failed to hide a look which translated into, "Oh my god, we're not going to hear the end of this."

However, I was brought down to earth moments later when a woman stepped by with her two young sons. The youngest, who could have been no older than two years old, took one look at my long(ish) grey hair and bushy grey moustache and let out a wail of terror. I smiled in the most condescending manner I could muster, which from a two year old infant looked like the sneer of Aqualung (a little Jethro Tull reference there for the initiated) and screamed even louder. Everyone looked round to see who was molesting this poor infant. Fortunately his mother could see the funny side of it and she just smiled at me as she passed.

We settled back in our seats. We were approaching Karwar so I stood up in order to take our two heavy rucksacks to the door. As I did so, the mother with her two sons passed by the other way. Talk about repeats. You'd think I was Peter Cushing playing the baddy in the first Harry Potter movie. I've never heard screams so loud and so high pitched. (No, that's a lie. I did once attend a woman's international hockey match at Wembley many moons ago, and there were 80,000 pubescent teenage girls in the stadium. Man, that was really scary!) She passed by as quickly as possible as Hélène and I and our luggage descended onto the platform.

Needless to say, our connecting train to Cochin was also half an hour late. We scrambled along the platform and miraculously found our carriage. My knee jerk reaction worked splendidly as I yanked our rucksacks up into the carriage. This being first class, a guard then helped us with our luggage and directed us to our seats.

Mmmm. Really nice and plush. Deep red cloth covered seats and air conditioning. We've cracked it. We exchanged pleasantries with the two people in the top bunks. One was a quiet Indian gentleman and the other a friendly, well-spoken young English woman who turned out to be a producer on BBC Radio. The aisle was wide enough to accommodate all our luggage and there were two sheets, a blanket and a pillow all neatly folded and waiting to welcome us "between the sheets".

Hélène and I made our respective beds, then with a quick kiss goodnight we separated. Her to her DSi and me to the land of nod. However, I hadn't yet discovered the result of our away fixture against Wolves and now we were on the train I couldn't get a signal on my mobile. This was damn frustrating and maybe contributed to the fact it took me ages to get to sleep. And I love trains. I don't know what it is about them, but for me the countryside always looks better from a train than from the window of a car or bus. There's that hint of romance perpetuated by those black and white movies your parents made you watch on TV after Sunday lunch.

And to sleep on a train. Wow! The little boy in me worked overtime imagining all sorts of scenarios from Brief Encounter to From Russia With Love. Having said that, it took me longer to fall asleep than I envisaged. The (lack of) Wolves result was obviously playing on my mind, and the motion of the train was not as smooth as those in Europe so I lay awake for some time playing with my Nokia. Would I be able to locate a TV showing our AC Milan second leg Champions League game in Cochin?

To break the monotony and calm my troubled brain I got up and went to the first class toilet. A good place for a LUHG sticker I thought. Many a tourist should pass this way I reckoned. (6 down, 94 to go)

Then back to my bunk for a fitful night's sleep.

TUESDAY 9 MARCH. COCHIN, INDIA
MANCHESTER UNITED 4 AC MILAN 0. CHAMPIONS LEAGUE LAST 16

India is hot. India coupled with a heat wave is fucking hot. Stepping off the train from our air-conditioned carriage we were met by a firing squad. In place of guns they held hair-dryers on hot, hot, hot. It hit us like a sauna, this wave of heat that made every pore on your skin leak instantly. We jostled and sweated our way through the crowd to the taxi rank and shared a pre-paid taxi with the young BBC Radio producer as it turned out our hotels were next door to each other. In fact our two hotels were in the same building, a colonial Portuguese construction that had been divided into various accommodation.

Hélène and I had decided to treat ourselves for our first night in the luxury part, then transfer to the hostel next door for the remains of our stay. Bliss.

I took advantage of every facility and freebie on offer, not knowing when we could afford to indulge again. Hélène didn't see it that way. She just thought I had no class. She's right, of course, but she still let me stow away all the toiletries. Double standards or what?

A strip of land between the Arabian Sea and the Western Ghats, Kerala's normally perfect climate and fertile soil allows everything to grow. We spent our first day wandering around this easy going and successful socialist/communist state (depending on what tourist guide you read). Down by the estuary the local fishermen operated their weird Chinese nets and we stopped for gallons and gallons of recycled pretend bottles of spring water at every opportunity. I haven't mentioned Indian bottled water before. It's bottled water, but not as we know it. They take water and add chemicals for health and safety reasons but it leaves a bitter taste in the mouth. Literally.

Hélène is always "encouraging" me to drink bottled water and not the artificial coloured flavourings of Coke, Pepsi, Tango, Sprite, 7 Up and the rest. She's right on every level except for one thing. Indian bottled water tastes foul and the above American monstrosities taste so good. This was re-enforced later that day when we stopped in an air-conditioned 5 star hotel for a bit of R & R. I ordered ice cream and water and was relieved to see they brought me a bottle of Evian. Water never tasted so sweet. The difference was enormous. Even at those prices it tasted sooooo good.

Cochin is famous for the backwaters of Kerala, a series of waterways and canals that meander their way through lush countryside. Here, spindly networks of rivers, canals and lagoons nourish a seemingly infinite number of rice paddies and coconut groves.

I had to make sure we chose a boat with a TV, as I didn't want to miss the return Champions League match against AC Milan.

Looking around we decided on a large luxurious looking double decker houseboat, complete with crew for cooking and cleaning, and a viewing platform/sunbathing area up top… and a television. This way we could enjoy the breathtaking views of the untouched and otherwise inaccessible rural Kerala that it offered while we float along doing absolutely nothing!

Unfortunately I wouldn't be able watch the match as the television didn't work! So why install it on board in the first place? Bastards! I suppose if the sun gets too hot, you could always switch it on and believe the snow was for real.

There were moments over the next couple of days when I almost forgot about AC Milan, which just goes to show how magical this mini cruise was. Our one night stop was by a canal bank and a short walk from a small settlement. As Hélène and I strolled amid the undergrowth we came across a couple of young English lads on a similar expedition. One turned out to be a Forest fan and the other a Baggie. Hélène couldn't believe that thousands of miles from home, in such a glorious setting, the pros and cons of the play-offs could generate such passionate debate. How the drama involved kept even mid-table teams and their fans on tenterhooks, whereas it made a mockery of natural justice where the team in third place could be ten points or more ahead of the team in sixth place and yet lose out. The fact that neither of them turned out to be ABUs was a bonus, so we parted firm friends, confident our paths would never cross again.

We continued on our walk, the subject of smiles and wide eyes from local children playing by the banks of the canal. Obviously they'd learnt their lessons as they immediately stopped playing and asked us for money. There was no cynicism in their smiles and our hearts were captivated. This time we didn't give money but pens from a selection Hélène always carried in her handbag for situations such as these. Hoping we had done "the right thing" and that it would encourage them for all the "write" reasons, we "spoke" to their mothers and lingered for a while.

A sanctimonious Western gesture or a genuine attempt to communicate, interact and encourage? I know how it may come across but we believed in what we were doing and it was done with the best of intentions. Believe.

The second day followed the pattern of the first. Eating, drinking, sunbathing and watching life drift by. Looking back I believe this was the brownest I got the whole year. Flashing my new dentures at the camera, my photos looked like they were in negative.

Suitably refreshed and incredibly laid back, as that had been my preferred position the previous 48 hours, reality hit us as the taxi we had arranged to pick us up and bring us back to Cochin failed to materialize. Much squabbling with local cabs resulted in a fare double that which brought us here in the first place.

C'est la vie, as they say south of Watford. Meanwhile I couldn't wait to get back and discover the AC Milan result. 3-2 up from the first leg, I wasn't totally confident despite Rooney's brilliant winning header as, according to reports, our performance hadn't been all that. Returning to our hotel the first thing I did was whip out my notebook and wait for it to connect to the free wi-fi.

At last. Manchester United 4 AC Milan 0 - YEEESSS!!!.

Make my day, you bastards! Reading on it transpired we had steam-rollered them, then the photos finally downloaded and there was Becks with a Green & Gold scarf round his neck. Aha! He knew what he was doing. Reading further he was quoted as saying, in all innocence, he'd just picked it up from the ground. Good boy. He knew that in those nano seconds photos of him wearing the Green & Gold would be flashed around the world. I doubt whether Fergie would have been pleased, but then I'd also read that there had been no mention of Becks in his programme notes, so I couldn't make out where exactly Fergie's and Becks's relationship lay. Did Becks do it to show affinity with our campaign or to get back at Fergie, or a combination of both? Being away from the day to day tittle-tattle of the red tops I could only speculate.

I gave both the benefit of the doubt and just revelled in the result and performance. I was delighted, yet also frustrated, as there was now no way

I could catch the highlights on TV. It's at moments like these that being so far away really brings it all back home. I'd contemplated at various intervals before leaving Blighty whether enjoying a once-in-a-lifetime experience or submerging myself in sensory and exotic overload, I might become aware of the diminishing affect Manchester United held over my very existence.

No fucking chance.

FRIDAY 12 MARCH CHENNAI TO PONDICHERRY, INDIA

Arriving tired, sweaty and exhausted in Chennai Airport around 22.00. By now we'd missed the last bus to Pondicherry on the south eastern coast of India, our next chosen destination. Unspoken signals between us led Hélène and I to the taxi rank outside the arrivals terminal where a group of men, each apparently bathing in their very own swarm of mosquitoes, awaited in battered cars of all descriptions.

A rip-off all-inclusive fare of 2200 rupees was agreed for the two hour ride, so we followed a young man to his car, squashed our luggage in his boot, but before we took off I said I had to go to the loo. (I didn't actually, but considering Chennai was a major centre for cricket and the IPL was in full swing, a LUHG sticker in the men's' arrivals toilet was called for. 7 down, 93 to go.)

Chennai, formerly Madras, at night is as frantic as during the day. Passing from the centre through the suburbs, the entire population seemed to be on the streets. A mass of seething humanity and bare lightbulbs as far as the eye could see. Once out into the countryside the driver stepped on the gas and we sped along at highly illegal speeds. But not before long he stopped at a petrol station to fill up, and asked us to pay the bill.

"OK." I thought. "I'll just deduct this amount from the 2200."

It wasn't the first time we'd been asked to pay this way so I thought nothing of it. Meanwhile the driver was picking up speed once more, so much so that Hélène and I had to hold on to the doors so as not to be thrown from side to side as in those old black and white Keystone Cops type comedies from the 1920s.

Relaxing it wasn't.

As is the way in India we passed though a number of check points and barriers, but at one the driver, who spoke very little English, crossed the road and spent around ten minutes in an office. When he came back he asked us for 300 rupees.

"What for?" I asked.

He pointed to a piece of paper that looked like a certificate and a fee of 300 rupees printed at the bottom.

"I thought the agreed price of 2200 rupees was all-inclusive?" I said to Hélène.

"Let's just get there. We'll deal with it once we've arrived. I'm tired."

So, reluctantly, I paid, and prepared myself for the "discussion" we would have with the driver upon arrival. Setting off once again I noticed a "Deviation" sign for Pondicherry passing by, but we sped straight on.

"This is going to be interesting." I thought, wondering what antics the driver was going to perform. I was not disappointed. He doubled back against on-coming traffic, then drove over rough ground that turned out to be a new road under construction, performing more Keystone Cops manoeuvres that resulted in us bumping and grinding against every contour of the vehicle. Eventually we arrived on the outskirts of Pondicherry where the driver began to ask for directions for the Queens Hotel, our sleeping venue of choice. I leant over and showed him my map but he wasn't interested. I leant back and let the driver get on with it.

Finally, at around 12.30 in the morning, and with the bar of the Queens Hotel still in full swing, we pulled up in front. We unloaded our luggage and the driver came round and asked for 2200 rupees.

"Here's 1750 rupees." I said. "That's 2200 less 300 for that certificate of yours and 150 for the petrol."

"No. You pay 2200. Look."

He pointed at some small print at the bottom of his taxi slip which stated that passengers pay for all additional expenses incurred. I informed him that we had been quoted an all-inclusive price of 2200 rupees and thus the stand off began.

Like a scene out of a spaghetti western we circled each other and spat out our respective arguments. The staff of the hotel came down the steps to see what the fuss was all about. The driver's lack of English diminished the entertainment value of the argument but everyone could see I wasn't going to budge. The hotel manager acted as go-between between the two warring factions and in the end I handed over 1800 rupees.

I think I won on points.

Exhausted physically and mentally we were led up to the first floor and offered a choice of several large colonial rooms. The Rough Guide to India had recommended the Queens Hotel for two reasons.

1) It was the place to hang out in Pondicherry. Correct

2) The rooms are spotlessly clean. Incorrect.

Our overwhelming desire just to collapse on one of the beds vanished in an instant as we were confronted by the filthiest rooms, walls, floors and beds you've ever seen.

Hélène immediately went into Kim and Aggie mode and launched an in-depth investigation into every nook and cranny. Now I didn't think we'd utilize EVERY nook and cranny but Hélène was not to be swayed. Much spraying later we spread our silk sheet on the bed, set up our own mosquito net and jumped inside.

Tomorrow (or later that morning to be precise) would be another day.

SUNDAY 14 MARCH. PONDICHERRY, INDIA
MANCHESTER UNITED 3 FULHAM 0

I'm possibly going to alienate a few readers here, but I witnessed today injustice and hypocrisy on a scale I was mentally prepared for in theory but not in practice. We took our first daylight stroll in Pondicherry, on the south east coast of India. The outskirts are just like any other medium size Indian town. Streets teeming with people all hours of the day and night, row upon row of rundown housing and makeshift accommodation next to open sewers that even Peter Rachman would have had second thoughts of renting out. However, just a few streets from the sea was the fading glory of French colonial architecture, with the most opulent buildings housing all sorts of French bureaucracy and the Governor of Pondicherry himself. Opposite were the beautifully manicured municipal gardens open only to the chosen few.

On the opposite side of the gardens was a small patch of grass knee deep in stinking rubbish and excrement, and a cross section of lower casts and down and outs living, eating, sleeping and shitting on any spare piece of land available. The surrounding pavements were littered with men, women and children, some as little as one and two, also living, eating, sleeping and shitting, but this time on the pavements and walls.

For me, what made this scene all the more galling was that, punctuated along various streets were a succession of temples and churches. Although of more interest to historians rather than lovers of period architecture, their facades hid treasure troves of priceless furniture, artefacts and the finest local masonry and textiles.

Now I may be a little naive here, but I thought God, in whichever form you believe in, was all caring and all seeing. Yet all these structures were man-made in mans' imagination of what God would like and appreciate. (Do you think they had focus groups thousands of years ago?) The taxes they derive from the masses and an ever increasing property portfolio (religious organisations are very often the largest property developers in many countries around the world) seem to go overwhelmingly into the construction and maintenance of these elaborate structures at the expense of the very people they are meant to help and support.

Meanwhile, every Saturday and Sunday afternoon, as the fierce sun begins to lose its intensity, families dress in their finest to stroll up and down the beach less promenade. The "joie de vivre" is infectious. Mobile stalls sell everything from little bowls of tempting fresh fruit, delicious hot and cold local savouries, ice cream and even candy floss. Hélène and I did the entire length, with me going off at tangents every time I spied a bar or café, in the vain hope of finding one that would broadcast our home game against Fulham. Failed. In the end I had to rely on a local internet café the following day to find out the result on BBC Sport.

United 3 Fulham 0

Another brace from Rooney who seems on fire at the moment. That's 32 goals in all competitions this season. Kerpow! Of course, it wouldn't be United without a little angst. Reading the Torygraph report it seems Ramon Calderon, the Real Madrid president (Booo!!) wants to add Rooney to Ronaldo and the rest of his Las Vegas style roadshow. Can't see that happening though. Can you imagine Rooney speaking Spanish? No, neither can I. On the other hand I never imagined dyed-in-the-wool Red David Beckham ever leaving United, so what do I know?

Of course, a win is a win and for that I was grateful. Since my last match in London before this great adventure began was a 3-0 defeat at Fulham, United have collected 29 points from a possible 36. Why did they wait till after I left? Bastards! It keeps us in contention for the title and there were bigger fish to fry in the coming weeks, so I put the game to the back of my mind and immersed myself once again in Indian culture and food.

Today we went to Auroville which describes itself as a universal town where men and women of all countries are able to live in peace and progressive harmony above all creeds, all politics and all nationalities. Appealing to my latent hippy philosophy it goes on to say... "to live in Auroville, one must be a willing servitor of the Divine Consciousness." Who's this DC guy then? Not another guru? India does seem to have a production line in gurus.

Suppressing the desire to take the piss, Hélène and I embark on an excursion that hopefully will dispel my cynicism and take me to a higher plain. A few days beforehand I had tried to book a hostel within the grounds but everything was fully booked. Only by staying within Auroville could anyone fully appreciate all that this ideal township has to offer. On a one day visitor excursion we would be on the outside looking in, one of a coachload of gawping tourists denied access to the inner sanctum and "the vibe".

Bearing this in mind we entered the site and were led past a magnificent banyan tree to a large concrete welcome centre with the Auroville philosophy available in all forms of written and visual media. Having read up on all things Auroville, Hélène was particularly looking forward to, if not exactly embracing, then at least experiencing the spiritual side. Yet the vision as embodied in the welcoming video made her uneasy and questioning the credibility behind the precision of the philosophy.

It seemed to us an awkward balance between freedom of expression and exclusions in place to stop disbelievers and religious fanatics from accessing the inhabitants within. Now the question I always ask is, "What is utopia?", and being as I'm in India it's time to think this through to its logical conclusion.

Utopia is what people imagine a perfect society to be, but as we are all different we all have different visions of our utopia. I envisage a world where it's sunny every day and it only rains at night when I'm in bed. There's no violence and women find me irresistible (OK, I've gone from idealism to fantasy, but bear with me) However, my world is filled with Manchester United and all the tension, stress, panic, agony and ecstasy that that entails. Nothing on this Earth comes close, which is difficult to square with the visions portrayed in science fiction novels and films of an all-seeing, all-knowing eye calmly at peace with the world.

United wouldn't be United if they didn't drag us from the pit of despair to the heights of ecstasy in the blink of a Charlton pile driver, a Bestie dribble or an arrogant Eric volley. I love having my insides screwed up in anticipation and my bowels relinquished as the ebb and flow of a match ensues. You can't tell me sex is as good as all those heart stopping last minute goals we seem to conjure out of nothing.

I thrive on the uncertainty, the invisible threshold between pain and pleasure. My common-sense cries out for the eradication of anguish. How to pay the rent when we get back? How to put food on the table for my family? Will I keep my job in these uncertain times? I'd pay a king's ransom for peace of mind on that score. The relief of a lottery win would be overwhelming, but it's not the be-all and end-all of my world. Manchester United plays such a disproportionate role in my life that I have no choice but to accept the emotional baggage that comes with it.

If I found inner peace it would mean United no longer dominated my world and I cannot let that happen, so Auroville, with all its good intentions, is not my heaven on Earth.

MONDAY 15 MARCH - PONDICHERRY TO GOA, INDIA

"The moment he walked through the door (boom boom)
I could tell he was… trouble."

Time to leave and get back to my dentist in Goa. The taxi driver arrived at 7.00pm in a small Suzuki hatchback. Doctor Who's Tardis it was not, so I was intrigued as to how he would fit our two giant and two normal rucksacks into his Dinky toy. The look on his face said it all - he was not a happy bunny. He huffed and he puffed. He puffed and he huffed, his semi bald head glistening with sweat under the street lights. Finally, with the combined help of a number of the surrounding entourage, and by removing his back parcel shelf, he got one of the giant rucksacks in the boot, one on the front passenger seat along with one of the normal rucksacks. Hélène and I took the remaining normal rucksack with us in the back. He then started a long animated conversation with the hotel manager while we perched ourselves on the back seat either side of the normal rucksack, glistening in our own sweat.

We wormed our way through the busy Pondicherry streets and out onto the two lane motorway, which in fact was just like a two lane main road in Britain, but if they want to call it a motorway that's fine with me. It soon became apparent the driver was having problems as, every so often, he world rub his hand across his forehead in an attempt to stay awake. Half an hour into the journey he turned to me and said, no demanded, six hundred rupees for petrol. We then came to our first toll booth.

"30 rupees".

I handed him a one 100 rupee note. The attendant in the booth gave him 70 rupees changed. I fully expected him to pass it back to me but no, he pushed it into a receptacle on the dashboard. Charming. I gave him the benefit of the doubt. He was obviously only keeping it for the next toll and towards the 60 rupees for taxis to enter Chennai airport. More efficient than to keep turning round. Silly me. At around 9.00pm he drove off the motorway onto a patch of land housing a small café and a couple of other low-key shops.

"Coffee. Five minutes."

Charming. Not, "Do you mind if I just pull over for five minutes? I really need to have a short break." or an equivalent. Without waiting for our response he disappeared from view. Luckily for us, and him come to mention it, our flight to Goa was not due to take off until 05.40 the following morning, but the driver didn't know that. We could have been in a desperate rush but that was inconsequential to him.

Fifteen minutes later he re-appeared, got back into the car and drove off without so much as nod in our direction. One more toll and then at just past ten o'clock, after much more rubbing of his forehead to keep awake, we arrived at Chennai Airport.

I got out to give him a hand as I knew he would struggle. Hélène found a trolley as I got out my wallet. I handed over the money and he went berserk. I couldn't catch most of it, his English pronunciation qualifying him for Barclays Bank telephone customer service, but I caught, "Haven't had any supper. Haven't had a coffee." (eerr, yes you have, don't you remember?) He knew how long it would take from Pondicherry to Chennai and back, I thought. If you miss your creature comforts, why accept the booking in the first place?

He threw a couple of the smaller ten rupee notes back in my face as though I had insulted him, then went away complaining at the top of his voice to anyone who would listen around the crowded and chaotic departure terminal entrance.

Let's just say it was a long hard night on the airport floor, interspersed with toilet breaks and the obligatory LUHG sticker in the mens' departure lounge toilet (8 down, 92 to go) but a price worth paying for a cheap flight back to Panaji in Goa and my final showdown with the dentist.

SATURDAY 20 MARCH. DELHI, INDIA

Our first day in Delhi and more than 36 hours before our home game against Liverpool, so I could immerse myself in this multidimensional metropolis populated by tenacious touts selling everything including kitchen sinks.

We decided to get up early in our £7 a night private room with hot and cold running cockroaches to minimize the effect of the intense heat and took a taxi to India Gate, the Marble Arch of India. Situated in spacious New Delhi, the city built as the Imperial capital of India by the British, it was originally known as All India War Memorial, the monument commemorates the 90,000 soldiers of the British Army who lost their lives fighting for the British Indian empire, or more correctly the British Raj in World War 1.

We arrived around 09.00am and it was already populated by ice cream sellers and street vendors. Families were picnicking or simply living on the vast scorched earth and beggars made a bee line for our TK MAXX/Primark clothed bodies.

Resistant to smiles wider than the elegant boulevards surrounding India Gate, we took our obligatory photographs before deciding to walk the two miles up the main aforementioned elegant boulevard to the imposing and imperialistic government buildings at the far end. Mistake.

As the sun rose higher in the sky so my will to live diminished in equal amounts. Did I say it was hot? It wasn't just hot, it was fucking hot, and humid too. Bravely waving away the enticing production line of taxis and tuk-tuks that descended on us like locusts, we spent the following two hours walking unshaded and hatless, passed the foreign embassies and tops of 5★ hotels until we finally arrived at a gloriously pompous sandstone building complex.

Looking back along the boulevard, the majesty of India Gate shimmering on the horizon must have inspired generations of those misty eyed occupying forces who remembered when a quarter of the globe was coloured pink. Shaking ourselves out of these dewy-eyed reminisces, we realized we were incredibly thirsty, hungry, sweaty and knackered. We hailed a tuk-tuk and asked to be taken to rambunctious Old Delhi, the capital of Islamic India.

"Be careful, sir. The place is full of thieves and murderers. Let me take you round. Don't walk. I show you everything."

Eerr…is he talking about Liverpool? I don't think so. Taken back by this overt display of religious bigotry, I chose my words with care, whilst assimilating the ramifications of his tirade.

"I'm sure we'll be OK. We walk everywhere, and we're old enough to be wary and use our common sense."

"Believe me, sir. It's not safe. I take you everywhere. I show you everything."

By this time I was getting angry. In my own mind I had tried to justify the strength of the driver's comments, but there was no disguising, as a Hindu, his utter contempt for Muslims. Was he representative of a significant number of his fellow Hindi? His blatant hatred came as a shock to me. I was ready for the segregation of castes, but this element knocked me back. I didn't want an argument. I was a guest in his country and maybe I had misinterpreted his comments (no chance) so I continued to smile and remained silent as he pointed out various landmarks such as the Feroz Shah Kotla cricket ground at Bahadur Shah Zafar Marg.

One last plea to drive us round Old Delhi fell on deaf ears as we bid him farewell and reflected on what he had said. The dramatic Red Fort lay before us, with the magnificent Jama Masjid, India's largest mosque dominating the skyline.

Did I say large? I almost said massive. Whoops! Just imagine a mind-blowing 25,000 people accommodated within its gargantuan red sandstone and white marble striped exterior. By way of contrast its majesty was further enhanced by the labyrinth of dark narrow passageways of medieval bazaars that seemed to cascade outwards on all sides. We could have been on the set of Michael Palin's Jabberwocky. We sat, ate and drank in our surroundings whilst we recovered from our excursions. Suitably refreshed, we made our way up the steps to the entrance.

An American couple were having an argument with one of two men in front of the main gate as we peered inside.

"Ticket. 500 rupees." The second man shouted rudely.

"Sorry." I said. "We just want to look inside."

"Stop. 500 rupees."

That was rather aggressive, I thought.

Before I could reply the man shouted at some people behind us.

"500 rupees. 500 rupees."

Was it me? I thought. I looked at the man. He had this angry, aggressive look on his face, just like his partner arguing with the American couple. I don't need this, I thought. Hélène and I looked at each other and descended a few steps.

Their attitude, coupled with more rip-off tourist prices, had really put our backs up. We discussed the situation and Hélène asked if I wanted to go inside. To be honest, I'm not into ancient religious buildings. I knew we'd be visiting a load more holy and military places before the year was out, so I made the decision to give this one a miss and spend more time wandering round the narrow winding streets of the bazaar. There was hardly a tourist in sight as we delved into the mayhem. It felt like a biblical film set as we were jostled between stalls and walls, diving under hundreds of loose and dangerous looking overhead electricity cables while keeping our wits and valuables about us.

This had certainly been a condensed day of Indian culture, both good and bad. We needed a few moments of reflection to bring it all into perspective. I couldn't sweep the negatives under the carpet. This year was going to be an eye opener, I knew that. It had always been my mission to separate myth from fact, away from the sanitised verbalisations of lofty travel writers. More Lonely Planet than Condé Naste, and certainly more Rough than Guide. Sometimes the truth is uncomfortable and it's not always politically correct. Often we think that the further away a place and its people are, the more exotic and alluring it must be.

I was determined to make the most every moment was to offer, yet I was not prepared to compromise on principles I held dear. On the other hand, who is to say that my Western ideals are superior to those of other peoples on other continents, whose very existence had evolved from a completely different set of values? This was going to be some learning curve, and I would have to learn when to open my mouth and when to keep it firmly shut.

I welcomed this comparatively early night as once we stopped talking I could re-focus on the Liverpool game tomorrow.

SUNDAY 21 MARCH. DELHI, INDIA
MANCHESTER UNITED 2 LIVERPOOL 1

The day started early as this time I woke up at 05.30. I tossed and turned (No, I did just toss and turn. No double meanings this early) I tried to go back to sleep but to no avail, so I decided to activate my brain and review my diminishing options on where I could possibly watch the Liverpool game that evening. The internet café round the corner said I could watch the game on one of his machines, which at 40 rupees an hour meant the whole match would only cost me £1.12. As long as their ancient machines had the software to run one of the feeds, so no guarantee there then.

We set aside the morning to sort out our family reunion in Thailand and made our way to a nearby internet café. Hélène attacked one machine whilst I began my booking mission on another, hindered by agonizingly slow and weak signals. After hours of Barclaycard cock-up induced rage Hélène and I agreed we'd had enough for one day and left to explore Delhi, only to discover one giant building site. Just our luck we had arrived at a time when two monumental construction projects were underway simultaneously. First of all they were building an extension to the metro system that was full to bursting every morning and every evening. On top of this they were preparing for the Commonwealth Games that summer and the whole of the centre was a hot, dust-filled cement mixer.

Thus we put sight seeing on the back burner and decided to utilize our time best by planning our onwards destinations. I approached a couple of guys to ask for directions to the official Indian Tourist Office. They smiled and beckoned us to follow them. We scrambled over broken masonry and rubble as they set a fast pace, taking turns to ask me the same questions as they led us on a merry dance around the backstreets of central Delhi until they pushed open a door of one of the myriad of "official" tourist offices that looked decidedly unofficial to me. I waited until Hélène came up behind, all panting, heat and dust, and we entered what was obviously just a travel agent run by a relative/friend of the two guys who led us there and earned a commission for every customer they introduced.

Once again it re-enforced the impression that everyone was on the make in India and nothing or no-one could be taken at face value. We sat down, in my mind we would at least get an idea of possible itineraries and have the basis for a comparable quote. We left an hour later having parted with over £1000 and a detailed tour involving low-cost airlines, a private air-conditioned car and driver and numerous 2 star hotels booked.

How did that happen?

Stepping outside I noticed Hélène had one of her faces on. I thought we had agreed the itinerary together so what could have brought this on?

Her. "You were so deep in conversation with those two guys as you rushed ahead you paid no attention to me."

Me. "But you were right behind me. It was just that with all the rubble and narrow passageways it wasn't always possible to walk side by side."

Her. "What you didn't see was that a lump of masonry fell on my head. It hurt like hell but I couldn't stop or I would have lost you, you were walking so fast."

Me. "I'm sorry. I didn't realize."

Thinks to myself. Why is it my fault a lump of masonry fell on her head? I'm just the easy target I suppose. Or in this case, she was. Mustn't laugh. It won't help my cause.

Back in our room I had time to think about the up and coming Liverpool match. I'd made arrangements with the manager of the internet café round the corner, who had assured me that a free download I had read about on one of the United fans forums would work on his machines. I had my doubts as his machines had been made before computers were invented. But, hey, needs must.

I got to the internet café just before 7.00pm. Armed with the link to the free download I registered and clicked on the link.

Nothing.

I tried several times but as I suspected the ancient computers didn't have software capable of showing the match live. I turned to the young guy who ran the place and was watching TV outside and asked him what time the (bloody) IPL game finished.

"Five or ten minutes. That's all." Hmmm. As I waited I switched on BBC Sport. Ten minutes gone, score 1-1. What the fuck! What's happening? Who, what, when, how....???

Finally the cricket was over and he switched to ESPN. I pulled up a chair outside on the gravel and joined him in front of the TV. Yup, there it was, 1-1. Whatever had gone on before, the match seemed pretty scrappy. Liverpool, as they had done in recent visits, were playing boring but effective football which seemed to stifle our midfield creativity. We were too slow and predictable in our build up and created few clear-cut chances. Surprisingly Park seemed our most effective striker, putting himself about in his normal busy fashion and continually harassing their defense. 1–1 at half time.

We'll have to increase out urgency in the second half, I thought, or the Scousers bogey will continue. And that's not nice. Meanwhile the manager was more than happy for me to put one of my LUHG stickers up on his wall. 9 down 91 to go.

In the second half we did indeed increase our urgency and Liverpool were confined to their own half. Their attacking forays diminished under the United onslaught, with Park again going close. Then justice was finally delivered when little Ji Sung dived bravely between two Liverpool defenders and headed a low cross into the Scousers' net. I jumped up and let out a yell.

"Yes, Yes, Yes! Go on Park my son. You deserve it. WE deserve it!" "Park. Park, Wherever you may be…" Passers by turned to look at what had caused all this commotion. I didn't care. Liverpool were now a spent force. I expected a fierce onslaught but they reverted to type as they lost another away match this season. Revenge was ours and I returned to our flea-pit a much happier, sweatier man than I had been a couple of hours earlier.

MONDAY 22 MARCH DELHI – VARANASI, INDIA

As the first part of our £1000+ package we had booked with the travel agent, we found ourselves in the departure lounge of the ultra modern airport in Delhi waiting for our flight to Varanasi, which for several thousand years has been India's cultural and religious centre in the northern state of Uttar Pradesh, not only for Hindus but also for Buddhists and Jainists.

We abused ourselves in the delicious, low priced restaurants (in an airport? There's a first.) and took advantage of the free Wi-Fi to catch up on friends, family and United gossip. I also considered this international arena an ideal venue for my next LUHG sticker, so one visit to the men's' toilet brought the score to 10 down, 90 to go.

An hour's flight later and we landed next to a shack masquerading as Varanasi Airport. Within half an hour the premises was empty except for us and a couple of taxis. Where was our driver? We asked in a couple of offices but no-one knew anything. I took the opportunity to adhere a LUHG sticker to a prominent information board. 11 down 89 to go. Every cloud, and all that. Half an hour later, one of the drivers of one of the taxis who we had already asked, shuffled up to us and asked our names. It turned out he was our driver but had been given a wrong name, so didn't recognize us when we first arrived.

No, I don't understand either.

He then took us in his Tata rust bucket to an office where a 70 year old local English speaking gentleman in a white suit introduced himself as our guide for our stay in Varanasi. He explained the programme as we drove through the outskirts of the town and came to a halt in front of a hotel.

"Excuse me." I said. "We asked for a hotel by the Ganges, within the old town."

He looked disconcerted. He went inside, then came out again a few minutes later and said he had made arrangements with another hotel. We drove on and entered the old town. The roads became narrower and I began to think the car would never get through.

I was right.

We stopped on a corner and told to get out. We waited until a horse drawn cart arrived drawn by a frail looking old man. They arranged our two large rucksacks on the floor then told us to climb up and sit astride the rucksacks and the seats. Once in position they placed our backpacks on our laps. I couldn't believe the old guy could pull us along and I offered to walk alongside, but this was obviously an insult to his manhood and his stare left me in no doubt what my place was.

We started off slowly but soon the narrow cobbled lanes exercised their almost mystical power and I began to slip forward on the plastic seat. This had the effect of lowering my bottom and raising my flailing legs into the air. Inch by inch I began my 180 degree transformation into Mr Upside Down man, accompanied by hysterical shrieks from you know who next to me who revelled in my discomfort.

Holding onto my bag meant I was unable to hold onto anything else and gravity and cobbles combined to make the day for the hordes of passers by who couldn't believe what they were seeing. To this day I can imagine the stories they would tell of this crazy upside down Englishman with his face where his arse should be and his feet where his head should be. At least I left my mark on the locals.

We went out for a stroll that evening to get a feel of the place. The Ganges in the failing light from our balcony, with the lights of the town on one river bank and absolutely nothing on the other was spooky and added to the mysticism of the place. A combination of mosquitoes, mystery and romance.

TUESDAY 23 MARCH VARANASI, INDIA

This morning we woke up at 05.30 and prepared for our pre-sunset boat trip on the Ganges by dousing ourselves in 100+ mosquito repellent. With no United match until the weekend I could totally immerse myself in this most sacred of cities. I'd read that Varanasi is one of the oldest continually inhabited cities in the world, but it didn't actually say "people". I think they must have been talking about mosquitoes. They were everywhere, like special affects in a Harry Potter movie.

Our guide was waiting for us outside our room at 06.00am and he led us through a maze of narrow alleyways and down the steps of one of the ghats to his small rowing boat. There was one other English girl in the boat already. A strange, translucent grey covered the Ganges and the flat narrow bank on the other side. The sun had yet to rise so the sky reflected this calm, still greyness. It was so peaceful as no motorised boats could be seen, or heard. One might even say it was "spooky", but in a lovely way if that makes sense.

The 100+ mosquito repellent was working overtime like an invisible force field. Swarms of the little bastards would attack us in waves, only to be repelled within a couple of inches of our bare flesh. Amazing. Thank you, thank you, thank you.

The young oarsman began to row, and all we could hear were the soft ripples of the water as his oars broke the surface. I looked around and became aware of other similar boats, some the same size as ours and quite a few larger ones bulging with tourists. I then realised that at this hour the Ganges was not overflowing with pilgrims from the four corners of the planet looking for purity, salvation and spiritual guidance, but tourists from the same four corners of the planet looking for pilgrims from the four corners of the planet looking for purity, salvation and spiritual guidance.

My western cynicism was extinguished however as we rounded a bend in the river and witnessed hundreds of men, women and children bathing, washing themselves and their clothes in one of the world's filthiest rivers. Kids were also laughing and playing while whole groups of women in the water were chatting and giggling like our mothers used to do over the garden fence in the old days.

As we got nearer to the famous Ganga Ghats the noise from the riverbank grew louder, the steps disappearing under the sheer volume of multicoloured humanity. It was actually quite moving and this devout atheist began to appreciate what this most holy of cities meant to so many people. Still, you won't find me swimming in the sewage polluted waters full of waste chemicals and the odd body part, but, hey, it takes all sorts.

By this time someone had switched on the sun, which had first appeared as a pale pink/grey ball but was now a glowing orangey red ball dominating the horizon. The intensity of the scene was having a deep affect on me and I wanted to somehow capture the bigger picture. We all had another moving experience as I stood up in the boat to take in the panoramic view on my camcorder, only to upset the delicate balance of the small rowing boat as it rocked dramatically from side to side, threatening to capsize at any moment. The other girl let out a pitiful little cry and my wife gave me a decidedly non-spiritual look. I attempted a sheepish sort of all knowing smile but only re-enforced my status as Frank Spencer act-a-like.

I sat down as though nothing untoward had happened but daren't look anyone in the eye. We then turned and rowed to the far end of the ghats where we were not allowed to take photos. This was the section set aside to burn the dead, offering various body parts to the river so the recently departed could liberate their soul from human body to the ultimate. It looked like a scene from a Quentin Tarantino movie.

We could make out individual limbs sticking out of the giant cauldrons like a scene from Macbeth and feel the heat on our faces from the flames that rose up into the sky. At the same time, hundreds of flowers and illuminated candles floated down the river. It was mystical, magical and macabre, all at the same time.

We had lots to reflect on as we wormed our way round the hot narrow alleyways of the old town for the rest of the day. Our musings were continually interrupted by breaks for drinks and a lunchtime meal in one of the hippy type cafes that populated the place. On a number of notice boards offering yoga and other holistic practices I strategically placed a number of LUHG stickers. 12, 13 & 14 down. 88, 87 & 86 to go. With all due respect, my Red religion was superior to theirs.

Every few metres delicious smells wafted from the street vendors cooking in the passageways. By the evening I couldn't stand it any longer.

"I just gotta try some." I said to Hélène.

"You know how weak your stomach is. Don't do it."

"But we've been passing these guys for six weeks now. Surely one of the wonders of world travel is to taste local street food?"

"You don't know what's inside it."

"But they're cooking it right in front of us. It must be fresh."

"Maybe, but how long have the ingredients been lying there in the heat waiting to be cooked. Don't chance it. You'll be sorry."

"But look at this guy. There's over half a dozen varieties of golden balls on offer. Let's just try one each."

Hélène let out a sigh.

"OK, we'll take two of each and take them back to our room for supper."

Yippee! A result.

Duly purchased, I carried our prized booty in my arms, savouring the warm delicious aroma that wafted along with us. Once inside our room Hélène went straight to take a shower but I couldn't wait any longer. I opened the bag and scoffed down my first golden ball.

Aah, I was in heaven. Beautiful. Such intense flavours danced on my tongue, intoxicated my mouth and settled in my stomach in a warm lump of cascading culinary contentment. I couldn't wait. I had to have another one. And another one. With Hélène still wet behind the ears, and other parts of her anatomy, I finished my portion and bathed in the embers of an edible explosion. WOW! That was something else! And to think Hélène had denied me all this time. (The food, that is) When she came out she had to agree my golden balls had been worth getting her teeth into. We sprayed the room and went to bed under our mosquito net, exhausted by the sights, sounds, smells and taste the day had assaulted our senses with.

Sleep didn't last long for yours truly though. At 02.30am my stomach started to fight back and my bottom responded to the calls for action. I let out a dump to end all dumps. A continuous stream normally associated with Rusholme on a Saturday night. I was glad when it was all over. I climbed gingerly back under the mosquito net, careful not to wake Hélène. The last thing I wanted was for her to roll over and say, "I told you so!"

I lay there for about an hour until I pressed the repeat button and renewed my acquaintance with the urinal. Then every hour on the hour throughout the night my golden balls came alive and a production line of Varanasi shit showered the porcelain. It wasn't very nasi. On the contrary, it was very nasty. (Yes, I did just write that. And you thought my jokes couldn't get any worse. Gotcha!) Yet Hélène didn't wake up once. How about that! By the morning I was but a shadow of my former self and I couldn't totally hide my nocturnal escapades. The first thing that hit Hélène was the stench. Then she looked at me and wondered why my suntan had disappeared. I couldn't lie. I confessed my sins and Hélène extracted her pound of flesh (mine had already been extracted) I felt awful but we had to go for breakfast on the roof terrace of our hostel.

The view over the Ganges was impressive but I wondered why the entire area was covered in barbed wire. I didn't have to wait long for the answer. A colony of wild monkeys swung through trees and clambered over the barbed wire in an unsuccessful attempt to nick our breakfasts. I know they must be pests for the locals but they were a wonderful sideshow for us travellers, swinging from tree to roof and back again (the monkeys, not the travellers).

That evening we booked a sunset boat ride, but before we got on the boat the boatman spent ages trying to hard sell us an extra two hours for 800 rupees which would cover a special Rama ceremony at the Hindu temple. By the time he realized no really meant no, the sun had already set and we had missed the sunset from the river. What's Indian for Knobhead.

The mosquitoes came out in force once more but fortunately the force was with us in the form of our 100+ mosquito repellent. I was amazed at how effective our invisible force field was. Other passengers suffered multiple bites but we remained bite free. Owing to the festivities at the Hindu temple there were a lot more boats on the river, the mood changing from calm to vibrant as a riot of noise and colour filled the air. Larger boats playing a variety of Bhangra, British and American dance music passed us on both sides. The waters were alive. We ended our boat trip and walked as near as we could along the side of the Ganges to watch the colourful Rama festivities for free. Highly enjoyable.

That night I went to bed without any supper, which, believe me, was a blessing not a punishment. The following morning we packed our bags and waited to be picked up and taken to Varanasi railway station for the night train to Agra and the Taj Mahal.

Forget golden balls, this was the second part of the famous golden triangle. We were dropped about 500 metres from the station entrance. Why? I looked at the rough ground, our two giant rucksacks and our two normal rucksacks. I weighed up the affect dragging all this along in the strength sapping heat would have on the remains of my anatomy and enquired why we couldn't be dropped a little nearer to the station.

"This is as far as we're allowed to go." was the unsatisfactory reply from our white suited guide.

"Lazy bastards." I thought. We bid them a curt farewell and commenced our army manoeuvres, bumping grinding our way over the rocks and stones, sweating buckets and without experiencing a single ounce of pleasure. Arriving at the station entrance we realized our platform was on the other side of the tracks and the only way to reach it was by lifting our full complement of luggage up the steps, over the bridge, and down the other side.

I looked around desperately for porters but there weren't any. This was weird.

Normally, wherever you go in India, hordes come out offering all kinds of goods and services, yet the one time we would welcome their advances they were conspicuous by their absence. I approached a couple of men leaning against a car. I put on my best smile.

"Hi. Would you two guys be willing to help us carry our bags over to the other platform?" They looked at each other, nodded, then clumsily tried to get hold of our two giant rucksacks. I was thinking these guys were almost as useless as me when two large red-shirted heroes appeared out of nowhere.

Porters! How wonderful. Please, have some money! Lots of money, only PLEASE help us with our bags. Smiling, the smile of hunters who have trapped their prey, they lofted our two giant rucksacks onto their shoulders whilst Hélène and I carried our standard rucksacks on our backs. We showed them our tickets and they dropped us right where our carriage was due to stop. Wonderful. We thanked them profusely, handed over our sweaty money, and waited for our train to Agra and one of the eight wonders of the world. The Taj Mahal.

However, I was in dire need of another wonder of the world, a toilet, so I left Hélène with the luggage so I could locate a hole in the floor. I was getting used to these urinals by now and like many travellers in India I always kept a roll of toilet paper about my person. Suitably relieved, I rejoined Hélène on the sweltering platform. When our train duly arrived I panicked, realising I only had seconds in my weakened state to lift all our "stuff" up into our carriage. Then like angels from heaven our two porters re-appeared and let us get on before handing us up our luggage. And they didn't even ask for extra money. They really were angels. We found our seats, which were actually two single plastic seats opposite each other by the window which together formed one single bed, whilst I would sleep in the plastic bunk bed above.

Opening another bottle of pretend spring water we began to converse with this nice young man in the seat opposite. It turned out he was from China, one of our future destinations, and he regaled us with stories of his home life. We took delight in detailing our travel plans while he took out his photos and was in the process of explaining each one to us when my arse and stomach finally succumbed to the dying throws of my decaying golden balls. I'm always in wonder when people, whether in real life or on the silver screen, are able to put a hand over their mouths when they know they are about to be sick, get out a few words of dialogue, then make their way to the nearest toilet or sink.

Not in my case.

I was at the mercy of involuntary spasms of violent vomiting. With no word of warning I let out a Guinness Book of Records, deep gut-wrenching, jet propelled projectile of vile stinking vomit, spraying the seats and floor of all those innocent passengers around us.

Hélène was horrified and deeply embarrassed on my behalf. I was just overcome by an overwhelming sense of relief. I had been expecting to open up more deposit accounts along the way. Instead I projected one giant, all-embracing lava-flow from my mouth, reminiscent of David Walliams as the racist English lady in Little Britain.

Boy, did that feel good when it was all over. I don't think the rest of the carriage felt the same way I did. I got down gingerly and Hélène and I used up the train's entire supply of kitchen towels and rolls of toilet paper in cleaning up my slimy lake, complete with Billy Connolly "diced carrots".

Finally I settled back to watch the countryside pass by. For some reason the young Chinese gentleman was not inclined to continue our conversation so I climbed onto my bunk and settled down for the night. Hélène did the same but déjà vu came back to haunt me as I got up around half a dozen times and made my way to the toilet at the end of the carriage. Holes in the floor, in the pitch blackness while the world moves all around you was a challenge I can tell you, which is what I've just done.

SUNDAY 28 MARCH. AGRA, INDIA
BOLTON WANDERERS 0 MANCHESTER UNITED 4

People usually come to Agra for one thing and one thing only. The Taj Mahal. There is also the Red Fort which is quite an imposing structure, but as it is situated in the centre of town, an ugly heavily polluted town at that, passing by in an air-conditioned private car on the way to our hotel was enough for us. Majit, our driver for the next few days, had met us at the station and we decided this was the way to travel. It took a sizeable chunk out of our budget but we thought we deserved a little indulgence. We were now beginning the second part of the well-worn golden triangle of Delhi-Agra-Jaipur in air-conditioned comfort, and I was going to sit back and think of, well, Delhi, Agra, Jaipur and Bolton away.

I had chosen accommodation as near as possible to the Taj Mahal itself as a dawn start was recommended to fully appreciate every aspect of the 420 acre site. We could see the roof of the iconic building from the terrace of a nearby restaurant. I was able to enjoy my first meal for almost a week, and an Indian meal at that! Lovely jubbly. I had goose bumps as I was about to realize one of my life's ambitions. I was also rather excited as I had verified that the TV in our room worked and I would be able to catch Bolton away before going to bed that night.

Things were looking up at last. My anatomy had settled down and all was right with the world. Hélène delved into her Sudoku and I turned on the TV to watch the match. No Rooney or Ferdinand, but with the Champions league quarter final first leg against Bayern Munich to come three days later, this was a calculated gamble, although in this Ferguson era it's come back to haunt us on more than one occasion.

Bolton, as expected, started off all guns and tackles blazing, then gradually our superior class rose to the surface. A bizarre own goal by Bolton's J Lloyd Samuel separated the teams at half time, although it wasn't till late in the second half that we raced away with the game. A Berbatov double and an 82nd minute strike from Darren Gibson secured the points to keep us in striking distance of free scoring Chelsea.

We had to be up at 05.00am so I only had three hours sleep to play with, but I was excited Tommy, so no chance of fatigue setting in I can assure you.

MONDAY 28 MARCH AGRA, INDIA

5.00am? No problem. As cars are not allowed within one mile of the main entrance to the Taj Mahal, our pre-arranged rickshaw would be waiting for us at 06.00am to take us to the main gate, so we wolfed down a simple breakfast and were waiting on the front step of our hostel in next to no time. Our rickshaw duly dropped us off at the main gate but there was already a long queue.

As we got closer it soon became apparent that the Indian two-tier system was in full operation. One line for Indian nationals and one line for foreigners. I left Hélène in the foreigners' queue and I went to the front to check things out. Agra has the reputation as the most corrupt of all Indian cities (and when you consider the level of corruption in India, that's quite an accolade)

Indians: 20 rupees

Foreigners: 750 rupees

Yes, you've got it. Tourists pay 37.5 times more than nationals. How could they justify that? Do all foreigners earn 37.5 times more than the average Indian? Shouldn't all people pay the same or should people from more prosperous countries pay more? If you think richer people should pay more, then by how much? India has one of the fastest growing economies in the world with a rapidly increasing middle class. Should locals be means tested? Whatever way I looked at it, the system stinks.

However, the authorities know that, despite making a lot of foreigners angry, they're hardly going to leave the queue, are they? Visiting the Taj Mahal is not what could be defined as repeat business for 99% of tourists, so they have us over a gold covered barrel. I was fuming as I made my way back along the queue. Hélène wondered why I had taken so long, and why I had my "angry of Mayfair" look on my face, to which I explained and she just shrugged her shoulders.

We slowly shuffled towards the entrance where men and women were separated, individually searched and reacquainted once inside. Then

I was asked to pay 200 rupees for the use of my own video camera, yet as soon as we passed through the impressive but conventionally constructed Darwaza (main entrance) and found ourselves in Bageecha (gardens) I was told the use of camcorders was forbidden. What's Agra for Bastards? Agra re-enforcing its well deserved reputation as the most corrupt city in India. Take a deep breath, David. Don't let it spoil your day. Now, move on.

Ah, there it was. The Taj Mahal stood majestically 400 metres in front of us, on a raised 50 metre square platform at the end of a beautiful long watercourse. No words from yours truly can adequately convey the perfection, the immaculate symmetry of design and construction with which the whole complex assaults the senses, yet after a lifetime's build up I was a little disappointed. I couldn't put my finger on it. Maybe it was the building's dull grey colour. I don't know. I had just expected more.

But then the sun slowly rose and so did the intensity of the light, and that's when the miracle unfolded before our very eyes. The stronger the sunlight and higher the sun, the whiter the marble became. By 10.00am the Taj Mahal was such a brilliant white that I literally cried at the beauty of it all. There are hundreds of books and tourist brochures and web sites describing the Taj Mahal, but only by being there can anyone truly appreciate the size and scale of perfection on earth that overwhelms the senses. To put things into perspective, I'd put it up there just behind Ole's goal in the Nou Camp, that's how magnificent it is.

I followed Hélène round the entire site, marvelling at every single element, every angle. At one stage we saw a number of armed guards surrounding a group of tourists.

"I wonder what's going on here?"

We sauntered over, hoping to be in the forefront of a breaking news story, It turned out to be just a group of paranoid American tourists who had hired these armed guards to protect them from all manner of imaginary catastrophes. Oh, how we laughed.

Of course, we both did the Lady Diana pose on the bench, but when I walked by the side of the structure that borders on the Yamuno river, the picture postcards for sale bore little resemblance to the sewage canal with its almost dry river bed and desert like conditions on the other side of the riverbank.

The Taj Mahal is a bit like Venice. It's sinking, yet I wonder how much of the money earned by tourism is ploughed back into saving the structure from decline? It is for me the most beautiful man made structure on the planet and it would be criminal if the powers that be failed in their responsibilities to maintain this legacy for generations to come.

The following day we set off in our air-conditioned Tata for Jaipur, the pink city. For lunch our driver stopped at what could loosely described as a motorway service station. Its cool, calm spacious interior was certainly a contrast to the vibrancy of everyday life on the streets, but its antiseptic blandness extended to the food which was also six times the price of local eateries. The only redeeming feature of the place was a wall bestowed with holiday company stickers, to which I added another of my LUHG sticker for fellow tourists to gaze at in awe. 15 down, 85 to go. We went to speak to the manager but he kept trying to hide, averting his eyes and walking away. But we wouldn't give up and eventually cornered him and confronted him about the price and quality of his food. He didn't give a flying fuck.

Meeting up with our driver, Majit, outside we asked him where he had gone to eat.

"In the dhaba across the road."

"Then Majit, that's where we want to eat next time. Wherever you eat, we eat, OK?"

"Yea, of course."

His English was actually more limited than we thought as he was out of his tourist speak comfort zone, so we explained that we loved Indian food, and not to stop for overpriced dumbed down tourist fayre again. He explained that he had to play safe with tourists which we totally understood, but we impressed on him that we wanted to experience everything India had to offer, as fellow Indians not as visitors to Disneyland.

Driving on the road to Jaipur we were engrossed by the clothes worn by the women working by the side of the road or in the fields. So colourful, so sparkly. A delight. Women were also working on the road itself, cleaning the tarmac with metal brushes with their babies on their backs.

We were then deposited in the centre of the pink melee; a chaotic and congested riot of traffic, people and bazaars, with a stunning backdrop of hilltop forts and glorious palaces. This was the epitome of a clichéd Bollywood Indian scene. It was wonderful.

At sunset, all the buildings within the city walls bask in a magical warm pink and gold glow. Although top heavy with tourists, nothing could take away from the magic of the place, transcending all the commercial activities that might otherwise have detracted from the very essence it unique.

"Oh we'll, drink a drink a drink to Jaipur the pink the pink the pink." Sorry, I couldn't resist.

The following day we forwent (is that the past tense of forgo?) the expensive elephant ride and asked Majit to drive us out of the city centre and up into the hills around Amber, 11 kilometres from Jaipur, to walk around the vast complex of courtyards, gardens and buildings that form the stunning Amber Fort, all built in white marble and red sandstone. Hélène and I (more I than Hélène if the truth be told) were getting a sense of monument overload, as one fort/palace began to merge into the next. Many people feel they have a duty to visit every piece of history on the tourist itinerary, and then bore friends and relatives back home with "look at me me me here here here". What about having fun, just like you would back home?

However, the Amber Fort had one saving grace. It had a lift! Eric be praised! One thing that was really getting to me by now was that the vast majority of historical buildings were constructed on hilltops. Logical, of course, in an era when location, location, location was THE major factor in the decision making process. Locate your enemy before he could attack you. Fine.

However, in this day and age, we all have to walk up these damn hills to get to them, and I swear I was walking up hills a lot more than I was walking back down again. I worked out that by the end of our year away, I should be halfway to the moon. I was always walking up up up. Just ask my thighs. To put things into perspective, I still prefer to stand at matches. I'm one of the original members of the Safe Standing Campaign.

Back in the 60s and early 70s I would be in the Stretford End, tunnel or right side, way before 1.30pm when the whole end would be rocking right up till kick-off and beyond. But now time has taken its toll. Whenever circumstances allow I will stand for the entire game, sing and chant, but as for jumping up and down for the full 90+ minutes... I wish. And so it is with walking. Anything which makes my life easier, I accept.

The Amber Fort had a lift, a modern day sacrifice that was worth its weight in steel. We all waited in line to be taken up to the top floor, and then begin our educated passage around and down without fearing the need for a lung transplant. As with all these visits I was on the constant lookout for football shirts, preferably worn by the locals. Just something to break up the monotony of monument overload. Nothing. Damn.

Any excuse for a conversation and bonding amongst locals and travellers alike I would jump at. It was my not so secret mission on this trip. I knew that not everything we did or saw would be as mind-blowing as the tourist brochures and travel guides would have us believe, but throw in a football conversation, especially with someone who loves or hates United, and spice would be added to the day. And with the Champions League quarter-final first leg against Bayern Munich in Germany coming up in a couple of days I was bursting to talk football with someone.

Anyone.

Not today though. Unfortunately.

MONDAY 29 MARCH JAIPUR TO PUSHKAR, INDIA

A distinct pattern was beginning to emerge here in India. The more religious a place, the more fundamental its followers and the more aggressive they are in their attempts to extort money from tourists. Today we drove the 168 kilometres from Jaipur to Pushkar. To be honest we'd never heard of Pushkar until it had been suggested as an important overnight stop on the way to Udiapur. A holy city with over 100 mosques and temples, all set along the shores of a lovely lake. At first Hélène and I were not convinced. Nevertheless we took the advice against our better judgement and agreed to stop for one afternoon and evening.

Our city centre hotel was right on the outskirts. In fact it was the hotel furthest away from anything, requiring a good twenty minute walk in the hot midday sun to reach the first sign of life. Talk about mad dogs and Englishmen. This was becoming a habit.

We walked past all the usual suspects, stalls selling tourist tat that look cool for five minutes in the sunshine of India but make you look a complete prat back home. Our mission was to find a restaurant overlooking the lake we'd spied only the previous evening on the internet.

We found the lake about fifteen minutes later, having survived a procession of people attempting to push flower petals in our hands. Actually we found where the lake used to be. In front of us was a waste ground with a tractor in the middle. At the bottom of the various steps (ghats) were small, square walled ponds with shallow pools of stagnant water and a few sad remnants of flower petals washed up in one corner.

Immediately a boy in black trousers and bright royal blue long sleeve shirt, who was no more than eleven or twelve, jumped on us and literally tried to pull us down to the edge of the lake to assail us with righteous fervour and a worryingly bright glint in his eye. He was selling religion but he could have been selling second hand cars or home contents insurance such was his slick spiel. Once he turned on the ignition, his mouth engaged and switched straight into overdrive.

Hélène gave him a dirty look but we had time on our hands now that the lake was an ex-lake, a lake that was pushing up daises (literally), a deceased lake. A lake that had met its maker. So I decided to indulge in a little what I intended to be friendly banter and debate. As I approached he gestured for Hélène to stay behind, as it would be bad for my karma (!) Have you noticed, the more vocal a religious fanatic becomes, the more intolerant he or she is of any dissenting voices. You would have thought if they believed so fervently in what they were preaching they would welcome disbelievers and try to win them over with sound arguments and spiritual superiority.

I had hoped he would enter into the "spirit" of a discussion and we could have an intellectual debate on the relative merits or otherwise of the relevance of religion in today's society. My hope was in vain. Just like those people trained in Mumbai or Delhi by Barclays Bank and employed at minimum wages as Customer Service agents (that's a contradiction in terms if ever there was one) he was not programmed to engage his brain outside of repeating his word perfect mantra.

He claimed my mind was closed and demanded I pay for the privilege of throwing a few of his flowers into the lakeless lake. I declined, which threw him as he'd gone straight to the "close that sale" pitch and wasn't used to people actually refusing his emotional and spiritual blackmail. I got up, collected my sandals and joined Hélène who couldn't decide who she was annoyed with more, me or the religious sales boy.

We calmed down by having a lovely meal in a rooftop restaurant overlooking the dried out lake. By this time I had discovered this wonderful fresh lime/lemon drink made out of freshly squeezed limes or lemons, to be drunk straight (Hélène's choice) or with a teaspoonful of this special syrup. A most refreshing concoction I'll have you know.

Later that afternoon we came across our driver as we were coming out of this impressive white marble Sikh Temple on the outskirts of town as he was going in. For the first time on this trip we saw the good work a religious sect could do. Majit took us round the complex and out the back where a number of men and women were cooking around a large fire. He explained that every Friday all locals, irrespective of religious persuasion, caste or credit rating, were invited by the Sikh Temple to sit and eat side by side for free.

Majit himself was a Sikh yet he had short hair. He told us that his father didn't agree and so he'd had to leave home. Ah yes, the tolerance of religion.

TUESDAY 30 MARCH. UDIAPUR, INDIA
BAYERN MUNICH 2 MANCHESTER UNITED 1 - CHAMPIONS LEAGUE Q-FINAL FIRST LEG.

I woke up, secure in the knowledge that our hotel in Udaipur had satellite TV in each room for the match that evening. I could enjoy the five hour car journey, my only real doubt concerned the water in Lake Pichola. After the disappointment of the non-existent lake in Pushkar, and having read numerous stories about the lake in Udaipur drying up after several years of drought, I was unconvinced by assurances from the tour company or our driver. My experiences so far had taught me that local people tend to say what you want to hear.

Our journey on the road re-enforced another image we had accrued, that of men sitting or lying around in the sun or the shade, drinking, talking or playing various card or board games whilst their women worked in the house, in the fields and on the roads with their children by their sides. India is being built, not so much on manual labour but womanual labour. (Yeah, that was bad, wasn't it!)

After an eternity of lost causes in the labyrinth of narrow streets surrounding the lake, we finally arrived as close as our car could get to the hotel. Two members of staff greeted us as we got out of the car and took our luggage into the hotel lobby. Another came forward with a tray containing two glasses of cold fruit juice. Heaven! I gratefully took a gulp of mine then turned to Hélène.

"Where's yours?"

"I've drunk it already"

Talk about land speed record. Wow!

After the formalities of registering we were led to our room on the second floor.

Nice. A large room with pleasant period furniture and, most importantly of all, a TV set. The view from the window was of a brick wall, not the lake as I had hoped. Disappointing, but there were more important matters to be considered.

"Excuse me. The television. Does it have satellite or cable?"

Blank smile.

"TV. Satellite? Cable?"

"Ah. I show you."

This was more like it. One of the hotel porters turned on the TV and started flicking through the channels.

"ESPN? Star Sports? I said, helpfully.

"One moment."

Lots of flicking. Lots of channels but no sports channels.

Suddenly he disappeared.

"What's going on?" I thought, doubt creeping back into my brain. I knew it. I had been too complacent. This was India. Don't take anything for granted. He re-appeared.

"Come."

I followed him into the room next door where he had found ESPN on its TV.

Phew!

I thanked him profusely and we transferred our luggage to the new room. Still only a view of a brick wall from our window, but more importantly, a view of the match from the TV to look forward to.

OK. Time for a quick meal before the match started. I suggested finding a local eatery within walking distance of the hotel, preferably with a view of the lake. Not wanting to waste time, I referred to our Rough Guide and a rooftop restaurant fitted the bill. It turned out the food and prices fitted the bill as well. Delicious flavours, twinkling lights shimmering on the black waters of Lake Pichola and a bill that complemented the proceedings nicely. Gazing out across the lake Hélène thought I was taking in the magical scene. Possibly anticipating images of Dawn Adams enticing Roger Moore into her room of the Obeiron hotel on the lake which masqueraded as a palace in Octopussy.

Wrong, of course. My stomach was in knots in anticipation of the match. Would we score the all-important away goal? Our record against German teams was not good, Barcelona '99 excepting. Was it about to change tonight? We came back to our room around ten. I pottered about for a while. We both had showers, then Hélène settled down with her DSi whilst I read up on Udaipur. The lake had indeed dried up for several years ago but the Rough Guide assured us that it was back to pre-drought levels. It didn't look like it to me but what did I know? I'd never seen it before, only in pictures in books or on the net. Oh, and the James Bond movie of course.

By now ESPN was showing highlights of the previous weekend's Premier League football for the umpteenth time, and although I had enjoyed immensely our victory over the inbreds, I had seen our goals a number of times, so I decided to get a little shut-eye and conserve my strength for the coming clash of the Titans starting 01.15 Indian time. I set the alarm on my mobile, stretched out and relaxed.

"You're boring." claimed Hélène as she sat hypnotised in front of her DSi playing Suduko.

I drifted in and out of sleep when suddenly I became aware of the fact that the flickering screen had, well, stopped flickering. I opened my eyes and to my horror the screen was a deep royal blue. The TV had lost its signal.

"NOOOOOOOO!!!"

I jumped out of bed wearing nothing but a look of horror on my face. It was now just gone midnight and the TV signal had decided to go walkabout. I missed the first half completely but commentators on Ten Sport such as Carlton Palmer (surely he doesn't speak like that in real life) were saying how, despite Rooney's header from a Nani free kick after just 66 seconds, we were fortunate to be 1-0 up at half time.

So what! This was the Champions League and the result was all-important. Of course I'd love United to play every team off the park, but reality dictated that from time to time grinding out the right result was the name of the game. In the second half Bayern continued to dominate possession but we seemed relatively comfortable. One or two scares but 1-0 away from home was more than I had hoped for a couple of hours back.

Then, after Franck Ribery (my personal choice as our next Roy Keane, despite his odious personal shenanigans) brought Bayern level with just five minutes to go, it was Ivica Olic, their version of our Ole who scored their winner in injury time. My misery was made complete when Rooney limped off in severe pain with an ankle injury in the build up to Bayern's winner. I was sick watching their players and fans over celebrating as though they'd won the bloody tournament itself. Would we be able to regroup, mentally, from this late setback, as we had a crucial Premiership defining match against Chelsea at the weekend? I was all of a quiver, I can tell you. So many permutations, how was a guy to sleep?

WEDNESDAY 31 MARCH. UDIAPUR, INDIA

Hélène and I went up to the covered restaurant on the third floor of our hotel in Udiapur for breakfast. Stunning views of Lake Pichola greeted us on three sides which instantly helped lighten my mood, then from the fourth side came the sounds of a cat being strangled. Sitting in an alcove were two young men in local costume. One was playing a side drum with a lovely deep clear sound, the other was playing a two hundred year old string instrument made out of a single piece of wood. It looked like a cruder version of the sitar and sounded like the strangled cries I omitted as Olic's winner hit the back of the net the previous night.

We sat down at a window table, hoping against hope these two earnest young men would not engage us in conversation. It was just too early. I also clutched my wallet in fear. Band playing music in hotel equals request for money. They smiled at us. We were now one of only two couples left and the other couple were further away. They're no fools, I thought.

A waiter came and we ordered our continental breakfast. The music got louder as they reached a crescendo. Dark thoughts re-surfaced concerning last night's result. Three days after wiping the floor with Bolton, we'd looked second best in all departments against an admittedly strong Bayern team. Sometimes you just can't explain it. Rome 2009 for example. After ten minutes we could have been 3-0 up before Eto'o squeezed one in from the narrowest of angles. From that moment onwards we just never got going. It was as though each one of our players decided to, collectively, have their worst game of the season, in their most important game of the season.

Last night was just the same. We never got our passing game together, allowing Bayern to take the initiative, equalise though a bloody deflected free kick late in the second half, then grab a winner in the last minute thanks to half hearted challenges from our defence which should have done better.

Despite Bayern's excessive celebrations, I consoled myself with the knowledge that our away goal could prove vital. All we had to do was win 1-0 in the return leg and we were through. However I was not Mr Sunshine that morning, and the last thing I wanted was to be nice to two uninvited musicians strangling a cat as I had breakfast.

Inevitably, without invitation, they began to explain the origins of their instruments, how they were both full time musicians. Their parents and grandparents were also full time musicians. They had performed in Dubai and Muscat. They had written the score for one of Bollywood's latest blockbusters.

I'm sorry, squeak squawk in any language is still squeak squawk, and with just three hours sleep on top of a bloody result, no amount of external beauty could outweigh their awful sound.

The rest of the day was spent wandering round Udaipur, getting lost in its narrow streets, sipping cold drinks and scoffing ice cream before taking a boat ride on the lake itself, which turned out to be murky and polluted. The James Bond hotel was also a disappointment close up, whilst only those with reservations were allowed to disembark. There was another building in the middle of the lake that we were allowed to disembark and have a look around. Quite posh it was, so LUHG sticker number 16 was deposited as discretely as possible in the cocktail area. 84 to go.

Once back on dry land we visited the old Royal Palace which had had an extension built by the British. Hélène commented that it looked like a pub down the Old Kent Road. The views from the top were breathtaking but there were stairs, stairs and more fucking stairs.

Eric, we must be so fit by now.

SATURDAY 3 APRIL. DELHI TO SRINAGAR, KASHMIR, INDIA
MANCHESTER UNITED 1 CHELSEA 2

Waiting in Delhi airport for our plane I had time to connect to the internet on my notebook. Hélène suggested I look up Srinagar in Kashmir on Google, as slightly worryingly, The Rough Guide to India made no mention of the place. Kashmir, and Srinagar in particular, had been suggested by John at Highland Travel as a suitable alternative to Nepal. It looked pleasant enough. It's main selling point being the Dal Lake and the unique rows of houseboats on its shores, one of which was to be our home for the next five nights. I then searched for our houseboat, "Heaven Queen". My heart sank as a review on Trip Advisor stated, "we thankfully sailed passed rickety old vessels such as the Highland Queen and the White Horse..."

Oh, great. Thanks a bunch. Our worst fears realised as once again John from Highland Travel had chosen the lowest common denominator as our accommodation.

We decided to grin and bear it as we usually only spend the minimum amount of time in our hotel bedroom. There's just too much of India to see to waste time worrying about "the small stuff".

One more LUHG sticker in the airside mens' toilet later (17 down, 83 to go) we joined the queue to board our plane. Due to a bomb blast the previous day in Srinagar, security at the airport was tighter than Susan Boyle's girly bits. Stepping off the plane, soldiers as well as airline ground staff directed us to the arrivals hall. I thought I had arrived back in Britain. There was a cold wind and a grey overcast sky to greet us.

As the only foreign nationals on the plane, we had to fill in extensive forms and be questioned by the security forces. Needless to say, we were the last people to leave the airport so it was easy to spot our driver cum houseboat owner, even though he didn't have a name card with him. It felt like we had entered a war zone. There were soldiers everywhere. On patrol, on rooftops, in various vehicles up and down the street. And each one was carrying a rifle. Hélène thought there would be fewer tourists here as the weather was poor and the troubles would frighten them off anyhow. So imagine my surprise to find that, for the first time on our travels in India, nearly all the shop signs and advertising posters were in English.

Soon we were driving by the side of the Dal Lake and there were rows of houseboats along the opposite side with names like 'Happy England', 'The White House' and 'Little Australia' and most were painted this dull beige colour. They were long rectangular constructions, with a terrace in the front and a variety of ornate woodwork around the outside. Behind three sides of the lake rose imposing hills with higher snow capped peaks in the far distance, hinting at the majesty of the Himalayas that lay beyond.

Finally we stopped and Galum, as he was called, lead us and our luggage to a Shikara, one of the fleet of brightly coloured wooden boats that acted as local transport for ferrying goods and people around the lake and its many canals. I was concerned about our luggage ending up at the bottom of the lake but we all arrived safely on the pontoon nestling between two houseboats, the 'Highland Queen' and 'The White Horse'.

I tried to keep an open mind, but then he opened the double doors in the front of 'The White Horse' and reality could no longer be held at bay. The dark depressing deep red patterned furnishings took me back to my grandparents' house 50 years ago. We had entered a time warp. It smelt 50 years old as well and was freezing cold.

"This is not good", I thought, as he gave us a tour of the place. Through the lounge and across the dining room and along the corridor on one side where he slid back a door to reveal our bedroom. The post WWII austere decorations continued, as did the relentless cold. And damp.

There was an old TV in the room.

"Have you got cable or satellite TV?"

"Oh, yes sir. No problem."

"Are you sure?" I asked, now world weary of locals saying yes when they really mean no, or when they simply don't understand.

"Yes sir. Cable sir. No problem."

I pressed home the point, as warm words were no substitute for cold hard facts.

"Can you get sports channels like ESPN, Star Sports and Ten Sports?"

"Oh yes sir. No problem sir. Sports channels, yes sir."

It suddenly dawned on me that he spoke at one hundred miles an hour in an Irish accent. How strange. Nevertheless I experienced little spasms of excitement as I realised that I would actually be able to watch the match from our bedroom. Things were looking up.

Hélène brought me back down as she asked if we could have a heater in our room and I was immediately reminded of the bitter cold affecting my bones.

"No problem. Heater? No problem." as he barked orders to one of his sons.

"What about hot water?"

"Hot water? Oh no problem sir. Hot water, yes we have hot water."

Not convinced I ran the hot tap.

Freezing.

I let it run.

Still freezing.

"Don't worry sir. It's an old wooden boiler on the roof. Very cold weather. Let it run sir. Hot water come sir."

"Hmmm. OK." I thought. I'll give him the benefit of the doubt, for now.

I asked him to show me the TV. I said nothing as he flicked from one snow scene channel to another.

"Don't worry, sir. It just needs tuning."

"Hmmm. OK." I thought. I'll give him the benefit of the doubt, for now.

Now passed and still no channels. I stepped nearer the TV and noticed that one of two leads emanating from the set itself was just dangling down by the side. I pointed this out and Golum sighed. He looked closer at a socket in the wall and we discovered that the cable had actually snapped and any chance of me watching the Chelsea match live had snapped too. I didn't even have a signal on my mobile so I couldn't tune into BBC Sport for two minute score updates. Life sucks.

With all hope lost I decided to bury myself in our lovely surroundings. Hélène and I agreed to let Golum take us for a boat ride on the lake. We put on our polar fleeces, stepped back down into the Shikara and spent a very pleasant, if cold, slow punt around the peaceful lake and its superb backdrop. The water of the lake was surprisingly clear, a welcome contrast to the polluted waters of the Ganges and the lake in Udiapur. The slow pace had a calming effect on me and we both enjoyed being at one with nature.

From the open lake itself we passed through narrow canals with floating land housing buildings and plots of land where the locals grew vegetables. Then we turned into a floating high street with shops on stilts in the water, selling all the usual everyday commodities as well as stuff just for tourists.

Throughout the ninety minute ride, various boats pulled alongside and their owners tried to sell us everything from tatty souvenirs to food and drink. When we returned to the houseboat Golum took us into his office to give us the hard sell on trips and tours he could arrange.

I got in first.

"Have you got the internet here?"

"Yes sir."

"Can I have a look, please?"

After his earlier failed promises I wanted to see for myself. He switched on his computer, but first elected to show us hundreds of photos of Srinagar, its surrounding countryside and hills. It was all very nice but by now it was almost 7 o' clock and there was only ten minutes left of the match. My insides were screaming as my professional exterior only displayed the odd twitch on my cheeks and neck. Finally I was able to connect to bbc.co.uk/sport. Click "Football", click "Live Video printer", click...

"Oh, Nooooo!!!"

Manchester United 1 Chelsea 2. 83 minutes.

I had tried not to think about it but my worst fears must have been realised at the end of the Bayern game that Rooney hobbling off was far worse than the actual 2-1 first leg defeat. Yeah, I know we had beaten Bolton 4-0 away only a few days before without Rooney, but with all due disrespect to Bolton, once you take away their attempts at intimidation there is little real talent there to fall back on. Teams like Bayern and Chelsea are another proposition altogether. Against Bayern we had simply not played well enough. We never got going, our passes went astray. I looked at the screen.

United 0 Chelsea 1. Cole 24

United 0 Chelsea 2 Drogba 79

United 1 Chelsea 2. Macheda 83

"Come Oooon!" I shouted to myself.

Golum was explaining all the tour options open to us and Hélène looked at me to contribute politely in the conversation. But my eyes were fixed on the screen.

The page wasn't refreshing every two minutes so I switched to "Live Scores". Still 1-2. I switched back to "Live Videoprinter". 85 minutes update. Still 1-2. Switched back to Live Scores". Still 1-2. Switched back to "Live Videoprinter". Still 1-2 and now Fletcher is the third United player to get booked. This is not looking good.

I continue to switch from one to the other, but to no avail. Finally, on "Live Scores" it reads, "Referee blows final whistle". We lose 1-2 at home to Chelsea and with only six games remaining they go two points clear and with a superior goal difference.

Fuck!

I turned back to Hélène. Golum was waffling on so I cut in.

"How much?"

Waffle, waffle, waffle....

"How much?"

Waffle, waffle, waffle.....

I was not in the mood for the bartering game.

"How much?"

He was uncomfortable with such direct questioning.

So fucking what!

In end he mumbled, "2800 rupees"

"2000" I replied.

Waffle, waffle, waffle.....

In the end we agreed on 2400 rupees for a day trip up the mountains to Gulmarg, 50 kilometres from Srinagar and above the snow line, and the following day we would do the three parks that make up Muglar Gardens.

That night Golum insisting on cooking us a meal. We put on our layers and waited in the dark dank lounge of the houseboat for our food to arrive. It was rather good but very heavy on the stomach. Conversation didn't flow and Golum could see we weren't enamoured with our surroundings. We bade him goodnight as early as was polite and went straight to a cold damp bed.

Fuck Chelsea. Fuck houseboats. Fuck the cold. And if you want to know, no, I didn't fuck. It was too fucking cold.

SUNDAY 4 APRIL SRINAGAR, INDIA

The boat was so cold during the night that when I woke up in the wee small hours I just couldn't go back to sleep. What made it worse the Chelsea result was swirling around my head. I tried to think of sex, drugs and rock 'n roll but losing at home to the Rent Boys and failing to watch it on TV I was overcome by pangs of guilt. Without an internet connection I couldn't even read any circumstantial evidence that would convince me that, unlike Bayern the previous Tuesday, "we woz robbed".

Hélène was fast asleep and it would have been wrong to wake her. Even the malaria tablet induced nightmares would have come as a blessed relief to the never-ending night. I tried a little hand shandy but my heart and other parts of my anatomy weren't into it.

Eventually the morning light filtered through the curtains and Hélène began to stir. Once she had rejoined the land of the living we agreed we couldn't spend another night sleeping in a fridge. This was meant to be enjoyable, not an endurance test.

We went for a walk that morning and found a nice but dated hotel overlooking the lake, with rooms at reasonable rates and cable TV, so we transferred our stuff from the houseboat. Golum was hurt, I could tell, but we had to make a decision. This was not an overnight stay but five days, and nights, and minimum standards were called for.

For the first time on our travels around India we were in a predominately Muslim town and I tried to analyse the differences. Surprisingly most people spoke superior English compared to people in the India we had already visited despite tourism being way down their list of priorities. One common thread was their insistence on selling us everything. Wherever we had been in India, no matter how poor or run down the people, their clothes or their homes, their cars were spotless. Here in Kashmir the cars were as dirty as everything else. People were still wonderfully friendly, a natural Indian trait. Fewer open smiles perhaps but just as welcoming.

The entire region was knee deep in soldiers, with three or more protecting every school and public building we passed, with special attention being paid to those where women or children were working or learning. Not something the repressive terrorists agreed with. This enabled us to really appreciate the area and the locals seemed genuinely pleased that a British couple had ventured past the headlines and were enjoying the body copy.

The following day we visited the original town centre, a menacing looking cluster of dark, foreboding buildings that would not have looked out of place as a Hollywood backdrop. I suspect we were the first "white" couple for some time to make for the focal point, a wooden temple where everyone inside and out wanted to be sure we enjoyed our visit and would take away positive images. In our naivety we had defied scaremongery, propaganda, assassinations and bombs and we felt undeservedly euphoric.

WEDNESDAY 7 APRIL. SRINAGAR, KASHMIR, INDIA
MANCHESTER UNITED 3 BAYERN MUNICH 2 - CHAMPIONS LEAGUE Q-FINAL SECOND LEG.

As we're due to fly to Mumbai tomorrow and re-acquaint ourselves with 40+ degrees heat, we decided to stay in our hotel room today and do absolutely nothing. My only worry concerned the occasional loss of Ten Sports, channel 17 on the hotel TV. All the other channels worked perfectly, just the one channel that was due to broadcast the Bayern game at 11.30 that night. Why always me?

We ordered room service for breakfast, then a few hours later we ordered room service for lunch. This is the life. Except that I was losing Ten Sports for longer and longer periods.

"Stop worrying." said Hélène. "It always comes back. Just leave it."

Just leave it? How could I "just leave it"?

Women.

I typed up this diary, made cups of tea and occupied my brain. But the feeling was gnawing away that lady luck was once again conspiring against me. I could wait no longer. At six o' clock I phoned reception and reported the problem and they sent someone up. Unfortunately he couldn't bring back the channel so he called a mate. He couldn't make it work either. They said they would be back in ten minutes. Two hours later and I was still waiting. I went downstairs to reception and confronted the manager. I told him his staff had disappeared and I still couldn't get any reception. I suggested he exchange my television with one from another room. He explained the whole hotel had a problem with Ten

Sports and there was nothing he could do. I felt this was his line of least resistance so I persevered.

"Can I try one of the TV sets in another room?" I ventured, "You never know, the angle of the room might effect the signal." I tried to keep a whimper out of my voice.

He sighed and called over one of his staff. He gave him a couple of keys and I followed him up to the third floor where our room was and we tried the room next door. But before we could even turn on the television there was a power failure, a common occurrence in India.

We made our way back to the corridor and waited for ages for the power to return. In the end I went back to my room and asked him to fetch me when power was restored.

It was almost nine o' clock when he knocked on my door and we went into another room down the corridor.

Nothing.

We went into a second room.

Hallelujah! A fuzzy, shadowy Ten Sports appeared.

"That'll do for me, Tom" I thought to myself. I over thanked him and returned to my room, relief flooding through my body at the thought that I was actually not going to miss possibly United's most important match of the season since the last one.

One chicken masala later I bid Hélène farewell, and armed with the heater and wearing my fleece and my mountain jacket (did I tell you it was fucking cold in Kashmir at night?) at 11.30pm precisely I crept along the corridor to the room with Ten Sports.

Just my luck. The only plug in the room didn't work so I couldn't plug in the heater. Damn. Then I remembered the porter had shown us that each bed had access to an electric blanket, so I switched it on and waited about ten minutes for the heat to permeate the layers of blankets, followed by my layers of clothing. Very soon my back was nice and warm but the rest of me was as cold as ice.

I went back to the television, only to see some Scottish bloke that used to be a full back with Celtic, discussing and predicting the game. What's that? Rooney was in the line up? Brilliant! Or was it? Was he fully fit or was this just tactical to unsettle the Germans. I mean, they don't like it up 'em, Mr Mannering, do they?

I then realised the match wouldn't start until 12.15am Indian time. My stomach was tied up in knots whilst my eyes defied the invisible matchsticks. Finally the game got underway. The Germans looked strangely nervous and after only two minutes Darren Gibson scored his first European goal, one which in all honesty their keeper should have saved. I let out a silent scream and leapt up and down like Woody in Toy Story 2. I couldn't believe it. 1-0 up, and with our away goal as insurance, we were now ahead on the tie. C'mon ref. Blow the whistle. What do you mean there's eighty-eight minutes to go! Who's counting?

Normally Germans are a so solid crew yet Bayern continued to make unforced errors. Just like United, I thought, not to take advantage of the opposition while they were reeling. How many times have we dominated possession but created few clear-cut chances? Surely Bayern would revert to type any moment now, so.....

AAAAhhhh!!!. A second goal! David, wash your mouth out with dirty water. recite one million Hail Marys. You've been thinking and talking shite. We're now 2-0 up and playing like men possessed. What a move. Valencia had beaten their full back and his cut back was flicked into the net by Nani with the inside of his foot. Fucking magic! Only seven minutes gone and we're 2-0 up! And playing brilliantly.

Now they were targeting Rooney, aiming for his dodgy ankle with relentless precision. Bastards. He wouldn't last the match, I could see that. Why couldn't the Italian referee? Yet, amazingly, especially after what I had read about our lethargic performance at home to Chelsea at the weekend, we were on fire. Nani was playing a blinder.

Surely any moment now the Germans would solidify and... AAAAhhhh!!! Nani's done it again! What a volley! AAAAhhh!!!. I don't BELIEVE it! What with all my jumping up and down, I don't know who's in the room directly below me but they must be thinking this guy's having the orgasm of all orgasms. And in a way I was. I tried to catch my breath whilst my heart raced n-n-n-n-nineteen to the dozen. I could hear Old Trafford rocking. Oh how I wished I was there.

Olic, Fucking Ivica Olic. Just like our Ole, he pops up from nowhere and almost immediately gets a goal back for Bayern. Instantly you could sense the hesitancy in United's play. Those super fast, super sweet movements now held less conviction. Then in the next minute Edwin did well to reach a curler from Robben that could have put Bayern ahead on away goals.

Fuck me, I can't take much more of this.

Half time. 3-1 ahead and into the semis. But, this is United we're talking about. Despite our recent history of grabbing last minute goals, we've occasionally grabbed defeat from the jaws of victory and my insides were all over the place. I was shitting myself from places not normally associated with waste products.

I went back to our room to thaw out a little, have a pee and make myself a hot drink. My hands were shaking as I trundled back to the other room. Talk about a game of two halves. This time Bayern started off like we had in the first half. It was complete role reversal. Then a major turning point. In the 50th minute the Germans conspired to get Rafael da Silva sent off, haranguing the referee when he innocuously tugged back Franck Ribbery's shirt. (Biased? Moi?)

Rooney was replaced by O'Shea and we lost our attacking verve. Our fluency disappeared and a sense of impending doom crept like the death of the first born. With barely a quarter of an hour of the match remaining Robben hit this wonderful/flukey (delete as appropriate) volley/punt (delete as appropriate) though a crowd of players and suddenly Bayern, who had been played off the park for the majority of the match, were now ahead on the fucking away goal rule.

Told you there was no God. We attacked in fits and spurts but the belief had gone, Extinguished. Then at 02.10am the referee blew his whistle and we were out.

Football. It was fucking and it was hell.

I lay back on the bed. I didn't know what to do or think. What would I say to Hélène if she had the temerity to ask the score? Would I be able to keep my emotions in check? I'm sure it's at moments like these a rock star would trash a hotel bedroom, but it's not my style. I have no style. I just turned off the electric blanket, the TV and all the lights and made my way back to our room and into bed.

Hélène was asleep. Thank fuck for that. Go on, sleep you bastard. Just you try. Sleep!

THURSDAY 8 APRIL SRINAGAR TO MUMBAI, INDIA

Today we flew from Srinagar back to Mumbai. With two sickening defeats whilst we were in beautiful Kashmir, now was not the time for calm reflection. I was dominated by negative thoughts and a hole in the pit of my stomach. Blackburn away at the weekend now took on gargantuan connotations and was temporarily taking the gloss off this wonderful adventure.

To counteract the negativity, I focused on the fact that the next time I'd be watching United would be in Thailand, with the rest of my family that we hadn't seen for two months. Or more accurately, we'd all have met up together, but it was unlikely they would actually be watching the game with me, if you see what I mean.

Thought so.

They say it's better to travel than to arrive. I interpret this as putting a higher value on preparation, so that you can appreciate more than can be witnessed purely on the surface. One way is to read books, and not just the obligatory travel guides but also novels set in the places you're going to visit. For me this certainly applied to Mumbai. Months later, during one of many book swapping exercises in a hostel somewhere in the world, I picked up Shantaram by Gregory David Roberts.

Wow! What a book. If I had known then what I learnt when I read the book I know I would have appreciated Mumbai more. This guy, a New Zealander who escaped from prison in Australia and fled to India, describes his incredible ride inside and outside the Mumbai underworld. Highly recommended.

Our base in Mumbai was a former Salvation Army residence just behind the famous 5★ Taj Mahal Palace Hotel overlooking the bay. Although run down, it was an excellent base from which to explore the city. Lots of young people 'do India' so I 'did' the notice board with another LUHG sticker. 18 down, 82 to go. It was dark when we arrived and by the time we had unpacked there was just time to wander down to the harbour, breathe in the stench and find a place to eat. Tomorrow we'd give Mumbai our undivided attention.

One of my overriding ambitions on this trip, if "ambition" is the right word – was to visit Dharavi, the slums of Mumbai. Only a few weeks before we left the UK I had watched a documentary fronted by Grand Design's Kevin McCloud. I had been fascinated by all aspects of this community of one million souls that Forbes magazine described as the second most efficient industry on the planet, as it recycles everything that it produces. In Dharavi, nothing is considered garbage.

All cities in India are loud, but nothing matches the 24/7 decibel level of Mumbai. Noise, however, is not a problem in Dharavi, the sprawling town centre slum where as many as 18,000 people crowd into a single acre (0.4 hectares) and there is one toilet for every few hundred people. As someone remarked in the documentary, "To use all that water for so few people seems a stupid, even sinful waste." Statistics show that more Indians have access to a mobile phone than to a toilet. They must talk some shit.

The following morning we traced the only "official" slum tour operator up some rickety stairs to the third floor of a nondescript tenement block. It was run by a young Chinese woman. The race to be the world's fastest growing economy was evident.

We were to meet our guide at 11.00am in front of the British built St Pancras Station lookalike Chatrapathi Shivali Railway Terminus, formerly called Victoria Terminus. A motley crew had gathered by the time we arrived. A young man made himself known and issued us tickets for a local suburban train.

His opening address included the expected reference.

"Has anyone seen Slum Dog Millionaire?"

Most hands went up.

"What did you think?"

Most people said they loved the film, that it was very inspiring. However this didn't satisfy our young guide.

"Residents here took exception to one major misnomer. The film portrayed these slums as desperate places rife with crime. What you will find is a close community where crime is much lower than the national average. The average wage here is also higher than the national average. You will also not come across any begging. Almost everyone here has a job. There is no need to beg. I ask you to keep an open mind but please let's all keep together."

We alighted at one of the stations nearest to the main slum entrance and he led us down to a main thoroughfare and before we knew it we were submerged in the labyrinth of narrow alleyways alive with people and industry. Sewage and the occasional rat accompanied us but there was far less pong than I had anticipated. However the overwhelming impression was one of community and industry.

Kids and adults came out to stare and smile, and significantly, for the first and only time in India, nobody was begging. He had been right. We were taken inside homes where people slept side by side on the floor. We were offered hot chai which was remarkably refreshing, even in this heat. Every possible commodity was traded and worked on. We visited one factory where ruined plastic toys were tossed into massive grinders, chopped into tiny pellets, ready to be refashioned into knock-off Barbie dolls.

Cardboard boxes, oil drums; you name it, they reworked it. You may think they only showed us selected workshops and foundries but there was no mistaking the progressive atmosphere pervading the entire site. Some things you can't hide.

In a clearing some children were playing on a mountain of rubbish. A few of us broke away and played kick about with them. It felt good. The tour finished with a visit to an educational project which was funded by money raised from our tours. A large room housed computers and other learning tools. We were informed that there was a minimal charge for lessons, as this gave them a sense of value as opposed to free lessons, and they found more people stayed longer this way.

As a concession to our temporary patronage I was allowed to put up LUHG sticker number 19 on the main window. That'll confuse 'em. 81 to go. As we were led back out of the slums we all agreed how inspirational it had been. In Mumbai more than anywhere else we had visited in India, the contrast between rich and poor was startling. The recently created aspirational middle classes now lived mostly in Manhattan priced, Stalinist styled, high-rise concrete monstrosities which dot the south Mumbai skyline.

Dharavi was an embarrassing eyesore in the middle of India's financial capital. Prime city centre real estate for which numerous plans have been submitted which would bulldoze the slums, divide the land into five sectors and replace them with tower blocks and all the inherent faults that we in Britain had witnessed in the 60s.

Profit before people. The death of community. That's progress.

Overall, in India the football front had been disappointing. Even in Goa with their influx of European tourists, they only paid snide T-shirt acknowledgement to our national game. Cricket was their number one sport. Fair enough, and maybe it was just my luck to arrive when the IPL was just starting. With a population of over 1.22 billion (Mumbai alone is home to over 20 million souls) and the second fastest growing economy in the world, I often wondered why United hadn't made more of an effort via summer tours to woo the locals. Maybe they've done their research and realized they won't get a return on their investment.

The current advertising slogan of "Incredible India" is certainly true. But it works both ways. India has incredible beauty, incredible hypocrisy, incredible people, incredible corruption, incredible food, incredible intolerance, incredible intensity, incredible dirt, incredible vibrancy, incredible poverty, incredible natural beauty, incredible driving and the people are simply amazing. I'll never complain about anything again. (That'll soon wear off, I can tell you)

Back at the hostel we packed our bags and made our way to the airport in preparation for our 04.45am flight to Bangkok, our family and my next fixture. Double barrelled excitement guaranteed. Roaming the airport I found two empty massage chairs. I raced back to Hélène to tell her the good news, only to find them occupied when we got back.

Doh!

So the floor it was after all.

THAILAND

SATURDAY 10 APRIL BANGKOK TO PHUKET, THAILAND

Today Hélène and I met up with our two girls and our granddaughter at Bangkok airport for ten wonderful days all together in Koh Phi Phi. Actually it was only nine days in Koh Phi Phi as the last ferry from Phuket to Koh Phi Phi leaves at 1.30 pm and we didn't land at Phuket airport until 2.30 pm. How inconvenient. So I booked a hotel in Patong Beach for our first night together.

They had told us to meet them by the Air Asia check-in desk as they arrived at 06.15 and we didn't arrive until 10.10, but they weren't there. I'm sure I read their e-mail correctly. We had no alternative but to wait in line when suddenly we heard screams and there they were, rushing towards us with trollies ablaze like the chariot scene from Ben Hur.

"Where were you?" was lost amongst hugs and kisses. Then the girls stood back and demanded to look at my new teeth. True gasps of amazement and approval greeted my Goan gnashers. Then an audible sigh as Lily exclaimed:

"Grandpa, I've never seen you so brown."

They then proceeded to all speak at once, telling us that as they had arrived so early, they had taken a taxi into Bangkok and done a few things. They thought the taxi driver had ripped them off but I told them that was par for the course and not to worry about it. I was actually impressed they had used their initiative and utilised the time so productively.

We all went for a meal in the ultra modern airport food hall before boarding our plane. I indulged in the luxury of a Dunkin' Donut doughnut. How I missed that combination of sickly sweet centre and moist outer. They beat Krispy Kream hands down. Heaven. Now there was just time for another LUHG sticker.

The flight to Phuket was swift, just one hour, ten minutes. At the airport, after a bit of a struggle, we found our contact with her well-hidden name board and we were directed to a waiting air-conditioned minibus, which took us on a forty-five minute drive to our hotel. A couple of minutes into the drive I turned to everyone and said:

"Can you hear that?"

"We can't hear anything."

"No, neither can I. Wonderful, isn't it? No incessant horns blaring 24/7. This is Thailand not India. What a blessed relief."

I had chosen the cheapest hotel I could find for our one night's stay, the criteria being:

1) They had rooms available at short notice.

2) It had a swimming pool.

Success on both accounts. Patong Beach was a hive of activity. The beach itself was lovely, A long semi-circular bay with a backdrop of green hills and trees. The resort itself could have been anywhere in the Med. All the usual suspects of discos, souvenir shops and western food competing with superior local fare.

My ears pricked up as I heard the strains of a few power chords wafting my way. Looking up, I saw a stage had been erected across the road on the beach and a band was rehearsing. I then became aware of hundreds of motorbikes and the fact that we had stumbled on a Harley Davidson convention.

Unfortunately the rest of my brood don't share the same superior taste in music as me so we passed it by on the way to our first meal together for over two months. The following morning, Lily beat us to the rooftop swimming pool after breakfast. Then it was time to get our 1.30pm ferry to Koh Phi Phi. Not only had the girls joined us, so had their luggage. We sweated and strained as we lifted it on to the boat and up onto the sun deck above, to fully absorb the rays on the two hour crossing.

As our magic island came into view I wondered how we would recognize our hotel representative. An animated melee of sweaty people and luggage dominated the jetty upon demarcation. It was only as things calmed down that we made contact with our hotel rep. He and his partner loaded our luggage onto a large railway station type trolley and we followed them thought the streets of the idyllic resort.

The girls couldn't take their eyes of all the colourful tourist tat on offer, and were beginning to lag behind as the two men began to mount the hill out of the centre of the village.

Damn. We're on the outskirts again.

I needn't have worried. Our hotel had magnificent views over the other bay and we had a choice of two completely self-contained individual cabins. Hélène, Jasmine and Lilyella immediately made the cabin their own, and within minutes the iPod and exterior speakers were on full blast.

Kids, eh? My first priority, of course, was to make sure the TV was working and the proposed cable TV actually existed.

It did. Phew! Now I could relax. Sort of. Everything was riding on tomorrow's game at Blackburn, and perhaps it was sad that here I was in paradise with my family, re-united (like that) after two months apart and with the likelihood of another eight months before we would be able to see each other again, yet my thoughts were dominated by four thousand holes in Blackburn, Lancashire. And though the holes were rather small,

ABUs were counting them all, hoping we would fall. Somebody spoke and I went into a dream…

Fuck it, let's get changed. Last one in the water, etc…

SUNDAY 11 APRIL KO PHI PHI, THAILAND
BLACKBURN ROVERS 0 MANCHESTER UNITED 0

This was truly paradise. Warm crystal clear waters teeming with all forms of sea life, sandy beaches, funky music blaring from numerous beach bars and all the tat you could wish for. After two months under a hot hot sun, Hélène and I had no qualms about sunbathing all day but we warned the girls incessantly about overdoing it on their first day. As the afternoon drew to a close a discussion began as to where to eat that evening.

"Ahem. Ahem." I ahemed. "Don't worry 'bout me. I'm watching the match tonight."

"Daddy!" was the instinctive response in perfect harmony.

"Sorry girls. Did warn you."

The girls were actually more understanding than Hélène, who to this day cannot accept the fact that United play such a dominant role in my life. And so it came to pass that, duly suited and booted, my female entourage made their way down the hill a little while later, leaving me and the TV to have a private one-on-one.

Wish I hadn't. Our new "most important match of the season" turned out to be an excruciating waste of two hours. My worst fears were realized in that the hangover from Chelsea and Bayern manifested itself in a lethargic Rooneyless United performance that never seemed likely to produce one of our famous last minute miracles. Berbatov's body language matched my own frustration.

Final whistle, 0-0. Now we were a point behind Chelsea having played a game more, and with an inferior goal difference. No amount of post match PR clichés could disguise the fact that an historic "four in a row" was no more. Let's be realistic, there's no way Chelsea were going to let this advantage slip.

Resigned to the inevitable I switched everything off and, just like United's chances of winning the Premiership, I went downhill to meet up with my brood.

17 APRIL KO PHI PHI, THAILAND
MANCHESTER CITY 0 MANCHESTER UNITED 1

A midday(ish) kick-off in Manchester meant a civilized 6.00pm kick off in Thailand. Even though I'd read all the build up on the net all week, in my mind the Premiership was as good as over. I just couldn't see Chelsea slipping up at this late stage. But the very fact that we were still in with a shout was a hell of a lot more than I could have wished for when I left England's green and pleasant land in February.

On our way back from the beach we once again passed the myriad of kosher massage parlours on both sides of the streets. The very idea of a pretty young Thai lady (real) running her hands over my body, kosher or non-kosher, was very pleasurable indeed, but knowing my previous luck with massages I approached this phenomenon with some trepidation. The whole family was up for it and we let Melanie choose.

Everybody knew which massage they wanted (where did they learn all about the variables? My only knowledge came from the adult channels on Sky, and they were encrypted so I only watched the previews after midnight) I have to admit, years of listening to heavy metal music at a Spinal Tap 11 has left me a little on the deaf side, so when Melanie said she recommended any of the messages except Thai massage, I picked out the two salient words, "Thai" and "Massage".

I chose a Thai massage.

My family gave me that funny look.

"What? What?"

Too late. This pretty little thing told me to lie face down on the massage table and she began to work.

Why was everyone looking at me? Who cares? I could enjoy this. She performed all the usual aspects, and I thought, laying flat I must compare favourably with some of the pot bellies she has to endure. We started to chat and she confided to me that the British like to "kissy kissy" but she wasn't that sort of girl and it wasn't that sort of massage parlour. I nodded (as best I could in the circumstances) in a sympathetic manner, as though to say "you're very pretty but I wouldn't because I'm not that sort of man. Your hands are safe with me. And, more importantly, my family's watching." but then she started to bend various bits of my anatomy further than they had been stretched since I was a kid and the massage began to go over to the dark side.

She twisted my neck from side to side that I had only witnessed once before in my life, the late night showing of The Exorcist. She then pulled both my knees up to my chin with such force that I thought all my joints had jumped out of their sockets.

Melanie called out, "How are you enjoying it Dad?"

"Well, apart from all the pain and discomfort, it's actually quite nice." Why does this happen to me? What should be, if not out and out sexual, at least sensual in the extreme. Why was I experiencing pain and torture when all around me were sounds of sighs and purring? I didn't cry out or anything. I assumed the girl must know what she was doing. Surely she had administered hundreds, nay thousands, of Thai massages before? It must be me.

When she finished my knees were aching, especially when I walked. My masseur gave me a brief kiss on the cheek for making her laugh and "being a sport", if being a sport actually exists in Thailand. My family continued to laugh at my expense as we left the shop. They continued to laugh at my expense all the way back up the hill to our hotel cabins.

Of course Hélène thought I was exaggerating, although she did say I had been warned to choose any massage EXCEPT the Thai massage. It transpired that the one little word, "except", proved my downfall. So much so, in fact, that I had trouble with my knees throughout the rest of our world tour and even now it can give me jip.

I've learnt my lesson. It's either a knocking shop massage or no massage at all.

End of.

With the massage aiding our girls getting over their jet lag, my suggestion of a late evening meal went down surprisingly well. I left them in the cabins as I looked for a bar for a bit more atmosphere than I could generate by myself in our own cabin. In the end I plonked myself down in a bar with a couple of local looking lads with United tops on in one corner. No City fans for a bit of banter though.

I ordered a drink and asked the barman if I could put up one of my LUHG stickers in his bar. "Sure." So I did. 20 down, 80 to go. I'm thinking, Koh Phi Phi is quite touristy. This sticker won't be wasted. I sat down near the two United tops. I nodded. They nodded. I said, "Hi." They nodded. Ah, Englishless United fans. I pointed to the LUHG sticker and said something. They just smiled. They obviously didn't get it. Will just have to concentrate on the football then. Create my own atmosphere.

As the match got underway in the not full up bar, I again marvelled at City's determination to perform like an away side at home. I respect Roberto Mancini. He'd won the Italian league title three times in a row with Inter Milan, but I thought he'd adapt his technique to the more attacking cut and thrust of the Premiership. Not a bit of it. United dominated possession without a cutting edge in the final third. Having said that, we could have been a goal or two up at half time with both Scholes and Berbatov guilty of not providing the finishing touch I craved and Rooney cutting in and missing when usually he scores from his favoured deep lying role. I also noticed that each time I was the only person in the bar to stand up and swear on these occasions. Did I say I was looking for a better atmosphere than my cabin? Forget it.

Obviously the possibility of beating City in their own back yard didn't mean as much to the locals as it meant to me. They couldn't even revel in my enjoyment and piss-takes at the anonymity of Tevez, that money grabbing whore, and Emmanuel Adebayor. (well, at least that rhymes) Craig Bellamy was thankfully a shadow of the player that caused my underwear to change colour in the orgasmic 4-3 at Old Trafford earlier in the season. A lovely slice wide of our goal was a moment to savour.

The second half was little better than the first. Any neutral observer would have been disappointed at the quality of play but I'm not fucking neutral and with the possibility of a double over our inferior neighbours, on top of knocking them out at the semi-final stage of the Carling Cup, substance was more important than style.

Then in the 93rd minute United lived up to their billing which had so painfully deserted them at Blackburn, with Scholes ghosting in from nowhere to head unmarked into the City net.

ROOOAAAR!!!

I jumped up and knocked my Pepsi Cola onto the floor. I looked around for someone/thing to hug but the two local United shirts were just smiling. I was literally the only one making a noise in the entire establishment, so I made enough noise for everyone. Repeatedly.

Final whistle. 1-0.

Looking at the bigger picture I still didn't think it would be enough, but if we hadn't won… No, it's not worth thinking about. I exited the bar still punching and thrusting the air. This was United for fucks sake. This was my team. My life. The icing on the cake was a double over City, we had denied them a trip to Wembley and dented their aspirations of entering the Champions League for the first time since dinosaurs ruled the earth. I hopped and skipped down the road to the agreed family meeting place. Not a bad day, at the end of the day.

SATURDAY 24 APRIL BANGKOK, THAILAND
MANCHESTER UNITED 3 TOTTENHAM HOTSPUR 1

A wonderful fortnight swimming, snorkelling, kayaking, sailing and sunbathing with the family had come to a tearful end at a chaotic Bangkok Airport the previous evening. Rumours abounded that our girls' Thai Airways flight to London would be the first allowed to fly with the lifting of the ban imposed due to the Icelandic volcano cloud. A gigantic rugby scrum at the Thai Airlines check-in desk was pure mayhem. Nobody knew what to do. It was a farce. I positioned our girls at the back and, armed with their tickets and passports I brought my Old Trafford elbows into play. (Home to Sheffield United circa 1972 comes to mind.)

Half an hour later I returned.

"Girls, I have some good news and some bad news. What do you want first?"

"Stop mucking about, Dad. Good news please."

"The good news is… I have your boarding cards. You're on your way home."

"What's the bad news then?" enquired Hélène.

"The bad news is, my dear, I have the girls' boarding passes. They're going home."

"Oh, very funny."

"Yes. I thought so."

A bitter sweet moment, I think you'll agree.

Tearful farewells and LUHG sticker number 21, 79 to go. Later Hélène and I were in a taxi on the way to the (in)famous D&D Inn in the backpackers' Mecca of Khaosan Road in the Phranakorn neighbourhood of Bangkok. The road itself turned out to be traffic free but people full, so we had to drag our heavy rucksacks in the heat and humidity of a Bangkok night.

It was hardly authentic Bangkok but it was really buzzing and I couldn't wait to get down and get with it. After waiting an eternity in line, the rude staff finally registered us and we made our way to our room overlooking the main drag. Immediately our ears were assaulted by the pounding beats of endless bars and our noses invaded by waft after waft of street food. You get the picture.

Obviously sleeping was only an optional extra, so I went downstairs to see if I could change our room but they claimed they were fully booked and tomorrow night was the earliest we could move. Hélène was not happy with this outcome and took her frustration out on me.

Obviously.

I was able to drift off once the booming bass lines had receded into my subconscious but Hélène assured me in the morning that she hadn't got a wink of sleep. Then to brighten our mood, once I opened the curtains we saw that brownish water was dripping from the ceiling directly onto one of our large rucksacks, and had possibly been all night. Of course, if it had been all night, Hélène would have heard it because she hadn't been able to get a wink of sleep. Obviously.

Diplomacy, and my desire not to be inflicted with another Jewish operation, dictated that I kept this killer evidence under wraps. With profuse apologies, one of the receptionists found us another room which we could move into in about an hour's time. We showered and dressed and went out for breakfast, deciding to grab every minute and not wait for things to happen, in this case, a new room.

We spent the day exploring Bangkok. We'd read on the net about the red shirt protest in the centre of Bangkok. Initially I had hoped these were Thai United fans demonstrating against the Glazers. However, it turned out to be a demonstration and sit in against the current authoritarian government which came to power in a military coup led by Abhisit Vejjajiva. The protests were organized by the National United Front of Democracy Against Dictatorship. (At least the word "United" had crept in somewhere) They were calling for parliament to be dissolved and an election date set. A couple of months previously security had been tightened in anticipation of the Supreme Court ruling to seize Thaksin Shinawatra's bank accounts, thereby depriving City funds for new players. Oh how we had laughed at another Bitter Blue banana skin. However, here on the ground things were altogether more serious. In fact Hélène and I had received e-mails from friends, family and the Foreign Office imploring us not to travel to Bangkok after witnessing scenes on TV of military crackdowns. We discussed the situation, but from what we could gather the protest was confined to a couple of blocks downtown, and as long as we gave this area a wide berth we should be alright.

We were also here for a week so there was no need to rush. Then I made a very important decision. I told Hélène I had to watch the United v Tottenham game that evening. She was more than welcome to join me, an offer I knew she would refuse, but by telling her early she had time to digest the information and come to terms with its implications. That evening she sent me down to the street to bring back some local cuisine which we could eat in our room, relax, then I could back go out to watch the match and leave her safe and secure in the arms of her Sudoku. I couldn't have put it any better.

Walking along Khaosan Road I was spoilt for choice. There were bars everywhere showing the game. This was such a blessed relief after the stresses and strains of two months of cricket dominated India. I plumped for a bar with the largest screen, sat myself down and looked around for any fellow Reds. There were European faces for sure, but no colours. I wore my Green & Gold and had hoped to engage in some serious footy chatter for the first time in two months. Then I noticed a couple of plain clothed lads talking and nodding in my direction. I raised my glass and they raised theirs. They turned out to be a couple of Manc lads who were both United fans. Brilliant.

I realised I must have seemed rather loud by their standards but that's just my way. I stressed the importance of the match and how difficult I thought it might be. Tottenham had recently beaten both Arsenal and

Chelsea playing some scintillating football so their confidence would be sky high, and I'm sure they felt this would be an ideal opportunity to end their dismal run of defeats at Old Trafford. On the other hand, if we won we would go top, although only by one point and Chelsea would have a game in hand over us.

It had all the makings of a very tense 90+ minutes. When the team was announced there was no Rooney and no Ferdinand. Shit, this could go either way. The first half started very tight. Not much in it. Not many chances. Spurs, thank Eric, were not playing with the flair and confidence I expected so very little pressure on our defence. Then a stone wall penalty as Patrice Evra was fouled and Giggsy converted to put us 1-0 up at half time.

Ordering a drink at half time, the barman was only too glad to receive my 22nd LUHG sticker, as a sort of kudos over other bars along Khaosan Road. I was gaining confidence when halfway through the second half Ledley King headed unchallenged into our net and suddenly it was 1-1. Out of nowhere I heard this shout, turned round and this young lad behind me had briefly celebrated their goal. I looked at him and across the table at his girlfriend. He immediately sat down. I suspect he thought it better to hide his allegiance in the face of three menacing Reds (Me? Menacing? Well, possibly my second glass of Pepsi in front of me convinced him I was a man to be reckoned with!)

United kicked off and continued to press forward, then a piece of magic from Nani lifted the gloom as he cut in and lobbed the Spurs goalkeeper and lifted me out of my seat. I jumped up and over to my two fellow Reds who, to be fair, weren't as demonstrative as me, and seemed a trifle embarrassed by my manly hugs. My satisfaction was complete as Ryan scored another penalty and the three points were ours. I had learnt my lesson and only hugged myself when the third goal went in. This was the signal for the Tottenham fan and his girlfriend to leave the building. I waited for the final whistle. 3-1. That'll do for me, Tom. Best we could have hoped for in the circumstances. Still in with a chance, at least that was what the papers were saying in order to sell papers, but in my mind only a miraculous Chelsea collapse could cement a record breaking four in a row.

And that wasn't going to happen.

The rest of our time in Bangkok was spent doing the usual tourist things, including the obligatory Grand Palace, which is actually 31 separate palaces, halls and pavilions. I expected to be blasé but the whole complex was magnificent. We visited a large open-air market where I bought an Einstein T-shirt. What with my growing flowing white locks, my family had taken to calling me Albert Einstein minus the brains, so I thought if you can't beat 'em, wear 'em.

WEDNESDAY 28 APRIL CHANG MAI, THAILAND

Today we took a tourist coach up the mountains to visit Wat Phra Doi Suthep, Thailand's highest Buddhist temple. We were driven at such breakneck speed up the winding mountain roads we were all car sick by the time he came to a grinding halt. We all gave him a piece of our minds. He couldn't give a shit. I could. My breakfast was about to come out the other end.

We queued up to be blessed by a monk with holy water, which I spied behind the curtain to be Evian. We were offered a lucky bracelet in the form of a cut off piece of string. What I hadn't realized was the women offered their left hand and the men their right. Every time I knelt down and stuck out my left arm the monk got more and more agitated. Where's his inner peace gone? I thought.

With an ever lengthening line of men behind me the monk gestured for me to move to one side. Hélène came over and explained what I had to do. How was I to know? We walked around the temple and surrounding area, then when we stopped for something to drink I planted LUHG sticker number 23, 77 to go on the café notice board. One religion for another. That's only fair.

The following day we went by minibus up the mountain to visit three tribes, the Lana, The Karen and the Long Necks that had settled in Thailand after fleeing persecution in Burma and China. In Lana, the first village, the tribe had been given a piece of land by the state and 40,000 Thai baht to build their homes. They were all constructed on stilts as the area was regularly flooded during the rainy season. There were no men there when we arrived as they all worked in the fields but we saw the women embroidering and selling the craftwork.

The second village, Karen, was bigger with lovely wooden houses, a church and a school. Spotting us passing by all the children came running towards us, arms outstretched, begging for money. I noticed that most of them wore T-shirts with slogans in English so I read each one out loud and asked the child in question to repeat after me.

They'd never encounter anything like this before and so our impromptu English lesson went on for some time. As they followed me up the hill, singing their own songs, I brought out my mobile, set it to video, then asked them to join me in MY song.

"Manchester, la la la. Manchester, la la la."

"U-NI-TED, clap clap clap. U-NI-TED, clap clap clap."

I have it on film so I can prove it! Their first English lesson.

A "REDucation". A triumph, even if I say so myself.

A short drive away was the third village populated by the Long Necks. Or more accurately, human zoo. This was embarrassing and demeaning. Behind two rows of stalls were elegant women and children, their incredible long necks adorned with dozens of gold rings, selling hand woven scarves (nice) and souvenir trash (not nice).

They obviously didn't live there but were bussed in for our entertainment. The guide then informed us that, not being Thai, none of the villagers from these three settlements could go to town or look for work outside their own communities. I don't think she registered our expressions which varied from mild discomfort to disgust. We finished off the day trip with a visit to the Tiger Kingdom tiger sanctuary in Chang Mai. Initially I was uncomfortable with the prospect. The Far East has a poor reputation when it comes to the care and exploitation of animals and prices for entry could hardly be labelled an impulse buy. I also have a problem with any animals kept in captivity. All the tigers here had been rescued and reared from birth so were completely at ease in the presence of humans. That doesn't necessarily mean this human was completely at ease in presence of tigers though. Meanwhile there was no programme for re-introducing them back into the wild so they would remain in captivity for the rest of their lives.

However, once inside, I was pleasantly surprised. There was reasonable space inside each compound. Facilities included play areas and pools and they appeared to play with their handlers without "performing" for the public.

Now I had a decision to make. Which tiger to play with? The younger, the more expensive the ticket, so I chose one of the magnificent fully-grown beasts as it was the cheapest option without being cheap, if you know what I mean. Hélène declined my invitation to join me in this unique bonding arrangement so stayed with my camera as I was lead into the waiting area.

Before I knew it I was in the enclosure and encouraged to stroke the tiger. He turned and gave me a look. I figured I wouldn't be in danger as long as I didn't do anything stupid (like shout "City are a massive club"). I mean, surely they must be insured in case I lose a limb or three? I relaxed and spent an awe inducing 20 minutes with my new best mate. I lay my head on his stomach whilst Hélène clicked away. I was up close and personal and felt immensely privileged. I continued to stroke him and even played with him as the keeper led him over to the pool.

All too soon my time was up and I was led out of the enclosure. I'm not sure the tiger will remember me, let alone keep in touch, but I shall never forget our time together.

I think I earned my stripes.

SATURDAY 1 MAY CHANG MAI - CHAING KHONG, THAILAND

We had a mostly lazy morning as our minibus to Chaing Khong on the Thai/Laos border didn't pick us up until 12.30pm. Opening the door we saw it was full of fellow travellers who had all booked the same two day all-in boat trip down the Mekong River to Louang Phabang in Laos.

I sat next to two pleasant girls from Southampton while Hélène sat on a solo seat behind. At the next stop two young guys got on, one wearing a Spurs top. A chance for bonding through a common denominator presented itself, and I looked forward to a little footy talk, especially since Spurs had recently beaten both Arsenal and Chelsea, then did the decent thing by losing to us at Old Trafford the previous weekend.

At the first twenty minute toilet stop I got into conversation with the Yid and he was infuriatingly nice. I was hoping for a little gentle piss-take but he was magnanimous in defeat, getting six points from those three games was more than he could possibly had hoped for, and he wished us luck for the remaining campaign. His mate was a Villa fan. (with an accent like that, it came as no surprise) I told him that my last game at Old Trafford before setting off on our trip was the 1-0 defeat to the Villa in December. That made his day, until he told me he was at Wembley to see Villa come second to United in the final of the Carling Cup. I told him how I had seen the match on a giant screen in a beach bar in Goa so 1-1 in anecdotes. Toilet stop for tourists could only mean one thing. You got it. Another LUHG sticker. 24 down, 76 to go.

We arrived in Chaing Khong later that afternoon and transferred to a really average guesthouse for the night. Hélène and I then took a stroll down to the river. The Mekong River. This iconic brown and murky river that had featured so prominently throughout the Vietnam war. You wouldn't know just by looking at it how significant this scene was. I was staring at history. Bloody history that had left its mark during my lifetime.

The trip included dinner, but the portions at the hostel were really small, so we had to ask for more, then the headmistress in charge took away the bananas after one hour and switched off one of the lights in the most unsubtle manner imaginable. Nevertheless we continued to chat with everyone around us. It's moments like these where travellers exchange stories and anecdotes; swap advice that enhances the travelling experience. However that night we had difficulty to sleep. Hélène put it down to the fact we had taken Malerone, a stronger anti-malaria tablet to our normal one. I slept fitfully but Hélène claimed not at all. On top of that we could both hear an incessant hen crowing throughout the night, right outside our front door. Bloody thing. When I asked others at breakfast how their night went, by common consent "slept like a log" was the overwhelming response. Bastards!

Breakfast was a minimalist affair requiring a magnifying glass to locate the butter and jam. I splashed out on a 40 baht cushion, one of my best ever investments as people had told me the wooden seats on the boat can give your ass a toothache. A minibus took us down to the jetty where the standard confusion reigned as documents were queued for at various windows, forms filled in and requests for additional weekend supplements requested. We declined and were not asked again. 1-0 to the travellers.

Waiting for our fellow passengers to be processed gave me ample opportunity to post LUHG sticker number 25 on the Thailand customs window, 75 to go. A significant moment this. One quarter of my way through my stack yet slightly less than a quarter of the way through our world tour. I mustn't get carried away with stickering. There was still Australia to come in June where lots of ex-pats would be following England in the World Cup. A golden opportunity to win over hearts and minds with some serious bantering with both Reds and ABUs. I "MUST" make these stickers count.

A long canoe took us and our luggage across the Mekong and our first landing on Laos soil. Looks just the same from this angle I thought as more forms were requested to be filled in. We were then directed to a first floor restaurant overlooking the river as a Laos official, a young man dressed in 80s boy band style clothes and hairstyle, warned us of the perils that lay ahead. Basically it came down to spend your money with him for such niceties as food and accommodation at inflated prices, rather than risk the unknown at inflated prices. Most decided to do their own thing and ignored him but virgins like us paid three hundred baht (£6) for a double room with en-suite facilities at the overnight stop at Pakbeng.

I just had time to stick LUHG sticker number 26, 74 to go, my first on Laos soil, (or restaurant window to be precise) before we were lead down the steep jetty to the boat. Balancing all our luggage at a 30 degree angle was a challenge in itself. Hélène was waiting for the inevitable splash but it never came. Yup, I had defied gravity and expectation.

All the comfortable seats at the back were already taken by the time we boarded so we chose a two seater wooden bench near the front. OK, we missed out on the comfy chairs but we gained by being well away from the noisy engine. Those with iPods/MP3 players at the back really suffered, although those with boney backsides like me also suffered, despite the cushion of a 40 baht cushion.

Travelling down the Mekong on a slow boat with 40 other travellers is one of the world's "must do" activities. I'm glad I did it, but for me at least it is a trifle over-rated. The scenery is green and pleasant enough but samey. At intervals, watching local fishermen or passing boats loaded with goodies or children playing in the murky brown water breaks the monotony, but many chose to sleep, read or listen to music. The passing countryside lost its allure quite quickly for the majority.

And those wooden seats! It took squirming to a new level. Meanwhile I had plenty of time to anticipate events at Anfield and the Stadium of Light twenty fours hours later. By now, our whole season came down to these two matches. I still hadn't changed my opinion that Liverpool, with only two and a half days to recover from a numbing Diego Forlan induced exit from the semi-final of the Europa Cup (Diego, whoa - o -o - oh. He came from Uruguay, he made the Scousers cry. Diego....) would fail to raise their game sufficiently to restrain a superior Chelsea team that had a whole week to prepare. Always the pessimist, I was mentally preparing myself for the worst case scenario. I daren't let myself believe, after a season including the disruption of our magnificent back four and a failure to find a formula to compensate for the loss of Ronaldo, and to a lesser extent Tevez, we were still in a position to win the league.

All the permutations kept swimming around my head but I came to no sure fire conclusion. For Liverpool and their fans, this was the ultimate lose-lose situation. Beat Chelsea and they virtually hand the title to their most hated rivals - us, and with it the title of the club with the most league titles. It was a Scouser's worst nightmare and one which during the wilderness years of the 70s & 80s I never thought I was remotely capable of witnessing. Lose or even just draw and their lingering chances of Champions League football would be over for another season.

Oh, joy of joys. How I was revelling in their agony. Oh, the delicious irony of it all. However, we mustn't forget United's part to play in all this. Even if Liverpool do the decent thing and roll over and die, we still have to beat Sunderland. With Chelsea scoring seven goals at home in two recent matches, they had a far superior goal difference. So even if Liverpool beat Chelsea, drawing against Sunderland was of little benefit. We have to win. Then of course, if Chelsea win, our match immediately afterwards will be flat for players and fans alike. But if Chelsea lose...

As the light began to fade we arrived by the banks of the one road town of Patbeng. The entire population seemed to be at the water's edge, falling over themselves in a bid to charge for the benefit of taking our luggage to the respective guesthouses.

Hélène and I refused all advances as we wobbled up the plank and river bank to the road with our luggage. Fortunately our guesthouse was the first building on the right. After registration, the smarmy owner led us to a room overlooking the river. The Mekong River. Wow. Look at that. I could just imagine Francis Ford Coppolla or Oliver Stone down at the water's edge, directing another historical scene.

Out we went again, in the remaining light we passed the saddest little market we'd ever seen. Old plastic sandals and other children's clothing, bathed in layers and layers of dust built up over the years. It was like the whole place had been asleep for 100 years.

LAOS

SUNDAY 2 MAY LOUANG PRABANG, LAOS
SUNDERLAND 0 MANCHESTER UNITED 1

On the second day our boat doubled-up as a taxi for the locals. I'm sure they didn't pay what we paid but it was a right slice of human life. We had lots of stops. Kids would clamber into the water and beg for money. We'd toss the odd coin into the water and watch them dive under the silt and gunge to retrieve their booty. Was I helping or was it just live entertainment. I'm not really comfortable with scenes like these, but I'm sure those kids didn't give it a moment's thought. They had other priorities. At one stage the boat got stuck on a sandbank and the captain had to wade in and under the boat to retrieve the propeller from the build-up of rubbish.

Finally, with my arse developing the mother of all toothaches, we arrived at Louang Prabang. If we thought the scrum at Patbeng was a bit over the top, the crowd that came to take out luggage and haul it up the river bank were positively mental. You couldn't talk to them. They just grabbed your luggage from out of your hands and brought them up the steep river bank and loaded them into a waiting tuk-tuk. We were just bit players in this live theatre.

Wait a minute, I thought. We don't even know what's a reasonable price to pay. Negotiations were not on the agenda.

"50,000 kips." Called out the tuk-tuk driver.

"What!" I thought. "That's a rip off."

"Too much. Too much"

"Two people. Two people."

Hélène was tired and said, "Pay the man."

"But I don't have 50,000 kip."

The tuk-tuk driver had heard this one before. His gesture left nothing to the imagination. Translated it meant "Hole in the wall." Resigned to my fate, we clambered onboard and the driver meandered up and down a number of streets until he stopped outside an ATM. I drew out a mountain of notes, returned to the tuk-tuk and finally arrived at our pre-booked hostel. I gave him his blood money, minus a tip as I was sure he had earned a month's salary at my expense.

Our room was nice and large but there was this nasty smell assaulting our nostrils. More importantly though the TV was working and we had cable. Having double checked it was actually functioning, we went out for our first evening stroll. What a lovely town. For such a poor country, the tourist dollar had certainly contributed to its air of class and sophistication. As a next door neighbour of Vietnam, its history was intertwined with France. Lots of low-lying French style housing and furniture abounded. As daylight disappeared and the lights came on it was almost like a fairy tale. OK, the high street was full of tourist shops and restaurants at tourist prices, but once again, a short walk either side of the main strip and it was possible to eat and pay like the locals.

We could see water glistening at the end of the road so went back once more to the river, only to realize our hostel was no more than 400 metres from where we had landed. The tuk-tuk driver had driven up and down all the roads, doing a number of spaghetti junction, figure 8 type manoeuvres in order to convince us our hostel was worth a 50,000 kip fare. We'd been well and truly tuk-tuked. Never mind. My stomach and not my wallet was the dominant factor right now.

MONDAY 3 MAY LOUANG PRABANG, LAOS
SUNDERLAND 0 MANCHESTER UNITED 1

I don't think I'll ever forgive Gerrard for that suicidal back pass that let in Drogba for Chelsea's first goal in their 2-0 capitulation earlier in the day. But I was encouraged by United's spirited performance in the face of that early result and also those of our fans in the Stadium of Light in their green and gold, singing till the end. Berbatov and Rooney were paired up front, but it was a beautiful goal by Nani that secured our 3 points. Berbatov missed a hatful of opportunities that nearly woke Hélène up, as I could not fully suppress my cries of anguish. After an even Stevens start, United dominated the match, so in the end I welcomed Monday with open arms. There are worse places in the world to contemplate the inevitable end to the season than the beautiful laid back town of Louang Prabang on the banks of the Mekong in Laos.

TUESDAY 4 MAY LOUANG PRABANG, LAOS

Set my mobile phone alarm for 05.30 as we wanted to see the march of the monks at 06.00. Apparently all monks from the various monasteries walk the streets at 06.00 and people give them food, and that is their entire meal allowance for the day. Hélène and I got out of bed, put on our respectful clothes of trousers covering the knees and shirts covering our shoulders and made our way onto the street. It was grey and overcast and a welcome relief from the heat of the previous day, when only mad dogs, an Englishman and his French wife went out in the morning sun.

We saw the monks disappear round the corner and we thought we'd missed it. I whispered some very un-monk like phrases under my breath, but then a local woman came up to me and forced a basket in my hand containing individual food parcels wrapped in banana leaves and a large bowl of rice.

"20,000 kips," she hissed at me. Damn, I'd only come to watch the phenomenon, not take part. I thought I had stood a respectful distance from the locals, but obviously not. Well, at least it meant they would be coming round the block again for second helpings. The woman pushed me down onto a matting on the side of the road to await their second coming. Soon a longer procession came into view and I offered my bowl up to them. The lead monk pushed it aside.

"Bloody cheek", I thought. "This lot just cost me 20,000 kips".

Then the woman came over and indicated that I should give individual portions to individual monks.

"Doh!"

It's not easy handing out individual portions whilst at the same time filming the event on a camcorder, but I resolutely stuck to the task and the resultant images of monks' thighs and feet will surely impress friends and family when I get home. Then Hélène took over my pitch and I was able to concentrate on filming the ritual with due reverence. I never realised Buddhist monks were exclusively Blackpool supporters, but to a man they wear bright tangerine robes all day long.

Just then the woman came back and urged me to accept more food for the monkfest but I had wised up by this time and (I thought) politely refused her offer. It began to rain, but it was warm rain so didn't affect proceedings. I then spied two kids on the opposite side of the street with a wicker basket each in front of them and they clasped their hands together when the monks passed.

"They're beggers", Hélène informed me.

"Oh yeah", I exclaimed, as some of the monks we had given our food parcels to dropped portions into the two childrens' baskets.

"Very clever", I thought. "This was real re-distribution of wealth". The people give to the monks who give to the poor. Very noble and a trifle humbling. The possession of monks grew longer with gaps in-between. The kids used these gaps as an opportunity to take their booty out of their baskets and hide it behind a bush, so that when the next line of monks appeared, all the monks saw were two children with empty baskets in front of them.

"Very clever", I thought. "Just like the Artful Dodger scene from Oliver. Very enterprising".

The main point of debate now was how best to get to Hanoi in Vietnam from Vientiene, the capital of Laos, Plane prices were remarkably high, but the flight only took one hour ten minutes. The alternative was the £40, 26 hour sleeper bus.

I suggested a quick internet session to keep in touch with our nearest and dearest and check out the options, as well as a way of getting out of the intense, strength sapping heat. However, my ulterior motive was to contribute to the fans forums in suggesting the most horrible and painful way to end Steven Gerrard's miserable existence on this planet.

A LUHG sticker duly suitably adorned the internet café's main wall (28 down, 72 to go) Thus duly exorcised, we made our way back to our guesthouse. Just outside we met one of the two Dutch girls from the slow boat and she told us of a travel shop up the road that arranged half day trips to the famous Kouang Si waterfall (No, I'd never heard of it either) for 50,000 kip each, but in an air conditioned minivan not a tuk-tuk. That sounded more like it. She also told us the same travel shop sold tickets for an air-conditioned minivan to our next destination, Vang Vieng, for 115,000 kip, cheaper than the so-called VIP bus. Sorted.

Thirsty once more, we went for a drink during Happy Hour before choosing the Coconut Garden for our evening meal. Superb. Hélène then suggested a massage before we went home. No, nothing like that, just a foot massage in one of the many respectable massage parlours in town. We both chose the one hour foot reflexology massage for 35,000 kip. We took adjoining chairs and let the masseurs do their thing.

Shit, why have I got the bloke? Hélène soon closed her eyes, but I desperately wanted to fart, a common reflex action on my part as a result of all the physical stimulation. So I kept my eyes open during the entire session. Whereas Hélène purred with pleasure at the appropriate moments, I let out gasps of pain as my muscles were kneaded with an intensity I considered unnecessarily harsh. Fuck me, this was Koh Phi Phi all over again. They finished off with a five minute head and shoulder massage. Bastards, they're at it again. Get off my neck. That hurts. Hélène tried to stifle her giggles as the expression on my face told the whole sorry story. Massages and me don't mix well. Either I'm too uptight and my muscles too rigid, or someone's got it in for me. I know which theory I'm going with.

Meanwhile, it's a knocking shop for me next time. At least I know what to expect.

WEDNESDAY 5 MAY LOUANG PRABANG, LAOS

Today, with the temperatures topping 40* C, Hélène and I took a minibus to the Kouang Si waterfalls, 35 kilometres out of town. Once again, the only people to put a blot on the landscape of a nation full of wonderful people were taxi and minibus drivers. This one drove like a man possessed, in a land where everyone else drives so calmly and carefully. We took the uphill mountain curves at speed, taking the gloss off what should have been a very pleasant ride with ever more breathtaking vistas. Then when we finally arrived at around 12.15, he told us to be back at the van by 2.00pm. Whoa there boy!

I took it upon myself to be the unofficial spokesperson and told him we had booked three hours at the waterfall. He smiled sheepishly and reluctantly agreed to 3 o' clock. But why try the scam in the first place? It just made his working day and our collective tempers shorter.

He was soon forgotten as we made our way along the paths to the waterfall. First we came across a bear sanctuary that saved bears from medicine men who use their bones and skin for ancient healing rituals, with no scientific merit whatsoever. Seeing them roam and snooze at ease in a large natural enclosure was both humbling and rewarding. Then we came across the waterfalls themselves. They looked delightful and so inviting as they cascaded down, forming pools at different levels where we could swim in their refreshingly cold, crystal clear waters. What a wonderful contrast to the searing heat of the day. Even the paths leading up to the highest waterfall were shaded and cool.

Hélène and I gingerly slipped into the top swimming area. Brrr! That was cold on first entry but then its refreshing powers invigorated us both. Down to the next natural pool and this time we just sat on the rocks with our legs dangling in the water. As we sat still, little fish swam up to us and started to nibble at our legs and toes. And to think I had paid 150 baht for a seven minute session two weeks ago on Koh Phi Phi and here we were having it free for as long as we liked. Deal or no deal? I'll let you decide.

Back in town we booked two $180 tickets on Vietnam Airways to Hanoi for Sunday 9 May. Now the only two things I had to arrange was our hotel for one night in the capital, Vientiane, and to find somewhere in

Hanoi to watch the Chelsea v Wigan and United v Stoke games.

Our plane wouldn't land until 18.40 Hanoi time, so finding a TV set took precedence over finding accommodation. I hoped Hélène would understand.

Another session at the internet café ensued, including me putting a request on the Red Issue and Red News fans forum for anyone who could tell me where I could catch the matches in Hanoi. I intended to go online once we arrived in Vang Vieng the following afternoon. You never know, amongst the expected abuse there may be one or two practical and not physically impossible suggestions.

THURSDAY 6 MAY LOUANG PRABANG TO VANG VIENG, LAOS

I set the alarm for 07.00 but woke up early, as we were due to take the 09.00 air-conditioned minibus to Vang Vieng. After breakfast across the road we met the two Dutch girls from the slow boat who were also coming on the minibus with us. Let's just say that one of them is not a morning person.

At 08.30 a clapped out minibus arrived outside our guesthouse. Oh My Eric, surely we're not going all the way to Vang Vieng, a five hour drive away, in that cramped rust bucket? The driver spoke not a word of English, but put our baggage on the roof and drove round to pick up a full payload of nine passengers. This is not happening, I thought, trying to make light of our impending doom laden journey. Fortunately, ten minutes later we arrived at the bus station where we were to transfer to more appropriate minibuses. Phew! That was close.

Our relief was short lived however, as chaos in Laos reigned amongst the transport staff as they tried to squash as many travellers into as few minibuses as possible. Customer comfort came second to profit as they delayed everyone's departure. We eventually left forty sweaty minutes later, the promised air conditioning a long lost fantasy created by over enthusiastic travel agents in order for us to hand over our loot.

"Truth. What is it good for? Absolutely nothing." Say it again, y'all. At least we all had reasonable leg room so we settled down physically and mentally for the road ahead. Soon we were slowly climbing up hills, which meant lurching from one side to another as the driver took the hairpin bends a little too fast. Some coped better than others, but I had to hold on grimly as my stomach and bottom let me know in no uncertain terms they were not 100% in agreement with proceedings. The scenery began to compensate for the driving, as the higher we went the more lush and spectacular the hills and mountains. From soft undulating hills to more dramatic mountain ranges the further we travelled.

Two hours in and we made our first toilet stop. My bottom led the rest of my body to the Glastonbury type temporary toilets by the side of this refreshment stop. Armed with my own loo paper I was soon adequately relieved and bought a drink and crisps for Hélène at a rip off 16,000 kip from the unsmiling woman at the counter. I half expected her to bring out a hammer and sickle from under the counter, sing allegiance to the Communist Party and behead us capitalist pigs.

The mountain road got tighter as the scenery became even more spectacular. Distant, jagged mountain peaks in the grey haze seemed like mythical lands come to life from the pages of a J K Rowling/J R Tolkien novel. (Right, that's covered all my demographics). Roger Dean graphics filled our windows as bend after bend brought another 70s album cover into view.

Forty five minutes after setting off we arrived in Vang Vieng. Our experience of being 1000 per cent ripped off by tuk-tuk drivers when we disembarked off our slow boat in Louang Prabang had left its mark. Whilst I waited for our luggage to be set down from the minibus, I could hear the tuk-tuk drivers gathering like vultures, offering the short journey into town for 10,000 kip per passenger. With eight passengers to each tuk-tuk, that meant they were making 80,000 kip per trip. Nice work if you can get it, but they weren't going to get it from me.

The last remaining tuk-tuk driver grinned smugly as he waited for us to succumb to his toothless charms. I turned to the page in my Rough Guide which showed our guesthouse just a short distance away. At the same time we were joined by a couple from South Korea who also didn't want to play their money grabbing game. Much to the amusement of the waiting tuk-tuk driver the four of us began to drag our heavy luggage over the rough ground a full one hundred metres to the road outside the bus station.

We were pulling our rucksacks along the street when we spied another tuk-tuk driver coming towards us.

"How much to the centre?"

"5000 kip each."

Victory for the common man. And thus we arrived at the Nana guesthouse at one end of the main road.

"We're miles away from the centre," complained Hélène, her timing wiping the smile of triumph off my face.

"No we're not. It's just down the road. Look." and I showed her the map. She wasn't convinced. Whilst we checked in, we saw a Brit complaining that he had no water in his room and he'd been here three days. Not a good sign. Hélène looked at me. It was my fault and I hadn't even done anything!

Top of our agenda though was the famous Vang Vieng tubing, opened originally by hedonistic backpackers and which has put this 3 streets and a bus station town on the map. If you remember, I wrote in the beginning that I wasn't one for extreme sports, but tubing had been on my list from the outset. Gentle-ish, but with a hint of danger. It sounded right up my street, or river to be more accurate.

Vang Vieng exuded an atmosphere of lethargy by day and debauchery by night. Who could ask for anything more? Tourists sprawl out in the pillow & mattress filled restaurants, termed "TV Bars", until the sun goes down and then party heavily throughout the night.

Hélène was concerned the tubing might be too rough for me, as I wasn't the swimmer I once was. (If the truth be told, I was never the swimmer I once was.)

We asked a guy running an internet café we were using and he assured us (but mainly Hélène) that it was perfectly calm and gentle as you drifted down the river for four kilometres. My main concern was what colour "I've tubed the tube. Vang Vieng" sleeveless T-shirt to buy.

One of my missions whilst online had been to find as cheap a guesthouse as possible in Hanoi that had cable or satellite TV, as my number one priority was watching the final week of the Premiership season. Chelsea held all the cards, having a one point lead over us and with a vastly superior goal difference, which meant they had to lose or draw at home to Wigan whilst we had to beat Stoke.

Yeah, I agree. A neutral wouldn't bet on us, and history shows that the team leading going into the final week invariably wins the league. Ourselves in 1999 being a prime example. Yet where there's United there's always hope, so I went through the list of hotels on hostelbookers. com until I came across a hotel in the Old Quarter of Hanoi within our price range and with cable TV.

Duly reserved we then strolled back to our guesthouse, ordering a takeaway to be enjoyed in our air-conditioned room as we were sweating more and more as the humidity increased. It was coming up to three in the afternoon when we decided to go for a stroll and suss the town out and find out about the tubing. On the way we met an Australian version of Family Guy. He boasted he earned 3 times the salary of the Australian Prime Minister for just 3 months work, in the excavation of rare minerals in the outback for export to China. He claimed he had a wife in Oz and one here in Vang Vieng, where he spent 3 months of the year and lived like a king.

He told Hélène not to worry about the current situation as we were coming towards the end of the dry season and the river was so shallow that the waters hardly moved along at all. He went on to explain that for the last few years construction companies had been excavating then re-filling the river bed to facilitate the building of up-market hotels and a gold resort. Tubing as it exists today will soon disappear for good. Hélène wanted to see for herself though, so our first experience of the river was in a motorized canoe.

The scenery was magnificent, with mountains rising directly beside the river. As we sped along we passed our first tuber, an American girl who bleated, "Where's the finishing line?"

It turned out she'd been in the water for almost 4 hours and was exhausted and bored rigid. The water being so shallow she kept having to get out of her tube and just walk along, cutting her foot to ribbons in the slippery process. Not the best advert for tubing I think you'll agree.

As we neared the starting line up river we passed more and more ramshackle wooden bars where people lay on plastic mats and drank Beer Lao whilst listening to dance and rock music blaring out from humongous speakers. Brilliant. The bars seemed to be competing with each other for custom and we were told prices are amazingly low as a consequence. Westerners employed by the bars hand out free shots and organize drinking games to encourage people to stick around. Many offer promotions to encourage you to visit their sister bars in town.

The down side is that a lot of tubers drink too much as they drift from one bar to another and drown along the river. What you might call the "drown side."

I'll get my coat.

At the same time we observed that there weren't many people on the river this day as it was so shallow, so once we arrived back we decided to put on our swimsuits and go and lie in the river to cool down and just watch school kids jump fully clothed into the river on their way home from school.

We grabbed onto some large stones so not to drift off and laying in the cool flowing water watching these kids, who couldn't swim, jump repeatedly into the water. They were laughing and shrieking, not just at their own activity, but at these two weird looking westerners lying in the water.

As the sun went down we retrieved our clothes and made our way back to our hostel. Food was now uppermost in our thoughts, so a slow stroll up the main street brought us to our restaurant cum internet cafe of choice.

As soon as we sat down, a wind whipped up from nowhere and

suddenly the lights went out, the Wi-Fi disappeared and the heavens opened up with a ferocity I'd never experienced before.

Wow! Where did that come from? This was obviously an everyday event for the people already inside the restaurant but for us it was a 3D Technicolor, wide screen, in your face nature lesson. The owners brought out candles and continued to cook. As Hélène and I ate our delicious and now highly romantic meal, the owner came over to make sure everything was fine and he turned out to be English (unfortunately not a football fan, so discussing the final week of the season was not on the menu) and let us in on life in Laos. People and life is sweet and cheap, but you never forget you are living in a Communist state so criticism of local or national politics is a no no if you don't want to disappear without trace.

SUNDAY 9 MAY VIENTIANE, LAOS
MANCHESTER UNITED 4 STOKE CITY 0

A relatively short 3 hour bus journey brought us to Vientiane, the capital of Laos. Anticipating two days of luxurious self pampering, imagine our disappointment when we arrived at a 60s communist concrete slab masquerading as a modern 3* hotel. Our room on the third floor did overlook the ever widening murky brown Mekong River, but only a narrow strip above the rocky defences. The TV was out of a 60s gritty northern drama but it worked and that was the main thing. Eric be praised.

At least tonight's entertainment was sorted. We changed and went downstairs and out onto the patio only to discover the swimming pool hadn't been cleaned since the day it was built. The water was filthy. Broken, rusty sunbeds littered the surrounding cemented grounds. It was like an up-market Scouse housing estate. We couldn't believe it. All that build up and then… this!

We marched straight back into reception to complain, yet I'm sure the venom of my arguments were diluted somewhat by my appearance wearing the only pair of Speedos I possessed. (I wanted an all over tan you see. I didn't feel the need to impress with my Billabongs or O'Neils) They say English is the international language. So is shrugging, as that's the only visible response I was able to generate from the formal staff. No attempt to appease me, not even tea and sympathy. They couldn't give a flying communist fuck.

Vientiane turned out to be a hot humid characterless dump so the desire not to linger aided my master plan of getting back to our hotel room to watch the Stoke game. Being realistic the tension had gone out of the game for me. There's no way I could see Chelsea losing at home to Wigan. They've been known to raise their game on occasion, in fact they had beaten Chelsea 3-1 at home earlier in the season, but the Rent Boys were on the sort of a roll that United are famous for and I just couldn't see it happening. Still it would be my last chance to see United in action for 3 months at least. There were the pre-season friendlies to look forward to, but I worked out the likelihood of any TV channel in New Zealand or The Cook Islands transmitting these games were as remote as the Glazers winning a popularity pole amongst the Green & Gold brigade.

Mentally I earmarked the Community Shield against Chelsea in August as my most realistic live match option. I would be in Australia for the World Cup though. Not a prospect that caused my underwear to change colour I have to admit, especially the way England had (not) played in the last few matches, but with bars and pubs full of ex-pats, I'm sure a reasonable atmosphere could be created.

So leaving Hélène to the joys of Sudoku once again as I switched on the telly and saw United stroll to a 4-0 victory. With Chelsea 3-0 up at half time I watched our match without any hint of tension, just resignation. Then when Rooney limped off with about 15 minutes to go I thought that just about summed up our season. Thank you and good night.

I could reflect on the championship changing moments throughout the season that could have brought 4 in a row back to Old Trafford, but what's the point? It won't change anything. As I suspected when I decided that this was the year to disappear. United would rue the combined loss of Ronaldo and Tevez. The very fact that we could have won it on the last day of the season says more about the character of our players and manager than money ever can. I'd sent my Champions T-shirt back with the girls in April in Thailand because I just knew. And now it would be another 12 months before I could possibly wear it again.

"Always look on the bright side of life."

Look at that. I'd made so little noise watching the footy this time Hélène was fast asleep. What an epitaph for the 2009/2010 season.

VIETNAM

SUNDAY 9 MAY VIENTIANE, LAOS TO HANOI, VIETNAM.

Call it men's intuition, but something in my water nagged me to check on our Vietnam visas as we were due to fly to Hanoi at 17.50 and I anticipated them to be the strictest among the communist countries we had visited so far. Our visas consisted of three typed pages issued by the Vietnamese consulate in London, listing all the people who had been approved that month and there were our names and the dates 8/4/2010 – 8/5/2010. Aaahhh!

It was Sunday 9th May. All the embassies and consulates would be closed and our visas had expired, by one day! Images of us rotting in Vietnamese jails, or even worse, being denied boarding our plane and having to remain in Vientiane. Hélène said it's only one day and we shouldn't worry.

"Only one day!" I exclaimed. "Don't you realise communist countries are slaves to paperwork. They'll go through everything with a fine tooth comb. (I assumed they had fine tooth combs). There's no chance they'll just wave us through." Hélène gave me a contemptuous look, conveying her belief I was exaggerating the situation. I was not.

We went downstairs after breakfast in our room and asked around. The duty manageress assured us everything would be OK. Hélène gave me one of her "I told you so" looks but I wasn't convinced.

At the airport there was nobody staffing the Vietnamese airlines office. I strolled down a corridor and found someone having lunch in the Air Asia office. I anticipated a few friendly words before I drew the conversation round to Air Asia's partnership with Manchester United. Any excuse for a football chat. It had been three months since I had left the UK and I even missed the abuse of opposing fans and ABUs. However, the conversation didn't go as I'd hoped. He was obviously annoyed that I had interrupted his lunch.

"You'll have to stay behind and sort it out with the Vietnamese embassy in the morning". Fuck! Surely not. I reported back and we decided the best form of defence was attack. Finally they opened up the Vietnam Airlines check-in desk and we showed them our passports and tickets, hoping against hope they wouldn't ask for our visas. I mean, they were only the airline, not customs or security or anything.

They asked for our visas.

Damn.

I gave the lady our three page visa confirmation letter. I could see she was confused so I pointed to our two names amongst the list and, with a long line of passengers waiting to be processed, she just ticked them off against her list and we were through. Phew! That was close. Power to the people.

The one hour flight to Hanoi was uneventful. Night had fallen as we came into land and I noted how few street or house lights were evident from the air. Security was the strictest we had encountered so far, and my visa fears returned times ten. Collecting our luggage we made our way to the visa department where there was a long queue of mainly well-to-do middle-aged French tourists complaining about waiting in line.

I thought to myself, waiting in line is what communist countries do. Who remembers trying to leave the United dedicated airport in Moscow after the Champions League Final? Wasn't that the queue to end all queues? Unsmiling, chain-smoking police holding us in confined spaces as dawn rose but our plane didn't? Fortunately we'd won. Imagine how Chelsea fans must have felt at their airport. In fact, that's quite funny when you think back on it. John Terry handing us the trophy and then waiting hours to board their flights back. Life has its compensations.

Confusion reigned behind the glass partition as Hélène and I already had visas stamped in our passports. The rest of the queue were queuing for visas. I'd paid extra to obtain our visa for Vietnam in London before we left and our visas for Laos and Cambodia in Bangkok, as a precaution against communist queues. Failed. The Rough Guide had explained that visas were obtainable at the border of each country but I just thought it was more efficient my way. Of course, every system is as strong as its weakest link. And apart from me, I hadn't bargained for Vietnamese customs unaccustomed to pre-ordered visas. That got 'em. Or more accurately, that got us!

Green uniformed men scratched their collective heads. Then one came over and said, "50 dollars."

"Excuse me. We already have a visa. We've paid for it already."

"50 dollars."

"Look, we've paid for it already. Look, here. (me pointing. Can you picture that? Good) Hélène, can you speak to them. They may speak French." She didn't get anywhere so reluctantly (extremely reluctantly in my case) we handed over an unnecessary $50 and proceeded to the lines of custom officials. We'd been scammed and there was nothing we could do about it, paying twice for the same thing, but at least they'd accepted our visa stamp.

Oh no they hadn't! Arriving at the customs desk, a thorough investigation of our visa revealed it was past its sell-by date. Uh oh. We were pushed to one side whilst they processed the rest of the queue. Another green uniformed man came forward and proclaimed.

"No entry."

"Pardon?"

"No entry."

"Sorry, there must be something you can do?"

"Wait please."

I felt sure we couldn't have been the first to be in a position like this and they must have a plan B. If there was any way to extract money from these Imperialist pigs they'd have made one up by now. They had. I utilized the wait to extract one of my LUHG stickers from my back pocket and adhere it to a large plain wall. 29 down, 71 to go. Wonder what the commies would make of that?

A non-uniformed man was summoned from behind the customs desk. He was introduced as a travel agent. It reminded me of the old advert on TV where a bank manager steps out of a bedroom closet. How convenient.

He spoke good English, expressed sympathy for our plight and suggested a solution if we didn't want to be put back on a flight out of Vietnam. And guess what? It involved marching me to the nearest hole in the wall and drawing out $130 x 2 for the privilege of 2 extensions to our visas. Capitalism? Communism? It's just another "C" word, isn't it! So much for political idealism. This was another reality cheque.

Handing over thousands of dong was a sobering experience, especially as I hadn't had the pleasure of spending any of it. Duly checked and counted we were allowed to leave the airport and enter Vietnam proper.

We were led to the pre-paid taxi rank and got into a taxi (what else?). I gave the driver the address of our city centre hostel written in both English and Vietnamese and, just like Elvis, we finally left the building. Rain had started to fall and there weren't many lights on as we approached Hanoi itself. Not the most auspicious start. We found our hostel down a quiet alleyway where we received a nice friendly welcome. A young guy on reception saw my United top and immediately claimed his "allegiance" to Chelsea. That's all I fucking need. And it's good night from him.

The following morning we took our first stroll round bike mad Hanoi. I was dying to burst forth with a "GOOD MORNING, VIETNAAAAAAMM!" at the top of my voice but Hélène was beside herself with the insensitivity of my suggestion. That is until we came across the first shop selling souvenirs and everything from army green T-shirts, caps to uniforms all had "GOOD MORNING VIETNAM" printed in red right across the front.

Capitalism, communism. If there's cash to be made, politics come second. It's that "C" word again.

TUESDAY 11 MAY HANOI, VIETNAM

We set the alarm for 07.00 as we'd booked a full day's excursion to Ha Long Bay, a World Heritage Site consisting of thousands of 20 million year old limestone karsts and isles sticking dramatically out of the water along the 120 kms coastline of Bai Chay Beach.

Around 170 kilometres east of Hanoi, it was one of the "must see" destinations on our round the world trip. The minibus duly arrived at 08.00 and we set off under an overcast sky. However, as it had pissed down at the same time yesterday morning I didn't complain. I was sure (i.e. I was hoping) it would brighten up by the time we arrived at Ha Long Bay four hours later.

Two hours in and we stopped at a sanitised service station just for tourists. Inside the concrete hangar a wide range of sanitised merchandise was available. Pretty young girls followed uncomfortably close (or comfortably if you're that way inclined) behind as we strolled around. They produced a non-stop barrage of Chinese type water torture drip drip information in an attempt to extract our dong. Well, at least my arse didn't complain. I needed to walk.

We weren't left alone for a second, so I failed to put up LUHG sticker number 30. As a tourist only stop, this would have been a useful addition to my guerilla campaign. Shame. At around midday we arrived on the outskirts of Ha Long Bay. Already we could spy clusters of limestone rocks in the mist, the weather enhancing the mysterious qualities of the geography. Side-stepping layers of people of all shapes and sizes attempting to sell us all shapes and sizes of rubbish, we stepped onto our wooden boat and said goodbye to dry land. As we left the port I was reminded of this as a string of dark brown wooden boats all left together, creating a traffic jam flotilla as they all vied for the best shipping lanes. However, I was not going to let this commercial reality spoil my enjoyment.

It was still grey, but dry and warm, and as the monoliths came closer, their spooky greyness only added to the ghostly atmosphere. Half an hour in and our first stop was at a floating fishing community who used to live and work on their boats, but now lived on floating wooden platforms. We moored alongside one of them and stepped onto their platform. Numerous water filled basins were overflowing with a vast variety of fish, including baby sharks (Boo!), squid and giant prawns, crabs and various shell-like seafood creatures. Small boats came by at regular intervals, their owners selling a cross selection of everyday supermarket goodies including the freshest fruit and vegetables. Who needs dry land? Kevin Costner, eat your heart out.

As we left this fascinating fishing community I captured on film one young man slipping between two floating planks and ending up in the sea. Made my day, that did.

On deck I was approached by a young man who had registered my United polo shirt. He turned out to be an Eintracht Frankfurt supporter on holiday with his fellow Die Adler (Eagles) mates. My sort of footy fan, planning his summer vacation around his team's pre/post season friendlies, in his case Vietnam and Thailand. I spent a pleasant half hour talking footy with someone who was a real fan and not a glory hunter. Respect.

Now it was time for another excellent meal. By this time the sun had come out to play and after eating we went up on deck to view the spectacular scenery and sunbathe at the same time. Who said men can't multitask! Our guide explained that some of the rock formations had been given names as they resembles various animals, such as the gorilla, lion and two birds kissing, (You'll have to take my word for this, they really did look like the animals in question)

On the way back we stopped and climbed up millions of stairs (OK, I'm exaggerating, but you get the picture) to enter Sung Sot Grotto (Grotto of Surprises). Having only been discovered in 1993, I was ready to be underwhelmed but I was astounded at their haunting beauty. The amazing shapes, colours, patterns and formations would have challenged the finest CGI graphics companies based in Hollywood. (My) words cannot do them justice. I definitely had a Condor moment as the sheer scale and beauty of the stalactites and stalagmites overwhelmed my imagination.

At four o' clock we slid slowly back into port where we disembarked and re-boarded our minibus for the four hour journey back to Hanoi. I had forty winks (yes, I did say "winks") on the way back as the effect of the sea air and all those stairs took their toll. At dusk we stopped at the same grey tourist hangar for tea and toilet but still no sticker opportunity. Finally arriving back in Hanoi at half past seven.

The rest of our time in Hanoi was spent walking and tuk-tuking around the bustling city, visiting the giant Ho Chi Min memorial, ("Ho Ho, Ho Chi Min. Ho Ho, Ho Chi Min". I remember chanting this at games, but for the life of me I can't remember why. Another senior moment I guess), walking round the lake and in the evening being impressed by Thang Long Water Puppet Theatre in which puppeteers stood up to their waist in water behind a curtain and the puppets performed in front of the curtain for our pleasure. One hour was short for the price but plenty enough as far as my concentration levels were concerned.

FRIDAY 14 MAY CHINA BEACH, DAR NANG, VIETNAM

Even before I lived and worked in the South of France at the turn of the noughties, I had taken the TGV a number of times from Paris and always enjoyed the final part of the journey from Marseilles to Cannes, Nice and into Italy. The views from the train clickety clicking (we can't say Chuff Chuff anymore) halfway up the hills of the Esterel were amazing.

This morning those vistas were knocked out of the water by our night train from Hanoi to Dar Nang. As light flooded our compartment in the morning I was like an eager child opening the curtain uncertain as to what I would see. The views weren't just amazing, they were A-MAAA-ZING!! From high up in the hills, from Hue all the way to Dar Nang, we passed slowly above one deserted bay to another, each looking as though no man (or woman) had ever set foot on their pristine sands. Stunning. There were no tell-tale shacks, let alone concrete and glass edifices to dollar domination. Each bay was perfect. OK, there were no paths, so it would be a challenge for all but the most enterprising. A good thing, surely?

Arriving in Dar Nang we took a taxi to Hoe's Place, the hostel that stood out from all the others in the guide books and online. The town, which had featured so heavily in news reports during the Vietnam War, looked characterless to the naked eye, and once we found ourselves on the coast road, giant hoardings bellowing out the virtues of Hyatt, Inter-Continental and Sofitel concrete and glass edifices obscured views of the sea.

I had spoken too soon, led into a false sense of complacency by the romantic train ride. Here was tangible proof that communist Vietnam, having whipped America's arse in the war, had succumbed to the Yankee dollar in peace time. You just don't know who the goodies or baddies are anymore.

Hoe's Place turned out to be a quirky little guest house squeezed like a Monopoly house between giant developments. David versus Goliaths. Soon this whole beach will be the private preserve of the rich and infamous, each paying hundreds of dollars a night for the privilege of strolling up and down the beach we and the locals had access to for nothing. You'd better get here quick folks.

Once disrobed, we met up with a group of students from Devon and Cornwall who, at 10p a pint, were playing drinking games seemingly oblivious to the beauty outside. Each to their own I guess. The notice board was ripe for LUHG sticker number 31, so up it went. Now just 69 to go.

Our first dip in the South China Sea was invigorating. The water was clear but the waves and strong current made it a challenge. By 5.30pm scores of locals came to jump and bathe in the sea, yet hardly any of them could swim. That evening we all sat round the table as the owner made supper for us all. As this was included in the price of the room, who was I to refuse.

The following day we took a taxi to Hoi An, the ancient riverside city of Vietnam that had largely escaped destruction of successive wars. The town oozed charm and history. It looked so pretty. OK, it's now definitely a tourist town with hotels, restaurants, tailors, and souvenir shops dominating the old centre. Despite this air of theme park unreality, Hoi An's charisma pervades.

We read that the local People's Committee periodically clamps down on touts. While this didn't mean a completely hassle-free visit, to stroll around was certainly more relaxed than in Hanoi. Hoi An is closed to traffic so we found it wonderful just to walk and try to get lost. If it wasn't for the heat, I'd definitely have rented a bike.

One historical event that still happens today we were happy to miss. During the rainy season in October and November Hoi An gets flooded. And I mean really flooded. The greatest flood ever recorded was in 1964 when the water reached all the way up to the roof beams of the houses, and in 2006 the town bore the brunt of the worst typhoon in 50 years. Everywhere we went we saw markings reminding us of nature's destructive powers. Standing in shops knowing you'd have been underwater just 4 years ago. Every year they just move things up to the first floor through a trap in the ceiling. And we stood in lots of shops. Not because of Hélène's insatiable appetite but because it was so damn hot outside.

SATURDAY 14 MAY. HO CHI MINH CITY, VIETNAM

Exiting the arrivals building in former Saigon, our eyes were bombarded with neon in all directions. On first impressions it looked as though the Americans had never left. Walking around the centre later in the evening it felt like almost any other city. Designer names, 5★ hotels, a sophisticated night-life, it was all very confusing, but as we walked around the city the following day, a deeper perspective made itself felt.

SUNDAY 15 MAY. HO CHI MINH CITY, VIETNAM

With so much to see in so little time we took a tuk-tuk along wide boulevards to the Ho Chi Minh Memorial. Wow! The locals must view him as some sort of Vietnamese Che Guevara. OK, snap, snap. No time to go inside. Now off to the War Remnants Museum, or to give it it's original snappy Communist name, "The House for Displaying War Crimes of American Imperialism and the Puppet Government of South Vietnam. The human rights violations and war crimes atrocities American and French forces committed in Vietnam."

For marketing purposes, and possibly to save money on ink, it was changed to the "Museum of American War Crimes", then in order to attract the first wave of inquisitive Americans wishing to return to the place where they came second, "War Crimes Museum", and now, as we saw in Dar Nang, having fully embraced the Yankee dollar, the "War Remnants Museum".

Yup, they beat 'em, then joined 'em.

Once inside I was expecting anti-American propaganda but this was much more than that. The predictable clichéd PR gave way to some interesting and horrific statistics. One particular caught my eye. I've always thought land mines the most cowardly of all military hardware. How revealing to discover during the reign of the much loved US President John F Kennedy, these little beauties were developed in the States and are now widely employed by third world countries and African dictators and guerilla groups.

The entire three floors is a catalogue of man's inhumanity to man, women and children, with neither side taking the moral high ground. Tiger cages, the effects of Agent Orange and other chemical defoliant sprays. It was all there for us to enjoy. Needless to say, but I'll say it anyway, there was no mention of the North Vietnamese or Viet Cong's massacres or atrocities.

Next stop was the old American Embassy. The elegant, neo-classical building was bulldozed by the Viet Cong when they over-ran American forces and personnel during the shameful (for the Americans) fall of Saigon, and today it is a one dimensional, rectangular, characterless Communist edifice to all things anti-American.

Walking around the grounds, and then looking out from one of the first floor committee rooms, it's easy to visualize the fear and terror in the eyes of the estimated 10,000 personnel as they were left to face the onslaught alone. It's chilling in the extreme.

Then it was off to the tunnels of Cu Chi, an immense network of connecting underground tunnels located just outside Ho Chi Minh City, and part of a much larger network that underlie much of the country.

Now, I'm a skinny runt, but they were too claustrophobic for me. No Leppings Lane experience for yours truly. Outside were examples of torture equipment and traps for American soldiers and their dogs. Yup, you read that right, torture equipment and traps for dogs.

The evening finished with a walk around the streets of a suburb where Hélène's mother and father had worked as headmaster and headmistress of a school at the time of the French occupation. Finally we located it, but, how shall I put it, we weren't exactly welcomed with open arms. We were escorted on our rounds whilst I sneakily took photos. This was closure for Hélène, so we left it at that.

CAMBODIA

TUESDAY 17 MAY PHNOM PENH, CAMBODIA

My mobile phone alarm went off at 07.00am. This morning we were going to visit Choeung Ek, the Killing Fields fifteen kilometres outside Phnom Penh city centre and then back into town to visit the Genocide Museum. Pol Pot and the Khmer Rouge were directly responsible for the deaths of around 1.7 million people. That's 21% of the entire Cambodian population at the time. And now 30% of all tourists visiting Cambodia visit The Killing Fields, the site second only to Angkor Wat in popularity.

This wasn't going to be a boring history lesson like those we learnt at school. These were horrors committed during my lifetime by people I may well pass in the street. How would I react? Just like our visit to the War Remnants Museum in Ho Chi Minh City in Vietnam and The Bridge Over the River Kwai in Northern Thailand, would I be able to separate cocooned tourism from catastrophic real life events? There was only one way to find out.

We negotiated a £5 return with a tuk-tuk driver and he drove us to the entrance. A guide took us round a football pitch-sized area surrounded by farmland and for one of the few times in my life, no jokes were appropriate. This was horror on a scale that had to be seen to be believed. The memorial park has been constructed around the mass graves of around 20,000 victims in this site alone. As we walked around we could see remnants of children's' clothes and even bones and teeth sticking out of the ground. We were told that after every heavy rainfall, more and more come to the surface. The bordering tress still held the nooses used for hangings.

In the centre a commemorative statue has been built, its outer glass walls showcasing shelf upon shelf of skulls of men, women and children. 8,000 in total. The sight just stuns you into silence. The guide explained that bullets were too precious to use for executions. Axes, knives and bamboo sticks were far more common. As for the children, their murderers simply battered them against trees. The Khmer Rouge realised that children would seek revenge for the killing of the parents, so they killed them as well!

In the afternoon we visited the Tuol Svay Pray High school on the outskirts of Phnom Penh, more commonly known today as S-21, the Tuol Sleng Museum of Genocide, which on April, 1975 the Khmer Rouge turned into a torture, interrogation and execution centre. The place looked benign from the outside, with palm trees and grass lawns in a suburban setting. It could have been a school anywhere in the world, but inside there were weapons of torture, skulls, blood stains and photographs of the 20,000 thousand men, women and children who were murdered.

The scene once back outside was also heart-rending. Amputees of all ages begged near the refreshment stalls, cafés and souvenir stalls. I asked the guide how come there are children here without limbs.

"Land mines" he said.

The horror lives on.

Back at the hostel we talked to fellow travellers, and around half couldn't face a trip to the Killing Fields. We live a sanitised life in the West. Everyone must realise the depth some humans will stoop to. So whether it's Nazi concentration camps in Germany and Poland, or here in Cambodia, denying what man is capable of will sow the seeds for more horrors in the future.

FRIDAY 18 MAY SIEM REAP, CAMBODIA

So, this is what 04.00 am looks like? Hope it'll be worth it. This morning we're due to watch the sunrise over Angkor Wats, another of life's "must see/do" experiences on our list. I put on the kettle and got out the pain chocolate & pain custard I'd bought the previous evening, so at least we had something in our stomachs to get us through the early hours. At 04.45 we went downstairs and met our tuk-tuk driver and we were on our way through the dark streets and open fields to the historic site. The only people on the road at this hour were local early risers and tuk-tuk drivers with other tourists.

After about ten minutes we arrived at the 2.2 mile moat surrounding the imposing early 8th century complex, which was only discovered by a Frenchman 150 years ago when he ventured into the forest and discovered the abandoned site by accident. The first light of dawn enabled us to make out the iconic ominous looking outline of the world's largest religious building, the centre of the Hindu universe. At the centre stood towers that appear on every postcard you ever see of Cambodia.

It was a bit nippy as we stood there and waited for the day to begin. We didn't have long to wait. The sky turned from dark purple to Day-Glo magenta with an intensity only nature can produce. Slowly the full Harry Potter backdrop came to life, a living 3 dimensional wonder on a scale that challenges the senses.

This is not a tourist brochure so I won't go into any more site details other than to say goose pimples turned to sunburnt goosebumps as the heat matched the intensity of the colours of the sky. Since the fall of the evil Pol Pot regime, tourists have begun returning to Cambodia and approximately

50% visit Anchor Wats, with the result that the government can afford to go into partnership with various foreign agencies to undertake continuous restoration work. In fact, 28% of ticket revenues across the whole Anchor site is spent on the temples themselves, and the good news is that the influx of tourists has so far caused relatively little damage, other than some graffiti and one strategically placed LUHG sticker number 32 (68 to go) near the entrance where tourists pay for their ticket.

We spent the whole day there climbing, clambering and sweating in equal measure. At one point the air was filled with a piercing scream as the two Southampton girls we first met on the minibus from Chiang Mai recognized us.

Lots of heavy sweating and smelly hugs ensued. Weird but wonderful, the fact that you can be travelling and meet people at such unlikely times and places. One of the joys of travel. This would turn out to be the last time our paths would cross. There would be no "next time" as the girls were returning to the UK the following day. We all spoke at once until the heat sapped our strength and we limply bade each other farewell.

We continued around the extensive site, more out of duty than anything else. We knew we were in the presence of something special but you can get sensory overload and we agreed to call it a day and make our way back to our waiting tuk-tuk driver.

HONG KONG

SUNDAY 20 MAY PHNOM PENH - HONG KONG.

We made it to Hong Kong twenty years too late. By that I mean the old airport. I'd fantasized for years about landing amidst the skyscrapers towering above us as opposed to the other way round. I'd seen photos on magazines and moving images on TV and in films. One of the world's "Wow" images. But that was twenty years ago. Today Hong Kong Airport is like any other modern efficient characterless airport so there's nothing to write about, except that we were detained for 45 minutes for no reason. We were marched to a small office where other unwanted entrants were already waiting to be interrogated. There were video cameras recording our every movement. Hope they captured my Julio Inglesias side.

How, what, when, why and how long were duly answered with a straight face, Hélène making sure I didn't revert to type by adding a little sarcasm, cynicism or simple puns that might get us into trouble. We were then frog marched back to customs with no explanation for our detour, then sent on our way.

They say it is every travellers right of passage to stay in Chungking Mansions in Nathan Road. Horror stories abound but it's all down to choosing the right hostel. A combination of Rough Guide, Lonely Planet, Hostelbookers and Hostelworld whittled us down to a hostel on the top floor that was like Doctors Who's Tardis but without the extra dimension.

Passing through the dingy crowded entrance hall to the lifts in our block, I became aware of black people hustling along with Indians, Arabs and locals. Apart from fellow tourists, this was perhaps the first time I had seen black people in the Far East. Significant? I think so. At the lift a middle-aged Englishman was waiting for us. He was the manager of the hostel we had chosen, and he always greeted first time guests here as unscrupulous touts had a habit of luring innocent guests to other hostels with similar sounding names and charging them commission for inferior accommodation.

Our room was light and airy and much of the furniture and fixtures were brand new, so I reckoned we had landed on our feet (mainly because there was nowhere to sit down. Boom. Boom) My feet stuck out at the end of the bed and only one of us could stand up at a time but it was spotless.

A quick change and a stroll along Nathan Road resembled the tackier stretch of Oxford Street in London. (You know, that bit between Oxford Circus and Tottenham Court Road. Ah, thought you did). Only a few hundred yards and there we were, in front of the famous vista of Victoria Harbour. There were not many Chinese junks plying their trade but a mélange of modern motor boats and ferries. The range of styles of skyscrapers in front of us was impressive. I couldn't wait to see what they would all look like lit up at night, but looking to the left there appeared to be nothing but white tower blocks looking like something out of sixties Britain. They don't show those on the photographs.

I'd told Hélène to change into "smart casual" back at the hostel. (I'd chosen a white polo shirt with the United crest embroidered on the left breast, and my beige Ralph Lauren slacks from TK MAXX. I know where it's at). The reason became apparent as we passed in front of The Peninsular, the 5★ hotel in Hong Kong. Just like The Ritz in London or George V in Paris, The Peninsular was the place for afternoon tea. To see and be seen. We passed by the row of impeccable Rolls Royce's in front of the entrance and swept into the air-conditioned luxury of the main foyer. To the left was the Tea Room filled with tourists of all nationalities and just a smattering of locals. I wasn't really surprised.

We chose a seat near the window and there followed an hour and a half of refined nibbling and sipping the most delicious sandwiches, cakes and English breakfast tea. I even followed the crowd by asking our waiter to take our photo. Hélène was embarrassed, and rightly so, but at least I wasn't the first. I mean, it's what waiters are for, isn't it?

We hovered around for as long as was acceptable, including visits to the loo (twice, always a good test of a luxury establishment), then made our way back out to find a good position overlooking the harbour, in anticipation of the "Symphony of Light", what the Hong Kong Tourist Office call the biggest and best free pyrotechnic light show on the planet.

But what a let down... I was expecting the greatest show on earth, yet what followed was like sitting in front of and in the middle of the ultimate 360*, 3 dimensional, HD IMAX cinema and watching a black & white movie in pastel shades with the sound turned down. Oh, and no fireworks. Rubbish only scratches the surface. All that build up and then... well, it was like watching Bebe's first match for United. So much promise, so little talent.

The following morning we agreed to do the obvious tourist trip to the top of Victoria Peak. We've all seen the photos. It's just something you've got to do, right? Having been brought up in a small fishing village in Brittany, Hélène is more of a country girl while I am more of a city boy (did I just write "city" boy? Must be some mistake). Anyway I like the energy large numbers of people and buildings exude, so I was really looking forward to this.

Before we walked to where the Peak Tram started from and joined the queue we went to a special travel agent where we ordered our Chinese visas for the next leg of our journey. These were extortionately expensive at 880HK dollars each (£70), and two, one week Japanese Rail Passes at 2500HK dollars each (£200), which can only be purchased before you arrive in Japan in order to obtain the 40% discount on the country's hideously expensive rail travel.

I don't think there was one local among us in the Peak Tram queue. Eventually we got ourselves in one and it began its ascent. The higher we went, the more luxurious the accommodation on either side. High-rise apartment blocks gave way to detached villas as the air became cooler and fresher. This is how the other tenth lives, I thought.

Surprisingly (to me anyway), at 552 meters (1,811 ft) it's the highest mountain on Hong Kong Island, but not the entirety of Hong Kong, an honour which belongs to Tai Mo Shan. At the top we're out onto a twin level square perimeter. It's sunny and warm but with a strong wind. The view is truly breathtaking and we're doing the normal tourist things when

I spot a light blue football top.

Yup, there's no mistaking a City strip. What sad bastard's wearing that? I wondered. It's the first one I've seen on this trip, so way down behind us, Liverpool and Chelsea, with Arsenal a distant fourth. (An omen for the coming season no doubt). I hover expectantly, trying desperately not to waste this golden opportunity to strike a blow for the Red Army. Hélène wonders why I don't come over to her. I point to the shirt but she doesn't comprehend. No, can't think of anything witty or pertinent, so I fall back on the tried and tested. I slithered up behind him and in my finest voice honed to perfection over many decades of football terraces I fill my lungs and let out a piercing:

"U-NI-TED!"

His girlfriend let out a scream to match mine as he swung round and his face broke out into a grin.

Shit. He took that well, I thought, as he shook my hand and laughed, which is more than Hélène did. She seemed the only one not to "get it." He was too stunned to come back with a vitriolic comment so I went away smiling, another notch on the side of my imaginary United fuselage. Hélène's look of "grow up" was dismissed out of hand. The City fan had got it. His girlfriend had got it. I had sure as hell got it. Hélène was out of it. She couldn't play. She didn't understand the rules. Boy, that felt good. Grow up? What's the point?

The next day we decided to take the world's longest cable car ride to visit the Giant Buddha, which sits serenely atop Ngong Ping plateau amid the spectacular mountain scenery of Lantau Island. As the cable car rises above the planes taking off and landing at the international airport, the Giant Buddha's compelling presence dominates the skyline. Needless to say, once we stepped out of the cable car there were more souvenir shops and restaurants to tempt us. The walk to the Giant Buddha itself was through a concrete maze that was under construction. I'm sure visitors in the future will appreciate it's layout and appeal, but for us cement dust coupled with the hot, humid air was a concoction guaranteed to attack both eyes and throat.

The final part of the trek was up 200 steps in the heat and humidity to the Giant Buddha itself. Inside there were signs everywhere stating "No photography", yet outside in the numerous souvenir shops there were postcards galore with images of the inside.

Mmmmmm…..

By the time we arrived back in Kowloon, nightfall had fallen so we took the famous Star Ferry which magnified the size and scale of the mesmerizing blazing skyline at a fraction of the cost of official night tours.

Then a stroll around the living breathing streets before eating a lovely cannelloni and retiring to our spotless shoebox.

MACAU

WEDNESDAY 26 MAY HONG KONG TO MACAU

Eleven years to this very day. Can't believe the years have flown by so quickly. As a kid I always thought all parents read from the same hymn book, learning the same parent type phrases and expressions, just to put the fear of Eric into children and to keep us quiet. "Just you wait till you're our age" meant when you reach our age you will see we were right and you were wrong. Wrong.

Most of the principles, values and beliefs I had as a teenager I still hold true today, but occasionally one or two utterings from my parents I can agree with. "The older you get, the faster time passes". How right they were. I still get the same chills as I visualise Ole's leg deflecting Teddy's header into the net as I did that heady night at the Nou Camp. Feelings so intense it seems only like yesterday. Every aspect of the three day drive to Barcelona and back, the walk round the side streets just to enter the stadium, the inflatables in the sun before kick-off, James and Freddie Mercury forever swim round my head.

And those final three minutes. Sex will never be as good as those final three minutes. Or as long! But through my watering eyes the alarm makes its presence felt.

Today we have much to cover before taking the fast ferry to Macau. As a last minute treat Hélène decided to visit the hairdressers to redo her roots. I took this as an opportunity to wander down to the harbour and stroll the entire length of the Kowloon side, this time eye-balling everyone I passed to see if they picked up on my United T-shirt.

Nothing. Ex-pats, locals…nothing! And this was the first "country" I had travelled to that United had blessed with a pre-season presence. There was not much evidence of them having made sufficient inroads at street level. Nevertheless I took the opportunity to whack up LUHG stickers 32-34 in locations I was sure ex-pats would surely pass. Now just 66 to go.

Looking spectacular, Hélène emerged from the salon reborn, all sophisticated like. After almost three months on the road this was like a start over, but with a suntan to boot. As we were leaving today I wondered who would benefit from the new, improved model? Our next stop was a couple of days and nights in Macau, so the casinos had better watch out.

The approaching vista of the Portuguese colony from our hovercraft was nondescript to say the least. A hotchpotch of old dominated by a hotchpotch of new. Once in the arrivals hall we were attacked by swarms of unauthorised taxi drivers demanding 150 HKD for a journey to our hotel that cost us 30 by metered taxi.

A curse on their first born.

I hadn't intended paying £50 a night for a hotel (you know me), but the Best Western Sun Hotel on the outskirts of Macau City itself was the cheapest one available at short notice. After settling in we walked the streets to the "strip", a poor man's version of Las Vegas, a mishmash of over the top hotels awash with neon, gaudy gold and Chinese punters doing what is illegal on mainland China.

Since her triumph/disaster in Las Vegas twenty five years ago, (Triumph – she really enjoyed herself. Disaster – she lost all our winnings) Hélène had been looking forward to "doing the slots" once again. Only after all this time the slot machines have changed. Instead of rows of three there were rows of five and neither of us could make head or tail of how to play. Hold or play? We seemed to have no control over events whirring in front of us.

A short period of noise and colour later, the machines had swallowed all our money. Quite unsatisfying. We took a taxi back to our hotel, Skyped and Facebooked as many of our friends and relatives as possible. Contributed to as many threads as seemed relevant on Red News and Red Issue fans forums, as the following day we would be plunged into a Chinese imposed Facebook free zone, not to come out of the darkness for the next three weeks.

Cambodia, Laos and Vietnam had all been Communist yet Facebook was freely available. Why was China different? What were they afraid of? What would China be like? What would the people be like? Would I be able to keep my mouth shut and not end up doing hard labour somewhere where even British intelligence couldn't find me? Separating fact from fiction and political propaganda is one of the fascinating aspects of travel, but would I live to tell the tale? At least I didn't have to locate a TV showing United matches so this pressure at least was off. We shall see...

THURSDAY 27 MAY MACAU – BEIJING

We had intended to stroll around the old Portuguese quarter in Macau, but a combination of "saw a bit from the taxi yesterday and we weren't that impressed" plus "let's have a much needed lie-in in a nice hotel with all the facilities and get ourselves together slowly" won the day. The hotel offered to drop us at the border crossing in their luxury 4x4 for the same price as a taxi. This time we were ripped off as the hotel charged us 170 HKD whereas a metred taxi would have charged around 30. 1-1.

The dark and depressing Macau airport hangar masquerading as their border crossing was slow but effortless as was the more modern Chinese section. We were expecting the Spanish inquisition (OK, Chinese inquisition) but we just sailed through.

Wow! We're actually in China! Made it! I came over all emotional, I can tell you.

Our next mission was to find the bus terminal in Guangzhou for a bus direct to Guangzhou Airport. We could have flown to Beijing more conveniently direct from Hong Kong, but a bit of searching online revealed flights from Guangzhou, just over the border in mainland China, were considerably cheaper. Anyone on a limited budget should bear this in mind.

The Chinese border crossing opened out into two multi-coloured floors strewn with stalls and shops selling every "shmockner" you can imagine. Asking for directions, it became immediately apparent that nobody spoke English, even though this giant shopping "souk" was right on the border. Interpreting conflicting sets of directions we eventually hauled all our luggage, dripping (us, not the luggage) up umpteen flights of stairs and into daylight. I saw a cluster of buses over the road so we sweated our way across and into the bus terminal.

Nobody spoke English.

I wrote the words "Guangzhou Airport" in English on a scrap of paper. I assumed/prayed the girl behind the glass partition understood as she issued us with two tickets and indicated for us to sit.... over there. A long, long time later we were invited to board our bus and slowly we made our way out of this border town and along the river to China's third largest town, Guangzhou.

A permanent pinkish haze hung over the city as the ring road to end all ring roads circumvented the sprawling metropolis and took us to the airport. Wow, first the Chinese side of the Macau/Chinese border and now Guangzhou Airport, the epitome of modern architecture. Instantly one pre-conceived image of Communist rule evaporated, that all constructions were dull grey concrete monstrosities, similar to those I witnessed in my 24 hour visit to Moscow in 2008 for the Champions League final.

Guangzhou Airport was the very latest in everything. Light, airy, spacious, and the equal of any airport in the West. I read that the city is home to numerous trade fairs, exhibitions and conferences throughout the year attracting a global audience, and their facilities match their ambition.

Just as impressive were LUHG stickers 35 and 36 I put up in the men's' toilet both ground side and air side. At 6.30pm we boarded our flight to Beijing which passed without incident and by 11.00pm we had landed in another ultra modern airport. Passing swiftly through customs and baggage reclaim we grabbed the only taxi in sight and gave him the address of our city centre hostel in both English and Chinese.

Just our luck. We had chosen a taxi driver that didn't know his way round Beijing.

The first flickers of dawn shot across the night sky as he finally located the side street housing the New Dragon hostel. Halli-fucking-looyah!

We rang the bell and obviously woke up whoever was inside. Poor thing. The taxi driver pointed to the metre but I explained, succinctly I thought, to the young hostel receptionist that we had endured an unwanted tour of dark wet Beijing suburbs and were only willing to pay the price printed in our Lonely Guide. It transpired the driver was one of many who had suffered from loss of agricultural income and came, unqualified, to the big city to earn a living and support his family. The only problem being, he must have only just arrived, as he knew as much about the Beijing road system as I did.

The young hostel receptionist sent him on his way and led Mr & Mrs Zombie to their private double room in the annexe that had everything we could possibly wish for at the price. The staff offered to bring us breakfast in bed at 06.30, but as that was only in a couple of hours time we requested 09.00am if possible. T'Pau! We had China in our hand and we were mightily impressed so far.

How long would that last, I wondered, as I drifted to sleep before my head hit the pillow.

CHINA

FRIDAY 28 MAY. BEIJING, CHINA

At precisely 08.30 we heard a commanding knock on our door and before I could move this woman entered our room with military precision and plonked a tray full of breakfast goodies on our bed. Hélène and I looked at each other. I felt we were acting on a film set so I took everything, good and bad, in my stride. When in Beijing.

So, our first day in Beijing. What to do first?

Let's get the Forbidden City and Tiananmen Square out of the way. Just like The Killing Fields and the Genocide Museum in Cambodia, the tunnels and War Remnants Museum in Vietnam, and the Bridge Over The River Kwai in Thailand I felt extremely uncomfortable visiting these sites of inhumane treatment on a scale I find both physically and mentally sickening. And now I was going to visit the scene of the Tiananmen Square massacre where untold thousands of students and intellectuals holding peaceful protests were massacred when martial law was introduced. The ultra conservative communist authority (conservative communists. I always have problems with that apparent contradiction of terms) sent in tanks and soldiers and opened fire on the estimated 100,000 protesters. Power corrupts, and absolute power corrupts absolutely. Wasn't it ever thus?

I looked at the map in Lonely Planet, then it came to me as a revelation. Instead of being weighed down by carrying the whole book with us each time, why not just tear out the relevant pages? Why hadn't I thought of that before? We're not going to need the pages once we're done and the idea of amassing books and weight when restricted to a maximum 23 kilos on most flights seemed ridiculous upon reflection.

Our hostel was within walking distance so we started with the Forbidden City first. An amazing experience. So many buildings, it vied with the Grand Palace in Bangkok for overdoingitness, although in June it's bloody hot so it can take the gloss off after a while.

Back outside I was taking photos of stern looking guards when I spied a United crest. Looking up I saw it adorned the left breast of a 30ish year old European gentleman in a party of three carrying professional camera equipment.

"Aha!" I thought. "A chance for some real United banter."

Dragging Hélène behind me I made my way over and introduced myself, simultaneously indicating the very same United crest on my shirt.

Did the floodgates of footy talk fill the air?

Eer...no.

This world-weary Scandinavian looked decidedly uncomfortable in face of my full-on onslaught. Polite one-liners diffused my pent-up enthusiasm somewhat. No life-long bonding here I'm afraid. He couldn't wait to get away quickly enough. Was it me?

Obviously it was. I just thought surely there must be thousands of United fans around Europe who share the same passion as me/us, or had my experience living and working in France been representative of Europe as a whole? Namely that football is purely a leisure pursuit, to be forgotten about once the final whistle blows? On my travels I'd already established what many of us already knew, that significant numbers of football fans around the world follow personalities more than a particular team. I've already lost count of the number of Beckham and Ronaldo shirts I've seen in both United and Real colours. But genuine Reds? Disappointingly few.

We made our way across the road and walked across Tiananmen Square. So spacious and quiet, with imposing buildings on all four sides, it was difficult imagining the horrors of eleven years before. Unlike the aforementioned sites of human destruction, here there was no tangible evidence, no statues, no plaques. It was as though it never happened, which is just what the authorities would like us to believe.

I'll tell you one thing that did happen though. There's a moving statue of rows of people (peasants) in one corner of the square, I can't remember the exact details, but I left LUHG sticker number 37 on the base of the square plinth. Knowing there were CCTV cameras covering every aspect of the square I was so discreet even Hélène didn't notice.

We kept on walking for walking's sake and soon found ourselves opposite a street I can only liken to a wider version of Carnaby Street in London, with European fashion stores and food outlets from McDonalds to Hagen Dazs housed in these dark grey, two story buildings that ran the whole length of the street.

Well, I had to, didn't I?

Hagen Dazs....mmmmm.....

SATURDAY 29 MAY BEIJING, CHINA

The following day was Great Wall of China day. But not any old Great Wall of China day. You see, I'd done my homework and read that most tourists elect to go to the nearest site where they would be knee deep in… tourists. So Hélène and I chose one of the few sections to retain its original appearance, Simatai near Chengdu, a three hour drive from Beijing. Our bus was mostly full of healthy young gap year type boys and girls. We stood out like sore thumbs, and other sore parts of our anatomies. The bus divided into two sections. Those that chose the 10 kilometre stretch… and us, who opted for the easier 4 kilometre section. We'd seen the photos. We knew how steep and uneven it would be. 4 kilometres would be more than enough thank you very much. Arriving at the base all the healthy young gap year boys and girls began their trek up to the foot of the wall. I was quite attracted to the cable car that took us ¾ of the way up. There was a lot of building works going on which detracted somewhat from initial impressions, but these were soon forgotten as the cable car began to move.

As it rose above the hills the scenery grew ever more fantastic with precipitous topography (I got that last phrase from a guide book. I'm sure you noticed). The wall itself was getting nearer, undulating as far as the eye could see. Knowing that the Beijing section of the wall alone is 542 miles long, it still doesn't prepare you for the immensity of it all. And here the undulating countryside was spectacular, simply spectacular.

What they hadn't told us though was that the remaining walk up the side of the hill to the wall itself was dodgy with a capital "D". A number of local women followed us, pushing postcards, brochures and books in our hands and demanding money. I demanded they stopped, not because I didn't want to buy anything (which I didn't of course) but because every time they touched me I thought that would be my last. They must be used to scrambling up and down but I was shitting myself and might have left my own souvenir on the hillside.

Sweating profusely we climbed through one of the dark crumbling watchtowers and out onto the crumbling wall itself. Made it. I'm here. Never thought this would happen to me. Wow!

I just stood there, taking it all in. Mind blowing. Hélène took my hand and...

"DON'T TOUCH ME!" I cried. "Fuck me, have you seen the steps? They're so steep and shiny and broken and ... slippery."

"You're joking...aren't you?" she retorted.

No I wasn't. Now I knew why this part of the Great Wall wasn't knee deep in tourists. We were so high up, take your eye off the steps for one minute and the steps would be knee deep in broken knees.

Seriously, I never realized it would be so steep, or that I would be affected so strongly by vertigo whilst Hélène glided up and down like a natural. At some points there was virtually no wall on either side of the wall to hang onto, just narrow strips of steep uneven steps with a sheer drop either side. Health and Safety Officers in the UK would be creaming themselves envisaging all the realms of regulations they could dream up to stop people enjoying themselves. I'm not saying I didn't enjoy it, I just took a hell of a lot longer to navigate our four kilometres, take in every vista and pose for every obligatory photo.

We had a lie in the following morning then took the glistening metro to the Olympic Park. First impressions – impressive. Second impressions – equally impressive.

The Birds Nest stadium looked a mesh of silvery grey web like structures. I wanted to go inside but Hélène couldn't be arsed. She was doing this for me so her arse didn't come into it. We found the correct entrance and were directed up to the first floor under one of the stands to where you could exchange your shoes for approved trainers and then let out onto the track. Wow! What sports grounds in the UK would let you walk out just like that?

I stuck LUHG sticker number 38 on a pillar opposite the trainer outlet before emerging out onto the track. I may be a professional United supporter but I'm useless as an athlete, yet the springy running track made me feel like a contender. I got Hélène, reluctantly (extremely reluctantly) to take a multitude of stupidly posed pictures and videos of yours truly performing all the sporting activities on offer. You should have seen my high jump. You should have seen my triple jump (No, you shouldn't. Couldn't even reach the sand pit) I made sure my United shirt featured heavily in all the filming though. Great fun.

Next stop was the cubic swimming pool building but unfortunately it was closed to the public the day we visited. We hung around for hours waiting for the sun to go down, and as we waited Hélène spotted an odd couple, one man and one woman. They were approaching people and offering to take their photos. They both carried oversized handbags which I thought a bit peculiar.

Not for long though. After taking a photo each of the couple would dive into their handbag and 60 seconds later a large colour photo would appear. I strolled nonchalantly over and inside their bags I spied the smallest 3-in-1 printers you've ever seen. How enterprising. And obviously illegal as they kept looking round and moving on whenever anyone in a uniform came along. Free enterprise rules, OK!

Then as the sun went down the Olympic complex came alive with all the buildings illuminated. The Birds Nest stadium in all its pulsating yellows and oranges and the swimming building in translucent throbbing blues against the darkening skyline. We came home exhausted but satisfied. So far we had been blown away by all we've seen in China, with one exception. The Chinese don't understand the concept of queuing. For anything. I soon learned, if you can't beat 'em, join 'em. My football fan training came to the fore as I fought for every open space on offer. I wonder what the rest of the country will be like?

That night, before going to sleep, I went downstairs to arrange for an early morning alarm call and early breakfast. The pretty young girl behind the counter wore a confused expression on her face as she complied with my request. I'd got on really well with her over the past few days so why this apparent change of attitude? When I got back to our room Hélène asked why I had gone downstairs without my false teeth?

Shit.

That explains everything. When I smiled, all the poor girl had seen were two Dracula stalactites descending from above and two anti-Dracula stalagmites protruding from below. She's now scarred for life, and it was my fault.

WEDNESDAY 2 JUNE BEIJING TO SHANGHAI

Today is marked with a bullet. And for good reason. We are going to take the new bullet train from Beijing to Shanghai. Ten hours in one seat is normally more than two buttocks can bear, but my childhood fascination with trains negated any foreboding. With an 11 o'clock start, we had time to panic quietly as Hélène barked instructions with regards to packing our two giant rucksacks and scolded me for still not getting the hang of it by now, almost four months into our trip. (You've spotted a pattern evolving long before now, haven't you dear reader?)

We said goodbye to the New Dragon hostel and took a taxi to Beijing South railway station. Like a giant squashed alien spaceship, the station is a marvel of cutting edge design and planning. It puts anything we have in Britain, including the new Eurostar section of St Pancras to shame. There's so much space and even, as Monty Python might have exclaimed, "comfortable chairs". Yes, proper armchairs and tables and things, as well the obligatory rows of hard seats near the check-ins themselves. It's more like an airport than a railway station. I was impressed. Again.

We treated ourselves to superb cappuccinos and delicious French style cakes before boarding the bristling white steed, its huge phallic engine throbbing quietly, exuding inner confidence and hidden power. Instantly you know, you just know, this engine is George Clooney, Brad Pitt and Jonny Depp all rolled into one.

I left Hélène in one of our seats as I just had to take a photograph or three of me with the beast. I walked to the front of the platform and mimed to one of the locals to take my picture with... it. Done. But not before one of my greatest LUHG sticker triumphs. Number 39 on the actual nose of the phallic beauty.

Back in our surprisingly comfortable "hard seat", i.e. second class, the train left right on time. We got some funny looks as the only Westerners on the train as the stewardess handed out free bottles of water and before we knew it we were purring our way thought the grey/green Chinese countryside. Although the scenery was nothing to write home about we were impressed that nearly all the buildings, both commercial and domestic, had solar panels on the roof. A one-off investment by local party councils that would have long lasting benefits for all in the community. We think we know it all in the 'West' but we have so much to learn. It didn't feel like ten hours as the train glided into Shanghai railway station, having sped along even faster than the famous bullet trains of Japan. We'd eaten, drank and dozed a little and felt fighting fit as we dismounted.

At the taxi rank outside we were blinded by the concentration of Western style neon signs, advertising western brands and height defying skyscrapers. It had the buzz of New York about it. We received a lovely warm welcome by everyone working at our hostel. They had prepared a dormitory just for us, Wi-Fi, TV, the lot. What a great start to Shanghai. And tomorrow we pay the first of our three planned visits to the World's Fair. I couldn't wait.

The following morning we took the bright modern metro to the World's Fair entrance. 4 yen (38p) What a rip-off, the metro had only been 2 yen (19p) in Beijing. We made our way round the confusing signs (in English) to the main entrance and bought our tickets. The theme of the expo was, "Better City – Better Life". I interpreted this as a countenance to all the negative publicity in the West to China's terrible record on pollution as a consequence of their race to be the world's fastest growing economy.

In front of us was the giant red imposing Chinese pavilion, but we thought we'd better follow a structured route so as not to miss anything. There were no queues so we went straight in, despite being led to believe by the hostel staff that it was sold out.

The first pavilion we came to was Cuba. This should be good, I thought. Two communist countries, I expected the works. What a letdown. Just one square room with piped Cuban music, no live music, and just photos round the walls. Oh, and no freebies, just a bar with drinks at inflated prices. Not a great start.

Suffice to say the whole site was an almighty damp squib. Predictable pavilions by country after country. Passive, very little interaction. Now I don't know whether the Chinese authorities had laid down strict rules and regulations that it all but squeezed out any creativity, but we soon got fed up by the whole thing. Then as it got more crowded and long queues began to form outside most pavilions, I got the distinct feeling that most of these people had no idea of what they were about to see or do.

And I was right. I started a conversation with a fellow Brit in one of the queues and he told me the authorities had been so disappointed and embarrassed by the low turnout to their multi-million pound investment, they had resorted to bussing in citizens from all over China to make up the admissions. Then I became aware of swarms of these people rushing around in groups and converging at entrance after entrance without entering. What's going on here?

Now you won't believe this (well you will, because I'm about to tell you) but they had all been issued with fake passports and were in competition to fill up their passports with as many of the pavilion countries stamps as possible. They'd descend like locusts, rudely pushing their fake passports under the noses of pavilion personnel and demand stamps. No please, no thank you. No nothing. I had to laugh, but some of the pavilion staff we spoke to afterwards were getting pretty upset that these people showed no interest in their country, just the stamp.

Now, I'm not being biased, just proud, but Hélène and I both considered the most creative and forward thinking pavilion was designed by the UK! Everyone stand up. As we approached it just seemed like a giant fuzzy light grey cube. It was entitled, "Seed Cathedral". Coming closer we discovered this 20 m3 cube was constructed with 60,000 slim, clear acrylic rods emanating from a central core. Each one containing seeds of different plants that were collected in a biodiversity project launched by the Royal Botanical Gardens in Kew in 2000, re-enforcing the notion that nature can live and enhance our lives within the big city.

The cube had been placed in the middle of what looked like a grey field, but was in fact meant to represent wrapping paper. Then who should I spy standing proud with his arm raised in celebratory salute but Wayne Rooney himself. Or rather a Madame Tussaud's waxworks. He was wearing a red England top but never mind. I thought he would look good next to me in my white United polo shirt so I waited until my patience wore thin and employed the Chinese principle of pushing my way to the front and pleaded with a reluctant Hélène (what other type is there?) to take my photo. I put my arm round Wayne's shoulder and the two of us were photographed with both our arms raised in salute. Oh, how the locals laughed, and snapped. Unfortunately there were too many tourists and security people around to stick an appropriate LUHG sticker here.

Hélène had hoped the French stand might be worth a visit, but we were both bitterly disappointed. Escalators brought us up to the top, then sloping gangways brought us past windows, the other side of which were people cooking, yet there was nowhere on the whole stand to buy, let alone sample for free, any French food or drink. On the walls were black and white photos of French icons such as Bridget Bardot and the Paris skyline (but no Eric Cantona. Heathens) A wasted opportunity.

The rest of the day was spent queuing for the sake of queuing, on the off-chance we may miss something, and the fact we certainly wouldn't be coming back again. I will give a special mention to the Cambodian pavilion though, with its detailed reproduction of Angkor Wat, and to the South African pavilion, if only for the fact it had a giant football outside in recognition of the forthcoming World Cup and I just HAD to get Hélène to take some seriously posed funny shots.

Oh, how the locals laughed, and snapped. End of story. And no, we won't be going back and I didn't buy a "Shanghai Expo 2010" T-Shirt.

SATURDAY 5 JUNE SHANGHAI

We started today in Xintiandi, one of the "cool" neighbourhoods of Shanghai, featuring an affluent, car-free series of reconstructed traditional shikumen (stone gate), low-rise buildings housing cool (i.e. expensive) boutiques, book stores, cafes and restaurants and the obligatory shopping malls. When in Shanghai, as they say, so we treated ourselves to an early brunch which was ace. The quality of food and service were impeccable, and the attractive, middle-aged manageress paid us a lot of attention whilst practising her English. Gastronomically satisfied, we walked a few blocks to the Taiking Road Art Centre, an even cooler labyrinth of traditional longtang alleyways full of genuine charm and vibrancy. This place was full of design studios, Wi-Fi cafés and boutiques, the perfect antidote to Shanghai's oversized malls and intimidating skyscrapers. And being relatively hard to get to by public transport prevented, it was not swamped by tour groups.

I purchased two prized processions that remain with me to this day. Luggage tags. One said "This is MY fucking bag" and the other said "Only Dirty Clothes Inside". Well, it made me smile. We ended the day walking round pretty Fuxing Park, smack-dab in the colonial-era French Concession, with its shady sycamore trees and stuccoed villas. Of course, it was the name that attracted me in the first place. I mean, I couldn't let it go, could I? In the park we found grannies in pyjamas belting out Chinese opera and Mao-suited men taking their caged birds for a stroll round the central lake. There were covered pavilions, fountains and glorious flowerbeds, and the locals seemed to be genuinely enjoying every aspect of their environment. They smiled at us and we smiled back.

I could get used to this.

SUNDAY 6 JUNE SHANGHAI, CHINA

So far, each day had surpassed the previous in China. The only downside had been prices, which were significantly higher than in the countries we had already visited in Asia. China's growing middle classes have pushed the cost of consumer goods up significantly, and with Shanghai the powerhouse of the Chinese economy, everyone creating the wealth has to spend, spend, spend. Everywhere you go in downtown Shanghai there are malls, malls, malls. Every Western brand was represented. In fact, central Shanghai felt the most Western of all cities in China. There was a buzz about the place, an energy that was tangible.

It is generally recognized that China is responsible for a quarter of the world's population. I can vouch for that. Walking along the main boulevards I think I met everyone of them. It felt like I was walking towards Old Trafford as everyone else was coming away from the match. Wave after wave of people coming atcha (thank you, Cleopatra. Long lost reference there). We made our way to the Bund (the word means Embankment in English) which runs along the western bank of the Huangpu River, facing the glistening high rise edifices to mammon, the god of wealth, in Pudong in the eastern part of Huangpu District. If I had been a little disappointed by the sights and sounds of Victoria Harbour in Hong Kong, then I was overawed by vistas The Bund exuded from every angle.

Did you know that Shanghai has one of the richest collections of Art Deco architectures in the world? You did? Oh. Oh well, I was impressed anyway. Initially a British settlement, the elegant buildings on The Bund were the original symbols of opulence financed by Britain making a killing (literally and metaphorically) smuggling opium into China so, armed with an explanatory handbook, Hélène was in her element as we attempted to gain entrance to each and every building in order to admire the OTT interiors.

As in all these situations, I find it hard to disassociate myself from the intolerable suffering of the masses for the benefit of the few, so I more than welcomed the opportunity to cross the river by the strange brightly lit underground tourist tunnel and view The Bund from the eastern shore. Even better was the positioning of a Haagen Dazs in a slightly raised position so that I could indulge my sweet tooth to my heart and stomach's content whilst watching the world go by on land and on the river.

As darkness fell and the lights came on, The Bund once again outshone Victoria Harbour with its very exuberance and over the top pyrotechnics . Pleasure cruisers sailed by in both directions, music blaring and performing gaudy flashing light shows that re-enforced the expression, "If it's worth doing, it's worth over doing". Utterly compelling.

Well done Shanghai, and goodnight.

MONDAY 7 JUNE ZHUJIAJIAO, CHINA

After a much needed lie in this morning I checked into my Lonely Planet and discovered Zhujiajiao, an ancient water village located in the Qingpu District of Shanghai. A bonus for me was the fact that the bus station was under one of the stands of the large football stadium, so I spent a few minutes boring Hélène rigid while I did a tour of the circumference. I wanted to go inside but we didn't have time. Working out the bus route, we arrived around 11.00am outside the walled town of Zhujiajiao. Obviously popular with tourists both local and international, the money they generate keeps this little gem in pristine condition.

It was baking hot as we wandered around, Hélène looking out for antiques and me for any tourist or local wearing a football shirt, preferable Eric's Disciples on Earth.

My vigilance was rewarded when I spied a couple of local looking lads down a narrow alleyway wearing United tops.

"Hélène. This way."

"Why? What's down there?"

"Voila!" "Hi guys, do you speak English?"

Grin. Grin. Grin.

In broken English their girlfriends' superior English vocabulary aided a conversation of sorts. Inevitably the cameras came out and they outdid me with the number of shots they took. Each one wanted a solo shot of themselves with me as well as the obligatory group photo.

As a parting shot I gave each of the two lads one of my LUHG stickers, (39 & 40, just 60 to go) and explained as best I could what demons the Glazers were and why they should stick them up in an appropriate environment.

Hélène took all this in good humour, which was a first, as she could see the joy I was bringing to the locals. Eventually my job here was done and we all moved on, leaving the two boys in awe of someone who had actually been to Old Trafford. I'm never complacent about any trip to OT, no matter how sanitized the experience has become compared to "the old days", yet encounters like this make me realize, as if I needed telling, that supporting United is a privilege that I should never take for granted.

The rest of the day was taken up by wandering around this delightful little Chinese Venice, scoffing ourselves silly in a restaurant overlooking the main canal and teaching a kid on the next table some English phrases as he wanted to practice his English whilst explaining the Chinese only menu to us. Sweet. Exhausted, we made our way back to the bus by sunset, only to meet up once again with my local United crew. Beams all round once again, but by this time I had no strength left so I just beamed back.

TUESDAY 8 JUNE SHANGHAI, CHINA

As we were due to fly to Xi'an, the home of the Terracotta Army, early the following morning, I had chosen a hotel near the airport for the night. Our taxi driver had great difficulty finding it, even though I had the address written in Chinese, driving up and down the same dark highway as I kept a close eye on the metre. Eventually the hotel was located, and the obligatory discussion over the fare began. By this time it was almost 1 o' clock in the morning but I kept my Mr Bean smile intact as I handed over what I considered a reasonable fare. The driver followed us into the hotel to exchange unpleasantries with us and the receptionist but my look of benign innocence won the day and he left the premises accompanied by what I can only presume to be Chinese swear words.

We were very tired by this point and my luck ran out when I went to clean my dentures and I dropped the bottom set on the marble floor. I instantly gained two pieces for the price of one. I looked like an inverted Christopher Lee, with just two pointed molars sticking up. There was only one solution. Get out the super glue and with Hélène's help, stick the two pieces together. I sat on the bed holding them in place until I thought it was safe to put them down. Unlike Eric & Ernie, you could see the join, but at least I wouldn't scare passing traffic. It was 3 o' clock by the time we got into bed and only three hours sleep to fall into. I fell asleep immediately.

WEDNESDAY 9 JUNE SHANGHAI TO XI'AN, CHINA

The taxi ride from Xi'an airport to our central hostel brought us down to earth. Well, to be accurate, it was the plane that brought us down to earth, the taxi just drove along it. The point I'm trying to make is that Xi'an, outskirts and centre, is a dark depressing grimy grey industrial town. This was the China of pre-conceived western images, a Salford of the Lowry paintings. Our spirits sank as we took in our surroundings. I'd allowed two days and nights in Xi'an and that might be one day and night too much.

Still, first impressions can be deceiving so let's give the place a chance. I'm like that, me.

Our hostel was fine, as have all the Chinese hostels been so far. India could learn a lot from these guys. Still we'd only come for one thing, so once we dumped our things in our room we made our way back to the reception and booked ourselves on the full day tour to see the Museum of the one and only Terracotta Army and Horses of Qin Shinuang. Would it live up to expectations? We'd soon find out, but now was the time to eat, and even in a boring looking mid-sized Chinese town the food was superb. Why can't Chinese restaurants in the UK be as good as these?

Back at the hostel we went back on the Facebookless internet. I couldn't help but overhear this podgy Cockney guy surrounded by his three sons as they tried to book onward flights. I contributed my two pennies worth and this time my Green & Gold T-Shirt provoked a typical ABU response. Hélène's eyes glossed over as light-hearted banter turned to piss-take and counter piss-take, but soon theirs' took on a darker tone and Hélène got up and left.

This was my first "proper" football conversation in four months. Passion, needle, humour, all the elements I had been missing. The Dad and two of his sons supported Arsenal but for some inexplicable reason that was never fully explained, the third supported Norwich City. This Canary nailed his ABU flag well and truly to the mast by declaring loudly that he hated Man U more than any other team, even Ipswich Town. Norwich might play in green and yellow, but the green of envy was evident in all his utterances.

I never found out what the family did for a living, but I bet you it wasn't one hundred percent kosher if you get my drift.

THURSDAY 10 JUNE XI'AN, CHINA

"Terra-cotta Army! Terra-cotta Army!" hasn't got the same ring to it as "Red Army! Red Army! Red Army!" but that wasn't going to stop me seeing one of the world's greatest man-made phenomena. First discovered by accident in 1974 by a local farmer digging for water, these hollow figures and horses of Qin Shihiang dating from the 3rd century BC (Before City won a trophy), and now approaching 7000 and rising, are responsible for putting Xi'an on the map. Without them it would just be another grey, characterless mid sized Chinese town.

We congregated in the reception of our hostel at half past nine, including the Arse with his fat arse and his three sons. A young girl came in and led us down our small side street to the main road where our minibus was waiting. The driver was asleep in his driving seat and didn't seem overtly concerned by our presence. The agitated girl took out her mobile and spoke rather crisply. The man didn't respond. One by one we realised she had led us to the wrong minibus, as a few minutes later another one pulled up on the other side of the road.

As we drove for an hour to the site of the Terra-cotta Army, she outlined the plan for the day. Hélène hates being in an organised group and made disquieting noises and grunts at regular intervals, but one fact she told us stood out for me. Each and every one of the thousands of workers who had sculpted the figures was systematically murdered on the orders of the emperor. That's one way to save on labour costs and pensions I suppose.

When we arrived at the site we ran a gauntlet of obligatory souvenir stalls before entering the first of three giant halls. The scene which greeted us in the first hall was simply breathtaking. Row upon row of army soldiers as far as the eye could see, each one sporting individual features. The phrase, "They all look the same to me" could never be applied here. They vary in height, according to their roles, with the tallest being the generals. The figures include warriors, chariots, horses, officials, acrobats, strongmen and musicians. Current estimates are that in the three pits containing the Terracotta Army there are over 8,000 soldiers, 130 chariots with 520 horses and 150 cavalry horses, the majority of which are still buried in the pits and yet to be excavated.

By rights the farmer that discovered this treasure should be a multi-millionaire many times over, earning a percentage from every ticket and souvenir sold, every hotel/hostel room booked and every meal consumed by the thousands upon thousands of visitors from all over the world. Instead he was just offered a small house and a piece of land. By Chinese standards this was more than the man could ever have dreamed of. By western standards he has been exploited left, right and centre, with others profiting from the simple man's good fortune.

The day we were there he was sat behind a desk in the souvenir shop, signing copies of a glossy, beautifully illustrated full colour coffee table book. I looked at him and wondered how aware he was of the global response his discovery had generated. Maybe he was happy with his lot. I simply don't know, but it did make me think. In fact it did made me think that as this place was full of tourists, a strategically placed LUHG sticker number 41 was called for.

On the way back on the bus, the young Chinese girl encouraged everyone to join in for a spot of karaoke. With my voice I shrank lower in my seat but then, as nobody came forward, I was inspired to go for a bit of one-upmanship over the fat Arse and his three sons. I beckoned for the microphone and to the acute embarrassment of my wife, bewilderment of fellow passengers and incredulity of the four ABUs I waded into…

"Take me home,
United Road,
To the place I belong.
To Old Trafford
To see United
Take me home
United Road".

A crescendo of guffaws, gasps, giggles and polite applause greeted my passionate but out of tune rendition of this United classic. In my mind at least, 1-0 to the Red Army.

FRIDAY 12 JUNE YANGSHOU, CHINA

Up till now, location, location, location and cheap, cheap, cheap have been the overriding factors in our decisions as to what hostel to choose.

On top of this I read customer comments via Lonely Planet, Rough Guide and Trip Advisor. Take out the 10/10 and 0/10 reviews on the basis people may have a hidden agenda and insert my internal gut reaction and this scientific approach has served us well so far.

Hélène and I both prefer central locations at the heart of the action, but for Yangshuo I had read of a new kid on the block that had knocked the long established number one hostel off the top spot. The Trippers Carpe Diem hostel was run by a young couple, he a Belgian chef who also taught Tai Chi and Kung Fu in town and Jenny, a local girl made good. Situated 2 kilometres out of town along the Li River, it couldn't be faulted. Our private double room was large and spotlessly clean, and the food was the best yet. Giant portions and superb flavours.

The only down side was the rain, and it was coming down with a vengeance. We had arrived around midnight in Guilin and took a one hour taxi ride in the pitch black rain to Yangshuo, yet this only added to the mystery of the place. Yangshou is the number one destination in China for the Chinese themselves to visit, an almost out-of-this-world experience, and in the pissing light of early morning we could see why. So many holiday postcards and up-market travel magazines depict huge limestone rocks jutting out from either side of the Li River, and even from our hostel the rain could not disguise the scene which was eerily moving.

We were told the most dramatic monoliths were down river so we booked a half-day trip on the river itself for the following morning. The rest of the day was spent wandering around the town, a mixture of the pretty and the ordinary, the centre full of overpriced tourist eateries and McDonald's and rows and rows of souvenir stalls. And here I have a confession to make. Despite the over commercialization of the town, the backdrop was simply stunning so I just had to get a T-shirt.

I just had to. Say you do understand.

SATURDAY 13 JUNE YANGSHUO, GUILIN, CHINA

"UNBER - FUCKING - LIEVABLE" I first uttered these immortal words on May 26, 1999 in Barcelona. I uttered them again on 26/27 May, 2008 in Moscow. I uttered them for the third time today as we floated down the Li River.

Why?

I'll tell you. Are you sitting comfortably?

Then I'll begin....

The day didn't start too well. The 20,000 limestone peaks known as the Yangshuo Fairyland were hidden by morning mist, low lying clouds and rain. And today I was due to realise another of my lifelong ambitions, boating down the Li River from Xingping to Yandi amidst scenery reproduced in every travel brochure on China. In fact, so iconic the Chinese have put the scene on the back of one of their bank notes.

After a gorgeous breakfast (me, banana pancake with overloads of syrup. Get in there my son!) Jenny approached us and said that one of their staff would accompany us into town to make sure everything went smoothly. That was a nice gesture but we said it's OK. Just give us the name of the tour company and we'll find it. She said they were right next to the bus station but as it was the first time they had used this particular travel company they wanted to make sure. She then admitted she didn't know their name in English, just Chinese, but they would be looking out for us by the bus station.

She also let on that most guests elected for the more energetic options of kayaking or hiking, whereas us boring old farts were the first guests of theirs to choose the easy way out.

"What could possibly go wrong?" I thought as we took the free shuttle cart from our hostel along the bumpy unfinished road to the bus station in the centre of Yangzhou, to wait for the travel rep to escort us to the boat. Two minutes later a bus pulls up and a woman shouts "Yandi".

We edge forward, not knowing whether the bus was to take us to the boat quay (good) or drive all the way to Yandi (bad). I was a bit suspicious as I was led to believe the boat quay was only a short walk from the bus station and the facility of a connecting bus was a bit over the top. But, hey, if it meant not walking, I was all in favour.

I showed the woman my boat ticket. A little conflab with the driver ensued before she waved us on. I showed my ticket to a bloke from "up north" who had a beautiful Chinese woman in toe and he said. "Yup. Looks good to me. We're going to Yandi too."

"OK", I thought. "They must know."

My boat ticket was written half in Chinese and half in English so Hélène and I settled down in our seats and the bus drove off. We'd been driving for around five minutes and I assumed we were going to pick other people up from other departure points. I voiced my unease to Hélène but she just shrugged in a Gallic sort of way that the French are past masters of.

Fifteen minutes later we came to a toll on the main road out of town and I thought, "This sketch is getting silly"

I spoke to the bloke from "up North".

"Where are you getting the boat from?"

"We're driving to Yandi and getting the boat back down the river to

Xingping."

"NOOOOOOOOO!!!!!!!!!"

My male instinct had been right all along. We were on the wrong ruddy bus.

"STOP" I shouted in English, which of course meant sweet fuck all to the driver and the woman who had beckoned us onto the bus in the first place. I tried to explain with the accompaniment of smiles, grimaces and exaggerated hand gestures that we wanted to get off. I showed them my boat ticket once again. There was a telephone number of the tour company on it. The driver stopped and called. He then passed his mobile over to me.

A distressed Chinese woman spoke in broken English that the boat was due to depart in a few minutes and we had to get back.

"But I'm 30 minutes out of town. I need to find another bus to bring us back, and I can't see a bus stop anywhere."

I can't recall her reply, but as Hélène and I got off the bus, the driver flagged down one going in the opposite direction. We ran across the road and boarded it. The locals on the bus looked at us like we were aliens from another planet, which for 99% of them I suppose we were. Hélène and I looked at each other and we got a fit of the giggles, and couldn't stop. What the locals made of us we'll never know, but I'm sure many a version must have been passed round the dining table that evening. One more bus fare and thirty minutes later we were back where we started from, in the bus station.

Now we had to try and find the travel company that our hostel had booked our tour through. And remember, we didn't even have a name. How frustrating was that! Third time lucky. A bemused girl was waiting for us as we approached.

"Thank goodness." I thought, "We've finally made it."

No we hadn't.

"I'm sorry, the 09.30 boat has departed."

"What?"

"Please, don't worry. There is another boat at 12.30."

"Aha. OK. Actually, that might work out better."

You see, every day so far in Yangzhou it had rained in the morning but let up in the afternoon. Still grey but warm. We might even get a better view of the peaks in the afternoon.

We accepted their plan B and decided to walk around town for a couple of hours. Just then Jenny from the hostel came running up, apologising profusely for the confusion and wishing she had accompanied us after all. We told her not to worry. It was all an experience and I'm sure we'd laugh about it later.

With two and a half hours to kill we decided to wander round the town, but in a different direction this time. Looking for a suitable establishment for tea and dunkers I was stopped in my tracks by a sign I spied up an alleyway.

"Fawlty Towers". Yes, you read that right. "Fawlty Towers".

Either an ex-pat with a sense of humour or a local with a sense of humour I just HAD to coax Hélène into taking my photo on the steps of the hotel. Just wait till I upload this onto my Facebook page, I thought to myself. "Basil. BASIL!!"

By this time we only had time for a quick McDonald's pretend tea and coffee before making our way back to the agency where we hung around until a man signalled for us to follow him. We walked for ages back along the river towards our hostel as the rain began to fall once more. Finally he stopped by the river bank and indicated this was where the boat would pick us up. There was an empty one some way along the bank so we imagined we must be in the right place.

We waited, and waited, and......you've guessed it...we waited. Boat after boat passed in both directions as the rain continued to fall, but none hinted at coming over to our place. What a day. When was our luck going to change? Eventually our man from the agency went over to the empty boat then signalled for us to come. It was our boat after all. It's at times like these that knowledge of local swear words can come in mighty handy. However I did my bit on behalf of western civilisation. I kept smiling in face of extreme provocation. A career in the diplomatic service will surely follow.

It turned out our hostel had been so embarrassed by letting us down in the morning, they had chartered a boat just for us! Hélène and I were King and Queen of our own fucking boat! Abramovich, Branson, Gates, eat your hearts out! We were escorted upstairs by the crew still in their pyjamas, to the viewing deck and the open balcony in front. We settled down and as the boat pulled away we waited for the jaw dropping fun to begin. Only it didn't.

The clouds were so low and the rain so thick that we couldn't see more than a few metres above the waterline. We sat back deflated, hoping against hope the weather would change. Little by little hope won through as the rain softened and the clouds began to part. Then, and only then, did the dropping of jaws commence. Not only that, my heart started to beat faster and my breath came out in short spurts. We were gliding through the middle of a scene from a science fiction movie. Nothing had prepared me for the sheer size, scale and immediacy of the vertical limestone monoliths shooting out of the earth all around us. Some so high they disappeared in to the heavens obscured by clouds (little Pink Floyd reference there). I could imagine the giant from Jack and the Beanstalk residing at the top.

We stood on the open deck as the rain continued to fall. And it went on for miles. I honestly felt I was on a different planet. Nature like this really puts man in his place. Man-made marvels such as the Taj Mahal may be one of the eight wonders of the world, but the eight natural wonders of the world, including this trip along the Li River, have a far more profound effect on me. I "Ooohed" and "Aaared" more times than I care to admit. I was soaked to the skin but couldn't care less. For four hours we sailed downriver, our senses forever assaulted by each and every curve and bend we encountered.

Boatloads of Chinese stopped at various mini islands along the way, buying up all the souvenirs on offer, to impress the folks back home that they had actually reached their promised land. I smiled and waved at all of them, mainly because I couldn't stop smiling. That's the effect the whole experience had on me. Just typing this brings it all back and I cannot mask the watering of the eyes. Grown men, eh? And I thought only United had this effect on me.

OK. It wasn't Barca' 99 but it was still pretty profound I can tell you.

When we finally got back to our hostel I turned on my laptop to check on how England had got on in the opening match of their World Cup campaign. Clicked onto BBC Sport to find England had only drawn 1-1 with the USA. Leading 1-0, Robert Green had done a Taibi and let a simple pass slip through his fingers and into the net and nothing our limp attack could do to change the course of events. I had been right not to make an effort to catch the match in real time and it seemed England hadn't made much of an effort either.

United > England.

Nothing changes.

MONDAY 15 JUNE YANGZHOU – GUANGZHOU – HONG KONG

Our time in China was coming to an end. (Sounds like The Secret Millionaire, doesn't it) We'd barely scratched the surface yet the three weeks had been mightily impressive, changing perceptions and wishing we had at least another month at least to do it justice. My only disappointment, considering United had played the China card a number of times in recent pre-seasons, was the lack of any noticeable support. Football shirts, let alone United shirts, were few and far between. In fact my only direct contact with any United fans of note were the two young guys from Hong Kong we met on a day trip out of Shanghai.

Neither had I had the opportunity to test out the level of Premiership matches broadcast in China as the season had ended whilst the World Cup in South Africa had yet to begin. My reservations about China's disregard for human rights and freedom of speech remain as strong as ever, but from my limited experience, day-to-day life for a quarter of the planet's population seems on a par with ours in the West. And in some instances, far superior, and not just from a financial viewpoint.

Today we took a taxi back to Guilin where we boarded a flight to Guangzhou, whose super modern airport once again benefited from a LUHG sticker, this time in the arrivals hall. 41 down, 59 to go. Then we benefited from a super efficient combined service of bus from outside Le Meridien Hotel in the town centre to the border and minibus through customs and onto Hong Kong airport, where we spent the night on the floor before boarding an early morning flight to Tokyo.

All in all we had less hassles with the authorities in China than any of the countries we had visited so far. We hadn't expected that. Credit where credit's due.

And now on to a country from the opposite end of the political spectrum. With Japan looking forward to competing in the World Cup finals later that month in South Africa, I was hoping for a more all-round football experience. Nobody told me the national sport in Japan is baseball, not football. I was soon to find out.

TUESDAY 15 JUNE HONG KONG - TOKYO, JAPAN

Hong Kong airport was the first on this trip to recognise and accept our Airport Angels membership card, one of the few benefits for paying an over the odds monthly fee as a Barclays Premier customer. This meant throughout the night we had access to a special lounge with free food and drink, free Wi-Fi and internet, and large LED screens showing the World Cup. With Business Class passengers making up the majority of the clientèle, two strategically placed LUHG stickers (42 and 43) would hopefully influence the movers and shakers. A hearty breakfast a few hours later saw us onboard our flight to Tokyo.

We were prepared for everything to be really expensive in Japan so we'd only budgeted for one out of our fifty-two weeks there. In Tokyo reasonably priced hostels were all in the suburbs, so I'd chosen a simple hotel for around £40 a night, a little nearer the centre. I say centre, everyone knows Tokyo doesn't have a "centre" as such but a number of must see neighbourhoods.

Although I didn't fancy having my first taste of Tokyo's public ' transport system weighed down with heavy luggage, lack of sleep and the possibility of getting lost, (I'd seen the Michael Palin programmes and that episode of Top Gear) the thought of those frighteningly expensive taxis was enough for us to brave the Tokyo underground. Before leaving the airport proper, however, we made our way to the special outlet in the airport where we changed the Japan Rail vouchers we'd purchased in Hong Kong for the real thing. Now not only the famous bullet trains but our impending airport special would be 40% cheaper. Good times.

As on every trip I make, long or short, I look out for floodlights and the possibility of recognizing the odd stadium or three. I tried to remember the names of clubs in the J league where Gary Lineker had plied his trade and Arsene Wenger had turned to management. Imagine my confusion then when out of the train window all I could see at frequent interviews were giant nets set at 90 degree angles. Golf ranges? Surely not. I know the Japanese are fond of golf, but why so many practice ranges when they could have the real thing. Of course, they weren't golf ranges, they were baseball cages.

Silly me. At the back of my mind (and that's some way back, I can tell you) I recalled having read/seen that baseball was their national sport, and nothing fills a Japanese with pride more than one of their own making it in the States. First India with cricket and now Japan with baseball. The world's gone mad, I tell you. Arriving at Skinjuku station we transferred from the airport express to a normal line. We congratulated ourselves on not getting lost and soon alighted at the nearest station to our hotel. As it was pissing down with rain (what else?) we rewarded ourselves with a taxi to the hotel. An old gentleman appeared out of nowhere and, to the accompaniment of surprisingly good English, helped us and our luggage to the nearest taxi. The driver was very polite and the fare was (only) £10.

And do you know what the nicest thing was? They both did it out of a willingness to please and not for additional monetary gain. How refreshing. We checked into our hotel where the manager didn't speak a word of English. Now I'm not saying our double room was small, but, boy, was it small! Maybe not as small as our hostel in Hong Kong but small enough for someone like me with two left feet to knock into everything and amass bruises like war wounds.

Still, with only two days and nights earmarked for Tokyo there was no time to admire the non-existent view from our window but throw ourselves once more upon the mercy of the metro system with its lack of English signage. With Lonely Planet as our guide I chose a "centre" and we just walked around.

I have to say, compared with the striking architecture of Hong Kong and Shanghai, Tokyo's skyscrapers were decidedly boring. With the exception of the huge Kenzo designed municipal offices and another with dubious leaning characteristics, most were merely functional and lacking in any individuality. Walking around, I noticed lots of boys and girls were sporting Japanese football shirts. Football may not be their national sport but the prospect of Japan appearing in the World Cup finals certainly filled them with a collective pride.

I persuaded Hélène to accompany me into a sports shop resplendent with said replica tops. Wandering around I let out a silent squeak of delight when I came across a small dedicated area just for United merchandise. What better way to enhance this display than by transferring LUHG sicker number 44 from my back pocket to the most prominent position possible, for all the passing trade to see. Duly executed with Banksy precision it didn't take Hélène much persuading to exit post haste and continue up the street.

I'd made a list and we rushed from one place to another, most of which meant very little to Hélène who detests large bustling cities. I persuaded her to come with me to the top floor of the Sony showroom as I'd read they display products not yet available to the general public. I was right. Most impressive were the 3D TVs without glasses. Cool. Every screen showed the Japanese football team in 3D. Second were a range of digital cameras with disproportionately large lenses. Brilliant pictures and not due out for another two years at most.

How much?

Shit.

On the other hand I'd also read about Tokyo's equivalent of Tottenham Court Road, in this case a labyrinth of streets with stalls selling all the very latest electronics. I almost bought one of said cameras being sold illegally from these shops, but our budget forbade me.

Yes, I still regret that decision.

Then we visited Harajuku, Tokyo's equivalent of London's Carnaby Street. Japanese teenagers in a mishmash of styles ranging from baby doll, gothic, Lolita, visual kei, decora, hip hop and punk. It was all style over substance but enjoyable to gawp at nonetheless. We even found a punk pet shop and bought stuff for Melanie's dog and cat back home. Should get a few tails wagging.

On a serious note we went to purchase our beds for the special sleeper train between Tokyo and Hiroshima as they sell out well in advance, only to discover the "bed" on this double decker train called the Sunrise Izumo Express was in fact a strip of rock hard, horse hair type carpet on which we had to use our sleeping bags. That'll teach me not to speak Japanese.

JAPAN

FRIDAY 17 JUNE HIROSHIMA, JAPAN

Careful not to miss our stop I had woken up needlessly early from a fitful night's sleep. The view from the carriage was of green countryside slowly becoming non-descript suburbs as we gradually assembled our limbs after a night on the rock hard carpet floor.

Descending gingerly onto the platform in the early morning light we followed what we assumed to be the exit sign and found ourselves in a large modern concourse.

I worked out we could save money by dragging our luggage around a few streets to our hostel. Fortunately it was not too hot this time in the morning and we arrived in one piece with just a slight sheen to show for our excursions.

We deposited our wares in our room. Today was my 62nd birthday but there was only one thing on our minds. The Hiroshima War Museum and Peace Park. We all have different levels of acceptability of black humour, and I tend to make a joke about almost anything, as contributors to Red Issue, Red News and my facebook page can testify, but something as horrendous as the dropping of the atom bomb that instantly wiped out 70,000 citizens, with another 70,000 fatally injured from radiation was off limits as far as I was concerned. My contribution was to take off my United T-shirt and put on a sloganless top so as not to invite comment. I did not want to downgrade the enormity of the triple A crime and its consequences by providing someone with a light hearted interlude.

The receptionist informed us what bus to take and soon we arrived at the end of the thoroughly modern main thoroughfare. Turning left into the beginning of the Hiroshima Peace Memorial Park I was instantly transported back 65 years. My insides were struck by the twisted shell of what is now called the Hiroshima Peace Memorial, commonly called the Atomic Bomb Dome or A-Bomb Dome. Originally designed by Czech architect, Jan Letzel in 1915 for the Hiroshima Prefectural Commercial Exhibition, it was designated a World Heritage Site in 1996.

This was no Universal Studios backlot. This was for real and the effect was chilling in the extreme. It's blackened skeleton framework contrasted sinisterly with the bright blue sky and healthy park in bloom that lay before us. It had been sunny that day too. How could it have withstood the blast when all around it was literally blown away in an instant?

The purpose of the Peace Memorial Park is to not only memorialise the victims, but also to establish the memory of nuclear horrors and advocate world peace. Totally agree, totally understandable, but the colourful displays outside produced by local children just seemed naïve in the extreme to me.

Inside the true horrors of the atrocity were graphically played out in 3D. Skin literally melting off bodies. Survivors in agony as passers by, following orders from the Japanese government itself, ignored their desperate cries for help.

Harrowing in the extreme, but essential for visitors like us, just like the England team's visit to the concentration camps in Poland prior to the 2012 European Championships. Travel is not all about sun, sea, sand, sex and souvenirs. Sometimes you have to dig a little deeper. It can be extremely uncomfortable but gives you a depth and understanding where people are coming from. Our future is determined by events in the past. It shapes our character and provides the inspiration for advancement.

It must never happen again.

SATURDAY 20 JUNE KYOTO, JAPAN.

You know those scenes in movies such as "The Day After Tomorrow" and "Ghostbusters", when something really bad is going to happen. Clouds race across the sky, getting darker before your very eyes. Well, it's just happened in the common room of our hostel in Kyoto.

Hélène's been typing for half an hour on Facebook in the internet café, updating our adventures to a close friend in France and was just about to press the "send" button when the computer blew time and she lost the lot. She rushed over demanding another 100 yen but it was too late. You should have seen her face. On second thoughts, it's better you didn't. Suffice to say I was in the firing line for all the understandable anger and frustration anyone would feel at a moment like this. And I should know. It's happened to me on many occasions.

Needless to say, it was all my fault. If I hadn't been hogging our own laptop she wouldn't have had to pay to use the hostel's internet café, and she wouldn't have been under pressure to finish before her time ran out. Instead of pointing out the deficiencies in her argument, one by one, I elected to play the role of the compassionate partner. I agreed with every outlandish accusation, then kept a low profile. That is to say, when she stormed back to our room, I stayed behind and attempted to get Melanie, Jasmine and Lilyella on Skype. I know that would have made her feel better, but as this was Saturday afternoon back in the UK, the likelihood of a connection was remote.

So I took the only sensible course of action any self-respecting United fan would take in the circumstances. I brought up both Red News and

Red Issue fans forums on my computer and spent the next couple of hours contributing to posts, plus starting a couple of my own. Bear in mind, this was the day after England's miserable 0-0 draw against the mighty Algeria in the World Cup and the oh so predictable backlash was rising to Beckham '98 proportions. This time, apart from the donkey Heskey, another United player was in the firing line. Our Wayne, for commenting on the OTT abuse by so-called little Englanders who had booed the team off the pitch.

And this is just one area where the United slogan, "Not arrogant, Just Better", comes into play. I've witnessed many a dire United display over the past five decades. Supporters who've only known the unparalleled success under Ferguson should have lived through the 70s and 80s. With the mind-boggling ineptitude of Alex Forsyth, Tom Sloane, Ralph Milne and the like, we've paid our dues. But no matter how much we would complain to each other before or after a match, during the hallowed 90 minutes we support the team to the hilt.

OK, we do get individuals who shout abuse at individual players, but you rarely hear organised chanting or booing a particular player or the team. That's one example that separates United fans from ABUs. Not Arrogant, Just Better.

This is what true supporters do, or should do. It's easy to rejoice when things are going well, but just like life outside the stadium, supporting someone when they're down is much more important, 'cos that's when they need it most.

I know England haven't won a major tournament since 1966, the year Eric was born (and I was seventeen years old) but the hysterical over optimism that accompanies every England campaign defies logic and analysis. So I posted something along the following lines:

"England & World Cups. The Good, the Bad and the Ugly"

The good news is that in many tournaments over the past forty years, England have started badly, scraped through the qualifying stage with their third and final match, then got better as the tournament progressed. Italia '90 anyone?

The truth is though that many British players play better for their clubs than for their country. As Paul Scholes wrote recently in his autobiography about, "the selfish attitude of some players. Too many individuals appeared to be there for personal glory. They were using the national team as a way to be noticed." On top of this English players playing in the Premiership play more hard games each season than players in nearly all the other leagues around the world. In fact, until 1992, there were 22 teams in the old First Division, more than any other league in

Europe except Spain. And until their Euro success in 2008 and subsequent success in the World Cup in 2010, Spain had gone even longer without winning a major tournament so the similarities are clear. Throw in two major domestic cup competitions and European football on top of internationals for our top clubs and you have a recipe for mentally as well as physically tired players.

We were told at the time that the Premiership was conceived primarily to aid the national team. With a constitution stating just 18 teams would be invited to participate, this was never going to get off the ground. Can you imagine four club chairmen agreeing to commit football suicide? No, neither can I.

Still, no other league can match the age old adage; "there are no easy games in the Premiership". On top of this, with all the money accruing from the sale of television rights for Premiership games, English clubs now attract some of the best players in the world, which further enhances the Premiership product. Wonderful for fans of those clubs blessed with such talent, but with many opting for a quick fix of Johnny Foreigner at the expense (literally) of investing in youth schemes to unearth local English talent, the knock-on effect is that England has less and less talented players to choose from.

Which brings us back to Heskey…

Now, where was I?

I tried without success to get our girls on Skype. Eventually I gave up and retired to a cold and frosty Hélène burying herself in the remains of her Sudoku book. She briefly looked up, murmured something that my mutton and jeff ears couldn't pick up, and said she was going to sleep. I welcomed the embrace of a single bunk bed but the clothes that had been hanging up all day in our room were still wet. This had the knock-on effect of increasing the dampness of our beds and it took me a lot of tossing and turning (I've done that joke already, OK?) to finally fall asleep myself. A damp squib end to what had been a lovely day in this beautiful city, a perfect mix of ancient and modern. Let's hope Hélène is in a better mood tomorrow.

MONDAY 21 JUNE MOUNT FUJI, JAPAN

When we mentioned to people we intended to visit Japan's iconic Mount Fuji on our way back to Tokyo they told us that we'd chosen the wrong month. June was rainy season and the mountain was nearly always bathed in clouds. We wouldn't see a thing, plus the authorities didn't allow the climbing of Mount Fuji until the beginning of July. We were 10 days too early.

"Chikusho!" (That's Japanese for "shit")

Still, we'd come all this way and will probably never have the chance to come here again, so let's give it our best shot and hope for the George.

Unfortunately our 7 day Japan Rail Pass didn't extend to the expensive, private Fujikyu Railway line train down from Otsuki to Kawaguchiko and when we arrived it was pitch black so we had no idea where the mountain was. A short taxi ride later we were in our hostel and ready for food. It was late, so Hélène sent me out to the nearest supermarket where I purchased two Japanese versions of Pot Noodles. In the hostel kitchen I looked at the pots. You'll never guess, but the cooking instructions were in Japanese.

Doh!

I looked round the kitchen. It was deserted except for two pretty tall Japanese girls (unusual for Japan. Tall, that is, not pretty. No, I mean they were pretty AND tall. Oh well, you know what I mean) They smiled as I approached. The Japanese do a lot of that. Smile, that is.

"Excuse me. Can you speak English?"

Yes, they could. Better than me!

They helped me with the cooking instructions and before you could say "nicky nacky nick nock, nicky nacky noo, nicky nacky nick nock, sold to Foo Man Chu" I was climbing the stairs with two steaming pots.

They were delicious!

The following morning we got up early as we'd only allowed one day to see Mount Fuji and get back to Tokyo for our night flight to Perth. We made our way down towards the stunningly beautiful Fuji Five Lakes (Fujigoko). In the morning sunshine they were the prettiest lakes I'd ever seen.

As we approached the bridge dividing Lake Kawaguchiko and Lake Ashi I took out my map and tried to figure out where Mount Fuji should be in relation to the lakes. Hélène and I studied the map, taking it in turns to turn it 360 degrees.

Eventually Hélène said, "It should be behind us."

I turned round.

FUCK ME! WHERE DID THAT COME FROM!

Someone had only gone and plonked a giant Mount Fuji right behind us. It towered above everything, filling our senses with awe and wonder. I'm not joking, it was like someone had got out a model village, inserted us in it like that scene from Beetlejuice and then decided to include an oversized model of a mountain. It was the most perfect mountain I had ever seen.

OK, it was the only mountain I had ever seen, but I'd seen photographs and movies of mountains of all shapes and sizes, but I'm sure if you asked a kid to draw his or her perfect mountain they'd draw Mount Fuji.

Yup, another (Japanese) Kleenex moment I'm afraid. Blubbered like a scouser at a Manc celebration party. The world stopped as Hélène and I took far too many photos. Then as we walked around Lake Ashi we were mesmerised by the beautiful landscape all around us. We snapped away like mad, which needless to say slowed our progress quite considerably. Just as I thought it couldn't get any better I stumbled across the aerial cableway at Mount Komagatake which overlooked the Hakone National Park and offered the perfect view of Mount Fuji half way up from the other side of the lake.

Result? More snapping overload until clouds began to form at the top of the mountain, and by mid afternoon it was (as Pink Floyd would say) totally "obscured by clouds". We'd been so lucky I couldn't believe it. And to round off a perfect day, we had a superb Indian meal in a restaurant not far from our hostel. Beat that!

TUESDAY 22 JUNE TOKYO, JAPAN – PERTH, AUSTRALIA

We flew from Tokyo to Perth on the oldest plane in Qantas fleet. We had been invited to stay with Red ex-Pat Graham Wyche, his wife Sue, and son David in Sorrento, but a phone call a few days earlier had established that a heavy hailstorm had rendered their home out of bounds to guests, so we had to dip into our budget for an unexpected three nights in a hotel nearby.

Graham and I had shared many a 400 mile round trip to Old Trafford and back in the 80s and early 90s, but then an opportunity arose in Oz and he and Sue had deliberated for ages like The Clash, "Should I Stay or Should I Go Now?" I didn't want to lose a good friend but I told him he'll always regret it if he let the opportunity pass him by. My killer line was something along the lines of "Don't worry if they call you a winging Pom. If it doesn't work out you can always come back."

I like to think I pushed him over the line and he subsequently emigrated and set up a successful publishing business as well as a Britain's Best, a shop selling football shirts, souvenirs and groceries from the UK. In addition, for many years he hosted a football show on Channel 9, a local TV station. He also set up the official Manchester United Western Australia Supporters Club which ran for many years until, as I wrote in the very beginning of the book, the club took away the official status of many supporters clubs around the world unless they agreed to unrealistic financial demands.

Graham was also responsible for making this man cry uncontrollably in May 1999 by being the first of my grovels to come home to roost. I'm talking Champions League Final tickets of course. A ticket earmarked for our very own Francis Burns became available when Franny was invited, all expenses paid by the club, to meet up with the 1968 European Cup winning squad. For once trickle down worked and something far more important than money was mine. The rest, as they say, is football, bloody hell!

AUSTRALIA

WEDNESDAY 23 JUNE PERTH, AUSTRALIA
ENGLAND 1 SLOVENIA 0

With Hélène holding the fort by entertaining Graham's wife Sue in a nearby hotel, Graham, David and me set off for The Sovereign Arms, a large pub in Joondalup, 25 kms north of Perth city centre, that was overflowing with ex-pats for England's final World Cup qualifying match against Slovenia. Anything less than a win and another tail between the legs exit was on the cards.

The place was buzzing when we arrived. I purposely wore my LUHG Green & Gold T-shirt hoping for a bit of a banter, even a bit of ABU baiting.

Nothing.

People were too pre-occupied with England. Oh well, if you can't beat 'em, join 'em. Set myself up by going to the loo and sticking LUHG sticker number 45 on the mirror. Don't know how long that will stay there, but long enough to make an impact. I hope.

The match began and England played as though it was a Premiership match. A high temp start radiated confidence and decibel levels in the pub. Our lack of finishing was again brought into doubt (no doubt for me, we're shit) but a strike by Jermaine Defoe put England in front and this was signal for beer shampoos amongst the pub's clientele.

With England unable to increase their lead, and with numerous heart stopping moments in defence, the match was played out amidst nervous tension until the referee put us out of our ecstasy. Phew! That was close, but at least we're through to the last 16, not that this performance would have the rest of the teams quaking in the football boots. On reflection, the best thing about this match was the stadium. It was named the Nelson Mandela Bay Stadium. Respect.

SUNDAY 27 JUNE CAIRNS, AUSTRALIA
GERMANY 4 ENGLAND 1

Whenever England played Germany at football, the old German joke used to be...

"England games are always hard and Germany always wins". Very funny. Yet in the last 27 matches between these two bitter rivals, England has won 12, Germany 10 and 5 have been drawn. And who will ever forget being in Munich when from a goal down we went on to a glorious 5-1 win?

Well, me for a start, 'cos I watched it on TV in a pub back home, but you know what I mean. Which brings us round to the first knock out stage of the 2010 FIFA World Cup. England's progress had been lacklustre at best, pathetic at worst. Still, the 1-0 victory over mighty Slovenia once again raised English expectations to unrealistic levels. After a slow start, would this be the catalyst to bigger and better things?

Surprisingly... no.

Still, I convinced Hélène to join me in Gallaghan's pub in Cairns where the joint was rocking with England fans, many painted head to foot in the red cross of St George. Most tables were stood upon and danced upon by jovial Ing-er-landers, with a smattering of Germans around the sides. I'll give them one thing though, their women were better looking than ours. (Mine's French, so I get out of that one)

LUHG sticker number 46 duly adorned the men's' toilets before play began.

Once the game started though, we could tell that England were second best in all departments, the singing subsided when Klose got their first in the 20th minute and Podolski added a second in the 32nd minute. A brief respite in German domination came when Matthew Upson scored for England on the 37th minute but the real talking point came a few minutes later when out of nowhere Fat Frank let go this hum-dinger that flew over the line before the German keeper had a chance to clear it.

Bedlam. I ran amuck around the pub screaming at the top of my voice. I don't know why she did it but Hélène rushed after me and tapped me on the shoulder. It's not like her to join me in goal celebration mode. If anything she runs the other way.

"Excuse me, the referees disallowed it."

"What the ★★★★!"

I concentrated on the giant screen. It was true. The ball had crossed the line in true Roy Carroll v Tottenham proportions, but this time MY team suffered the ultimate injustice. Countless replays from all angles showed beyond a shadow of a doubt, the ball had clearly crossed the line.

Where's a Russian linesman when you need one? Where's the fucking goal line technology? Where's Sep Blatter, I want to tread on him.

Bloody Germans. 1966 and all that. I bet they engineered the whole thing. (They're good at engineering) 44 years to get their revenge. How petty. How pathetic.

What do you mean, we didn't deserve it. I know that. We'd played poorly and the Germans fully deserved to be leading but that's not the point. Who knows what would have happened if that second goal had been allowed to stand. Imagine how the Germans would have collapsed in the face of such a comeback.

Ok, maybe not, but doubts would have crossed their Teutonic minds and we'd have snapped out of our self-induced stupor. Ok, maybe not that either, but who knows what affect a rush of adrenalin to the head may have created? They don't like it up 'em, Mr Mainwaring.

How about OUR revenge for 1970 in Mexico. Fancy taking our Bobby off while we were still leading. Sir Alf Ramsey? What had HE ever won? Didn't have a clue, did he?

It was just so bloody unfair. First Bayern Munich in the Champions League where we'd blown them off the park three months beforehand, and now this. They say things come in threes. What next for Germany, a Formula 1 world championship driver instead of our Lewis? (What's that? Who shouted Sebastian Vettell?)

Told you so.

Meanwhile the second half had kicked off and the Germans put the boot in two more times to run out comfortable 4-1 winners. The writing had been on the wall a long time before the referee blew to put us out of our misery. The pub had gone from subdued to deathly quiet. The Germans in the pub hardly celebrated at all, at least not like we would have done.

They were polite, well behaved, sympathetic, and outnumbered. They weren't stupid.

"Let's get out of here." was all I could say. Not very romantic for late on a Saturday night I admit, but on top of United's so near but so far season, this just took the icing off the cake. The streets were dark and empty as we made our way back to the hostel, and so was I.

FRIDAY 2 JULY INNESFAIL, QUEENSLAND

We decided to see Queensland from the ground up, so we hired a second hand station wagon from Autobahn for AUS$35 a day including camping equipment and mattresses. We planned to save money by sleeping in the back on our way down to Brisbane and Tony, ex-pat Red number

2. Despite the fact Australia has gorgeous weather and grows some of the best fruit and vegetables, prices in the shops were disappointingly, disproportionately high, so any savings were to be appreciated.

Much to Hélène's annoyance I placed LUHG sticker number 47 on the back window, so as to "REDucate" the natives on our way south.

We started by going the wrong way, on purpose, taking the delightful coast road up to Port Douglas. Superb. Australia do some of the best beaches in the world, and this was the second of many to take our breath away. (We'd already been to Perth, remember) We then made for Tully and the Australian rainforest, the wettest spot in the whole of OZ. Spent two nights sleeping in the station wagon, in the same rest area by the same roundabout. Despite waking up each time I changed position I withstood the nocturnal call of nature, even though the loo had manifested itself into a small plastic bucket inside the car. With my Frank Spencer dexterity, the odds were not in my favour in such a confined space.

One perennial question remained unanswered though. Why is it when you finally settle down, be it in a car, camper, tent, etc... after completing all conceivable ablutions, emptying waste from every possible orifice, you start to fart? And not just me you understand, her ladyship as well.

On top of this it had rained Australian cats and dingoes all night. The condensation that had built up inside the vehicle resulting from the necessity to close all the windows fused with the natural gasses emanating from yours truly plus one produced a force so powerful we were able to briefly create an additional hole in the ozone layer.

What's more, any clothes and seats on the perimeter of the interior were wet through, so this morning's breakfast started with recriminations all round, followed by the leftover of the two day old Danish sweetbread and two cups of tea from the van that operated from 09.00 to 19.00 each day on the rest area.

The Australian cats and dingoes continued to rain down on us as we discussed our plan for the day. It was decided that a visit to the Art-Deco town of Innesfail, just two kilometres down the road, would be our top priority. From there we could buy a mobile phone charger for the car, e-mail our girls, I could e-mail then phone travelling Red, Steve Chadwick and hopefully make arrangements to finally meet up, Facebook myself silly, catch up on the World Cup results, and see who else Fergie would be unable to purchase this summer and discover the latest on any possible takeover of the club by the Red Knights or any other interested party.

I set off for the men's' toilet with a sense of purpose, leaving the memories of the previous night behind me. I set up my toilet bag, hooking it over the corrugated iron window. I took out my false teeth and set them up on the narrow ledge under the window. Not hygienic I know, but at least the insects were not moving.

I washed as best I could in the tiny sink in front of the toilet. I then cleaned my false teeth and left them to dry on the narrow ledge under the window. After cleaning the four remaining teeth of my own, I went back to dry my dentures, only in my haste to speed up proceedings I dropped them on the hard tiled floor and, yes, you've guessed it, I broke the bottom set in two again!

Claiming they had come apart under my strict brushing regime, a visit to the dentist was added to our Innesfail shopping list. The idea of Australian pricing filled me with dread. There would be no anaesthetic here to soften my wallet.

We drove into town and would you Adam & Eve it, opposite the supermarket car park I spied a shop sign... "Denture Repairs". I never knew such a shop even existed. I just thought dentists performed this service themselves or sent them away to a specialist.

Well done Australia.

We crossed over the road and went inside. A local woman greeted us. I could see a harassed gentleman through a window behind the counter. He looked up and came round.

"What's the problem?" he asked.

"Actions speak louder than words." I mumbled, and proceeded to take out my split bottom dentures.

He smiled but said he was already late. He had two nursing homes to visit then he was off to Cairns and wouldn't be back for a couple of days. No wonder he looked harassed. However, I was going to add to his harassment.

"I can wait." I suggested helpfully.

"It's not that, you see. I'm late already."

He turned to his assistant.

"Maybe you could just repair them for me. You know, stick them together or something?"

"Sure." she replied. "Come back in 45 minutes."

We left the shop, relieved to know at least a temporary repair would be done and I could walk and talk almost like a normal human being. (I heard that!) Having completed our shopping mission we retuned to Denture Repair Man. Even more harassed than before, he asked us to wait five minutes, then produced a perfectly repaired set of dentures. Relieved to resume my George Clooney persona I asked him where he was from, as clearly his was not an Australian accent.

"Manchester."

"Wow!" I exclaimed, pointing to my green and gold T-shirt.

"Read any good T-shirts lately?"

"Read any good tattoos lately?" he replied and pulled up his left arm sleeve to reveal, Oh no, a City tattoo! I'd been dentured by a bitter!

He turned out to be a sound bloke. If he'd had more time we'd have developed some serious banter but he had to be on his way and we weren't hanging round so we parted

SATURDAY 3 JULY MISSION BEACH, QUEENSLAND

This morning we drove the short (by Australian standards) distance down the Bruce (you couldn't make it up) Highway to Mission Beach, and my mission was to finally meet up with Steve Chadwick, erstwhile United fan, Glazer disillusionist and a front runner in all things FC United.

Like me Steve had taken a year off from Planet United, only he had worked for three months in Sydney before "doing Oz", coming up the east coast while I was coming down. After a flurry of Facebook false starts, Mission Beach was designated our Camp David. (Be fair, who's ever heard of Camp Steven?) Yet even at the eleventh hour fate attempted to intervene and deny two true Reds a meeting down under. Hélène and I had strolled along the magnificent and almost deserted Mission Beach itself. Encased in a semi circle of palm tress, we gorged ourselves on a vista that would not be out of place in the Caribbean or South Pacific.

Tearing ourselves away I attempted to phone Steve on my mobile but there was no signal so we went searching for an internet café where I could finalise arrangements. Aha, another barrier. Message from Steve. "No signal on mobile. Am staying at Absolute Backpackers in South Mission Beach".

Armed with his directions we drove up and down the main drag until I located the hostel. Jumping out of the car I made contact with the receptionist who told me Steve's room number. Went round to the large windowed chalet where four young men were all asleep.

Lazy fuckers.

I knocked two or three times before I saw a body stir. A mummy like apparition slithered towards the door. He slid it open and a wide grin transformed his features into a human being.

"Lucky for some." I said.

You're joking, Mr Blatt. (he keeps calling me that. Where's the disaffected youth we keep reading about? Too much respect I think you'll agree) We've all been skydiving. We got up really early and we're knackered."

That told me.

"Come and meet the wife and our station wagon." I said, as a way of changing the subject. "They'll both be pleased to see you."

Steve was certainly pleased to see both, especially our station wagon adorned with another of my LUHG stickers on the back window.

"Cool, Mr Blatt. That's class."

My wife's not bad either, so we asked Steve the best place to talk all things Red and Oz. He pointed to a pub cum restaurant opposite where we took pride of place near the window. Hélène and I ordered some pub grub but it was too early/late for Steve so he stuck to liquid refreshments.

We gossiped for a couple of hours, covering all things United, FC United, his three month stint working in Sydney with some politics thrown in for good measure. With Steve to the right of centre and me to the left a lively discussion followed that somehow turned into the benefits of studying Latin at school. At this point I was relegated to the substitute's bench as Hélène and Steve bestowed the benefits of learning Latin as a base for mastering so many other languages. All I could muster was the age-old repost… "What's the point of learning a dead language?" to which they mustered point upon point which left my arguments floundering.

We finished by going outside and photographing each other with my LUHG station wagon in the background, but with the sticker taking pride of place. We then said our goodbyes and pledged to keep in touch, which we have. Steve continued north whilst we continued south along the coast road.

It would be almost two weeks before I would be able to talk all things United again, with ex-pat Cockney Red (well, Sidcup to be more accurate) Tony in Brisbane and a surprise Manc Red guest. But let me not get ahead of myself. There are lots of Aussie highlights to come before then, but perhaps too many for a publisher of a United book to allow me to mention. Let's just say the Queensland coast is absolutely stunning and we drove the entire length of it, but I can't leave without mentioning the Whitsundays.

I'd seen dramatic colour photos in travel magazines and Sunday supplements, but nothing prepared me for the majesty of the sweeping swirling sands below me from the Hill Inlet lookout, the same vantage point that professional photographers use. And when brochures talk about white sands, white sands usually turn out to be cream, yellow or even grey. But let me tell you, Whitehaven Beach is the whitest beach the world (i.e. me, that is) has ever seen. You need sunglasses just to look at it.

THURSDAY 15 JULY BRISBANE, QUEENSLAND, AUSTRALIA

Is there any better activity on this planet than talking all things United? Silly me, of course there is. Watching United. But when option one is not available, option two fills the void.

A couple of days ago I received a message on my Facebook page from Stephen McKay, ex-Manc. now resident in Brisbane.

"How about meeting up?"

How about meeting up indeed. It transpired Thursday evening after work was the only time available to Stephen, so we agreed to meet under Brisbane's equivalent of The London Eye on Brisbane's South Bank.

I texted him my description of black trousers, black pullover, black Regatta (Manchester brand) fleece and longish grey/white hair. The march of time can be so cruel. I brought Hélène with me, even though I knew 99% of the conversation would be United related, on the off chance Stephen would bring his partner with him.

He didn't. Tough Hélène. That's the way the Aussie pie crumbles.

He bounded up, all grins and light blue tracksuit top (Light blue? Surely a character defect?). Despite five years in Auckland and now resident in Brisbane, not a trace of Oz marred his Collyhurst to Middleton accent.

We spent a delightful hour talking at 100 words per minute, regaling each other with United matches and experiences. So many games and so little time. Hélène smiled gracefully, totally out of all the footy talk, but contributing to "How each of us arrived in Oz".

In one respect Stephen is just like me. When recounting an emotionally filled incident, he gets tingles all over just recalling the details. With United, the match could have been years ago but the emotion is still Red raw. Only United can do this, because United reaches parts other teams cannot reach.

We could have rabbited on for ages, but Hélène and I had agreed to meet Tony and Leanne at 7.00pm to catch the catamaran up river for a Lebanese meal, so a flurry of photos later we exchanged United hugs and got on the cat. Great bloke.

Our hosts were waiting for us as we drew into New Farm Pier so they got on our cat and together we made our way for a couple of more stops. By now it was pitch black and a cold breeze was blowing as we walked along the side of the river for some posh Lebanese nosh.

We sat down and decided, with a little help from our waiter, to choose one mixed grill and one mixed platter. This way we could have a vast diverse range of Lebanese goodies to choose from and everybody should be satisfied.

When the food arrived everyone agreed it was all lovely. Halfway through though I had a Mrs Doubtfire moment and brought our table to the attention of the entire restaurant.

Never having the best co-ordination in the world has been re-enforced ever since I've had to adapt to my George Clooney Indian dentures. The co-ordination required for chewing, eating and swallowing, and differentiating between liquids and solids has been sorely tested. And tonight I struck new depths.

During one particular pleasant interchange I took a lump of something, chewed it, then swallowed. Only this time it wouldn't go down. It stuck in my throat, with the same sensation you get when you swallow a boiled sweet too soon. I tried to swallow again and again without bringing attention to myself. All the while I had stopped breathing so I took a sip of water hoping this might do the trick.

It didn't.

With United failing to bring home their 19th league title a couple of months earlier and therefore realising every Liverpool fans' worst nightmare, I was not ready to leave this mortal coil. I stood up and with Hélène's questioning/concerned look in her eyes, I squeezed myself and this (to me) enormous falafel flew across the room and landed on the floor, followed by an assortment of Lebanese fare.

Nobody knew what to do or what to say. Leanne, Tony's girlfriend looked away, Hélène looked genuinely concerned whilst Tony quietly asked for a cloth from a passing waiter. I sat down, assuring everyone that normal breathing had been restored and everyone should get on with enjoying their meal.

Hélène didn't know whether to be angry or relieved. She chose the latter, then burst out laughing at me. I deserved it. Being a posh restaurant all the other tables carried on as though nothing untoward had happened, but you can be sure they were all talking about this Pom who couldn't hold down his food and made a falafel out of nothing.

SATURDAY 17 JULY. BRYRON BAY, AUSTRALIA
MANCHESTER UNITED 3 GLASGOW CELTIC 1

Tony and Leanne wanted to make an early start today as we only had one day to see and do everything in Byron Bay. I was in total agreement, so as soon as the alarm went off on Hélène's mobile phone I got dressed and turned on Tony's computer in the study for the pre-season Celtic result. Nothing.

The match in Toronto hadn't started yet, so I'd have to wait until we settled into our hostel that evening to find the score and all the gory details. Putting that to the back of my mind (never an easy thing to do, even for a meaningless, pre-season friendly) I loaded all our bags into the boot of Leanne's car and we set off. It was sunny but cold, ideal conditions for an excursion down the Gold Coast. Tony drove sporting an air-conditioned straw hat. I say air conditioned, the fact was his hat had giant holes both front and back and had obviously seen better days. I suggested giving it a decent burial but he wouldn't hear of it. Sentimental attachment and all that.

Tony drives for a living and he's a very careful driver. Such a careful driver in fact that every other vehicle on the road overtook us. It was an hour before we made our first stop at Coolonga, a lovely beach on the other side of the bay from Benidorm, I'm sorry, Surfers Paradise. The hideous grey concrete spires mocked us from the distant skyline but we were oblivious to their charms. I spied a café called "Pancakes in Paradise" but was shouted down by the other three. Damn democracy.

We took our shoes off and walked on the soft, wide sandy beach down to the gentle waves lapping the shore. Hmm. Cold but not too cold. Coffee was suggested then almost immediately withdrawn, as it was decided that arriving as soon as possible in Byron Bay should be our top priority and we could always have drinks and dunkers there.

Back in the car it was another hour before we found our hostel in Byron Bay town centre. We registered and put our luggage in the room, then with two hours free parking to take advantage of, walked the 100 metres or so to the beach.

And what a beach. Everything a beach should be and more. No high rise monstrosities to spoil the view, just miles of sand and surf, backed by tree-lined peninsulas. I know this was winter but there were very few people or dogs on the beach. Ideal.

We met up with Tony and Leanne and ordered take away elevenses and sat ourselves on the rocks overlooking the beach. What a wonderful way to start our day in Byron Bay. Suitably refreshed and re-energised, we strolled around the one and two story shops, full of new age gear, clothes and surf related items, notwithstanding some enticing cafés and restaurants.

Meanwhile the charms of Byron Bay were working their magic on Tony and Leanne as they decided to spend the night there too. We went back to the car and drove in ever increasing circles to find a cabin/caravan park someone had recommended. For AUS$130 they secured a pretty green and yellow cabin with all mod cons ensuite.

Now for the big one. Off up to the lighthouse, the most easterly point of mainland Australia and its incredible 360★ views plus the possibility of catching sight of whales as they migrated north to breed, only to return in September with their young 'uns.

What a sight that must be. Would reality match the brochure? Match it? It exceeded it!

From the moment the first vista came into view we were captivated, our senses overwhelmed by the sheer size and scale of the beauty below us. This wild wide beach disappearing almost to the horizon, continuously pounded by resurgent waves bombarding the shore. And almost deserted.

I looked down. How did those surfers reach the beach? And look at those hand gliders. Where else could they land but the beach? Then how would they get off?

I looked out to sea. We all did. Where were the whales?

We made our way slowly up the road, constantly on the lookout for tell-tale white foam splashes out to sea. A few false dawns later and we were at the top.

Breathtaking. Simply breathtaking. The brochures had been outdone.

I zipped up my fleece as the gusts made themselves felt. Some men were still in singlets and T-shirts. Either they were extra tough or I was a wimp.

Yeah, I was a wimp.

Then we all started peering out to sea in a concerted effort at whale watching.

Hélène saw it first.

"Look, to the right of that small boat", she exclaimed.

I looked. I waited. Then I saw it too. A white plume of foam and...

"Yes! I saw it! I saw it! It soared straight out of the water."

I became all Vinny Jones. "It's been emotional!"

Such a long way away out to sea yet such a pull on the heartstrings. My first live whale, in the majesty of the ocean where it belonged, not in one of those artificial water parks performing tricks for our entertainment, or one of a thousand each year cut up on Japanese whaling ships for "scientific purposes". Scientific purposes my arse!

We stood transfixed as binoculars were passed round, bringing this extraordinary ritual of nature into focus. Even from this distance the very presence of the whale was mesmerizing. We've all seen fabulous pictures of whales on TV and in colour supplements, or up close in some superficial water park, but to see one in the flesh in its natural environment, even at this distance topped the lot.

We stayed as long as our stomachs would allow. Now it was time for lunch. With a reluctant farewell and overloaded cameras and camcorders, we walked back to our car and drove down into the centre of Byron Bay and fish and chips. They tatsed SO good!

The afternoon was spent walking along the spectacular beach before we retired to a vantage point above to watch the sunset and lookout for dolphins. We witnessed the first but not the latter as the sunset behind the hills to our left, its rays forever changing and softening the hue around us.

The dropping temperatures told us it was time to move so we walked to the Railway, a large bar in front of the old railway station where Hélène and I would take the 07.33 bus in the morning.

On the way, purely by chance, we came across an American Graffiti procession of old American cars lovingly restored by their owners. I spent ages videoing them all, only later when playing it back did I realize that it went on so long it would bore the pants off those not totally enamoured by this sort of thing, so I edited it down to 10% of the cars.

But what cars!

By now my internet café time had passed so the United v Celtic result would have to wait until we were back in our own hostel. Meanwhile Leanne found out that a recommended bluegrass/hill billy band were going to play that evening and it was free.

I can't stand country and western music, but country rock, and in the past such bands as The New Riders of the Purple Sage, The Nitty Gritty Dirt Band and Commander Cody and the Lost Planet Airmen had been known to cross my turntable, so I thought I'd give it a go. Plus I had been missing live music more than I had realised. Only the previous evening I had joined in two "metal" debates online, one on Facebook and one on Red Issue, bestowing the virtues of Metallica, Anthrax, The Pixies et al.

A number of times on this trip I've met people and when the conversation turns to music they come out with phrases like.

"I like all types of music except heavy metal". Heavy metal/true rock is the purest form of musical primeval expression. Give me a power chord and I'll give you the man. But I digress.

We found a table outside although the temperature had dropped alarmingly. We ordered barbecue type fare and chunky chips (real chips, yeah!) and settled down for the band. They came on stage half an hour later and began to play. The first song was an instrumental and they weren't bad musicians. But then the lead singer came on stage.

What a twat.

What a tall, thin strip of liquorice. Was he full of himself or what?

Dressed in a red military jacket and jeans, he waddled (I'm sure he would have called it "danced") across the stage. He strutted as though he was playing in front of thousands of hero worshipping devotees at a headline concert instead of this half full Aussie pub full of disinterested drinkers.

What a ponce. One of those, "it was so bad it was good" nights.

We all laughed at him not with him, but he was totally oblivious to it all. He thought we loved him whereas the only one to love him was himself. It was entertaining for all the wrong reasons but made our night.

Finally Tony and Leanne drove us back to our hostel and promised to get up early the following morning and drive us to the bus terminal for our 45 minute bus ride to the railway station for our connecting train to Sydney.

What a day. The good had far outweighed the bad, and beautiful Byron Bay itself will remain in my consciousness forever.

Yes, it was that good.

SATURDAY 18 JULY BYRON BAY TO SYDNEY

I love trains. Even at my advanced age the countryside always looks better from a train window than from the window of a car or plane. Maybe it's the "boy" within me, I don't know. When it comes to alcohol, football, music, food, you know, stuff like that, whatever turned me on as a teenager still gets my juices flowing at the three quarter stage of my time on this planet. For example, when it comes to food and drink, if we're talking posh then I've got an immature palate, or quite simply, a sweet tooth. Keep your red wine, give me Ribena any day. Music? Give me Muse or Machine Head to go along with Pink Floyd, Led Zeppelin and Rory Gallagher. None of your repetitive house music. I'll leave lift muzac to others. It's got its ups and downs, but I prefer the stairway to heaven.

In Japan I had realized one of my boyhood dreams by travelling on the Bullet Train. Top that. I did, in China, on the almost 400kph Beijing to Shanghai train which was even newer and faster.

So what does Australia have to offer?

Something out of Thomas The Tank Engine. A quaint 80 kph locomotive that wouldn't be out of place pre Dr Beecham. I couldn't believe it. Was this the extent of Australian railway engineering?

Strewth!

Nevermind, we settled down for another 10 hour journey, which this time covered less than 400 miles with a number of stops en route. Let's just say it was pleasant, OK.

SUNDAY 19 JULY SYDNEY, AUSTRALIA

Well, there was only one way to start, wasn't there? Hélène and I walked in the cool Sunday morning winter sunshine down the deserted city streets of the financial district hemmed in by skyscrapers and through the Royal Botanical Gardens to Bennelong Point and the world famous Sydney Opera House.

I'd read that it had been designed by the Danish architect Jørn Utzon, who never actually saw the completed project in person. That must have really pissed him off.

Wow! It's not as white as in the photographs but cream, yet still mightily impressive nonetheless. An iconic global building and here we were coming up from behind. Needless to say we did the full 360 degree circumference, taking photos of every angle imaginable. The view across the water was impressive too. Lots of delightful bays with green hills all around.

Housing here is said to be some of the most expensive in the world and I could see why. What a view to wake up to every morning. I was dying to see inside and listen to those world famous acoustics, but could we find a door that was open? We could not. That was disappointing to put it mildly.

Meanwhile we had the majestic vision of Sydney Harbour Bridge on the other side of the narrow headland to enjoy. To me it looked just like a blown up version of the Tyne Bridge in Newcastle, which came as no surprise when we learnt it had been constructed by the English firm of Dorman Long and Co from Middlesbrough that had not only been responsible for recently completing one of Britain's supreme feats of engineering but later went on to build the Forth Road Bridge in Scotland.

So, let me get this straight, the ultimate symbol of all things Australian was actually designed and built by the British.

Pommy bastards rule, OK! Ha Ha!

We walked back round the bay to the Harbour Bridge itself, with the intent of walking up and over the top of the single span structure. Then we found out the price. 225 Australian dollars each for the privilege.

Double strewth with knobs on. Sorry, we were on a budget, and being the height of the Australian winter, the cold, high velocity winds that whip round you up there cooled our desire. We ended up climbing one of the four towers at a fraction of the price and from an even higher viewpoint we were still able to take in the magnificent 360* views.

WEDNESDAY 21 JULY – SYDNEY, AUSTRALIA

Today is Hélène's 60th birthday. I couldn't let it pass without a bit of a "do", now could I? My 60th the year before had been a bit special so I felt compelled to rise to the challenge. I'd realized ages ago that we would be travelling somewhere in the Southern hemisphere when Hélène's momentous day would arrive so I'd begun to formulate and hatch my plan whilst still at home in London. I'd checked our flight schedule and worked out that the 21st July coincided with our early morning flight from Sydney to Auckland with LAN.

Subsequently I began a flurry of e-mails with the airline, in order to celebrate her birthday whilst 36,000 feet up in the air. Not exactly the mile high club fantasy that festers in my subconscious but at least I could cast iron guarantee she would not be expecting anything on this scale. She'd be thinking, "He's forgotten", only to be cruelly reminded that the score so far for forgetting birthdays and anniversaries lies 7-2 in my favour. Then with just one week to go I received an e-mail from LAN informing me that our flight had been cancelled and re-scheduled for the following day.

Bastards! Now what can I do?

I always think panicking helps, it's a great way of channelling all that pent up frustration. Once the emotion subsided I looked for a substitute on the bench. Where would we now be on the 21st? Ah, Sydney. Right, let's have a look.

I won't bore you with the details of my investigations but I settled on the world famous (what do you mean you've never heard of it?) sea-food restaurant, Doyles On The Beach on Marine's Parade, Watsons Bay, with superb views of Sydney Harbour Bridge from the beach side tables.

I checked out the menu online.

HOW MUCH?

Fuck that. Oh, wait a minute, they have a special all-in, 3 course winter menu for 26 Australian dollars. That's more like it.

My wallet breathed a sigh of relief. When Hélène wasn't looking I phoned and booked a romantic table for two right on the beach. The only problem now was, how to lure Hélène there without her realizing? I would have to come up with a cunning plan, and we all know about the type of people who come up with 'cunning plans', don't we?

With an extra day and night on our hands we poured over our Lonely Planet and planned our Sydney sightseeing. With so much on offer Hélène couldn't understand why I was so insistent on doing the harbour ferries and Watson's Bay on the 21st.

Watson's Bay is located on the southern head of the entrance to Sydney Harbour. To the east is the Tasman Sea and to the west is the wharf with a glorious view of the city of Sydney in the distance. It is a narrow headland with superb views from both sides, various walks being indicated in the book. It's recognised as Australia's oldest fishing village, having been established in 1788. Doyle himself originally sold his daily fish catch in 1845, although how history knew he began at exactly a quarter to seven remains a mystery. (Yes, you have just read one of my worst jokes ever. That's teach you for sticking with me for more than

100 pages)

Working backwards from our table booked for one o' clock I manipulated our morning so that we would catch the 12.15 ferry from Harbour Central. Once on board I checked the route map to make sure I had correctly counted the number of stops and would recognize our stop.

We left the shelter of the harbour and made our way around the various bays. A bit like the Staten Island ferry in New York, we could enjoy the views but at a fraction of the tourist boats. We came to our first stop but there was no sign to indicate the name of where we were. I just hoped and prayed it corresponded to the map.

I'd worked out we were the fourth stop en route so relaxed a little and enjoyed the spectacular view of the Sydney Harbour Bridge from the water. As it receded into the distance we came to stops 2 and 3. We took what I thought was an interminably long time at stop 3 and I was getting excited at the prospect of seeing Hélène's expression once my master plan came to fruition.

Finally we took off again but strangely Sydney Harbour Bridge was getting bigger, not smaller.

"Something's wrong." I thought to myself. According to my cunning plan this shouldn't be happening. We should be heading round the bay, not back towards the centre. BACK TOWARDS THE CENTRE! What the ★★★★!'"

"Excuse me, darling, I just want to have a quick word with one of the crew."

"Why?"

"Oh……nothing….just want to check on something…eeerr…"

"Excuse me, Mr crewman, sir. When will we be arriving at Watsons Bay?"

"Watson's Bay? Just been there mate. We're on the way back now."

"NOOOOOOOOOOO!!!!!!"

But there had been no sign. How was I to recognize Watson's Bay? A death to all your first born.

Fuck! Quick David. Panic!

Right, panic again!

Nano seconds passed as I tried to get my brain in gear and come up with some sort of credible plan B to keep eight months of planning from going overboard.

Failed.

I went back to Hélène who could see from the expression on my face that something was wrong.

"What's wrong?" (See. Told you)

I had no option but to confess and beg for forgiveness. In a torrent of platitudes I admitted my subterfuge and the failure to keep my secret plan a secret. The only thing to do now was to scrounge a free trip back to Watson's Bay out of the ferry company.

I played the sympathy card and they let us re-board the ferry back at Harbour Central without paying. I phoned Doyle s on the Beach and they agreed to keep my special table where they sell sea shells by the sea shore.

Phew! Sorted, but minus the element of surprise.

We had a superb seafood meal that lived up to all expectations. My clam chowder especially was out of this world. Then, fully bloated, from the restaurant we walked north past the nudist beach called Lady Bay, although there were no nipples on display as the weather itself was nipples. We climbed up to South Head and saw the Hornsby Lighthouse. Then, buffeted by high winds, we walked passed The Gap and took in Signal Station and the Macquarine Lighthouse and saw the wreck of the Dunbar. What's Australian for "bracing"? So, it turned out all right on the night/day, but I could have done without the underwear changing crisis that lead up to it.

THURSDAY 22 JULY. SYDNEY, AUSTRALIA
PHILADELPHIA UNION 0 MANCHESTER UNITED 1

Today was our day for visiting Bondi Beach. It was sunny but cold as we made our way to Circular Quay and worked out the right bus for Bondi. Although the bus had been full of kids clutching surfboards as though they had been born that way, forty five minutes later we appeared to be the only ones on the beach itself. A certain Mr Groom had dismissed Bondi Beach as a "f*****g load of old w**k" but he had obviously visited it in the summer where I guess the place can be overrun by pink bodies, a bit like Blackpool just after the war. (No, I wasn't there, I've just seen pictures, that's all. Don't be cheeky).

Hélène and I were mightily impressed. A sweeping bay of clean yellow sand, hemmed in by gentle green hills. Minus the tourists, I could see what attracted the tourists in the first place. A brisk stroll along the windswept beach and back along by the edge of the surf developed a craving for food that could not be ignored. We made our way back up and across the main road to one of the roadside cafés and purchased a pie each and chips. Not the dreadful stick insects you get at McDonald's but real chunky chips made from real potato. We then descended back onto the beach and chose a spot by the wall, protected from the wind. Perfect.

This was the life. Cold wind, warm sun, hot pie and chips. Top that.

Now we were ready for the famous coastal walk around the bays to Waverley Cemetery. We started from the right hand corner of Bondi Beach where a sea water swimming pool had attracted a number of participants that perhaps didn't fancy the strong waves of the open sea. A number of surfers clad head to toe in wet suits clambered around the swimming pool to get a short cut access to the waves, risking the rocks as they manoeuvred themselves out to sea.

We walked round the first bay towards Mackenzie's Point and south to Maroubra. Great views, with the constant sight and sound of the boiling sea and waves crashing against the rocks as we left the beaches behind. Nobody was swimming here. From our elevated vantage point we could see jagged rocks just beneath the surface.

We briefly glimpsed the fading Aboriginal rock carvings in Marks Park before rounding the next bay and coming to the delightful Tamarama Beach, a small beach used mainly by locals. Time for tea and dunkers I suggested, as I had spied a cake shop with views of the sea. I think I've told you already how surprised and delighted I have been to discover that many Australian cakes and gateaux match their more illustrious French counterparts. This was an ideal spot for refuelling.

Satisfying my stomach we continued round the coast. Each bay providing spectacular, ever changing views. Finally we came to Westerly Cemetery high above the surf, with the graves of lots of famous Australians that we had never heard of, but we were so invigorated that we continued past and on towards Coogee Beach, a full six kilometres from Bondi.

Once again we seemed to climb more than descend but by now, six months on the road, I'd built up the stamina to cope, and I didn't have a strength sapping Indian heat wave to contend with. Finally we arrived in Coogee. I could see why the monied men and women of Sydney chose Coogee as one of the preferred places to live in Sydney. What stunning views of the sea yet only 30 minutes from the city centre by car.

We took the bus once again and observed how the passengers reflected the ever changing neighbourhoods, from ladies who lunch to loud Jewish kids coming home from school. I felt I was watching a 3D documentary. With all the energy we had spent during the day, our last supper in Sydney dominated the bus ride home.

"We just have to try Harry's Café de Wheels." I said.

"What's that?" enquired Hélène.

So I gave her the full background story of my love affair with pies To be honest, when I make my way to Old Trafford from the Chester Road or Sir Matt Busby Way I'm torn between a jerk chicken, rice and peas in the mobile Jamaican stall opposite the Bishops Blaize or a meat and potato pie with chips in curry sauce from one of the many eateries dotted en route. They don't do meat and potato pies "darn sarf" and it's one of my anticipated treats as I motor along the boring M1/M6.

Now I'd read on various blogs and guide books about Harry's Café de Wheels in the notorious Kings Cross neighbourhood of Sydney. An Australian institution that had begun during the depression in the 1930s, it had changed its name after the war from simply "Harry's", on account of the local council insisting all street vendors without the required paperwork move at least 12 inches a day. And that's how Harry's Café de Wheels was born. Neat, huh? So to round off another perfect day we ventured down the hill from the hostel we were staying in on our last night in Sydney. Wonderful vistas of the dramatic Sydney skyline lit up at night greeted us as we descended some really steep steps down to the water's edge.

A thought immediately came to me.

"We're gonna have to walk all the way back up to our hostel. The pie had better be worth it!"

It was... and more. We hit the jackpot.

The stall was lit up with tacky 1950s American style neon, photos of numerous celebrities adorning the walls. I made a couple of circuits until I found a spot to adhere LUHG sticker number 48. I knew it won't last long up there, but hopefully enough Brits will pas by who will "get it". I joined the queue and we deliberated over an extensive menu with couplings that sounded dubious in print but I guessed tasted OK.

OK? They tasted fantastic! For less than 5 Australian dollars we had a mammoth circular pie each drowning in gravy. Superb. And as the temperature had dropped alarmingly, just holding the hot pie was a pleasure in itself.

All the way back up I munched and dripped, dripped and munched. Hélène finished hers before me but I like to take my pleasures n i c e and s l o w. Mmmm.... My jacket was testament to my edible orgasm, which I'm sure Hélène will comment on in the cold light of morning, but for now I'll just revel in the afterglow.

Back in our hostel bedroom I quickly switched on my laptop to get United's latest tour result. To be honest, I wasn't going to spoil my last day in Sydney pleading to stay in and catch it live by streaming. I need to store a few brownie points for use at a later date when more important matches are on the agenda.

Made sure Hélène got my drift. Won 1-0. Not even bothering with the details. Goodnight Philadelphia.

NEW ZEALAND

FRIDAY 23 JULY AUCKLAND, NEW ZEALAND

What can I say about Auckland other than it rained for virtually the whole time we were there. The town is nothing to look at architecturally but the people are really nice, if a little old fashioned. The shops certainly were.

The hostel we were staying in advertised free (yes, FREE) city tours for newcomers by Stray Travel.

"I'm having some of that." I thought to my wallet, so Hélène and I booked a wholedayer on this rickety old bus powered by used chip oil. The two guys running it were really cool and friendly and the whole eco vibe sat comfortably with me. They cracked the same anti-Aussie jokes as us, played AC/DC and Crowded House and made us feel right at home.

Our first stop was at the Sky Tower when Hélène almost pushed me forward to volunteer to sky dive down the outside of the tower. I stopped myself just in time. We were meant to do the Harbour Bridge and cruise the waterfront, but the rain came down so hard we could hardly see a few metres in front of us. We did see the New Zealand entry for the next America's Cup yacht race though down at the harbour.

Wow! Then they took us to one of the oldest pubs in town and we had a lovely pub lunch. Already I've noticed prices here are a lot lower than in Oz. However, apart from food and drink, there's nothing I really want to buy. You see. They give with one hand but take away with the other.

SATURDAY 24 JULY AUCKLAND TO LAKE TAUPO, NEW ZEALAND

After our success touring and sleeping around Queensland in an estate car, we opted for the same mode of transport and accommodation for the North Island of New Zealand. Originally we had hoped to take in the stunningly beautiful South Island as well, but July being winter in the Southern Hemisphere, and as neither Hélène or I could be even loosely described as partakers of extreme sports, we knocked this idea on the head. Travelling with someone is all about compromise but we were both in agreement on this. The South Sea Islands were beckoning, one of our dream destinations, so NZ had to make way. Rightly or wrongly we only allowed ourselves one week here. Even with a year's travel to play with we knew we had to prioritize, so this green and pleasant land of the wrong shaped ball had felt the full force of our itinerary scalpel before we even left England's green and pleasant land.

It was also two weeks before the Community Shield season opener against Chelsea, so the possibility of missing a couple more pre-season friendlies in the States wasn't worth losing sleep over.

So with LUHG sticker number 49 adoring the back window, to amuse and "Reducate" the natives, our first port of call was Waitomo, home of the glow-worm caves. The brochure had shown cave ceilings lit up like the night sky with glow-worms taking the place of stars.

Would it live up to the hype? Yes it did, and more!

We descended some stairs down to an almost pitch black cave with black water running swiftly along the bottom. As we waited in line whilst they prepared a boat for us they told us no flash photography was allowed as this would disturb the glow-worms.

Once gingerly aboard the boat it gently drifted with the current. This really was black. As our eyes adjusted to the darkness we became aware of hundreds, nay thousands of bluey, greenish yellow dotted lights all around us.

This was brighter than anything in the brochure, which went on to inform us the life cycle of a glow-worm is about a year from larva to fly. During that period it casts the luminous glow for which it was named. The light is often an eerie blue and is stronger when the worm is hungry. From the ceiling of the caves, the worm suspends lines of sticky beads to trap prey, which are attracted to the light. Once prey is caught, the glow-worm pulls in the line to feed. Looking at a ceiling of glow-worms is like gazing at the stars on a clear night. A mature adult glow-worm fly has to be careful not to get trapped in a glow-worm line itself, and be eaten!

Just goes to show, even a glow-worm can never totally relax.

When we came out we drove to Lake Taupo, the largest freshwater lake in the whole of Australasia, where we intended to stay the night. It was pitch black when we got there so we drove around the lake for a suitable place to park and sleep for free.

Failed.

Had to settle for a motel with special rates for motor caravans using their extensive back garden. So it was out with the sleeping bags and blankets. It was going to be a cold, damp one tonight folks.

SUNDAY 25 JULY LAKE TAUPO – HUKA FALLS, NEW ZEALAND

Woke up to wonderful views over Lake Taupo. The air was so clear and fresh we could see the snow capped mountain ranges way off in the distance, on the other side of the lake. The washrooms were still locked so it was a dirty couple that made their way down to the edge of the lake. Some people were setting up a floating golf range by the shore, with a hole and flag out in the lake for a hole in one challenge. For 10 New Zealand dollars you had three balls, and the money went to charity.

My money went to charity and my balls went to the bottom of the lake. Breakfast was now on the menu so we drove round the lake till we came to the main town and chose a crowded place called Friends. We soon found out why it was so crowded. It was superb. So much, so fresh and so tasty. And warm inside. Coupled with the aroma of freshly ground coffee, bacon, toast, quiche, freshly baked warm muffins and views over the lake, we defrosted from our night in the boot of our car.

I could have stayed there all day, but this was no time to slow down. Places to see, people to meet. OK, forget that last bit, I was getting carried away.

From Lake Taupo we followed the Waikato River to Huka Falls, (Huka being the Maori word for "foam") a set of waterfalls on the Waikato River that drains Lake Taupo

At the top of the falls is a set of small waterfalls dropping over about 8 metres. The most impressive, final stage of the falls is an 11 metre drop. The drop is technically six metres (cliff beneath the water) but the water flow raises the level to 11m. OK, I agree it's not exactly Niagara, Victoria or Iguaçu Falls, but they are the most visited natural attraction in New Zealand, and within the context of the gentle north island it was still an impressive natural site. Appearances can be deceptive though. Did I say "gentle"?

The falls featured in a national scandal in February 1989 when the body of cricket umpire Peter Plumley-Walker was found downstream with wrists and ankles bound. The resulting investigation exposed the Auckland bondage scene. Dominatrix Renee Chignall was acquitted of his murder after three trials. Who says there is no night life in New Zealand?

Meanwhile, we had a choice. Either the exhilarating but stomach churning Huka Jet which twists, turns, performs 360★ theatrics and skids (well, that's what it looked like to me) at 50mph up and down the choppy river, or the standard tourist passenger boat.

You're ahead of me, aren't you? Yup, that's right. We chose the latter, boring old fart mode of transport. Both craft take tourists within a few meters of the base of the cascading falls so why take extra risks? (I'm losing a few of you young 'uns here, aren't I.)

We found the mooring of the BOF boat and spoke to the one man skipper. Turned out he was an ex motorbike racer from the UK who had spent his last remaining years in London repairing bikes in Ravenswood near Hammersmith. Split from his wife and got away as far as possible.

Loves New Zealand and wouldn't change a thing.

It's always nice to find people who are happy with their lot.

Once unmoored (is there such a term?) we chugged along the river, passing swirling pools of geothermal heated water that looked but didn't smell inviting.

"Don't even think about it." The skipper's voice came from behind. "The currents will pull you down. Nobody swims around here."

From water level the oncoming falls seemed bigger and badder than the brochure had suggested. The noise and unique blue hue of the boiling water seemed to entice us.

"Come closer. Come closer. That's it. Just a little bit closer…"

Enough! With a roar of its engine, our boat did a pretty nifty 180 and we were on our way back. Enjoyed that.

MONDAY 26 JULY ROTORUA, NEW ZEALAND
KANSAS CITY WARRIORS 2 MANCHESTER UNITED 1

Today we visited the impressive sulphur lakes in Rotorua. Renowned for its geothermal activity, notably the Pohutu Geyser at Whakarewarewa and hot bubbling mud pools, Rotorua has the nickname "Sulphur City". But nothing could take away the rotten egg smell of the Kansas City Warriors and they trampled, literally, over United in this pre-season friendly. I seethed with righteous indignation as I read about the hosts "over zealous" (journalist speak for 'dirty') challenges.

Even though they had one of their players, Jimmy Conrad, dismissed for a reckless tackle that lead to our penalty, United were once again caught on the hop. Both Giggs and Gibson were booked for retaliation but nothing awarded against the persistent fouling by Kansas City players.

Having said all that, we were shit. Although the home side's winner, scored

just one minute after Berbatov had equalized for the Reds from the penalty spot, never actually crossed the line, this abject display by United doesn't bode well for the season ahead. It's always disappointing when muscle triumphs over skill, yet United have had enough experience of this kind if treatment not to let it get to them. On top of this, we didn't seem to have created many clear cut chances in the 80 degree heat against a team 5th in an 8 team MLS division.

Very disappointing. Let's hope it's a wake up call. It's a MLS select eleven next. We shall see…

WEDNESDAY 28 JULY AUCKLAND, NEW ZEALAND – RARATONGA, THE COOK ISLANDS

Hélène had a bad night, which of course meant I had a bad night.

"Sing me a song!" requested her majesty at 02.30 in the morning doesn't have the same ring about it as... well, anytime now I come to think about it. This wouldn't be so bad were it not for the fact that the alarm was set for 05.30 as we had ordered a taxi to take us to the airport at 06.15.

Before you could say "City are a massive club" the alarm went off and we were up. The driver was waiting for us downstairs and we drove (well, he drove, to be precise) in the rain with dawn just breaking on the horizon. 35 NZ dollars later, as opposed to the rip-off 75 NZ dollars the airport taxi rank taxis had charged, we were standing in a small queue for Air New Zealand NZ46 to Rarotonga, capital of the Cook Islands, our first South Sea island destination.

For the first time this trip it looked as though we weren't going to get a window seat. Damn. And our first stop in the South Pacific to come. All that azure blue water, all those dusky maidens... (sorry, my imagination was running away with me there. Have you seen the size of those Cook island women? Not very PC I know, but have you?)

Then the old Blatt charm worked its magic and we were offered two emergency seats, one being a window seat.

Yes!

All that extra legroom. Planet nod, here I come. Two hours later and we boarded the plane. Now let's see....11e and 11f. Shit! They were just normal seats, only with an emergency door to my right. Never mind. I'll just check out the reclining factor in readiness for....

What the fuck! The seat doesn't even recline! I've, I mean, we've been done! Now I come to think about it, if I'm going to sleep, what do I want a window seat for anyway? You can see why I never made it far up the corporate ladder. Forward planning was never one of my strong points.

No, you're not going to spoil my day. The beguiling South Pacific islands are calling me (I don't know what they're calling me, but they're calling me nonetheless.) and you shall not break me.

We touched down at 14.55 on the 27th, a full nineteen hours before we took off! I know I'm backward, but this is ridiculous! By crossing the dateline we've gone back in time. Eat your heart out, Dr Who! Now, if only I had tomorrow's racing page (or is that today's? Or yesterday's?) I could make a fortune. But then why hasn't anyone done it before? Oh, bollocks. It's too early. Let me out of here.

The view as we disembark was tear-jerkingly beautiful. Lush green mountains bursting with health and vitality in the aftermath of a Cook Island shower, the sun revealing a kaleidoscope of colours and hues. Small private planes that you associate with South Sea Islands just waiting on the tarmac to take some rich businessman or drugs dealer to another exotic rendezvous.

I get a couple of shots in before the customs people can arrest me, then we queue, pass security and trolley our luggage out into the South Pacific landscape.

"Where's our driver?" I remarked as our surname was conspicuous in its absence from drivers' nameboards. We made our way over to the Rarotonga Backpackers (our pre-booked hostel) stand in the airport forecourt.

Forty five minutes later we are driven almost half way round the island before turning into our hostel by the sea. The first views were divine. Just like every image you've ever seen of a South Pacific island. The second view would have to wait though as we had to check in.

"Name?"

"Blatt. David & Hélène Blatt."

"Sorry, we don't have a booking for Blatt."

Oh oh!

"You must have. Here, I've printed out the confirmation booking. Look."

She looked. Or, to be more precise, she looked at the date.

"You're booked in from tomorrow."

Shit. This losing a day routine had struck home with a vengeance.

"Surely you could squeeze us in?" I said, showing her my best denture smile. She looked at her book, then at her husband out the back, then back at me. She could squeeze us in. Phew! That was close.

Now for the second view.

Not so divine this time. The narrow beach lead down to the shore, and we were immediately aware of razor sharp rocks under the surface as far as the eye could see. Paddling, let alone swimming, was out of the question. Damn, the aerial shots and text hadn't mentioned this on their web site.

With three weeks scheduled for the Cook Islands, as it was the cheapest of the South Seas destinations we had chosen, we decided there and then to find another hostel in a more favourable location. Easier said than done, as we were to find out.

COOK ISLANDS

WEDNESDAY 28 JULY RARATONGA, THE COOK ISLANDS

Sergeant-Major Hélène made sure we got up early in order to drive around the island to Vera's backpackers at Muri Beach and try to secure a room. Although considerably more expensive than our current location, reviews on the internet had put this hostel at numero uno on most backpacker's lists, mainly due to its location on the only truly sandy beach on the island.

Vera's wasn't much to look at from the outside but there was no denying the location, right on the sandy beach, was superb. Within a secluded, tree lined bay, the gentle turquoise waters lapped gently against the shore. One or two little boats were moored within touching distance.

Heaven on Earth I thought, as we entered the low key reception. Somebody else's heaven on Earth I mused a few moments later, as we left with the phrase "full up" still ringing in our ears. Driving back along the coast road, all the reasonably priced accommodation was unavailable so we resigned ourselves to Raratonga Backpackers. Don't get me wrong. As a hostel in a developing nation it was adequate. The couple that ran the place were friendly enough but for 3 weeks in paradise it's all about location location location. Never mind.

This evening I joined in a rugby v football discussion. Told them about my first book. Spoke to an Aberdeen supporter who had just done South America with his New Zealand girlfriend. He'd loved Peru but couldn't live there. Buses from Chile were superb. People were very friendly, even if you didn't speak Spanish. Less so in Bolivia as the population have actually been told not to speak to tourists/travellers unless they speak Spanish.

Agreed with me that Fergie is the greatest manager of all time. Up went LUHG sticker number 50 on the hostel noticeboard. 50 down, 50 to go. Five and a half months and halfway round the world. LUHG stickers bearing up well. Will have to ration myself just a little to make sure they are seen in the most effective places. I admit I'd got a little carried away in the beginning, and with 5 months in soccer mad South America still to come I shall have to be a little more strict with myself.

THURSDAY 29 JULY. RARATONGA, THE COOK ISLANDS
MLS 2 MANCHESTER UNITED 5

Got to get my football head on. After the disaster of Kansas City, we have to get back on track against the MLS team. I know they're only friendlies, and the way we play is more important than the result, but did you see the way we played in Kansas? No, neither did I, but I read enough reports from Reds online to know it wasn't pretty. I got up and booted up my laptop.

Ah, here it is. MLS 2 United 5 in front of over 70,000 spectators in Houston. That's better. So, what happened? With our new signing, Javier

"Chicharito" Hernandez on the bench, as he'd only met his fellow team mates for the first time on Monday, we'd started with Macheda upfront together with Obertan and Nani. Not the most lethal attack in the world I grant you, but pre-season friendlies are all about fitness and trying out new combinations. Yet within 22 seconds Macheda, himself not 19 until next month, intercepted a sloppy backpass from an All Stars full back and slotted the ball home.

In the 12th minute Macheda leapt unmarked to head home a Nani corner. I'd read that the MSL XI players had been picked as the twelve best as voted by MSL supporters. This meant, of course, they'd hardly played together as was evident by their sloppy marking. Yet it gave United the confidence to bounce back after the horror show in Kansas.

The MLS team stepped up their game in the second half and brought the score back to 1-2 before Darren Gibson did the only thing he's any good at by scoring a belter from a direct free kick 20 yards from goal. Three minutes later Tom Cleverly made it 1-4 with a close range shot, but the goal most of the stadium, and certainly the United contingent had come to see, arrived in the 84th minute when Hernandez ran onto Paul Scholes's long pass and scored from 20 yards out. Final score 2-5 United.

Our Little Pea had arrived in style, and later watching him on You Tube it made me feel even better. Now for the serious matter of trying to bring forward our flight to Papeete in Tahiti from the 10th of August to this Saturday, the 31st of July.

Why?

As lovely as Raratonga was, what the brochures don't tell you is that it rains every day in July and, as I've mentioned before, the rocks under the sea which look so picturesque in full colour aerial shots, come right to the shore and I'd stubbed my toes numerous times as I waded through the surf. After the strenuous but highly rewarding three months travelling throughout the humid heat of India and South East Asia and the bright crisp cold of an Australian and New Zealand winter, a few lazy hazy (forget crazy) days of sunshine were called for. The locals we spoke to told us this had been their best winter for ages. And they all loved the rain.

I could see their point of view. They need the rain to accompany the sun in making the land so lush and green, only I didn't come here for my shin to turn lush and green. I wanted David Dickenson/George Hamilton golden brown, and from a suntan, not rust! Hélène and I wanted to do nothing but recharge our batteries in the sun and sample local cuisine.

With the cost of flights to the beautiful outer islands of the Cook Islands out of our reach we contacted Travel Nation to pay a routine £30 admin charge to change our flights, only to be told that the South Sea

Islands leg had been outside of our special Round The World tickets and we had to contact Air Tahiti themselves. Went to a local travel agent in the capital, Avarua, to make arrangements, only to be faced with a bill of £125 EACH, as the ticket we held was a promotional fare and none of these remained.

What's Tahitian for 'Bastards'? Never found out. Hélène and I had a quick board meeting and decided, as rip-off as this surcharge was, a once-in-a-lifetime trip demanded sacrifices to make things happen so I unlocked Fort Wallet and extracted the plastic.

Spent our last night attending a Cook Islands cultural evening cabaret that turned out to be a real belter. Genuinely welcoming hosts, superb food and captivating music, dancing and drumming (there's always drumming, isn't there?) that was way above the standard bland fayre you come to expect on tourist excursions. Yup, the joint was really Cooking!

Sorry.

TAHITI

SATURDAY 31 JULY.
RARATONGA, THE COOK ISLANDS - PAPEETE, TAHITI, FRENCH POLYNESIA
CHIVAS DE GUADALAJARA 3 MANCHESTER UNITED 2

The good thing about being in this part of the world is that United's kick off in the 50,000 all-seater Estadio Omnilife stadium in Mexico was only two hours ahead of Cook Island time, so I got out my untrustworthy laptop and attempted to get a signal for streaming.

Out of interest the Omnilife Stadium was formerly known as Chivas Stadium, and before that Templo Mayor stadium. Construction originally started in 2004 but a combination of financial problems and "other issues" meant that today's match was the official opening of the stadium. Adding to the excitement was the fact that our latest addition, Javier 'Chicharito' Hernandez was going to play for both sides. Arrangements had been made that he would play the first half for his old team Chivas del Guadalajara and the second half for us.

But could I get a signal? Could I f★★★! I mean, no, I couldn't. Hélène sent me out of our room as my temper shortened in direct correlation with the impending kick off. In the end I had to throw in the towel and resign myself to finding out the score once we had checked into our hostel in Tahiti in the evening. I suppose there are worse things in life than spending our last morning on an exotic South Sea island staring at the Pacific Ocean, even if the weather was decidedly iffy. Warm, but iffy. We sat and had a drink overlooking the sea opposite the airport in a hotel where the word 'service' had been struck off the staff agenda. They knew that folks only stayed one night so why bother making them feel welcome?

The three and a half hour flight to Papeete, the capital of French Polynesia, was in a small twin prop plane that gave me a buzz for all the wrong reasons. I had the hippy shitty shakes. However, this was offset somewhat by the incredibly intense pink sky we witnessed at sunset as we came in to land. Arguably the most beautiful islands in the world had opened the show with arguably the most beautiful sunset in the world. If this was a taster of things to come then I was just going to lie back and think of... where I can find a bar or café showing Premiership football. I mean, Papeete is the capital, right? Surely there would be somewhere in town with connections to the outside world. I discreetly fumbled in my pocket and drew out my pocket diary.

Oh, I see. We're not due to play our next friendly until four days later, by which time we'd be installed in a hostel along the coast. Oh well, I had just better concentrate on immersing myself in the hedonistic pleasures of the capital of French Polynesia. But first I had to find out the result of our match against Chivas. Then I could let go.

It was strange to feel as though we were back in some small provincial French town far away from the glamour of Paris, but then that's exactly where we were. Papeete, and indeed the whole of French Polynesia is just another French 'departement' (county). Unlike citizens from the remaining countries of the British Commonwealth, everyone living in a Dom Tom, (French dependant territory) is a part of France and can vote in French elections, not just ex-pats who have registered to do so. So, fundamentally, we were back in France.

The food should be good then. The husband who had picked us up at the airport dropped us in front of the hostel where his wife welcomed us and beckoned us into the lounge. Three pregnant girls were sitting on the sofa watching a French soap opera. I recognized their faces. (the actors in the soap opera, not the three girls. Careful or you'll get me into trouble) The girls looked rather young. I could have sworn one was no more than 15 or 16 years old. I couldn't help but enquire as to the circumstances that brought three unrelated pregnant young women to a hostel in the back streets of the Tahitian capital. It transpired that many French Polynesians, from all over the islands, come to Tahiti for medical care. Only in the capital is there sophisticated facilities to treat people. After depositing our bags in our room, I took advantage of the hostel's Wi-Fi and found the score.

3-2 to Chivas. Shit. What happened? Javier "Chicarito" Hernandez happened. Playing for his former club he scored against us in the 8th minute. Should I be pleased or annoyed? How about both! Then I read that our other new signing, Chris Smalling, a defender from Fulham, had scored with a powerful header to equalize.

Yin and yang I suppose. I'll take that as a plus. However Chivas raced into a 3-1 lead before Nani scored our second ten minutes from time after good work from Tom Cleverley. Hmm, seen Cleverley a few times on MUTV. Hoping for good things from the lad. So, not all bad then. And it was only a friendly, and United had been away for three weeks, and they had done a lot of travelling. Yup, I'm good at making excuses. Isn't that what football fans do? Red Eyes and all that.

Now I could lie back and think of Tahiti until United's last pre-season friendly against the Aitricity League X1 in Dublin on the 4th August. (What sort of fucking name is that for Eric's sake?) Not going to even think about that now. I'm starving, Hélène is waiting and Tahiti is calling. A combustible combination. The husband drove us 900 metres back towards the quayside which was buzzing with the sights, sounds and smells of dozens of roulottes (mobile food vehicles) selling French Crepes, Chinese, Vietnamese, Burgers, Seafood, etc. but at non French Polynesian prices.

After a brief walk round the port in the balmy night air we chose to eat some French crepes. Mine was Nutella, banana & chantilly with vanilla ice cream. And do you know what, despite having lived in Brittany for five years and the south of France for six, this was the best crepe I had ever tasted in my life! Jealous?

WEDNESDAY 3 AUGUST PAPEETE, TAHITI, FRENCH POLYNESIA

When you say the words French Polynesia, Tahiti, Bora Bora, etc... doesn't it conjure up fantasy images of pristine beaches, dusky maidens, gorgeous backdrops and glorious sunsets? Well, they do for me anyway. What I didn't expect was a characterless, almost run down capital. Papeete (which incidentally means "water from a bottle") is nothing to write home about, even though I'm writing home about it now.

Yes, I know it has streets, a port, a waterfront, but it's, it's.....nothing. No architectural buildings of note. There are no beaches. In fact, reading my Lonely Planet I realize there are very few beaches on the whole of Tahiti. And when you consider the largest island in the Windward group of French Polynesia, located in the archipelago of the Society Islands in the southern Pacific Ocean was formed from volcanic activity, perhaps it's not all that surprising. I just had those Sunday supplement images in my head. I should have done more research before we arrived.

The rapid growth of the capital has been as a direct result of the French Government's decision to move their nuclear weapon testing range from Algeria to the atolls of Mururoa and Fangataufa, some 1,500 kilometres east of Tahiti. Careful planning went out of the window as the race for immediate economic benefits took precedent. Traffic jams are the norm here as the busy streets in the town centre are too small for today's volume of vehicles.

So, does Pepeete have anything colourful or different? Well, yes. One touristically conventional and one decidedly and irrevocably unique to French Polynesia. Let's get the conventional out of the way first. What can be more practical and appealing than a beautiful, multi-coloured sarong. Images of exotic Polynesian birds, flowers and sunsets, as well as original Tahitian art adorn these attractive and not too expensive souvenirs. Close inspection however, reveal that they are all made in Indonesia.

The second though was a real eye opener though. Let's talk about sex, or more precisely, the 3rd sex, for that is what the Rae Rae are. Homosexual or transgender, rae rae are accepted here. There's no shame and never has been. It makes western hang-ups obsolete. Homosexuality has been common throughout Polynesia for centuries and is considered a casual form of sexual expression. The rae raes are simply another element of Tahiti's exotic and sensual history. To see these creatures glide around the markets, shops and hotels is an eye opener but quickly becomes an everyday occurrence.

According to ancient tradition, the first or third son in a family was feminized to help with large numbers of siblings and was dressed and treated as female from infancy onwards. Others say that warring tribes captured females for sacrifice so men were disguised as women and trained to turn on their captors.

But whatever the historical truth, the level of acceptance by family and society is unusual and Hélène and I were delighted to discover something truly "different" on our travels. It seemed to us that most of the people we had met so far in India and throughout South East Asia had wanted to appear Western, wearing fake designer labels from head to toe and keeping their skin as white as possible. Here people were proud of their culture and heritage and displayed it with pride, and not just in hotels as part of package tour entertainment.

Which brings me neatly to that very essence of the package tour, a cultural evening in a big hotel. With only a limited time on our schedule for French Polynesia we had chosen the 5★ Marriot just along the coast aimed at monied American tourists and not the Hotel Costa Packet,

Los Wankos brigade. With the cost of meal + show at Glazer butt-clenching levels, we chose the late, unobserved entrance + loitering on the stairs option. As this was Tahiti and not Tenerife or Torremolinos we anticipated a sophisticated Las Vegas style spectacular.

It was spectacular alright. Spectacularly amateur. With all the money lavished on the production, it was like watching, "The X Factor" outtakes. The dancers kept banging into each other, the jugglers kept dropping their whatever they throw, the fire-eaters kept burning themselves, Oh, and dropping their flaming sticks as well. It felt like an updated Polynesian version of Mel Brook's, "Springtime For Hitler." This really was one of those "it's so bad it's good" evenings.

Hélène and I laughed and applauded in all the wrong places. With hindsight it was just about value for money, and when you consider we didn't pay a penny as we sneaked in late, you get my drift.

Cook Islands Cabaret 1 Tahiti Cabaret 0

THURSDAY 4 AUGUST PEPEETE TO PAEA, TAHITI, FRENCH POLYNESIA

Got picked up by the husband of a couple running Pension Te Miti in Paea, about 30 kilometres along the coast from the capital. Discovered he was from Ploemel in Brittany, only a few kilometres from where Hélène was born. (First one to mutter "small world" has to close this book immediately) Settled in our room, then after lunch went to the beach. Not the nearest as this public beach was dirty and naff. Walked about 500 meters along the coast road. New beach was OK, a mixture of white and black sand and hidden rocks to stub your toe(s) on. Weather cloudy but warm. Water acceptable but not warm. Dark clouds hovered above the lush green hills but never descended into rain. Across the sea we could see the island of Moorea with its own cloud hovering above the central mountain, just like a child would paint a cloud on top of an island. I almost expected to see bats and Dracula's castle atop the mountain peak.

Sunbathing wasn't really on so we went for walk along the beach for 3 ½ km. Consumed cocktails and ice cream sundae at Le Meriden for 3220 CFP (£22) Pretended to be posh as I sat there in my discreetly embroidered United polo shirt. Went to reception to change the last of my New Zealand dollars but given a really hard time by the receptionist. "No, we're not (fucking) guests." I exclaimed. "Just gimme the (fucking) money (bitch).

"OK then. Just this once." she eventually condescended, a frozen hotel receptionist smile on her lips as she handed over less CFPs (French Polynesian francs) than I was hoping for. By this time it was almost dark outside so we walked back along the road. An interesting day, but so far

Tahiti has not been the "paradise on Earth" we had been led to believe.

WEDNESDAY 4 AUGUST. PAEA, TAHITI, FRENCH POLYNESIA
AIRTRICITY LEAGUE X1 1 MANCHESTER UNITED 7

Sorry, but despite first impressions being less than awesome, here we are in one of the most exotic destinations on the planet, and I need to accrue a few brownie points for leverage in "discussions" with the other half on the non negotiable, "must see" United matches in the coming season. So, if I am being totally honest, with Pepeete ten hours behind Dublin, getting up for a 05.00am kick off was a sacrifice I could live with. As long as Hélène registered the fact that a sacrifice had been made by yours truly I was satisfied.

Woke up naturally, had a long, lazy breakfast with our Breton hosts, then asked to use the hostel computer with a faster connection than my laptop to look up our result. United's 7-1 rout in Dublin against what in the old, less commercial days would have been called the League of Ireland XI made the scoreline even more impressive. Turned out it was Rooney's first competitive match since England's dismal showing in South Africa and he displayed no ill effects. Didn't score but ran all over the pitch appearing fit and hungry. But the story of the match has to be the growing star from Mexico.

By all accounts he seems to have hit the ground running, which not many United purchases do. Within 2 minutes of coming on at the beginning of the second half he swept home a low cross from John O'Shea. Goals were shared out (which was nice), whetting the appetite for the first real competitive match of the coming season, the Community Shield match at Wembley against fucking double winning, Drogba fucking offside goal at Old Trafford, fucking Chelsea.

I could feel the venom searing through my Red veins. Hatred, what a wonderful emotion to stir a football fans passion. I'm alive again. Roll on Sunday. Alarm clock? Bring it on I say. Bring it on.

SUNDAY 8 AUGUST. PAEA, TAHITI, FRENCH POLYNESIA
MANCHESTER UNITED 3 CHELSEA 1. COMMUNITY SHIELD, WEMBLEY.

At Last. A real football day dawns – at 04.00! The Community Shield may kick off at 15.00 in Wembley, but that translates to 04.00 here in Tahiti. With alarm set at 03.50 I wake up like the perfect male in a television advertisement, eyes bright with anticipation. I put on my pre-Glazer United polo and trot over in the pitch-blackness to the other building in our hostel where resides the television. Setting the volume to almost zero I turn on Tele Polynesia and there are Manchester United and Chelsea lining up in the tunnel. Perfect, except for the incessant duo French commentary which doesn't let up for the whole match. A combination of low volume and limited French means all I hear is a low drone like a fly that wants to be put out of its misery.

As they line up ready to be presented to Gianfranco Zola (?) I squint at the screen.

"What's Mickey Phelan doing in our line up?"

A closer look reveals Rooney resplendent in his receding hairline. Phew! That was close. As the two teams kick-about prior to kick off I once again squint at the screen.

"What's Wes Brown doing sitting next to Ancelotti on the bench?" A closer look reveals Ray Wilkins resplendent with no hair whatsoever, just an orange sheen at the top of his bonce. This comes at watching a match at 4 o' clock in the morning.

After a couple of minutes Chelsea settle into their boring short passing game and we have trouble getting hold of the ball. On the other hand, the Rent Boys are being easily contained by Captain for the day Vidic and his teammates. By contrast, when we attempt a breakaway, our game is faster and a lot more attractive, but moves breakdown if our passing is not 100% accurate. For me one disappointment is Rooney back out on the left attempting crosses and not in the centre just behind Owen, where I believe he is much more effective. After half an hour Chelsea have had greater possession but we've looked more dangerous on the break.

Scholes is now finding his range and a couple of superb 40 yard passes out to Valencia on the right by-passes Chelsea's normally tight defence and results in chances. Then it's third time lucky as five minutes before half time another 40 yard exocet missile lands at Rooney's feet as he's drifted out to get more involved, and an immediate low cross finds Valencia running in unchallenged to tap in our first goal.

I jump up and mime a celebration whilst everyone else in the hostel remains fast asleep. (Thinks. I'm getting better at this) Valencia once again leaves his smile back in the dressing room as he acknowledges the crowd with his right arm.

Half time arrives, as does my visit to the loo. When I get back the adverts have finished and the French based sports emission is now direct from the European swimming championships in Hungary. Thanks but no thanks.

No half time analysis or replay of our goal. I don't know whether this is good or bad but they don't 'arf go on a lot about the swimming. After an inordinately long time it's back to Wembley and my armchair for the second half.

Berbatov on for the getting fitter after one month in the Caribbean Rooney and "Little Pea" Hernandez on for the ineffective Owen was the start of the inevitable array of substitutions that managers use games like this to test out different formations and to ease players back to full fitness.

The second half continues much like the first with boring boring Arsenal, sorry Chelsea (habits die hard I'll have you know) passing as though they believe they gain extra points if they complete more passes than us. So much good it did them for another brilliant Scholes 40 yard cross this time sees Valencia beat his man and send over a low cross which Hernandez, all arms and legs, slides in and knocks the ball via his feet, arm and teeth into the net.

Queue even noisier silent jumping from me as I witness a smile as wide as the Wembley pitch on the young Mexican's face. He momentarily looks round to see if the goal stands then runs off as though he cant believe he's actually scored a goal on his first appearance at the famous Wembley Stadium for the famous Manchester United. His face was a picture, one that will go on my bedroom wall when I get back home.

More substitutions follow from both sides. With six minutes to go, Van Der Sar, who's played a blinder so far, parries a long shot, only for Kalou to tap in the rebound. 2-1 and now Chelsea began to play as though playing meant something, whilst the camera scans the Chelsea end of the stadium where I spy around a dozen Chelsea fans standing up trying to wake up the Neanderthals around them. Farcical and funny as fuck.

Fearing United complacency was misplaced as we kept possession, minus one or two hiccups, till a lovely passage of keep-ball resulted in a through ball to Berbatov who lobbed the Chelsea goalkeeper with aplomb. 3-1, and the Chelsea pensioners are extinguished. Thank you and goodnight. Or should I say good morning.

No, really. As soon as the final whistle went, the cameras immediately transferred to the swimming championships in Hungary and I didn't get a chance to witness Vidic holding up our first trophy of the season. Never mind, as a prelude to things to come this was a nice way to start. The time was now 06.00 and dawn was breaking.

"Ow! That hurt!"

Sorry, the old ones are the best. On second thoughts, probably not.

I made my way back to our room with a Cheshire grin on my face, where I was greeted by Hélène with... "Come to bed and keep my kidneys warm. I'm cold."

Hardly top shelf stuff I know but this is real life folks. I wrapped her in my arms and dreamt of Fergie's smile at the end, The Little Pea's smile in celebration and Scholes's Charlton like precision passes. Next thing I knew it was 10.30 and we had missed our free breakfast, but I was still feasting on my nightime goodies.

MONDAY 9 AUGUST PAEA, TAHITI, FRENCH POLYNESIA

Today we hired a small car to do a circuit of Tahiti Nui and Tahiti Iti, the larger and smaller elements combining to look like a tadpole. The word spread and soon two tall recruits asked to tag along. I knew Hélène preferred to have the car to ourselves but we couldn't think quickly enough of a polite way of refusing. Anyway, I reckoned if they both did the decent thing and contributed to the hiring and petrol, it would be a welcome aid to our draining resources.

One guy was a tall elegant Englishman by the name of John. Almost older than me, the poor bugger was rather tall, and our petite Suzuki forced him into some rather contortionist positions on the back seat. He disclosed that he was a poet and author and had had a number of volumes published. Of even more interest was the fact that he lived in Coalville, a small mining village between Derby and Leicester and that last season he had seen the local derby between Hinckley and Kettering.

It turned out he actually supported Leicester City, so we passed the time quite amicably whilst we waited for our second passenger, a mid 30s Canadian who we had dropped off at the Air Tahiti offices in central Papeete. I ventured some anecdotes such as my first game at Old Trafford was in the spring of '67 against, would you believe it, Leicester City. A glorious 5-2 victory for the Reds, including a double by the original King, Denis Law, includes one delightful lob over the world's greatest goalkeeper, Gordon Banks. This contrasted with the agony of seeing David Herd break his leg whilst in the act of scoring a goal at the Scoreboard End, having been sandwiched between two burly Leicester defenders.

John was suitably impressed, by that I mean he remained awake during my entire ball-by-ball account of my first visit to the Theatre of Dreams. Once our Canadian friend returned we eased our way out of ramshackle Papeete's perpetual daytime traffic jam and drove clockwise towards our first stop, Point Venus, a disused lighthouse on the east coast headland. Entry was forbidden as the lighthouse was closed, but even so the view from the water's edge was superb, although strong winds made taking photos precarious. The views of the multicoloured water, waves a choppy, with a little island or "motu" in the middle of the bay were a complete contrast to the characterless concrete of Papeete which we had left behind merely fifteen minutes beforehand.

Thoughts in the car turned to food, but everything was closed as we searched for the turning that would take us inland, between striking valleys to our first waterfall. We came across Arahoho Blowhole, a unique natural phenomenon whereby churning waves crashing into a cavern force themselves into a hole which then force the water out of another hole in the form of spray like a geyser, accompanied by a loud noise similar to a whale blowing off. Quite disconcerting when you hear it for the first time. (I claim Hélène was more frightened than me.)

I caught the right turning but soon we could go no further than a car park. A noticeboard informed us that one waterfall was a five minute walk through the valley to our right, with the other two a twenty minute walk to our left.

The first one was easy, and we were greeted by a wonderful vista of water cascading from on high down to a rock pool below. I commandeered one of our passengers to take a photo of Hélène and me with the waterfall in the background. It looks like we are both standing as the water falls directly on our heads. Of course, it's a good photo because I didn't take it, but at least I'm, I mean, we're in it.

The second and third waterfalls were more of a trek up and down slippery undergrowth, with the added obstacle of legions of mosquitoes out to attack us at every opportunity. Hélène had had the foresight to bring the insect spray with her and we drowned ourselves in the stuff. To any fellow explorers we radiated the healthy glow of two bodies bathed in a sensuous sporting sheen of perspiration. Until they got too close that is, and their nostrils picked up our whiff.

We drove round the smaller Tahiti Iti until there was literally no more road left. Very basic, very green and a million miles away from the concrete, noise and traffic of Papeete. Look at the water. When have you ever seen colours like that in real life? This was full colour, Sunday supplement Tahiti. This was French Polynesia. This was what the South Pacific was all about.

We lingered until the light began to fade and then we made our way slowly back to base. Now we were on Tahiti time. What's the rush?

MOOREA

TUESDAY 10 AUGUST TAHITI – MOOREA, FRENCH POLYNESIA

Got up at a reasonable time this morning as I had to return the hire car before 10.00am. Had a quick session on the internet before Freddie, the hostel owner, drove us and our two passengers from yesterday to Papeete. The French Canadian turned out to be the bad guy as he never offered a penny towards yesterday's full day trip, plus I had to fill in with petrol which cost another 2500CFP.

We were dropped off first at the ferry port with all our luggage. We bought two tickets for the fast ferry to Moorea, the island just 18 miles from Tahiti, but somehow we boarded the slower one instead. Never mind. The crossing took less than an hour and soon we were aboard a local bus motoring around the only road on the island, offering delightful glimpses of the bluest blue water finally matching the postcards in the tabacs.

We soon came to Moorea Camping, the cheapest accommodation we could find. 2500CFP (£17.50) a night for a double room with shared bathroom, which if you know anything about French Polynesian pricing, was the bargain of the century. We soon found out why.

The campsite looked to have seen better days. On second thoughts, it looked like it had never seen better days. There was a depressing, decaying air about the place and virtually deserted, but beggars can't be choosers, and with two weeks ahead of us, sparing the cash was the motto of the day. I had read that there was a dispute in the family about ownership, so whilst the dispute raged on the place went downhill.

Our small cell consisted of one double bed, a small shelf and.......... sorry, there is no "and". That was it! Of course I could mention the fading cream painted walls and the small grill to let the mosquitoes in.... but I won't. Whilst we still had the energy we put up our mosquito net, one of the best buys of the whole trip, and only a fiver at TK MAXX, then we went for a stroll to get our bearings.

The place's one saving grace was that it was right on a narrow white sandy beach and we had it almost to ourselves. The view was heavenly. A huge expanse of coral punctuated by turquoise blue sea and sky, broken only by a backdrop of coconut and palm trees. No high rise concrete slabs to spoil the illusion of a south sea paradise. This really was picture postcard stuff I had dreamt of all my life. A couple of hundred metres along the road was a low key cluster of high priced restaurants, snack bars, an adequate supermarket, a smattering of expensive souvenir shops and an electrical shop that sold wi-fi cards. At least there was civilisation.

On the way back we popped into Nelson Camping where Stephanie, one of our acquaintances from Pension Te Miti in Tahiti, had elected to stay. It certainly looked a lot nicer than ours, but was 2000CFP (£15) a night more, and the owners were a right pair of misery guts. We decided to stay put, only we would have to return the following day as Stephanie had lent me a very useful book on Easter Island, our next destination after French Polynesia.

As we had eaten late, we stopped off to buy provisions and a pastry each in the supermarket for our supper. And very nice it was too. I put our fresh and frozen shopping in the larger of the two sad fridges in the campsite kitchen, then we went back to the beach for our first swim and to sit and take in an awesome sunset.

Wow! A deserted South Sea island beach all to ourselves. We couldn't believe our luck. Believe. That night we went for a cool stroll, and looking up at the night sky as we walked back we saw more stars than I had ever seen before in my life. And they were all so blinkingly brilliant. Great clusters forming all the shapes and symbols that anyone studying astronomy would recognise.

We stood staring up in wonder at the night sky. I strained my neck, hoping at last to see a shooting star before I lost my balance and fell over backwards. The good news was I never fell over, but the bad news was that I never saw a shooting star either.

Tomorrow is another night.

WEDNESDAY 11 AUGUST MOOREA, FRENCH POLYNESIA

For the next few days Hélène and I did our best to impersonate the seven dwarfs, busy doing nothing, working the whole day through, trying to find lots of things not to do. Torquoise seas, sandy beaches, cloudless skies, basic accommodation, simple cooking, strolls along the beach and into the village. Sunbathe – swim – eat – sleep - sunbathe – swim – eat – sleep - sunbathe …. You get my drift as one day drifted into another. Back to basics I think they call it. The opening home game of the 2010/2011 season against Newcastle was not until Monday, so I had six days and five nights to fill. Hélène and I competed with each other to see who could do everything at the slowest pace.

If only real life was like this. I looked around me. This WAS real life and I was right slap bang in the middle. But I tell you this, after a world of work; chasing yesterday's deadlines, pleading with clients for payment, suffering suppliers who cocked up and left us in the lurch and all that office politics shit, I reckoned I had earned it. Guilt was not one of the emotions that filled my mind and body at this moment in time.

The population of our camp site had recently doubled with the addition of Andres, he from Colombia, and Jenny, she from Chile where they both now lived. With their muscular torsos, beautiful breasts and white teeth (you choose who owns which) they could have stepped out of a Mad Men TV advertisement. Hélène and I paled into insignificance on all levels. But they were lovely people. In fact Andres waxed so lyrically about Colombia, dissolving many of our preconceptions that Hélène and

I decided there and then to change our plans and include Colombia in our itinerary. In the end they only stayed a couple of days but we made arrangements to meet up when we touch down in Santiago in September.

I bought a wi-fi card to get an internet connection on my laptop and guess what?

Didn't work. Went back to the small electrical shop in the village which claimed "It'll work on the beach." and "They're adding new signal points all the time." Hardly satisfactory but there wasn't a lot we could do about it. Apart from my United fetish, we needed to keep in touch with our two daughters and they needed to keep in touch with us. We needed to plan our onward travel and check the outside world was still functioning in our absence.

Mmm… five days until the Newcastle game. Let's hope I have it sorted by then.

The following day we hired the cheapest car for a day. Renault Clio £90 + tax. Drove completely round the 62 km circle coast road. Could have done it all in 2 hours, but where would the fun be in that? Stopped for breakfast in a boulangerie on the other side of the island. Whipped out my laptop and… nothing! Grrr! Angry of Moorea.

Drove round to the Toatea View Point above the Sofital Hotel in Ora where we admired limitless variation of blues in the lagoon and a breathtaking view of Tahiti. Next stop was the famous Cook's Bay framed by jagged mountains, where large cruise ships and luxurious yachts were anchored, then round to Opunohu Bay where Captain Cook actually anchored in 1777. However, the best views were from the Belvedere View Point (790ft) with spectacular views of the two bays, separated by Mount Rotui, the sacred mountain of Ancient Polynesians.

Stopped off at the only supermarket on the island, Carrefour, near the airport and stocked up on "stuff" not readily available in the little shops by the side of the road. Meandered back, returned the Clio on time, then walked back to our camping only to find someone had stolen our frozen prawns. Grrr! Angry of Moorea.

I'm sorry. There's an unwritten rule when you stay in a backpackers hostel or a campsite. You respect other people's belongings. The real world filtered through my dreamlike revelry to remind me that bastards operate in paradise as well.

MONDAY 16 AUGUST MOOREA, FRENCH POLYNESIA
MANCHESTER UNITED 3 NEWCASTLE UNITED 0

Despite mosquitoes setting up home on my ankles, I must have fallen asleep eventually because a pale light was shining through the prison bars as I opened my eyes. I needed to know the time. Was it time to turn on the netbook and bring up BBC sport? I squinted at Hélène's watch. No good. I can't make it out.

I lay there and thought about how the game would go. Newly promoted teams often seem to harness an extra "umph" until the adrenalin wears off after about half a dozen matches, especially those that haven't played at this level for ages, a la Burnley last season. However, I didn't put Newcastle in this category. I'm sure they felt they were a Premiership club that had just had one bad season, only this would work against them this morning/tonight as without that extra "umph". Our greater ability and desire to right the wrong of Chelsea spoiling our "four in a row" would ensure a comfortable 2-0 victory. My only concern, carried over from last season, was who was going to score our Ronaldoless goals?

The Community Shield and England's victory over Hungary in midweek had shown us that Rooney is not yet back to full match fitness. He seems to get mad with himself when things don't come off, and anyone else who gets in his way as he sets himself such high standards. Will Berbatov have used the summer break to work out exactly how he should harness his undoubted talents for the good of the team? Will "Little Pea" Hernandez start and bring his speed and quick thinking, something we've sorely missed since Tevez left. And if Hernandez and Rooney do form a lethal partnership, what happens to Berbatov?

Who'd be a football manager?

ME!

Ah! Hélène's stirring. No pretending to sleep this morning so as to get out of my breakfast duties. I'm raring to go. We make our way to the open kitchen overlooking the lagoon. It doesn't take me long to make two cups of tea, butter up four slices of bread and spread jam on mine. All the while my netbook is coming gently to the boil, as the oh so slow wi-fi connection recognises my user name and password.

We check our e-mails first, to find out the latest on our winter reunion with the girls in Mexico, and their ever increasing list of mates who'll be joining us. A flurry of e-mails and some home truths later it's time for the footy. I click onto BBC sport minute by minute update and after an age it reveals a 2-0 scoreline to Eric's Disciples on Earth after 40 minutes.

YAHOO!

I quickly read the comments up till now and it seems my prophecy was 99% accurate. Sloppy passing by Newcastle together with sublime 40/50 yard passes by Scholesy had put us in a winning position, with Berbatov and Fletcher scoring in the space of eight minutes towards the end of the first half. We were dominating possession and clearly a class above the barcodes.

Halftime arrived and I suddenly had an overwhelming desire to try one last time to get live streaming of the game. Entering "live streaming" into Google, one of the first companies to come up was Live-tv.com. Right, let's give it a go one last time.

There's sure to be some of you out there reading this mocking my abysmal attempts, but you have to understand I'm only on the first rung of the internet ladder, and what comes second nature to you guys is like quantum physics to me.

I click on the site and find the option of our game. I click on it and after an eternity a small screen appears and slowly loads the match, only when I click on the arrow and template comes up saying, "OOOPS!. You're not a member? Never mind. Click here and you can be watching the match of your choice in just a few minutes. Damn.

OK, I can do this. It's still half time. Let's begin. I click where they tell me to click and I fill out all the forms, enter my credit card details, blood group and inside leg measurements for one year's subscription of $19.95 for as many matches as I want. As long as this site is legitimate, and bearing in mind I won't be back in the UK till February next year, it seems like a good deal to me.

What's that? Verify my e-mail address. OK OK, leave it out. Go to my e-mail account, click on confirm e-mail address. Go back to Live-TV. com.

Still nothing.

Start watching within a few minutes it said on their web site. What's English for lying bastards? Give up. Second half is now well underway. I shall just have to make do with BBC Sport and their 2 minute updates. With only United (there's only one United) names appearing on the updates it was evident we were in total command. Rooney was substituted after 63 minutes and Giggs rounded off proceedings nicely with a lovely volley in the 85th minute. With Chelsea having walloped West Brom 6-0 the day before, nothing less than a comfortable victory would have been acceptable. This was acceptable.

Now for breakfast and...nothing but sweet dreams on the beach for the rest of the week until Fulham away next Sunday, save for the occasional twinge of regret as Fulham away is one of the few grounds where I have connections, and not to be inside Craven Cottage for the first time in years left a vague hollow feeling inside.

I now had six days to get acquainted with my streaming service. Surely I would iron out any foibles by then? Don't you fucking believe it.

SATURDAY 21 AUGUST MOOREA, FRENCH POLYNESIA

A strange couple rode into our campsite this afternoon upon their funky moped. A local couple who Joel, the local gossip, claimed to have nine children and booked a room once every so often to engage in S & M, which I think everyone will agree is the complete opposite end of the spectrum from M & S.

As Hélène and I entered the shared kitchen facility this evening I gave them a glance. Normally everyone in a hostel or campsite says "hello" in one form or another but these two sat at a far table and never looked up. I took a closer look. He was small and thin, around forty I'd say, with a wiry moustache and a furtive look like a low-life crook from one of those early 50s black & white British movies. She was a mountain of a woman, quite capable of devouring him in one go. She was whispering in his ear as I passed, or perhaps sizing him up for their nightime rituals.

I didn't give them another thought as Hélène prepared the evening meal. My contribution was to charge our mobile phone then set the alarm for 04.40 so I wouldn't miss the start of the Fulham match which was due to kick off at 05.00 local time. This was going to be the first match I was going to watch via a live stream onto my notebook. The site advised switching on at least ten minutes before kick off to make sure the steaming was working properly. Add another ten minutes for me to translate computer talk into simple Janet & John English then we should be away.

After the meal we went back to our cell. I began reading one of my digital books on my notebook but my mind naturally drifted towards the forthcoming Fulham game. With Chelsea having scored six goals for the second week in a row they had thrown down the gauntlet. Admittedly against weaker opposition in West Brom and Wigan. We had demolished Newcastle the previous Monday but "only" scored three goals. Sir Alex had been quoted as saying Berbatov could have had a hat-trick, and although a Scholes inspired United had played brilliantly, at the back of my mind I kept asking myself, "How many goals would Chelsea have scored against them?"

And that really is the crux of the matter for United. In my mind we still haven't adjusted for the loss of Ronaldo and his phenomenal goal tally, and despite what Sir Alex may claim publicly, I believe the lack of transfer funds resulting from paying off the Glazer debts will seriously hamper our chances of monopolising silverwear this season.

I was mentally preparing myself for a 04.40 alarm call when I could hear raised voices from outside our room. It soon became clear the newly arrived local couple were having a mother and father of a row. Now, I couldn't tell whether this was some elaborate foreplay designed to arouse the senses for their forthcoming nocturnal whips, bangs and crashes or they were really having a fight. All I knew was that it was destroying any hope I had of an early night as I would need all my mental powers to combat the forces of sleep.

As their argument got louder and sleep was denied me, I had a very very naughty thought. For the first time in fifty two and a half years, since I first became aware of the wonder that is Manchester United, I contemplated missing a match I could see.

I know. One million Hail Marys. Another Jewish operation. Wash my mouth out with soap and water, anything that would and should cleanse impure thoughts.

It was now 01.30 in the morning and they were still at it. I must have drifted off but now I was wide awake. And I had to pee. I unravelled myself from the mosquito net (not easy in the pitch blackness of our cell, but I didn't want to wake up her majesty and risk decapitation by turning the light on) opened our door and walked across the dimly lit campground to the outer toilets.

There he was, sitting on the step of one of the toilets whilst his other half (the much bigger half) verbally abusing him from her cubicle. What sort of fucking game was this? I felt like giving them a piece of my mind, but then I thought, what if they thought I wanted to join in their elaborate charade? So I kept my thoughts to myself, gave him my fiercest "angry of Moorea" look, peed, strode back to my room.

It was now less than four hours to kick off and my resolve was waning. I couldn't go back to sleep. I tried to ease my conscience.

"It's only the second game of the season. There'll be time to make up any shortfall."

What the fuck are you thinking, David? For six months, throughout India and the whole of South East Asia you have moved heaven and earth to watch every United game. OK, you hadn't always succeeded, but your conscience was clear, you'd risked divorce and pushed your luck to the limit, but for all things United you had given 110%.

And what do you mean, "make up any shortfall"? How can you think we will not leave Craven Cottage without three points? OK, it has been an unhappy hunting ground the past couple of seasons. You were there. You know what happened. But look at how we played against Newcastle. Don't you think we'll carry on where we left off against the sorry barcodes? Pull yourself together man. You should be ashamed of yourself.

Yeah. I know. I hear you, but I'm tired. I could search for the result the minute I wake up and nobody would be any the wiser.

Who are you kidding? You'll never be able to live with yourself. Getting chubbed for mouth-watering away games is one thing. You can always blame "the system". But to voluntarily miss a game because "you're tired". Fuck me David. You're a disgrace!

Leave me alone. Leave me alone. I want to go to sleep. It's almost 02.00. Get out of my head.

SUNDAY 22 AUGUST. MOOREA, FRENCH MOOREA
FULHAM 2   MANCHESTER UNITED 2

This morning I did a very very bad thing. When the alarm went off at 04.40 I turned round, switched it off, and lay back in my bed. Now the fucking chickens had begun to crow. Cock a fucking doodle doo. Again and again… right outside our room.

David, the match starts in twenty minutes. You know you'll fuck up the live stream. You'll need every second you've got.

Leave me ALONE! I know. This is killing me. I don't need you to put the boot in. Get out of my head!

Heavy of eyelid and heavy of heart I stayed in bed. I now wanted to go to the loo again but that meant getting up. My conscience was playing with my waterworks.

Suddenly the alarm on the mobile went again. I twisted round so as not to wake Hélène, switched off the alarm and gave myself a hernia in the process. Light was coming in through the prison bars. The mobile screamed 06.08.

OK. You got me. Let me go for a piss and I promise to come back, pick up my notebook and go sit outside the kitchen area facing the lagoon, the only place I can get a signal.

"Where's my false teeth?"

Shit. I put them next to my pillow last night. Where are they? I frantically felt around my pillow, at the same time doing everything in my power not to wake Hélène as she doesn't know I sometimes take out the bottom dentures at night. She goes to bed next to George Clooney and I don't want to spoil the illusion.

Fuck it. There's no time left. I'll just have to find them when I get back and hope against hope Hélène won't have woken up by then. Or even worse, found them! I pushed this worse case scenario to the back of my brain as a more pressing engagement filtered through my consciousness. I opened the door and ran to the loo.

Duly relieved of my liquid assets, I went back, picked up the laptop and made my way over. The sun had yet to rise but there was a lovely

Lady Diana, eat your heart out. Well, I had to, didn't I! Taj Mahal, Agra, India.

It's moments like this you don't forget. Tiger sanctuary, Chang Mai, Thailand.

Halong Bay, It's been good to know you. Vietnam.

Olympic Stadium, Beijing. Imagine the jobsworths at Old Trafford allowing fans on the pitch

Me and Wayne infront of the award-winning at the UK pavilion. Shangai World Fair, China.

'Basil! BASIL!' Fawlty Towers. Yangshou, China

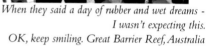

When they said a day of rubber and wet dreams -
I wasn't expecting this.
OK, keep smiling. Great Barrier Reef, Australia

Can you kick it? Outside South Africa
pavilion. Shanghai World's Fair, China

Is it a massive spliff?
No I'm learning the didgeridoo,
Sydney, Australia

At least they've got the
colours right!

Maupiti, French Polynesia - the world's most beautiful island knocking Bora Bora into second place. Wouldn't you like to be me?

'Daddy!' Me and Moai, Easter Island.

Now that's what I call a rock solid defence. Easter Island.

The Bolivian Salt Flats. Our first hot bath in 8 months. Wonderful.

Made it! One of the most iconic views on the planet. Machu Picchu, Peru.

Tena, Ecuadorian rainforest. A holiday romance or just a little monkey business?

My first iceberg, Ushuaia, Argentina. Awesome (pity it turned out light blue!).

Would you like lemon with that? Perito Mereno glacier, Patagonia.

The Super El Clasico - River Plate v Boca Juniors. A great way to learn Spanish.

Red-ucating the natives. Boca Juniors souvenir shop. Buenos Aries, Argentina.

Don't cry for me, Argentina. In front of Eva Peron's subtle grave, Buenos Aries.

Giving Kaka a run for his money. Maracana stadium Rio, Brazil.

What a load of rubbish. The Maracana under re-construction, Rio, Brazil.

Nothing Compares… Awesome from both the Argentinian and Brazilian sides (forget Paraguay) Iguazu Falls - Argentina.

Surprisingly tasty fare at the local shell station, Galapagos Islands.

The family Blatt onboard Dragonheart, a brilliantly restored Indonisian sailing boat. Koh Phi Phi, Thailand

The Glazers can run but they cant hide. Medellin, Colombia.

Here I am bonding with some Colo Colo supporters in La Serena, Chile.

Wayne soars as City's defenders look on. Of course "I was there" - the three most important words anyone can say on planet Earth.

rosy pink glow in the sky, which after the previous day's solid grey clouds and intermittent rain was a welcome relief.

I switched on my computer, waited for a hideously long time, entered my password, and waited more hideously long seconds until the desktop was ready. Clicked the icon to connect me to the hideously slow Hotspot-WDG Wi-Fi internet connection. Brought up my e-mail inbox and noticed three e-mails from Gerry Byrne, a United fan from Ireland that had been one of my first United contacts on the internet through Red11.org. One of his e-mails was the half time score. Oh, all right then. What's this, Scholes cracker. United one up at half time.

Great. Now I clicked on Primus, the company that I had paid my £15 for one year's free football from around the world on Live-tv.com. Fearing the worst as this was the first time I really would be able to watch live footy on my laptop I was amazed to realise I had followed all the correct links. I entered the members area, and scrolled down for Fulham v Manchester United.

Ah. There it was, and I had over two dozen links to choose from. First of all there was Media Player Splonge, then Media Player Zabock, then Media Player Umpapa. How the hell do I know the right one to choose?

I chose the first one. I waited ages but no image filled the screen, just an advert and blackness.

And mosquitoes. I'd forgotten all about the fucking mosquitoes, and those tiny lethal fucking nonos. In my pre-dawn state I hadn't put my thinking head on and now I began to suffer wave upon wave of insect attack.

Keep calm. Keep calm. Try the second link. I tried the second link. Ah, this is better. Here there's an advert, a large black screen, but a symbol going round and round in the middle. Promising.

At last! May Eric be praised! The screen was half filled with jerky images of the match. I checked the score at the top left hand corner of the screen.

1 – 1.

Oh, fuck. How did that happen?

I flayed my arms about in an attempt to keep insect free as I turned my attention back to the match. After a few jerky minutes I had to admit Fulham looked slightly the stronger team. Infuriatingly the screen would freeze for a few seconds then resume with the ball and commentary in a completely different place. Well, at least the commentary was in English.

Then the screen froze altogether. Tap tap here. Tap tap there. Here a tap. There a tap. Everywhere a tap tap.

Nothing.

I went back to the member's area and tried a different Media Player link. After what seemed an age another slightly smaller image came up. I could make out the Canal Plus symbol and I could hear French commentary. C'est la vie. What's the score?

Fulham 1 United 2

Brilliant! That's better.

However, this picture was even jerkier than the last and the insects were advancing. Then the screen froze again. Pity I couldn't say the same about the insects. Back to the members area and a different Media Player.

Failed. The minutes were ticking by as one by one the Media players....didn't.

Finally I got one to play. Aha, English commentary. Now, what's the score?

Fulham 2 United 2.

How the fuck did that happen?

Every time I look away someone scores. I'm cursed. They play out the final few minutes but the score remained 2 –2 and I'd missed all four goals.

Damn. Two points dropped. Now, after only two games we are two points behind the leaders and seven goals behind on goal difference.

They replay the goals. Wow! Scholes's really was a cracker. Just like the Scholes of old. So why did we let it slip?

Ah. Their equaliser. That's why. Our defence was shit. Ah. Now for our second. OK, an own goal. Well, they all count, but once again my prediction about our forwards not scoring enough goals comes back to haunt me.

All right. Show me their second.

Where's our fucking defence? Johnny Evans! What are you playing at? It's certainly not defending. Eric give me strength. I'm going back to bed. Sod the lot of you.

I gazed out to sea as I closed down my notebook. The tide was low and a lot of dead brown coral broke the surface. Not the scene on the pretty postcards they sell everywhere. At least it was going to be a sunny day.

Must remember to keep my mouth shut if I meet anyone. You never know, I may risk bumping into some unexpected early riser on his/her way to the toilets and wash area and the last thing I feel like doing at the moment is smiling. I wouldn't want to give them a Dracula type scare first thing in the morning. It was now 07.00.

My disappointment at the result was now giving way to panic as I remembered I still had to find the missing dentures before Hélène woke up. Will the British army get there before the Indians attack? I don't need this additional pressure. Not now.

I enter our room as quietly as possible. I frantically search and feel around my pillow again. This time there is the grey early light filtering through the prison bars and, lo and behold, there they are. Right on top of our dark brown silk mosquito repellent sheets, looking as though they were about to leap up and attack Hélène's neck with vampire like venom.

Overwhelmingly relieved, I popped them back into my mouth and crawled under the mosquito net and alongside Hélène. She stirred.

"Where've you been?" (as if she didn't know)

"Football" was my monosyllabic reply

"How'd you get on?" (she couldn't care a flying fuck. Why is she torturing

me so?)

"2 – 2. A draw. Now go to sleep."

She goes back on her side. Phew. I don't have to talk any more. My teeth are back where they belong.

I lay still. Sleep won't come so I repeat those scenes I had just seen on the screen. ("scenes", "seen", "screen". Not bad, eh? OK, please yourself) I try not to analyse it but my brain won't take no for an answer. Eventually I drift off.

We both awake around 09.45. Breakfast. We get up slowly and make our way to the kitchen area. I help by keeping out of the way and re-connect the internet. I go straight to BBC Sport.

What! Nani missed a penalty! Where was I? In no-man's land between feeds. Damn. But who was on the pitch at the time? Let's see, Berbatov, Owen, Giggs. So why did Nani take it? Oh, it's not even worth answering. It's done now.

Just don't do it again!

I have a feeling in my water, at 2-1 ahead, if that penalty had gone in Fulham would never have come back from two goals down and only minutes left to play. This will come back to haunt us at the end of the season, I know it will. You mark my words.

I check the fixture list. Our next game is West Ham at home on the 29th. It's a 17.30 kick off, which I have a love/hate relationship with back in the UK. I can lie in bed in the morning and leisurely get myself together before meeting mates and assaulting the M1 and M6 with my driving and my mates ears with my music. The downside is that I get back to London really late from the game and have to get up early for work the following day. And is it just me, but hasn't the traffic leaving the ground towards the M56/M6 got worse the last couple of seasons? It's a conspiracy I tell you.

All I can do now is read the contributions to various United fans' forums, try to make myself feel better, then go for a swim and sunbathe in my very own South Sea bubble.

FRIDAY 27 AUGUST MOOREA - BORA BORA, FRENCH POLYNESIA

Bora Bora. An island so good they named it twice. In fact, for the first time in French Polynesia we've come to a place that lives up to all the hype.

I awoke from my laboured slumbers on the hard deck floor of the cargo ship transporting us from Moorea to Bora Bora. (No, not the two bars in Ibiza. This is the real thing) In my mind I'd envisaged arriving by luxury yacht, but have you seen the prices? They ran out of zeros! In my research I'd discovered many locals travel on the inter-island cargo ship that delivers supplies to the outer islands and ferries people from one island to another.

There used to be three such ships, but they'd tightened up the regulations since my Lonely Planet guide was printed and now only one boat plying these waters actually accepts passengers, and then only 12 per crossing.

The bright sunlight was piecing my red eyes. I had no idea of the time but I didn't want to miss a second of arriving in Bora Bora. I stood up, not sure whether the creaking I heard was coming from the decaying wooden decking or my own bones and made my way to the side of the deck.

"Wow!"

There was no other word to describe the view. We were slowly sailing passed small green motus on either side with white beaches to die for. A couple had the obligatory 5★ huts over water accommodation. In front, rising dramatically like a giant green goddess out of the sea, was the island of Bora Bora itself.

Lush, fertile, shimmering in the early morning sun, no picture postcard can convey the jagged intensity of colours coming closer with every second. I woke Hélène up so she wouldn't miss our grand entrance. We stood in awe as the boat gently glided into the small harbour and docked, then we made our way down the four flights of steps to the cargo deck, re-acquainted ourselves with our two giant rucksacks and made our way past the crew unloading their wares and onto the island proper.

It was already rather warm and we couldn't see anything like a "truck" that our pension had promised would be waiting at the dock for us. Little did we realise that we had arrived almost one hour early (very unPolynesian) so when the truck did arrive ten minutes later it was in effect early as well.

I say "truck". It was actually a small bus with two rows of seats along each side. It drove us along the spectacular coast road to Chez Nono, our home for the next seven days. We came to the southern most point of the main island, namely Matira Point, where the truck turned down this narrow lane, passed the Hotel Intercontinental Bora Bora Le Moana Resort on the left and turned right into the opening for Chez Nono.

Paradise, I thought. An identical beach to our more illustrious neighbour, but at a fraction of the price. Mr Blatt. Give yourself a pat on the wallet. You've surpassed yourself with this one. We made our presence known at reception, who were expecting us one hour later, and to be honest, so were we. No problem. The woman just gave us our key and led us to a room on the ground floor (Thank Eric, no stairs) where we could just dump our things, and chill.

Suitably dumped, we strolled down to the divine private beach and knew we had hit the jackpot. A real soft white sandy beach and a lagoon so blue City fans would want to be buried here... alive! The water was so clear, and no dead coral to stub my toes on.

We emptied our rucksacks as this time we had shelves to put things on, then agreed we should have breakfast before doing anything strenuous, like sunbathing. In reception I read the notice board, then added my obligatory LUHG sticker (51 down, 49 to go) Across the road was a permanent roulotte which served breakfast, lunch and dinner. We asked about breakfast but they had stopped serving, plus the manager told us you have to order in advance if you want the complete works. When he told us the price, 1500CFP (£10.50) we happily accepted half works, which consisted of fresh mango juice, French coffee that didn't make the leather of your shoes curl at the ends because it was too strong, fresh sliced mango, toasted baguettes, butter and jam. At 800CFP each (£5.75) this was actually extremely reasonable.

What an excellent start to our day. We then strolled down the road to a local grocery store for some provisions, as eating out would be a rare event for the next few days. I spied a loaf of sliced bread. The sign read 625CFP (£4.50). Naturally I thought this must be a mistake, because the exact same loaf of sliced bread on Moorea had cost 310CFP (£2.20).

"Excuse me"! I enquired of the assistant loading the shelves. "How much is this loaf of sliced bread?"

He pointed to the price written underneath.

"625CFP".

"Why, thank you my good man."

What's Polynesian for rip-off? How can they get away with this? Answer, because they can get away with this. What's that old maxim in business? What's the maximum price any company can charge? Answer, the maximum price people are prepared to pay. Which is good up to a point, but in French Polynesia, and especially here in Bora Bora, being greedy is actually driving people away. According to a recent article in the local press, tourism for 2010 is so far more than 10% down on the previous year, and pricing has to be a major factor. Most of Europe and the States are only just coming out of recession, yet the cost of air fares, accommodation and everyday necessities in French Polynesia are pricing tourists out of the market. From Europe you can get to Bangkok and then onto the wonderful islands off southern Thailand for half the price of an air fare to Papeete, whilst the cost of living in Thailand, even in the built up resorts, is a fraction of the costs in French Polynesia.

Add to the melting pot the fact that no other group of islands in the South Pacific are as expensive. They all have to import a lot of raw materials and other essential goodies, so greed has to be a major factor.

Speaking to various locals, the government of French Polynesia receives a healthy subsidy from the French state, yet the politicians pocket the money in one form or another and very little trickles down to projects for the benefit of the local population.

"Trickle down." I always break into a cold sweat when I hear that expression, reminding myself of the Iron Lady who decimated much of British industry and whole communities in the north of England in the 80s. Leaner and fitter maybe, but at what a cost to people? Real people in real communities?

Trickle down doesn't work because the money emanates from the wealthy. And the wealthy are wealthy because they keep their money, that's why they're wealthy. Or spend it by and large within their own kind. Here in French Polynesia there are large 5 star resorts where the occupants live, eat and drink within their cocooned walls. Very little of their wealth passes into the local economy.

When cruise ships dock, their three meals a day (and more) passengers have little need for local eateries. Some partake of a local excursion or buy overpriced trinkets by the quay, but that's about all.

The French Polynesian government's tourist policy is exclusively aimed at the monied classes, so campsites like the one we stayed in on Moorea are closing down. Yet their blinkered policy is also hurting the ones they love best, the 5 star resorts. With the recession cutting into even some of the deepest pockets, those that can are making their money go further by choosing less expensive destinations where they can still enjoy the same level of luxury.

Club Med has disappeared on both Moorea and Bora Bora whilst the famous Hotel Bora Bora has recently closed down. When walking along the beach, Hélène and I saw many bungalows were unoccupied and this was August, the height of the holiday season in Europe.

There wasn't much we could do about that now, so we put our overpriced groceries away in our room and the fresh stuff in the communal fridge, then plunged straight into the oh so blue lagoon. Splashing around, Hélène and I looked at each other with the sort of look that said, "We've made it. We're actually here." And started grinning, or in my case, giggling with glee because I am just a big kid at heart.

Bora Bora. Not the open air club in Playa del Bossa in Ibiza that my two daughters wouldn't be seen dead alongside a boring old fart like me, but the real thing.

Bora fucking Bora.

Suitably refreshed and sunbathed, I dried myself off in order to retrieve the laptop and get on the net. With the salesman's words ringing in my ears.

"The signal is so much stronger on Bora Bora than here on Moorea. You won't have a problem, sir. Especially not where you are staying as you'll be surrounded by lots of 5 star resorts all offering internet access."

I believed him. Wouldn't you? So, I turned on my laptop and once the desktop was up and running I clicked on my internet connection.

Nothing.

Surprise, sur-fucking-prise.

Try as I might I couldn't get a signal. With twenty hours remaining on my wi-fi card I wasn't a happy bunny. Plus I still didn't know the draw for the group stage of the Champions League. Reds would have been commenting and planning trips to the sun and snow for over 24 hours now, and I was still in the dark. Not that I would be in a position to join in until next February at the earliest, but I needed to know so I could make my own mental plans.

And what about West Ham at home on Sunday I hear you cry. Yes, I'm crying too. Without an internet connection, how was I going to watch the streaming? You can almost envisage the veins throbbing on my face as the knowledge hit home.

So who's on the substitutes bench?

Wi-fi Tiki, that's who.

Wi-fi Tiki claimed to have the strongest signal of all the possible providers so I asked at reception how I could get connected.

"Hotel Matira have a connection. They're about two hundred metres down the road." Hélène and I decided to take a walk together along the beach and get them from behind. We strolled through their grounds, passed their run down bungalows until we found their reception.

"Bonjour", I said in French. "Can we buy a Wi-Fi Tiki card, please?"

"We don't sell them anymore."

Brilliant.

"Where can we buy one from then?"

"If you walk about fifteen minutes along the road, you'll come to Snack Matira. They sell them there."

"Merci." I said in French. (oh, you noticed)

Oh, well. At least this gave us a reason to do our obligatory afternoon constitution, so we meandered along the almost deserted coast road, imagining which villa we would buy and imagining living here all year round. Given the wedge, Hélène could but I couldn't. Not enough cultural variety or flights back to Manchester. Even paradise has its drawbacks.

And Snack Matira?

Don't ask.

SATURDAY 28 AUGUST BORA BORA, FRENCH POLYNESIA
MANCHESTER UNITED 3 WEST HAM UNITED 0

Despite her almost all over itchy body rash, Hélène had a good night's sleep, which meant I had a good night's sleep. However, our early morning slumber was broken by the sounds of a really heavy rainfall right outside our window. I got up to pull back the curtains and saw a mini waterfall landing in a growing pond right outside. What with the noise of the raindrops bouncing off the corrugated iron roof, sleep was impossible so we just lay there with our eyes closed.

Finally the rain subsided, so I got up and walked to the lounge, which opens on to our private beach and the lagoon. The scene was bathed in bright sunlight and there was a perfectly formed mini rainbow on the horizon of the sea. I rushed back to get my camcorder and recoded the happy scene. I took what I hope would be the perfect award winning holiday photo. A lone catamaran in the distance, crowned by the rainbow, with the shadow of a palm tree reflected on the water in the foreground. Perfect for blowing up and framing once we're back in Blighty, and to prove to ourselves we were really here and this is not all just a wonderful dream.

With Hélène still dozing I took the laptop and went to sit by the water's edge, the only place I could get a wi-fi signal. My machine decided to play silly buggers with me this morning and it took me ages to get connected. I scanned both our e-mail accounts but there was nothing of real interest. I then clicked on BBC Sport and the headline read,

"United ease to comfortable win over Hammers"

What! The match is tomorrow morning, surely?

Fuck me. Mr Blatt. You've done it again. You've cocked up the dates, haven't you? Too bloody right I had. The sense of jubilation at the result was tempered by the fact I had missed the match itself.

"I'm having too many of these senior moments", I thought. This has got to stop. I shall have to instigate some military type manoeuvres. It's bad enough fighting Hélène for the best way to spend two hours in paradise, but for me to self inflict an own goal is unforgivable. Queue self loathing when I should be rejoicing. I calmed down enough to read the report of Rooney's first goal since March, albeit a penalty.

Hélène didn't want to trust her skin to too much direct sunlight so we decided to rent a bike. Well, two bikes to be precise. Balancing her majesty on my handlebars was not ever going to happen. "Raindrops keep falling on my head" in the background as Paul Newman takes Katherine Ross for a ride in that scene from Butch Cassidy and the Sundance Kid was not going to be reproduced here in Bora Bora. We went to the roulotte across the road where we had had breakfast the day before and asked for two bikes. Nice people but not nice bikes. No brakes for a start.

"Just peddle backwards to stop."

Hmmm. I took mine for a test ride.

No chance. I could see myself falling in slow motion under a lorry as I tried to work out how to stop the bloody thing. Thanks, but no thanks, we said, and strode off down the road to rent from a lady who had bikes with brakes.

We started to peddle along the coast to Vaitape, the main town on the island. Hélène wore normal clothing as she didn't envisage going swimming whereas my more adventurous streak soon came back to haunt me. I had decided to wear my swimming shorts.... and nothing else. Soon the friction between me, my unmentionables and the saddle were beginning to chaff, and not in a pleasant way. After half an hour I could take no more. I called out to Hélène to stop. We had to find a solution or I would become celibate before her very eyes.

I've got to hand it to her. Necessity is the mother of invention. She took off her sarong, folded it into a strip and I poked it down my shorts, between the remains of my Jewish operation and the saddle.

What a relief! Peddling along became a pleasure once more as the wondrous scenery slowly slid by. On one side the lagoon constantly changing its hues of blues and green whilst on the other the evergreen mountain peaks mysteriously covered with hovering clouds.

I spotted Bloody Mary's, the famous seafood restaurant by the side of the road. On two wooden boards either side of the entrance were columns of "personalities" who had dined there. Everyone from Janet Jackson, Rod Stewart, Stephen Stills, Rowan Atkinson, Ronny Wood, George Michael, Kurt Russell and Goldie Horn, Commander Cody (but no mention of his Lost Planet Airmen), Paris Hilton (shit, there goes my appetite) and many more.

I looked at the menu. OK, if we have a burger or one of the lunchtime specials we can just about budget for this.

"Let's treat ourselves." I suggested to Hélène.

Forever the sensible one, she said, "We have to go to town first. I need to get to the pharmacy before it closes. If we have time we can always eat there on the way back".

Which is exactly what we did. Hélène had a fresh fish burger whilst I had Mexican chicken with lots of side dips. Then I thought, if something is worth doing it's worth overdoing, so I chose warm chocolate pudding with vanilla ice cream for desert.

All the while people were posing and photographing themselves, something Hélène hates doing, but she was going to have to do it with me. Once we paid I stood outside the main entrance and made her take photos with her camera and mine. I expect the phrase, "I was there." will once again appear under my Facebook upload in the near future.

Back at Chez Nono the first thing we both did was unload our goodies then plunge straight into the water.

Bliss, especially for my sizzling unmentionables. (have I mentioned them before?)

After showering to get rid of the salt, we went back to our room where I spread the new anti-itch cream all over her infected area. (No, that wasn't top shelf speak. I meant that literally) I then volunteered to make tea, 'cos that's the sort 'o guy I am. An American guy who had been talking to an Italian couple passed by, and I used the opportunity to have another chat in English. Turns out he had worked for two years in England, first in Northampton, then in London and finally in Oxford. I pointed him in the direction of my Green & Gold T-shirt.

"LOVE UNITED HATE GLAZER"

Oh no, he exclaimed. It turned out he was an Arsenal fan. Had been converted by a colleague when working in London. At least he understood the message. I'll give him brownie points for that. But then he blows it by saying he was in Cardiff for the championship final (his words.

F A Cup Final – my words) where Arsenal beat United.

"Not 2005!" I exclaimed in disbelief. How could he have got a ticket when I couldn't? And he went on to praise the Arsenal defence that day, in a match we slaughtered them in before losing on penalties. The last match before the Glazers took over. That's why we all wore black shirts.

This affinity thing was wearing thin. Hands across the water and all that, but come on! Fortunately we then agreed that the atmosphere at matches in the UK beats anything they have in the States because it comes from within, not generated by plastic pom pom girls and marching bands.

We ended as buddies and I looked forward to continuing his "Red"ucation tomorrow.

TUESDAY 31 AUGUST BORA BORA – MAUPITI

The pace of island life was shattered by Hélène's mobile phone which went off at 05.50 this morning. Nobody there, of course. I'd just settled back down when the robotic sound of a message received filtered through my grey matter. Needless to say there was no message.

All this wouldn't have been so bad but I had already set the alarm for 06.30 as we were going to take the 08.30 Maupiti Express from Bora Bora to, you'll never guess, Maupiti!

Everything I'd read until now suggested Maupiti would be what Bora Bora was like fifty years ago, before the tourist dollar hypnotised the latter with its all-persuasive power. On Maupiti the elders had decided not to allow the global hotel chains to set foot, concrete or glass on their island. Respect.

Accepting my short night's sleep had come to an abrupt end I got up and prepared breakfast before waking Hélène. By 07.40 we were waiting outside our pension for "Le Truck" to take us to the port. Surprisingly the boat departed on time, and as soon as we left the sanctuary of the harbour a school of dolphins came alongside and jumped with us for a full five minutes. This was a first for me. It filled my heart with wonder and my eyes with tears. A grown man, I ask you! Yet where would we be if we WEREN'T affected by moments like these?

Not long afterwards, another first. My first flying fish. I thought I'd seen flying fish before, schools of fish taking short hops out of the water. I was wrong. These were tiny exocet missiles flying with computer aided efficiency in a perfect straight line a few inches above the waves, their fins or gills acting as wings. Extraordinary.

The rest of the journey passed with me lying on the bench on the upper sundeck, pretending to sunbathe but in reality masking the affects of the swell of the ocean on my delicate stomach.

As we approached Maupiti and its motus a strong wind sprung up out of nowhere. Fortunately we were navigating the entrance to the lagoon so I was able to stand up and enjoy the spectacle of another perfect Polynesian island rising majestically before us.

The seemingly endless variety of blues and greens was spellbinding. No CGI graphics needed here. This was for real.

Docking was a relatively simple affair. Dozens of people were waiting on the quayside, brandishing pension brochures or offering bike rentals. Some acted as taxis but Hélène and I were oblivious to their charms. I had worked out that our accommodation, Pension Manu, (Yes, Man U. I know) was just a five hundred metre walk along the coast road into the only village on the island.

I remembered reading that Chez Manu was right behind a snack bar but nothing like that description appeared to us. No sign, nothing, and we were now in the centre of the village. We had just passed a hut on the right selling paninis when I remarked to Hélène.

"We may have passed it you know. Let's ask someone."

Hélène called out to a woman cycling passed in the opposite direction.

"Chez Manu? Ah, that's my sister. It's just there, behind the man selling paninis."

It would be, wouldn't it!

A large bulging woman appeared, all smiles and stomachs.

Cheek kissing all round, she had sent her boyfriend down to quay to meet us. Not having been pre-warned, and thinking everyone who stopped just wanted to make money out of us, I had dismissed him with a polite...

"C'est tres gentile, mais nous preferon marcher".

More fool us. When was I going to lose my Western cynicism?

She showed us to our room which was dated but adequate. We agreed to pay five hundred francs each on top for breakfast but declined the two thousand francs it would have cost us each for dinner. We reckoned we'd take a chance and do better, i.e. cheaper, in the one restaurant in town. We asked where the nearest beach was and she gave us confusing directions. In fact her Tahitian accent when speaking French was so strong even Hélène couldn't understand everything she said.

We thanked her and decided we'd do our own thing. A path by the side of the school next door lead to a seawall. There was no beach, just a few local boats hoisted up out of the water. A few hundred metres across the most turquoise stretch of water I had ever seen, a deserted motu with an inviting beach was mocking us.

"Swim across if you think you're hard enough" it seemed to chant.

Alas, the water was too deep and the current too strong to cross on foot so, admitting defeat, we turned right, back to where we had disembarked earlier that morning. Arriving at the little dock the seawall ended so we took the road.

Climbing steadily for half an hour we came to a fork in the road. To the left a rough track was signposted "plage" whilst the road proper continued up the hill on the right. Allowing gravity to get the better of me I decided to follow the rough track and only hope the "plage" or beach was not a too far away.

May Eric be praised. We came out by a rocky beach filled with black lava rocks of various shapes and sizes. The sea looked magnificent but the sea bed looked a toe stubbing nightmare. In fits, slips, slops and starts we made our way round the bay by the water's edge for about another half an hour. Little by little the rocks began to thin out and soon we were walking on a beautifully silky soft white sandy beach, the only one on the island as it turned out.

I would have been happy just to plonk our things down here and jump in the water. But not Hélène. Across the incredible aquamarine lagoon rose another motu, and this lagoon was walkable. Taking off my uncool but immensely practical professional walking sandals and holding them in my hand, I lifted our shoulder bag over my shoulder and we began to wade across.

We spotted large black rays gliding regally in one direction or another, and even some lemon headed sharks, but we rose to the challenge and forty five minutes later, feeling very Robinson Crusoe, we stepped onto our first motu.

Picture postcard perfect. A thin stretch of soft white sand, swaying palm trees and two men and a woman drinking a milky white liquid from an old Coca Cola bottle. Swaying in time with the palm trees, they gestured for us to join them. I don't drink, but even Hélène was disturbed by the look of their moonshine so we politely declined and made our way along the beach.

We found a spot as ideal as could be, set out our towels and accepted the welcoming waters lapping at our feet. It wasn't deep enough to swim so we spent the next hour or so just lazing in the water, sunbathing the bits not covered by H2O and trying to think of ways to top this.

Hélène admitted she was falling in love with the place and could live here forever. It was everything she had ever dreamed of. Warm waters of varying hues no camera could do justice to, a distinct lack of concrete and glass development, fruit just demanding to be picked in a French Polynesian garden of Eden, and a soil so rich, any vegetable would grow.

Nature would be our weapon to counter the incredibly inflated prices in the shops. Even heating bills would be a thing of the past.

I had to admit, she painted a highly attractive picture. But she had omitted one vital ingredient. How was I going to watch my United matches? Satellite and cable channels were available on the island itself but not on the motus, most of which didn't have electricity. But then, none of the channels showed Premiership football.

My only chance would be if I could get matches streamed onto my laptop. The first and last time I tried, away to Fulham now over a week ago, hadn't been an overwhelming success. England's opening European Championship qualifier against a Berbatov-less Bulgaria hadn't been enough to get me out of bed. Only United could provoke such a reaction, and our next match wasn't until next Sunday, away to Everton.

I looked around and admitted I was living the dream. I never thought in a million years I would be lying here in the South Pacific, with warm water gently lapping over me, the sun on my face and 360° views that anyone other than film/pop stars, mafia dons or captains of industry would only ever see in a travel magazine or on TV.

For anyone who isn't a football fan, a real football fan, my thoughts will appear flippant, ridiculous, even slightly unhinged. Even as I write I admit they wouldn't stand up in court in front of a jury comprising twelve sane men and women from a cross-section of our society. Yet paradise for me wouldn't be paradise unless Manchester United was a part of it. A living, tangible part. i.e. watchable. If not in the flesh, then on the substitutes bench of live TV.

Life without Manchester United for me would be like the twenty six years of MUFC before Eric. Some wonderful players, wonderful matches, wonderful atmosphere, wonderful camaraderie, but pre '92-93 a vital piece of the jigsaw was missing. Eric was that final piece, just as MUFC is that final piece for me. You can fill a bath full of water or you can fill it full of champagne, but without a plug it all washes away. Manchester United is my plug. The reason I was put on this planet was to follow the Reds at home, away and in Europe.

The great (yes, great) Bill Shankly once said words to the effect that football was more important than life or death. In the face of global crime, terrorism, corruption, racism, religious persecution, famine, drought, etc... where thousands, nay millions are affected each and every day, any rational man or woman would dismiss Shankly's comments out of hand. Yet, as individuals, our emotions are stirred more by what we perceive affects us personally and what we can affect ourselves than by gargantuan statistics with noughts on the end we cannot relate to.

The fact that Jordan's breasts are up one minute then down the next will make more front pages than the news that thousands are suffering in some far off country which offers no strategic, political or economic benefits to the West.

There's no logic in the fact that how our football team performs directly affects our mood, but it does. Stirring victories at the weekend inspire men and women on the shop floor and in offices on a Monday, whilst heart wrenching defeats provoke absenteeism and lower standards of workmanship.

Despite growing competition from all forms of online gaming, and slightly less from my other great passion, music, football is the catalyst that binds us. For me Manchester United has taken me to higher highs and lower lows than any other activity on the planet, including sex. Of course, this tells you more about me that the relative merits, or otherwise, of football and sex.

I love Manchester United with all my heart, soul and wallet, whereas the club itself doesn't know I exist and wouldn't care a damn even if it did. All football fans, not just United fans know this. It's the optimum definition of a platonic relationship, where one side is truly, madly, deeply in love but the other side couldn't care a toss. Our emotions are spurned, our requests for tickets ignored, entry prices raised far above the level of inflation. Used and abused by the very force we love so much. A Greek tragedy for the modern man. Yet we still come back for more.

Some have made the ultimate sacrifice and walked away from their greatest love, yet in doing so have created a model of purer, simpler, higher virtues, i.e. FCUM, FC United of Manchester.

All I know is, I couldn't live or breathe without MUFC. As I wrote in the beginning, wherever I am in the world, once the season starts I have to get back. This is a once-in-a-lifetime trip and I'd be a fool to jeopardize my marriage or the wrath of non football friends and family in the process. But when it comes to the rest of our lives, well, I'll compromise as any good husband and wife should, but I won't capitulate.

Manchester United has been an integral part of my life for over fifty years and will remain so till the end of my days. Oh, and beyond. Didn't I tell you? I've made arrangements with the Museum Department at Old Trafford to have my ashes scattered on the pitch. Obviously I want them at the Stretford End but they informed me it would be up to the groundsman on the day where I end up. I won't be in a position to argue and I realise Hélène will want to get out of there as quickly as possible so I'll just have to hope for the George.

I've worked out the music I would like played as they carry my ashes out from the players tunnel. Unfortunately, as the ceremony is conducted on non-match weekdays when fans and tourists alike take the stadium tour, "they" don't think it would be appropriate.

Shame. I'd have started with one of my favourite Pink Floyd tracks of all time, "Comfortably Numb". Good choice, don't you think? Then I would have squeezed in a medley of, amongst others ... Faithless – "Insomnia", Muse – "Knights of Cydonia", AC/DC – "Heaven & Hell", All Saints – "Never Ever", Stackridge – "Slark", "Take Me Home United Road" and the obvious cliché, Led Zepellin – "Stairway To Heaven". There'll not be a dry eye in the house I tell you.

The only thing that hasn't been agreed yet is the date, and I'll keep them guessing until the last moment, or until 18-5 has been achieved and surpassed. Now let me just lie here for a moment.....mmmmm.......

WEDNESDAY 1 SEPTEMBER MAUPITI, FRENCH POLYNESIA

We spent today being taken round the islands by the pension owner and her boyfriend in their little motor boat. First the boyfriend dropped us on a deserted motu, then a few hours later they both returned with our meal consisting of fresh fish and salad. As they stepped off the boat however I was more than a little perturbed to see the short, squat woman wearing a pair of shiny red Arsenal shorts.

WTF!

I tried to elicit a confession but the poor woman couldn't understand a word I said. So I'll never get to know how those chunky thighs adorned with varicose veins came to be wrapped in fake, market stall gear. Weird.

After lunch we visited various other motus and even helped our hosts go fishing in the shallow waters where we caught our evening meal.

This was the life. Just another day in paradise.

THURSDAY 2 SEPTEMBER MAUPITI – BORA BORA, FRENCH POLYNESIA

Walked the other way round the island today. Chatted to locals along the way. It seemed everyone was related to everyone else. Houses pass from one generation to another. Life drifts along slowly and everyone seems content with their lot.

Of course, my western eye may have missed intrigue and drama, Maupiti style, but from where I stood, sat and lay, this was as near to heaven on earth as you can get. I felt really sad to say goodbye to the new "most beautiful island on earth" but needs must and Bora Bora was calling. As we left the shelter of the motus the Maupiti Express boat began to fight the swell and this time we were in direct conflict with its current. For the next two hours I just sat on a crowded bench on deck and fixed my eyes on the horizon. Hélène's attempts at conversation were impolitely ignored as survival mode took over and became my number one priority.

Wimp? You got it. Sea sickness? I got it.

Finally got back on dry land and "Le Truck" was waiting to take us back to Chez Nono where all our food had disappeared, including my beloved Frosties.

What's Bora Bora for Bastards? They even have bastards in paradise. Do you know how much a packet of Frosties cost on Bora Bora? Fucking cereal killers.

HUAHINE

FRIDAY 3 SEPTEMBER BORA BORA - HUAHINE, FRENCH POLYNESIA

Today we took the cargo ferry to Huahine, often called the overlooked paradise in French Polynesia. Using it as local transport, when the ship docked in Uturoa on Raiatea, the second largest of the Leeward Islands for a thirty minute unloading session, I hopped off for an ice cream. How casual was that! Island hopping in the South Seas for an ice cream.

Cool.

And the thing is, by going by boat, we were able to see each island as it gradually came into view and truly appreciate its beauty. All thrusting green peaks surrounded by iridescent coronas of blue and green. Yet to put things into perspective, whilst Hélène and I drooled over each breathtaking, life changing vista, the locals were just going about their daily lives as it were service 86 to Chorlton/Altrincham via Stretford, Sale and Ashton-upon-Mersey.

It was dark by the time the boat docked opposite Chez Guynette in Fare yet we could actually see the hostel from the deck of the ship. Just like the picture on their web site. Have a good feeling about this. We were met by Olivier, one half of the French couple that had recently taken over the place from the original Guynette as mentioned in Lonely Planet, and simply walked the 100 yards from the ship to the hostel. How cool was that! Nice double room with ensuite and hot shower. Bliss. With no United matches until the 13th I can totally lose myself here. I may even stop thinking about football for a while.

Ha Ha. No chance. Get me that wi-fi link....now!

SUNDAY 5 SEPTEMBER HUAHINE, FRENCH POLYNESIA

Read about Rooney and the call girls on the internet. I won't go into the details as I don't know all the facts, just what I've read in the Red tops, but I would like to raise one point. We can all pontificate about the rights and wrongs of rich and famous men and women having affairs but the one thing I can't stand, and I personally find this unforgivable, is the call girl/mistress/ex-lover selling his/her story to the tabloids. I'm sorry, when two people have been as physically imitate as it's possible to be, I don't care whether they had sex out of love or money, but blowing the story to the lowest form of media for money makes the whistle blower the scum of the earth in my eyes.

I am the father of a famous daughter yet telling stories about her is the furthest thing from my mind. How could I jeopardize our relationship for cash? These people are scum. I was also a mini cab driver for a few years in the 90s and again some well-known personalities in my cab revealed personal secrets as I was their regular driver, but no amount of money would induce me to talk. And I could do with the money a hell of a lot more than more of these squealers. Scum.

Today we hired a car for 24 hours and drove round the two islands, Huahine-Nui and Huahine-Iti (Big Huahine and Little Huahine) connected by a bridge. Found this restaurant overlooking the sea and ate our first traditional Tahitian meal where the food is cooked in a "hima'a", a man made pit filled with hot coals under the ground. With a table for two right by the water's edge this was truly heaven on earth. Again I had to pinch myself that I was actually here, doing "stuff", sat next to people who I suspected did "stuff" all the time.

"It not be for the likes of me." and "I know my place."

How gloriously wrong I can be.As always, life is a balance between yin and yang, so when they presented us with the bill the zeros stabbed at my conscience as well as my wallet. I'd allowed for so much but not SO much. Ah, well. We only live once I suppose.

WEDNESDAY 8 SEPTEMBER HUAHINE, FRENCH POLYNESIA

We woke up to the sound of the wind and rain howling outside our window.

"Great.", I thought. "Fucking great. We can't cancel our boat trip but this is all I fucking need."

I loved the programme, "Trawlermen" on BBC 1. Having been Advertisement Manager for an international fisheries magazine in the '80s while living in Brittany, I knew how tough these men have to be just to survive, let alone earn a living from the cruel seas that no man or woman in their right mind would voluntarily leave the safety of dry land for. Even the camera crew deserve a special mention for their courage in filming in a Force 8 or 9 gale in the North Sea.

At the other end of the spectrum is... me. Getting in and out of the bath can sometimes make me feel queasy, so the thought of spending a whole day on a little pirogue in an area of the South Pacific prone to cyclones every so often didn't fill my heart or shorts full of good cheer.

But a promise is a promise so we duly met our guide outside Chez Guynette at 09.00. But not before we had phoned home to find out how Lilyella's first day at senior school in Hampstead had gone. She was upstairs playing with a friend when we called, which was obviously more important, so Melanie filled us in. Everything had gone well so we were all relieved.

Lighter of heart but still nervous of bottom, we took a 4 x 4 to a little port where our pirogue and two other couples were waiting. A French Polynesian pirogue, by the way, is like a super slick, long thin canoe or kayak, with a thinner balancing arm all along the left hand side. Many are used in races in October, when crews from numerous South Sea Islands converge on Huahine for the annual tournament. Very colourful and passionate it is too. Pity we won't be here to witness the events.

We pushed off from the quayside and sped around the coast. All the land was so lush and green, simply bursting with good health. Our first stop was at a pearl farm in the middle of the bay. Such a seductive setting for lowering the defences around my wallet. But I held firm and none of the overpriced black pearls found their way into our luggage.

The couple running it though were living Hélène's dream. A young Californian male had met and married a local girl and left the rat race to enter the pearl jam, competing with locals for this lucrative sector of the jewellery trade. To combat the daily threat of mosquitoes that descend in the late afternoon on land, they had built their own house in the middle of the bay and their workshop a 100 metre pirogue ride away.

Their business had grown to include pottery and even their eight year old son was helping with the designs. Hélène's utopia, if only this land lubbing United fanatic could change his ways. Don't hold your breath.

I'd love to fit Hélène's idea of a knight in shining amour, but it ain't gonna happen. I do feel bad about it though. Sometimes. I don't know what attributes she saw in me all those years ago, but her "womens' intuition" was surely misfiring in our early years if she thought I'd develop into some kind of super do-it-yourself hero that could fend for himself and support a wife and kids a la Swiss Family Robinson.

I read some time ago that when a woman first meets a man she loves, she thinks she will be able to change him over the years, whereas when a man first meets a woman he loves, he hopes she will stay the same for the rest of their lives together. Whoops.

I've surely been a bitter (not blue) disappointment to her ever since she realised "it ain't gonna happen" happened. Don't get me wrong. We've both made sacrifices and compromises in the course of our (I believe she'd agree) successful relationship, but dreams have to be based on some form of realism. To realistically expect me to give up Manchester United like Adam was prepared to sacrifice his own son, Issac, is one parallel too far. I'm sorry, Adam's religion doesn't hold a candle to mine. Mine is stronger, all powerful and all consuming.

United I stand and United I fall.

Now, where was I?

Ah, yes. Shark feeding. The highlight of our local excursion was to witness shark feeding with us actually in the water as they raced towards us, consumed by nature's instinct to create a feeding frenzy. The sharks that is, not us. Hélène and I held onto a rope that was strung out just below the surface and floated about as the sharks and other large, intensely multi-coloured exotic creatures (no, I'm not doing that joke. It'd be a little too obvious, even for me) zoomed by, first one way then another, as a local fisherman threw their supper in the water right next to us.

Hélène was genuinely worried that the sharks would consider us a tasty morsel, but I held onto the belief that if they allowed us to be in the water at the same time as the sharks, surely they must know that we would be safe. On the other hand, we've all read stories of things going wrong, especially in less well-developed tourist areas, so it certainly provided an edge to proceedings. They say sharks have very poor eyesight. I just hoped their instincts could differentiate between tuna and tourist.

No worries. Our front rope seat allowed us to get up close and personal as this real life extravaganza played out literally inches before our very eyes. We were encouraged to stretch out and touch the fish as they swam by, as they were oblivious to our charms in their all-consuming quest for food.

What a wonderful end to the day. No fish or humans were hurt in the writing of this episode, and all except the bait lived to fight another day.

Once back in our room I couldn't wait to post a brief description on Facebook, to be immediately contacted by David Diley, my "officetoocean" shark filming and conservation United buddy, who claimed he almost choked on his own vomit as jealousy filled his reading eyes. But don't worry, dear reader, as 2011 was to see David realise his dream in the most remarkable fashion. But more of that later.

Melanie confirmed that our Villa in Tulum, Mexico has been secured for Christmas and New Year, the owner agreeing to a lower deposit. Yay! Let's have more days like this, please.

SATURDAY 11 SEPTEMBER PAEA, TAHITI, FRENCH POLYNESIA
EVERTON 3 MANCHESTER UNITED 3

Back in Tahiti, the internet connection was down all day. My fucking luck, so there was no way I could catch the Everton game. In the tiny village of Paea, asking for an internet café was like asking for snow. It just didn't exist.

Physically I enjoyed my surroundings but my mind was thousands of miles away on Merseydive. I went through the motions of eating, talking, swimming and sunbathing (not a bad alternative when all's said and done), treading water, until I finally got connected in the evening.

Right, straight to BBC Sport for the result.

3-3

First reaction? Oh well.

Then I read the opening paragraph: "Everton stage stunning comeback to score twice in injury time to deprive Manchester United victory after Sir Alex Ferguson dropped Wayne Rooney for his comeback to Goodison Park"

Second reaction? WTF!!

My anger and frustration knew no bounds. I didn't know what to be angry about first, the giving away of two injury time goals or the dropping of Rooney. I was a conflict of emotional spasms. Grrr!!! Talk about clutching draws from the jaws of victory. First Fulham and now this. The script is meant to read, "United score. They always score." not the other way round.

Well, one thing's for certain this season. We're gonna win nowt with a defence like this. I put my brain into crisis management mode. What's the worse that could happen? Surely we'd finish within the top four so guarantee qualification for the Champions League. And, hopefully, Fergie and his backroom staff will iron out our defensive frailties in time for a good cup run.

I checked further. Both Chelsea and Arsenal had won. After only four matches we were already four points behind the leaders Chelsea who were also ten goals better off on goal difference.

Looks like number 19 will have to wait for another season at least. Last season, if it hadn't been for that atrocious Drogba offside goal at Old Trafford we'd have been champions. Now we seem to have gone backwards and, 10,000 miles away, there was little I could do to affect proceedings.

I shall have to bury myself in paradise and hope things look better when I wake up in the morning.

EASTER ISLAND

MONDAY 13 SEPTEMBER PAPEETE, TAHITI - EASTER ISLAND

From Papeete airport I phoned best Red mate, Mick Shenton in Southampton, using the remaining credits on my Tahitian phone card. After ages hanging around we had an uneventful flight to what is claimed to be the most remote inhabited island in the world - Easter Island (Rapa Nui). The usual suspects of hostel reps touting for business greeted us as we exited the small customs hall/baggage claim with our rucksacks. However we'd made our minds up to go with a hostel recommended by a young, ginger haired Swiss lad we'd met in Tahiti and Moorea. Turned out the first desk at the airport was the said hostel. We must have been the easiest sale this woman had ever made. £50 a night for a private double room wasn't cheap but is the going rate on Easter Island, and at least it included what turned out to be a substantial breakfast.

Driving in her rickety car along pot-holed streets the place looked pretty run down compared to the idyllic beauty of French Polynesia. It could well have been the end of the world. It was also noticeably cooler. The buildings we passed reminded me of a western with simple wooden housing on either side. The hostel was located a 20 minute walk outside of Hanga Roa, the main town, in an elevated position that gave out views over the cemetery to the sea in the distance from the terrace of our little hut.

And there, in the distance to our right, was our first sight of a line of the world famous extant monumental statues, or "Moai" to you and me. I have to admit to another Kleenex moment as another of my life's ambitions came to fruition. I couldn't wait. I literally couldn't wait to get up close and personal with these iconic figures that had captured my imagination when I first set my eyes on photographs in my children's encyclopaedia all those decades ago.

Waiting for us (or so it seemed) was the owner's Alsatian, which acted as our personal guard cum guide for the duration of our stay. It followed us everywhere we went, and curled up on our terrace whenever we went inside our hut.

It led the way for our first excursion into town, past the rough and ready playing field which doubles up as the national football stadium, and on to the small harbour. A fisherman was cutting up some rather large fish and throwing bits back in the sea. There seemed to be a commotion in the water. We looked more closely and we were greeted by the sight of three giant turtles squabbling over scraps.

Giant turtles! Here! Amazing.

Giant turtles on Easter Island are a lot like London buses. You wait a lifetime and then 3 come along at once. This was another one to cross off the list. We stood and stared at this free spectacle, spellbound by seeing these marvellous creatures in their natural habitat. An everyday occurrence for the locals but a lifetime achievement award for me.

Finally we tore ourselves away from the scene and went across the road to a little café recommended in Lonely Planet as having home-made ice cream to die for. I don't know what type of homes it was made from but it tasted exquisite. Accompanied by banoffee pie, a superb banana and gooey caramel cake I was in heaven… and still alive!

TUESDAY 14 SEPTEMBER EASTER ISLAND
MANCHESTER UNITED 0 GLASGOW RANGERS 0. CHAMPIONS LEAGUE

With Easter Island being six hours behind the UK, our Champions League home tie against Glasgow Rangers was fighting a losing battle with the once-in-a-lifetime opportunity to see one of the true wonders of the world. I was a conflict of contradictory emotions as I'd set myself the goal of not missing a single "important" United match in this incredible calendar year. Of course, "important" is subjective. First of all, this was a group match, which meant that it was unlikely to provide edge of the seat thrills and spills. I mean, we're talking Glasgow Rangers, hardly silky smooth football, right? Secondly, even if we weren't up for it and gave a below par performance against second rate opposition, there would be opportunities to rectify the situation in future group matches. On paper, any sensible person would choose Easter Island without a moment's hesitation. I'm not sensible so I wrestled with this dilemma as I went to bed, yet knowing in my heart it was really a no-contest. Easter Island 1, Manchester United didn't.

Boy, did I make the right decision. Back at our hut I switched on my laptop and it made for depressing reading. I feel sorry for you lot who travelled up midweek. Seems like Rooney was invisible in the aftermath of his off field exploits and with ten changes, no wonder we were so ineffective. How many times has Fergie made wholesale changes and they've failed to come off? That's certainly one of his Achilles heels. When I read that Gibson's long range efforts were our best chances that said it all. And to make matters worse, Valencia was stretchered off with a serious leg injury. Oh, well. As D-Ream once sang, "Things Can Only Get Better"

WEDNESDAY 15 SEPTEMBER EASTER ISLAND

Pre-hired the cheapest, dirtiest 4 x 4 I could find for a tour of island and as many of its 887 Moai created by the early Rapanui people. The day I thought would never come to fruition was coming to fruition. With Hélène taking responsibility for the route via our tourist map we set off for the Orango Ceremonial Village from where we walked halfway round the almost perfectly formed circular volcanic cinder cone called Rano Kau Crater Lake.

Birds swooped down as we watched, skimming the surface looking for fish.

We then took the east coast road with rugged scenery on both sides. Quite a contrast to the lush backdrop of French Polynesia. Not beautiful in the exotic long haul holiday brochure sense but in a natural weather-beaten way that would appeal to people at one with nature and like keeping it real. And Bill Oddie.

We could see many Moai dotted on the hills as we arrived at the Ranu Raraku National Park, the biggest and most valuable archaeological site on the island with 397 moai in various forms of construction. It was a quarry for about 500 years until the 18th century and supplied stone from which around 95% of the moai were carved. Unreal. These weren't in a line but spread all over the place. We settled on a dry over-priced dogburger from a van parked outside before entering this sacred place.

One word of warning though. Entrance ticket for the two largest sites is US$60 per person so it's not cheap. But to be fair, the rest of the sites on the island are free. There were marked paths that you're not meant to stray from, but, hey, we were only going to be here once in our lifetime so a little diversion and silly posing was in order. Those that followed our travels on Facebook will have seen my little whimsies, with my protruding nose an exact replica from one the natives had made earlier.

Next we came to a row of moai on the coast road, with their faces facing inland and not out to sea. No satisfactory explanation in our guide book, but an Eric given opportunity to pose on a piece of raised turf in front of them that gave the illusion that Hélène and I were standing alongside them. If I tell you a picture is worth a thousand words, then please believe me when I tell you it actually looks quite funny. My caption on facebook read "United's rock solid starting XI".

Well, it seemed funny at the time.

WEDNESDAY 15 SEPTEMBER EASTER ISLAND

Today we decided to walk round the island in the other direction. Came across members of the indigenous Hitorangi clan occupying the deserted Hangaroa Eco Village and Spa which had slogans sprayed outside, on its walls and on banners. The Hitorangi allege that the hotel had been bought from the Pinochet government in violation of a Chilean agreement with the indigenous Rapa Nui in the 1990s. They claimed their ancestors had been cheated into giving up the land.

What's new? Join the long queue, local lads and lasses. History is littered with Imperialistic violation of human rights, of invaders seizing lands and assets and reducing indigenous populations to slaves or second class citizens in their own land.

They were extremely friendly and invited us in. A young American girl greeted us and explained the situation. She was helping their cause by spreading the word to the outside world. I contributed a few suggestions and Hélène and I promised to do our bit once we had internet connection ourselves.

I looked around. This was obviously intended to be an up-market hotel for the more affluent traveller. It looked odd, seeing natives dressed in original costume inhabiting the concrete, glass and internal plastic set aside for the American Express brigade. Their naivety was attractive but I knew it would only be a matter of time before the authorities would instigate dawn raids to evict their embarrassing rebels.

(Later on I read a BBC report on December 3, 2010, that at least 25 people had been injured when Chilean police using pellet guns when attempting to evict them from these buildings. The occupation finally ended in February 2011, when up to 50 armed police broke into the hotel to remove the final five occupiers. They were arrested by the government and no injuries were "reported".)

We said our goodbyes. Lots of hugs and wishes of good luck. Fight the good fight, etc…

After lunch we continued our walk, then took a break by lying on the grass. I rested my head on a stone that turned out to be decaying horse shit that was being devoured by ants.

Aahh!

Back at our hut, armed with drinks on our veranda, we began talking with the quiet couple from our first day on Easter Island, who turned out to be really nice, just shy. They were doing a similar trip to us. Both had left respective jobs and flats. He was Australian and she was French, from Lille, which gave me the opportunity to regail them with my United adventure a couple of years back when United had played Lille in the Last 16 knockout stage of the Champions League.

CRS, tear gas, Ryan's crafty winning free kick when the French team weren't looking. How I kept them awake I'll never know, but I enjoyed my little reminiscing.

CHILE

THURSDAY 16 SEPTEMBER EASTER ISLAND – SANTIAGO, CHILE

We were met, early evening, at Santiago Airport by Andres & Jenny, the lovely couple we first met in our camp site in Moorea, but not before I'd gone down to the café by the port in Easter Island for ANOTHER Banofee pie and home-made ice cream. My philosophy – it's it's worth doing, it's worth overdoing.

Easter Island, we'll never forget you. Moai is another day. As we left the Santiago airport the cloudless sky was a glowing pinky purple with the dark, brooding backdrop of the Andes in the distance.

The Andes. That means we've arrived in South America. South America! Like, Wow, man! (cue Neil from The Young Ones).

I stared out of the window as we made our way into the centre of Santiago. So this is South America. It looked… just like any other city in any other country. I was searching for images of South America without knowing exactly what I was looking for. To be honest, it could have been anywhere.

In fact, only six months before Santiago had been rocked by a powerful earthquake, yet you wouldn't have known it from the buildings we passed. Investment in quality construction had paid dividends as virtually all of them had withstood tremors that consistently flatten whole communities in places like Haiti, where corners are cut and regulations openly flouted. What's the loss of thousands of lives compared to the fortunes that can be earned by the villainous leeches in power? Nuff said.

Andres found our B&B in a quiet, well-to-do suburb not far from the city centre. It was a nice house run by a genteel old lady and her single, balding middle aged son. Large rooms with dark period furniture, I felt like I had gone back in time. No wi-fi in our room, only in public areas.

Hmm. Bit of a grind that, as our next match is home to Liverpool and kick-off is at 08.30 in the morning, Chilean time. I noticed they had a computer for guests in the breakfast room. With the problems I'd been experiencing so far with streaming on my laptop, I felt an early breakfast would be called for tomorrow.

SATURDAY 18 SEPTEMBER SANTIAGO, CHILE

Today was the 200th anniversary of Chile's independence from Spanish rule and there was going to be a big concert in the national football stadium today with the cream of Chilean musicians and singers performing for our delight.

Music and football, not a bad combination.

I'd gone through the list of artistes on the official web site and I can safely say I didn't recognize any of them. Nevertheless it was an opportunity to witness Chileans at play, take a conducted tour of the national football stadium and grab some culture on the way. We made our way to what I had worked out was the nearest metro station to the stadium, but it was still a good (or bad, depending on your point of view) 25 minute walk away. I commented to Hélène that there didn't seem to be many people on the street, and you'd have expected the area to be heaving.

Something didn't quite add up, but as we were within walking distance it seemed foolish to turn back now. It was bloody hot, so we stopped at a refreshment kiosk on the way, and whilst paying well over the odds for a couple of cold drinks, we asked the thieving bastard who sold us our drinks why there were so few people.

"Today, President speak. Tomorrow, celebration."

Fuck. We'd (that is to say… I'd) got it wrong.

Immediately the alarm bells began to ring. Tomorrow United were playing at home to Liverpool and there was NO WAY I'd be missing that. Then the moment passed as I felt sure the festivities wouldn't start till around lunchtime at the earliest and kick off was 08.30 Chilean time.

Phew! That was close. I could now have the best of both worlds. Oh yeah? I hadn't allowed for the other half to throw a spanner in the works. We made our way to the stadium proper and asked one of the security guards on the gate where we could buy tickets. He pointed in a general direction and said something that included the words "9 o' clock."

Coming away we attempted to decipher what the security guard had said.

"Tickets go on sale at 09.00 tomorrow morning." was Hélène's interpretation. However, as an English teacher to foreign students, I am well aware that one word in a whole sentence could change the meaning significantly.

"FROM 09.00, not AT 09.00." I replied.

"No. AT 09.00."

"Hélène, think about it. That's not logical. It means they start selling them at 09.00 sharp, and then what, stop selling them at 09.01?"

"I'm just repeating what the man said."

"No, Hélène, you're just repeating what you thought he said, but don't you see? Taken literally, it's not possible. They can't sell tickets at 09.00 exactly. It has to be 'from'. Anyway, it's just your interpretation of what he said. Neither of us can be sure."

"Either way, we have to be here at 09.00am if we want to have a chance of a ticket."

"That's out of the question. If you remember, I've arranged with Max (the son and co-owner of the hostel) that I'll be watching United v Liverpool on their desk top computer."

"You and your bloody football! What time does it finish?"

"Around 10.30."

"Well, if we get there and all the tickets have sold out it'll be your fault."

"But Hélène, don't you see. The guy must mean 'from' 09.00."

"I'm just saying. If it's sold out it's your fault. You and your bloody football. We've come halfway round the world, and it was YOUR idea to see this concert in the first place."

"I know. I know. But how was I to know it would clash with the Liverpool match?"

"All I'm saying is......"

"Yes. I heard you. For fucks sake..."

The rest of the walk back to the metro was in stony silence.

SUNDAY 19 SEPTEMBER SANTIAGO, CHILE
MANCHESTER UNITED 3 LIVERPOOL 2

Despite not being able to reset Hélène's mobile to Chilean time, I was still able to set the alarm and wake up at 07.30 as the match was scheduled to start at 08.30 local time.

I duly padded round to Hélène's side of the bed and whispered as gently as possible:

"Do you want to wake up and have breakfast with me downstairs?"

"What time is it?"

"07.30."

Let's just say she declined my offer so I got dressed and made my way downstairs. Normally Hélène and I are the last ones to come down, which means we have our breakfast in peace, but at this time a motley Spanish speaking weekend ensemble was gathered around the large wooden table. And no-one spoke a word of English, whilst my Spanish consisted of Futbol (football), Hola (hello), Adios (goodbye), Buenos Dias (good morning), Buenos Tardes (good afternoon), Buenos Noches (good evening), Hasta Luego (see you later), Si (yes), No (no), Por favor (please), Gracias (Thank you), No Entiendo (I don't understand), Banco (bank), Centro (centre), Quanta Costa? (how much?) and Es Muy Caro (that's too expensive). Oh yes, most of the numbers between 1 – 10 and Spanish teams in La Liga..

Your almost impressed I can tell, but this was still not enough to hold a conversation first thing in the morning with native Spanish speakers chatting at 100 words per minute. I smiled politely, nodded my head and mumbled the best I could, desperately wishing they would become discouraged at my inability to interpret even the most basic of sentences.

Hélène is much better at this sort of stuff than me. With French as her mother tongue, the Latin base makes it easier for her to work out what Spanish, Portuguese and Italians are saying, whereas my Anglo Saxon base, coupled with my total inability to pick up foreign languages (I call it my ineptitude) puts me at a distinct disadvantage.

Eventually they left me to my own devices, so I scoffed down my breakfast before asking the mother of the house if she could switch on the internet. Although a little surprised at my early request, she barely flickered an eyelid and unlocked the cupboard next to the computer and switched it on.

There were surprisingly few e-mails for either Hélène or me, so I clicked on free-football.tv, logged in the members area and chose our match from the myriad on view.

"Which channel?" I asked myself, remembering the sickening episodes surrounding the Fulham game where I missed half the match and all four goals. Well, on only my second try, the disjointed figures of the players came on screen, less 30 seconds for the obligatory advert.

By now it was fifteen minutes into the game and the score still 0-0. United were playing by far the better looking football, as Liverpool continued where they left off last season, with short boring passes reminiscent of Chelsea but without any goals to show for it.

Fergie and I were both incensed when Nani was elbowed in the face on the blind side of the referee and his assistant during another of our flowing moves. A flash reveals 5 attempts on goal by United and zero by Liverpool. Typical.

Forty minutes into the game Hélène comes down for breakfast. I acknowledge her presence without taking my eye off the ball, then realised we could go in at half time scoreless despite our superiority in all things football. Then a cross comes over and Berbatov directs his header powerfully into the scousers' net. I'd promised Hélène I wouldn't make a noise. So I didn't. I just stood up and did silent speeded up windmill impersonations for a full two minutes.

Half time I was a much relieved man. Even more so as I went to the loo, something I had forgotten to do before leaving our bedroom in my excitement to go online.

A second cup of tea and a banana yoghurt later the players came out for the second half. The cameras picked out Rooney and Torres shaking hands as they lined up which I thought was a nice touch all things considered.

"Did you see that, Hélène. Rooney and Torres shaking hands? Nice touch."

"That little shit!"

"Why? What have you got against Torres?"

"No, Rooney."

"Oh. I see." (he he!)

Having finished breakfast, Hélène said she was going up to wash some clothes. Well, if that turns her on as much as United turns me on, who am I to stop her? Left alone in the breakfast room, I was now free to express myself more creatively, although with my own volume stuck at nought. The second half was only a few minutes old when Berbatov attempted a Denis Law type back-to-goal scissor kick and............

GOOOOOAAAAAAAALLL!

An even louder silent scream as my face contorted and my arms fired like pistons. I recovered in time to see the replay, only to piss myself at Giggs's expression which said quite clearly: "Fucking hell. How the fuck did he do that? Fucking magic!"

Of course, I have no means of verifying whether Ryan used as many expletives as me, but the look on his face was a joy to behold.

United were now rampant, but then so was Howard Webb, the referee. He began to book one United player after another, finally awarding Liverpool a penalty. (It was a penalty, but don't tell any United fans I thought so.)

Gerrard scores and it's now back to 2-1.

We're still on top and playing much the better football but the referee was adamant Liverpool deserved all the breaks going. John O'Shea was judged to have fouled Johnson just outside our penalty box. Who should take it but the one and only camera kissing Steven Gerrard. He didn't let us down. An admittedly excellent free kick went in low at the corner making the score 2-2 and queue Gerrard giving the camera tongues, larynx, teeth, gums and throat. Scouse Bastard!

For fucks sake, United! Get a grip! Don't let the scousers or Howard Webb get to you. You're better than all of them. Better skills, better character, better football.

Remember, the best form of defence is attack. Attack. Attack. Attack Attack Attack!

And that, my friends, is exactly what we did. And for once justice was done. Cometh the 85th minute cometh the man. Another cross and

Berbatov comes of age by powering another glorious header into the scousers' net and earning a United career defining hat-trick and there's no way back for the vermin.

Gerrard's OTT celebrations stuffed down his tongue, larynx, teeth, gums and throat. Even with no sound on the computer, I could just imagine Old Trafford rocking and I was rocking silently with them in my Santiago hostel. By this time I had cleared the breakfast room and I was free to stand up for the ex-champions. The highly polished wooden floor amplified my erratic celebrations until the final whistle brought about the creeping reality of a day at the national stadium celebrating Chile's 200 years of independence from Spain.

I bounded upstairs, washed, and within half an hour we were on our way. Me with a murderers grin on my face, renewed hope in my heart and something hot in the Thermos flask, 'cos the temperature here doesn't half drop something rotten at night.

At the Chilean National Football Stadium we purchased two tickets within a minute of our arrival. So, I had been right all along (a rarity, but I'll revel in the afterglow of victory and rub it in as childishly as I can get away with). There were all sorts of stalls surrounding the stadium but the stadium itself was closed.

Damn. I wanted to have a look around. Just like a train spotter, I wanted to tick another one off the list. I did a circumference of the stadium, looking for an unofficial opening. Then Hélène spied a couple entering by a pair of temporarily opened double doors and we slipped in behind them, following them up flights of stairs as though we had every right to be there.

Found ourselves outside the security room with wall to wall monitors and a uniformed jobsworth sitting at a central console. I tapped gently on the window pane. He slowly rose from his chair, came over and opened the door. I could see a section of the pitch below from behind his dandruff.

"Habla Ingles?" I enquired

"Grunt." Followed by a stream of Chilean Spanish which left us in no doubt that our presence wasn't welcome and we should run away in small jumps, immediately. He locked up and followed us downstairs to make sure we didn't sneak off in another direction. Perish the thought.

Outside once more I thought, "Fuck it.", let's just enjoy the day. I'm wearing my Green & Gold, I'd already spotted a number of locals in various Chilean club shirts as well as the national team colours. Surely I'd find the odd ex-pat or Brit on vacation and partake in a little banter. None whatsoever, which was a disappointment. With the warm glow of victory over the vermin still surging through my veins I was dying to take it out on someone. As Hélène and I did a slow circuit around the perimeter of the stadium I kept an eye out for any British football shirts. Nothing.

In the end we found a stage with rows of seats in front and decided this was where the musical festivities would take place. Once settled along the side Hélène sent me to find some food. I wandered alone around the stadium, this time 100% focused on British football shirts and an appropriate place to adhere some LUHG stickers. A large, blue, double-doored entrance to the stadium proper was selected and LUHG sticker number 51 was duly given pride of place.

I stayed behind for a few moments to see if my efforts had mobilised the natives.

Eerr…no.

Oh, well.

Still no British football shirts so I chose one of the food queues and began the long, slow, stop start shuffle. A good 45 minutes later I was only three people from the front when this tall black American, who had been impressively switching between English and Spanish the whole time, turned to me and said,

"Where's your ticket?"

Cold daggers in my stomach.

"What ticket?"

"You need to buy a ticket from that booth over there, then exchange it for whatever you want to eat."

Fuck!

"Don't worry. I'll hold your place, but be quick."

I thanked him profusely. I'd been dying to join in his conversation with a mixed group of boys and beautiful girls but hadn't found a way to worm my way in, and now they all saw this "Inbetweener" type novice with no clue as to how the system worked, and not a word of Spanish.

I rushed over to this new, but thankfully shorter queue, bought what I hoped to be two correctly priced tickets and rejoined my original queue. When it came to my turn, even after 45 minutes I still hadn't made my mind up, so I chose two different pies with "queso" (cheese) in them.

Armed with these piping hot spoils of war I made my way back to Hélène who genuinely thought I'd got lost, that's how long I'd been away. The rest of the afternoon was spent watching a selection of traditional Chilean folk groups and singers in national costume. Some entertaining, some not.

Topping the bill was this aging Shirley Bassey look and sound alike, but without the voice. Her dress was something out of Sunday Night at the London Palladium circa 1972. By the way the nationalistic crowd responded to some of her songs, she was obviously the Chilean Mireille Mathieu. She put on a real old fashioned cabaret type act which the audience, whose average age was well over one hundred, lapped up.

Let's just say this was the type of entertainment my parents used to enjoy, and even though I am now a grandparent myself it still sounded as naff as it did when I was a child. On the way out, another plea to redistribute my liquid assets led to the stadium's nearest men's loo and LUHG sticker number 52. 48 to go.

TUESDAY 22 SEPTEMBER VALPERISO, CHILE

Our hostel was high up in one of the safe favelas. You know, those shanty towns which started on the hills outside Rio de Janeiro in the 1800s where former slaves with no land ownership and no options for work lived, and can now be found in many cities throughout South America. We were told there was only one place in Valparaiso not safe to wander round and that was the favela above the port. So we didn't.

Didn't stop three grown up French students from our hostel ignoring the warnings though and getting mugged. All their flash camera equipment gone in 60 seconds. What's French for Twats?

One of the few proverbs I'll subscribe to, and it works for many situations is, "if you fail to prepare, prepare to fail." This is certainly true when it comes to travel. There are many clichés surrounding South America and one of them is the rampant lawlessness.

This is simply not the case. There are certainly no-go areas but with a little homework you can travel safely throughout the continent. So why ignore simple advice?

Favelas offer amazing views. Hélène and I worked out a route circumventing the circumference of the semi circular suburbs, each turn offering new and spectacular views over the bay. We reached one square when I spotted a group of smart, young, short haired, white American men and women. Some of the men were wearing short sleeve shirts and ties. They all had earlobes.

"Christian bible bashers!" I muttered. Had to be. I'd muttered correctly.

A young, well scrubbed couple made their way over to where Hélène and I were enjoying a quiet moment in the shade. The young man opened his mouth and spoke in perfectly polite American English, introducing himself and his wife/ girlfriend/fellow bible basher? Take your pick. I responded politely in English English thinking, "I could have a little fun here."

Normally when people like these confront you on the street, or worse, at home, I usually tell them to kindly run away in small jumps. One couple even had the temerity to knock on my door one night during the week when United were live on the telly and there had been no way, as a Cockney Red, I could have got time off work for that particular game. How I restrained myself I'll never know. I'm not normally an "effing and blinding" sort 'o guy. I just uttered a one word retort and retreated back inside.

Many older Reds will remember throughout the 60s and 70s this thin, Charles Hawtrey look-a-like dressed in a black mackintosh and bowler hat, whatever the weather, standing near the top of Sir Matt Busby Way. He held a placard proclaiming the end of the world if we don't repent and allow Jesus into our hearts (or something like that. Time plays funny tricks with the memory. I was only saying yesterday to…oh… you know……….oh, yes, the wife…)

But today we had all the time in the world. A little gentle, non football banter might while away a pleasant few minutes, and give me a chance to converse for the first time with Stepford Wankers and their earnest, brain washed rhetoric.

After almost thirty seconds of pleasantries the young man inevitably brought God into the conversation, which gave me the ideal opportunity to bring Eric into mine. Having never encountered a response like mine before, the look on their healthily scrubbed faces was a joy for a cynic like me to behold.

I then began to draw on my sermon, which was basically to let them down gently with the knowledge that God, (their God BTW) didn't actually exist. A concept I knew they would find hard to accept. We then went through all the usual arguments for and against (I don't need to list them all here. As a devout, practising atheist you can quite accurately predict mine) with me proclaiming that religion, all religions, were responsible for more wars, deaths, suffering and poverty than the Mafia, Hitler, Pol Pot and the West's insatiable pursuit of the world's natural resources at the expense of third world countries, put together.

OK, I admit it. I got a little carried away there. I know I said in the previous paragraph that "I don't need to list them". Well, I lied.

The nice thing was though, these people were so used to aggressive confrontations that to have a civilized conversation with two people of opposing views, without the need to resort to words beginning with "F" or "C" and finishing with "off" must have been like a breath of fresh air. Many of my piss-takes went over their heads (remember, Americans have little or no sense of irony) and I was enjoying myself immensely. Hélène didn't know whether to laugh or scold me for going too far, but I'd waited years for a moment like this and I was relishing every thrust, every parry, and without Nicky Campbell rudely interrupting.

They came out with every cliché in the book (I take that to be the Bible) and obviously didn't get my references to United as THE religion, Eric's Disciples on Earth, Bobby, George & Denis as the three wise men, Sir Matt Busby and Sir Alex Ferguson as God, his son and the Theatre of Dreams. I was on a roll and came out with every joke and piss-take you can imagine, whilst making serious points along the way. We parted on good terms, both sides having enjoyed the cut and thrust of a good debate.

I'd love to know what they said about us to their colleagues.

THURSDAY 24 SEPTEMBER VINA DEL MAR, CHILE
SCUNTHORPE UNITED 2 MANCHESTER UNITED 5 CARLING CUP

Took longer to leave the hostel this morning as we talked to a cool Chilean guy who was studying philosophy and we discussed life, the universe, and why there are no jobs for philosophers advertised in the Jobs Vacant columns. Just as we were preparing to leave, an Australian mother and daughter combo sat down opposite and we struck up another interesting conversation. I know it's wrong, but you can tell so much about people just by their appearance. With her short, silver grey hair and butch clothes, I could tell the mother was either a woman in comfortable shoes or a left wing activist.... or both.

She turned out to be a Socialist through and through, having returned to Oz from the UK a few years into the Thatcher era. Interesting woman. Would like to have spent longer chatting but Vina Del Mar was calling and it was getting on.

Hélène and I made our way down the hill to estation Bellavista and the 300 CLP trip round the industrial bay to Vina Del Mar. We started by the main park which certainly didn't live up to its Lonely Planet billing as one of the most beautiful parks in Chile. Perhaps the March earthquake was responsible for the restrictions in place but we saw all there was to see in an hour. Strolling down the main boulevard wasn't all that inspiring either, re-enforced by Hélène ear-bashing both my ears with insults relating to the fact I left our map of Vina Del Mar behind.

"How are we going to find all the beautiful colonial buildings I read about?" she exclaimed.

I'd noted down two eateries we just had to try. The first was called Entremasas at 333, 5 Norte which specialises in over forty different varieties of savoury pies, some of which are found nowhere else in Chile. A perfect choice for a low cost lunch I thought.

An additional benefit of its location was the fact we had to walk along the raised sea front overlooking the churning ocean cascading over jagged black rocks below. And what had looked like dark oversized seagulls from a distance turned out on closer inspection to be pelicans. Hundreds of them. On the rocks and swooping low over the waves looking for fish washed up by the strong currents. My first view outside of a zoo of this elegant bird in its natural habitat. Impressive.

As we strolled down the street, looking out for number 377, a vision came walking towards me. A United logo adorning this garish reddish striped polyester top that only the megastore would have the nerve to sell.

"Don't you dare!" hissed Hélène as I tried to work out how to greet this young man.

I dared.

"U-NI-TED!" I cried, whilst maintaining a welcoming smile.

An initial look of confusion gave way to a wide (almost said 'massive' there. Phew! That was close) grin as the young man recognised the discreet United enamel badge on my black, V neck Marks & Spencer pullover as I thrust my left breast in his face. His English was good so we spent a pleasant sixty seconds before he made it clear he wanted to escape from this English nutter.

Every other café seemed to be a pie shop but I was not to be swayed. Entremasas was what I was looking for and Entremasas is what I found. It looked like all the other cafes, but the pies....mmmm....I forget the combination I ordered but if I could sell them down Sir Matt Busby Way I'd make a fortune.

Walked back towards the railway station but when I saw this posh hotel with people sitting outside on the terrace I just HAD to stop for another OTT ice cream and watch the pelicans swoop down on the fish in the bay. You should have seen the pastries on offer but ice cream took precedence. Wherever I am in the world I need my sugar rush.

Back at our hostel in Santiago I searched for our Carling Cup result. After blowing hot and cold in the league, I couldn't give a flying fig leaf about the least important competition our first team is involved in, although as the whole world knows, we use the Carling Cup as a stepping stone for some of our younger players. It's nice to win it, of course, as we had done the past two seasons, but for season ticket holders to be forced by the Gimps to pay for a ticket through the Automatic Cup Scheme sticks in the throat.

Well well well. Father Christmas has come early this year.

United survive an early shock opener by the home team before running out 5-2 winners. But that's not the end of the story. Much chortling was to be heard as I read that City lose away to West Brom, Chelsea lose at home to Newcastle and, hold my sides somebody, Liverpool lose at home to the mighty Cobblers of Northampton.

Ha Ha Ha, Ho Ho ho. Pity there's no-one about to share my joy. Thank Eric for Red News and Red Issue online.

"It's OK, dear. You go to bed. I've just got a couple of things to do…"

SUNDAY 26 SEPTEMBER. LA SERENA, CHILE.
BOLTON WANDERERS 2 MANCHESTER UNITED 2

The 05.45am alarm went off right next to my right ear and had the desired effect. I woke up with a start. Yesterday's results, with defeats for Chelsea away to the Bitters and Arsenal losing at home to WBA, had given me renewed optimism. Normally the Carling Cup can throw up mini shocks, but unlike the FA Cup this second rate cup competition is no barometer of league form, therefore more defeats for our nearest rivals in the Premiership had stirred something deeper within the Blatt psyche.

After a slow start, we could finally get into our stride and cut back Chelsea's lead. After all, the Premiership is a marathon not a sprint, and we shouldn't read too much into early results. However I have to admit our inferior goal difference is a worry. Despite the joy of last week's victory over Liverpool, we hadn't been scoring with free flowing football and our defence was causing my underwear to change colour with alarming regularity. Two seasons ago the Ferdinand - Vidic partnership was rock solid. Since then, injuries and loss of form had made us vulnerable at the back and Johnny Evans was beginning to look out of his depth.

Let's hope last week was the turning point and the season starts here. A moment's hesitation later and I was out of bed and putting on every layer of clothing I could find, including my new, funky RipCurl ski style hat that a man of my age should have stopped wearing years ago. I quietly opened the door and, without waking "her" up, stepped outside into the open air corridor. At the end on the right sat the hostel computer, still asleep with a tea towel over the CPU and monitor. Aah, bless.

"Now, how do I switch the bloody thing on?" I thought to myself, as my eyes adjusted to the darkness. I pressed numerous switches but to no avail. I felt along the front and came across a variety of slots, one so large it felt like a toaster, but still the bloody thing wouldn't turn itself on. I fucking hate computers.

Eventually I had the bright idea to have a feel around the back and, lo and behold, I found another switch. I switched it. Success!

A triangular blue glow emanated from the centre of the CPU and finally the mouse responded to the abuse I had inflicted on it and the screen came to life.

After what seemed like an age the desktop appeared and I clicked on Internet Explorer. Quick check of my e-mails then it was all systems www.free-football.tv

Member login went smoothly and I was in. Under Bolton v United was a list of around twenty channels, the first few all on Media Player.

I clicked on the first one. Standard screen with 30 seconds of advertising prior to the feed. Thirty seconds later... no feed. I waited. And waited. Experience has taught me you have to treat these channels extremely gently, as they are highly sensitive and take offence at the least sign of provocation and crash without warning. But you need a picture before a crash and I wasn't getting a picture.

"Brilliant!" I thought. "Par for the course. I'll have to go through the channels one by one until I find one with a picture."

I fucking hate computers.

It was now 06.10 and the match was ten minutes old. "Not again." I thought. "I'm not giving up. This is United we're talking about. I shall go beyond the call of duty. First let me just check the score on BBC Sport before I try again."

Now, let's see. Live videoprinter. "What's this? Live preview! Where's the score? Wait a minute… Fuck me! I've woken up one hour too early. No wonder I can't get a match feed. They only come on steam fifteen minutes before the game starts."

"Shit! Shit! Shit! Shit!"

What an idiot. I could have stayed in my warm bed for another hour.

Self loathing in a grown man is not attractive, but I gave myself one hell of a bollocking before surfing around to pass the time before the bewitching hour of 06.45 approached. There was very little traffic on either Red Issue or Red News fans forums as most contributors were at the game. News of the Screws wasn't very revealing and there was nothing to report on Facebook, whilst my head wasn't into anything too serious. And it was fucking freezing! So much for Chile's second oldest city having a "pleasant year-round" climate! Fucking brochure writers.

Eventually 06.45 arrived and I re-logged in to my steaming site. "What the fuck!"

It was happening all over again! Not one of the feeds was allowing the match to appear on the monitor. There could only be one explanation. The fucking computer didn't have Windows Media Player installed.

Why me!!!

Bastards!

There was only one thing for it. Two hours of BBC Sport two minute text only updates. What a wonderful way to spend a Sunday morning in chilly Chile, sitting in front of a computer in the freezing hallway of a hostel waiting desperately for news and scores whilst looking like Michelin man...with a ski cap.

By now almost half an hour had been played. The score came up. 1-1.

Shit!

OK, let's have a read...

"Lively start by United... Bolton open the scoring after only 6 minutes following a corner kick. What! What was our defence doing letting Zat Knight, that tall streak of liquorice, score with a shot barely six inches off the ground. Hmm, no Rio I see. Rested for Valencia away no doubt, but we need him now! Nani wonder goal. Beats three men before shooting home. That's more like it. Half time. 1-1.

OK, I'm going for a piss, although I daren't handle the crown jewels my fingers are like ice, and to see if Hélène is awake.

She was, and ready for breakfast.

"Just another forty five minutes to go, then we can eat together." I thought that was a fair offer in the circumstances.

"You've been gone for ages. Isn't the match finished yet?"

She's pretty sharp you have to agree. I could have sworn I left her fast asleep at 05.45am and it was now 07.45am. How did she know two hours had passed?

I couldn't think of an excuse so I told her the truth. I'd got up an hour too early. She didn't know whether to take this piss or laugh. She settled for a yawn and went back to sleep.

The second half didn't read any better. Our defence still sounded shaky and Rooney, who has only scored one goal so far this season, and that a penalty at home to West Ham, was substituted after 61 minutes by Macheda.

The vision of our first away win of the season receded somewhat when Bolton's Petrov scored the inbred's second. And there was nothing I could do. I felt hopeless in my darkened corridor with no means of affecting the result.

When the going gets tough, the tough get Owen. Sorry, I have been looking for ways of using that for ages and now seemed the time. With 20 minutes to go, the man who scored 2 goals in our midweek 5-2 victory in the Carling Cup, scored with a glancing header from a Nani free-kick.

Whatever people say about Michael Owen, he does know where the goal is, and this draw eats away slightly at Chelsea's lead. But I can't help feeling it was a missed opportunity that may come back to haunt us next May.

I didn't have time to thaw out 'cos no sooner had I got back into bed for a bit of warming slap and tickle, Hélène reminded me we had a 10.15 bus to catch to Pisco Elqui.

Now, for those of you that like gazing at the stars at night. (No, I don't mean reading Heat magazine in bed) Pisco Elqui has, reputedly, the clearest skies in the world. A two hour bus ride from La Serena, at 1,300 metres above sea level this Andean village in the beautiful Elqui Valley surrounded by vineyards and the magnificent mountain range of the Precordillera of the Andes is THE place to watch the sky at night. Many of the world's most famous scientific observatories are in this region.

I was told by Hostel El Teroso de Elqui that if we told the bus driver where we were staying he would drop us outside. He didn't. He dropped us at one end of the town square and we had to walk up this really steep road pulling our two giant and two normal rucksacks. Met Sam and Julie, the couple we first met on Easter Island at the top, finally found our hostel but it was deserted. Eventually Hélène found someone cleaning one of the rooms and we were given our key.

Lovely cabin with a partial glass roof to stargaze. That night we lay the wrong way round in bed to gaze up at the millions of stars, galaxies and constellations in the Southern Hemisphere. More stars than sky, or so it seemed. Absolutely spellbinding.

We looked at each other. The bed was no place to be. We put on a Michelin Man layer of clothes and went outside to sit in a couple of the deckchairs in the hostel ground and just stared for ages up at the sky.

Double Wow with knobs on. This is going to take some beating. Back in bed I finished my diary and turned off the light, but by this time the sky had been obscured by clouds. My luck.

TUESDAY 28 SEPTEMBER PISCO ELQUI, CHILE

Last night I made the earth move for Hélène. No, seriously. We were lying in bed when we heard and felt this deep low rumble all around us. At first I just thought it was a lorry thundering by, but the sound was too consistent and lasted too long. Couldn't have been me then. Hélène suggested that maybe it was an earthquake. No chance I thought.

The rumble lasted for more than five minutes before gradually dying away. We drifted back to sleep and thought nothing of it. In the morning we went down for breakfast and the usually jolly lady owner was strangely quiet. We mentioned the rumble we had felt during the night and she immediately said, "Earthquake."

Well she should know. The major earthquake six months previously had shaken more than just the buildings and she was genuinely nervous and not her normal self. She told us that many people now run for cover or go down into basements at the first tremor. My flippant remarks fell flat, unlike the buildings in Chile that remarkably showed little evidence of the natural disaster.

We had a lovely breakfast, then made our way to the bus station which, thankfully, was all downhill this time. By midday we were back in La Serena and just left our luggage in the bus station ready for our next overnight bus to San Pedro de Atacama, a town on the border with Bolivia.

WEDNESDAY 29 SEPTEMBER LA SERENA - SAN PEDRO DE ATACAMA, CHILE
VALENCIA 0 MANCHESTER UNITED 1

The curse of overnight coach travel meant that I never stood a chance of catching our opening away Champions League fixture. A disappointing home draw against Glasgow Rangers two weeks earlier had dampened my already lukewarm expectations brought about by our stuttering start to the season. My only consolation so far was that I had chosen the right year to travel round the world. United glory would just have to wait till I got back next year.

Sorry lads, I know it's my fault for pissing off and pissing you all off, but a man's gotta do what a man's gotta do. If it meant a wait of one year for more silverwear then I accept my responsibility for what's (not) happening on the pitch, but I'll be back in time for City at home on 12th February, OK?

After getting up for a pee in the middle of the night, I settled back to sleep on the bus and the next thing I knew there was light streaming through the curtains and we had stopped in Afamagusta, a really characterless town on the Chilean coast boasting polluted waters. I got off for another pee. Once back on board they came round and served a hot breakfast. Wow! Chilean coaches are really cool.

Leaving the coast behind us we began to climb and climb for hour after hour. Vegetation slowly disappeared as we entered the driest desert in the world. Fifty shades of grey and beige passed for mile after mile until at around four o'clock in the afternoon we finally arrived in the frontier town of San Pedro de Atacama.

With it's rough and narrow uneven streets and low lying brown knobbly dwellings for all I knew made out of plasticine, it looked like something out of a spaghetti western. Any moment I expected Clint Eastwood to come out of the shadows and challenge me to a dual. This was real frontier territory. I'd never been in a town like this before. As Rory Gallagher one sang, this seemed a million miles away.

We dragged our heavy luggage over the cobbles to our hostel and discovered there was no wi-fi. Thanks guys. What about my Valencia report? What about Sunderland on Saturday. When will the world catch up with United demands. Stop the world, I want to get off. No, not really.

Leaving our luggage in our cute little cottage style room we ventured out onto the mean streets and straight into an internet café. Reading a match report at least I could console myself with the fact that we won where it was obvious the current Spanish league leaders had been the better team. That was more like the United I knew, grinding out results against the odds. I know it's a cliché, but it's true that United always perform better in the second half of the season, so as long as we qualify for the knockout stages…

Hmmm. Looks like Javier Hernandez could become our 21st century Solskjaer. After just seven minutes on the pitch his first competitive goal was enough to be our late winner. Yes, I'll leave it there for the moment. I'm too long in the tooth to go shouting the odds. Too much Grecian2000 has passed under the bridge. On the other hand I couldn't leave without putting up LUHG sticker number 53 on the internet café wall, to mobilize all the travellers into action.

SATURDAY 2 OCTOBER. SAN PEDRO DE ATACAMA, CHILE
SUNDERLAND 0 MANCHESTER UNITED 0

Days and nights drifted by as our bodies acclimatised to the 2000 + metre altitude, ready for our 3 day, 2 night assault on the Bolivian Salt Flats. Good food, better people and the best scenery. I counted down the days to the Sunderland game, though quite simply, a lack of signal this high up meant that I didn't even attempt to get up in the middle of the night and swear at my laptop for this game. If I had to miss one game this turned out to be the game to miss. From what I read the following morning we were definitely underwhelming and a neutral could claim Sunderland deserved to win. But we're United and at least we didn't follow our early season pattern of grabbing a draw from the jaws of victory. Even so, after seven games this left us 2 points behind Chelsea who are yet to play, so one game more played and a goal difference of 12 behind the Rent Boys.

Our chances of regaining the Premiership were drying up faster than the Atacama. It was not looking good, Houston. At least there was now an international break which meant United wouldn't play a competitive match for two weeks. I could fully immerse myself in all things Chile and

Bolivia and hope and pray (to Eric) that we could get our act together in the meantime.

MONDAY 3 OCTOBER SAN PEDRO DE ALCAMA – BOLIVIAN SALT FLATS.

After five days and nights in San Pedro we thought we'd allowed our bodies enough time to get used to the thinner air at this high altitude. As a precaution I had stocked up on Coca Leaf Tea, illegal all around the world except in Bolivia, Peru and Ecuador, as it is basically liquid cocaine. Said to alleviate altitude sickness, if it's good enough for the Pope and Queen Sofia of Spain, it was sure as hell good enough for me. As a back-up we purchased some Acetazolamide tablets too. We also spent a fair amount of time researching the tour companies as some had awful reputations for drunk drivers and poorly maintained vehicles, and unlike their equivalent on the Bolivian side, Chilean tour operators are not regulated even though they are more expensive. We took these warnings seriously.

As I got dressed to go and make ourselves a 5.00am cup of tea, Hélène stepped into the shower, as we wouldn't have hot water for the next three days and nights. I was almost out of the door when I heard a scream from the bathroom. I rushed inside to be confronted with my wife starkers, save for shampoo suds cascading down her body and freezing cold water raining down from above.

"There's no more hot water! Do something!"

I'm just the sort 'o guy to call in a crisis like this. I panic.

"What should I do? Who should I call? Showerbusters?"

"Try and find someone in reception. I'M FREEZING!"

In reception there was a young lady sitting by a stove (no heating in our room I should add). She didn't speak a word of English but reluctantly got up and by a combination of exaggerated gestures I successfully conveyed the problem. She shuffled outside, looked at a couple of taps and shrugged. Shrugs in many languages means…"I'd like to help but I can't be arsed."

I conveyed an expression which translated into…. "I paid top whack for a double room with ensuite facilities and hot water, and I want hot water. Now!"

Meanwhile Hélène was getting her death so I ran to the kitchen and put a kettle on the boil. Not for tea but just to get some hot water. I rushed back to Hélène and told her of my master plan.

She was not impressed. "I'M FREEZING AND SOAKING WET!!"

Just as I'm about to leave our room there's a knock on the door. The receptionist had returned with a bucket half full of tepid water from another unoccupied room.

Better than nothing so I thanked her very much and brought it into the bathroom, together with a cup so Hélène could use the water sparingly. I then went back to the kitchen to finally make two cups of tea.

Once we were dressed and ready to leave, the manageress came over to apologise and assured us she would sort it out soon. The words "Horse" and "Bolted" came to mind. That's all very well and good, we thought, but we're leaving now. Oh well...

We said our goodbyes and dragged our luggage along the unpaved dirt tracks to the travel agency that had organised our tour. Soon there were eight of us in a minivan off to the customs hut on the outskirts of San Pedro that handles the border crossings for both Bolivia and Argentina. As we approached the window I spied a wall full of travel stickers.

"What a great location for a LUHG sticker" I thought, so I mumbled some sort of excuse and ran back to the minivan, found my personal rucksack, withdrew said sticker and made my way back to our place in the queue. With so many people milling around I bided my time until I thought no-one was watching then stuck the sticker number 54 in a central, prominent position. "My work here is done."

Soon we had cleared customs and were motoring along towards the Bolivian border. With eight people in the minibus, we realised this was very good news, because at the border we were going to transfer to 4x4 vehicles, and each seven seater was only allowed a maximum of six passengers. In reality, there would only be four to each 4x4 so lots of space. Yippee!

We were introduced to our young driver guide who could hardly speak a word of English, but as the tour was more visual than anything else, this was no big deal. We all had Lonely Planet and other books with a wealth of information inside so we knew what to look out for, although we were totally unprepared for the sheer size and scale of everything on the menu.

We paired up with Sam and Julie again and made the 4x4 our own. The young driver put on some Bolivian pop music which added to the authenticity of the occasion.

Soon the town and its suburbs gave way to a bare backdrop of a cold sun and sandstone hills in the distance. There was no road as such. We just bumped along the ground for mile upon mile, marvelling at the vastness of it all.

Without realising it that much, we had been steadily climbing since leaving San Pedro towards the high plateau of The Altiplano. As we approached Laguna Verde, or Green Lake, the circular lake set against a backdrop of barren mountains, the driver pointed out our first flamingos in the bluey green water. They seemed to be delicately treading water with their long, spindly legs carefully monitoring their next move. We could make out pink markings but they weren't very pronounced. The jeep stopped on the crest of a hill so we opened the doors and jumped down.

The first thing we noticed was the bitterly cold wind which almost blew us off our feet. The second thing I noticed was how short of breath I became just scrambling down the hill. So much wind yet so little air. "How could that be?" I asked myself.

The answer of course was that at over four thousand metres above sea level, the amount of oxygen is reduced and this has a direct affect on your breathing. It certainly had an affect on mine. I'd read numerous times about thin air at altitude but never thought it could have such a pronounced affect.

Not only was I having trouble breathing, I was having trouble standing as well. The wind was so strong it was a struggle to remain upright. However, the sight in front of us made it all worthwhile. Dozens of flamingos going about their everyday business, seemingly oblivious of our attempts to make them pose for our photos. They poked their heads under the water when they wanted, not when we were ready.

Our next stop was truly a moment to savour. Hot springs. Natural hot springs. Hélène and I had our first hot bath together for almost eight months and it was wonderful, just wonderful. And the other people watching thought so to. In fact they joined in.

Celebrity Big Brother had nothing on us.

In the middle of this barren lunar type landscape nature had created natural steaming hot pools of sweet smelling water. Unlike in New Zealand where the overwhelming stench of sulphur permeated every aspect of mind and body and the only way to get clean once you got out was with a freezing cold shower. Here the water was just perfect. Nectar from the Gods for us to bathe in to our heart's and body's content. But not before some careful planning. Our guide set the scene.

The outside temperature was well below freezing. The water temperature was literally like a hot bath. We would not be allowed to spend more than twenty minutes in the water otherwise it would be bad for our health, especially our skin. For a moment I thought, well, if this is the end, I couldn't think of a more pleasant way to go. But then 18-5 came to mind and I knew now wasn't the time.

With military precision I measured the distance from the draughty, corrugated iron changing huts to the edge of the hot spring, about 50 metres over some pretty slippery rough ground and no railings. One false move, one stubbed toe and I'd become a human iceberg. Having been compulsory conscripted into the French army in her teens, Hélène is much tougher than me at withstanding extreme forces of nature, so she ridiculed my efforts to diminish my naked body's exposure to the elements.

But I would not be swayed. When the coast was clear I hopped, skipped, jumped and bumped my way to the edge of the natural spring and plunged into the hot hot water.

Aaahhh! Fuck me, that was hot! It had only taken a few seconds for my skin to unwittingly acclimatize itself to the below freezing air all around, so by the time I immersed myself in the water the contrast was a little more pronounced. Fucking hot to be precise.

But then I quickly became accustomed to the heat and I nearly melted with pleasure. My first hot bath for over eight months. Wonderful. The warmth permeated my very bones, my whole body alive and tingling. Soon my shorts were getting in the way of nature's sensuous calling. Couples all around were frolicking about. What an ideal setting for an orgy. Mind and body overflowing with energy. Limbs taking on a mind of their own. This reminded me of all that "free love" I had read about and missed out on when I was a teenager.

My fantasy scenario was working overtime, but the spirit of that naive but wondrous age has long passed and I resigned myself to the reality before me. Intent on enjoying every last second, we almost counted 20 minutes out loud before I put my return plan of action into operation. And this time it would be even more critical to get every element working in my favour. One false move, one unintentional detour and for every second not accounted for, the hot water dripping from my skinny body would turn to ice and I would be like Lot, forever turned to ice (as opposed to stone as in the bible).

Needless to say Hélène got out first and simply strode to the changing hut, but I didn't let this put me off my stride. With the precision of Joan River's plastic surgeon I bided my time then entered the Guinness Book of Records for the naked 50 yard dash over rocky ground in bare feet. I was fully clothed before Hélène had exchanged her one piece bathing suit for M & S knickers and bra. I was Michelin man once more.

I felt fantastic and ready to take on the world, but not before LUHG sticker number 55 was fixed inside the rickety changing room. And what a world. Our 4x4 covered miles of multi-coloured, barren rocks, sand and hills as far as the eye could see. A cliché I know but this really was a different world. A vast empty 12,000 ft plateau, like something out of the opening sequence from the original Planet Of The Apes, but to the accompaniment of Bolivian pop music.

Our next stop was also our stopover for the night. Laguna Colorada or Red Lake, where the solid pink flamingos reflected the colour of the water. More Lowry walking against the phenomenally strong wind to get as close as possible to these elegant creatures. The contrast with the Green Lake was striking. Just a few miles separated the two lakes yet nature had a mind of its own. Despite the lack of oxygen, we stayed as long as we could before we were driven to our hostel, a one story brick building where the word basic would be classed as luxury.

Freezing cold, with no heating, and temperatures dropping to -14*C at night. It had been a brilliant day but this was going to be a long, long night.

BOLIVIA

TUESDAY 4 OCTOBER BOLIVIAN SALT FLATS

Whenever they ask you on Facebook, your CV, or anywhere else for that matter, to list your favourite hobbies and pastimes, I always try to find a little space to add to the overwhelming vacuum Manchester United take up in my life. You know, music, travel, sex, etc....

But it only occurred to me last night, as I lay in my bed trying once again to try to get to sleep at four thousand metres above sea level, that breathing is one of my most consistent activities. Every time I lay on my side with one nostril pressed against the pillow, the restriction of my airways, already hampered by excessive dry, hard snot that insisted in returning seconds after blowing or picking my nose, the dependence on air, and in particular, oxygen, caused me to rethink my priorities.

The Bogie Man had well and truly got me. I was in a Bogie Wonderland. It's often said that you don't miss something/someone until they're gone, as you've taken it/them for granted for so long. I'm now going to add breathing to my list. I've now decided I like air, and I know I'll miss it when I'm gone. Cue the Hollies.

I thought it was just annoying that I couldn't sleep, but Hélène and the couple sharing our hostel room at -14 C were concerned enough to get up and see if I would be able to survive the night. They claimed the noises emanating from my person were the equivalent of a deflated tyre about to burst. I thought the noises inside my head were for my ears only but I was selfishly sadly mistaken. But no matter what they suggested or what I tried I couldn't breathe freely enough to fall asleep. A really hard day's night but without sleeping like a log.

No matter. Light slowly dawned and breakfast beckoned. I was still alive.

Soon we were back in our Toyota Landcruiser and mile upon mile of beautiful desolate scenery was passing us by. Halfway through the day, the driver's Bolivian pop music was driving us round the bend, even though there weren't any, so I gesticulated that perhaps he (we) would appreciate some of the music I had on my iPod. He nodded enthusiastically (good lad) so the rest of the day was accompanied by Muse, The Prodigy, AC/DC, Foo Fighters, Kasabian, Faithless, Oasis, early Quo and other guitar based heroes of mine. We were literally rocking all over the world.

Next we came to Arbol de Piedra, described as a stone tree, one of several giant rocks that had evolved into strange and formidable shapes by the howling sandy winds. We really felt we were on another planet.

Our hostel for the night, which incidentally was one of the few legally constructed entirely out of salt, (This is important. Others are illegal as, not being part of the water grid, they pollute the environment) was rationed to just one hour of electricity a day and all guests had to pay extra for the privilege. One could accept this as a consequence of living in one of the poorest countries on Earth, except for the fact that the hostel's staff and our drivers spent their entire time in heated leisure and sleeping quarters. I thought guests were meant to treat staff like shit, not the other way round. Damn colonies.

What's Bolivian for Bastards?

Meanwhile there was a farcical stampede for hot showers and the charging of laptops and mobiles. Diaries were written up and stories exchanged round the communal tables as we ate our basic rations supplied by the tour company. The consensus was that no matter how disappointing our accommodation and food had been, the sights that nature was providing meant that everything else was mere detail. But the best was yet to come. The Bolivian Salt Flats themselves, situated in Southern Bolivia near the country's Tunupa volcano and covering around 11,000 square kilometres, the world's largest salt flats.

We dragged our two drivers away from their warm sanctuary and involved them in our heated debate. We had divided ourselves into two camps. Those that wanted to set off at 5 o'clock in the morning in order to watch the sun rise over the vast flat whiteness of the salt flats, and those that didn't.

History will record that I made the wrong decision, but I was exhausted after two days and one night without air and very little sleep, so I joined the 'didn't' camp. Hélène joined the 'did' camp.

Our two young drivers 'ummed and 'arred. This was against the rules and they didn't want to lose their jobs. Their pay wasn't great, but any job in this part of the world was a lifeblood for their families and to jeopardize it would be suicidal. On the other hand, for all of us pampered Westerners, this was an opportunity of a lifetime. The chances of a repeat performance were remote and sacrifices were not just requested, they were politely demanded.

We offered to throw money at them, paying the driver who stayed behind the same amount as the driver that got up early, so neither felt they were losing out. In the end our collective force of will overcame their resistance and they agreed amongst themselves who would volunteer to take the early group.

I elected to stay behind and try to get a couple of hours extra sleep, consciously missing out on a phenomenal sunrise for the sake of a few extras zzzzzzzz's. Writing this I know it sounds petty and I will live to regret my decision, but you had to be me at the time to understand where I was coming from (or not going to, to be more precise)

Hélène continued to try to change my mind but my mind was made up. Maybe I was getting blasé, but I had already witnessed some of the world's most wondrous sights, sounds and smells. Surely missing out on just one more wouldn't confide me to everlasting hell, torment and damnation? And there were still more on the horizon.

No, I needed a little recuperation in order to be firing on all cylinders and fully appreciate what was on offer.

When I awoke the third and final morning I was alone with a pompous, middle aged German couple whose sole topics of conversation were about the places they had visited and how they were roughing it with us. What did they want? A medal? It was as though they were gracing us with their presence and we should all be grateful. They clearly hadn't done their homework as they spent the whole trip complaining about the facilities, or lack of. Tough shit.

Meanwhile my iPod assured a pleasant drive out under a clear blue sky into the heart of the salt flats themselves, drowning out their droning. On the way we saw brightly coloured locals herding flocks of goats and llamas by the side of our tracks. Then we turned right at an invisible sign, the hills receded and soon the earth was just a flat, almost hallucinogenic white as far as the eye could see, sky and ground merging into one dreamy landscape. Colours so intense and pure like a Hockney painting. I had visions of Sir Donald and Sir Michael Campbell attempting world land speed records on the Bonneville Salt Flats outside Salt Lake City in the States, yet here, to give it its proper name, the Salar de Uyuni salt flats were 25 times bigger!

This was just how I envisaged it, yet the scale of the whiteness and nothingness were far in excess of my imagination. And to think that only 30,000 years ago it had been part of a great prehistoric lake, Lake Minchin, later renamed Paleolake Tauca and having a maximum depth of 140 metres. Half the world's supply of lithium, 5.4 tons, is found just below the surface in the brine here and is used in batteries for mobile phones and computers, as well as being a key element in electric cars. (Not a lot of people know that. I certainly didn't)

We drove for about half an hour when we spied some tiny dots on the horizon. It was the other Toyota Land Cruiser with Hélène and our new best friends. As we drew nearer we could see them frolicking about and I couldn't wait to join in.

Our 4x4 ground to a halt, and after the customary hugs and kisses associated with young people whose emotions have been overwhelmed by nature's beauty, they regaled us with stories of the most amazing sunrise they had ever seen. I had a tinge of regret (which would grow in the months to follow) but, despite the cold, I was too engrossed in the hypnotic scene before me to reflect on what might have been.

On close inspection, the entire landscape was formed by salt in stunning hexagons which evolved after the salt pan had dried up. We sent each other 100-200 yards away and made predictably silly poses. Mine consisted of holding my arms out wide and photos showed I had a girl in the palm of each hand. I then ran away and Hélène got one of the girls to take a picture of me dancing on Hélène's head.

Up close and personal, funny images of Hélène and others were reflected in my sunglasses a la Los Angeles, Hollywood, Beverly Hills. David Lynch, eat your heart out.

Back in the 4x4s I swapped my middle aged Germans for more vibrant young people and we boogied and head banged for miles in the absolute flat whiteness of it all, until suddenly out of nowhere there appeared a brown desert island of green cacti rising steeply into the air.

Unreal.

In the middle of literally nowhere stood Incahuasi Island, a mini island of unusual and fragile coral-like structures and deposits that consisted of fossils and algae, as well as vegetation and dramatic cacti. You had to see it to believe it. We saw it but we still had difficulty in believing it. Our driver's English was insufficient to explain the biological phenomenon before our very eyes. Fortunately I had read that this "island" was actually the remains of the top of an ancient volcano which was submerged during the era of Lake Minchin. We stopped here for lunch, where one of my first actions was to stick LUHG sticker number 56 on the window of the only café on the island. I bet that one is still there.

Don't believe me? Go and take a look yourself. Hopefully some more adventurous Reds in the future will come across my legacy and remark in whispered tones, "The Blattmeister was here".

After a really average lunch we all clambered up to the top of the hill for amazing 360° views over the vast hypnotic whiteness all around us. Everything I had read about the salt flats was surpassed at that moment. I just stood and stared. Most took their obligatory photos and descended but I persuaded Hélène just to stand here and take it all in. Wow!

Many may be able to write more lyrically or poetically than me, but "Wow!" sums up better than anything the emotions and sensations at moments like this.

Three kilometres from Uyuni we came across the biggest train set in the world. The antique train cemetery where rust laden engines and carriages came to die. However, for the boy in me this was amazing sight.

I ran as fast as I could to clamber on board one of the locomotives. Hélène at the age of sixty suddenly discovered a little more about me and my childhood passions. I'd always wanted to be a train driver and here I could act out my fantasy. She couldn't believe how I skipped from one engine to another, and I wasn't the only one. This was short trousers and Tizer time. Thomas the Tank Engine meets the Royal Scot. The Mullard meets The Fat Controller. Luvly jubbly.

Sadly all good things must come to an end as the car horns brought an end to our childish games. I almost hugged my last engine as I reluctantly clambered down the rusty metal ladder and back onto Bolivian soil.

It was nice while it lasted.

We came to our final halt in the main street of Uyuni and we were all really sorry to say goodbye to our two young drivers. It had been a truly mind blowing trip and we all felt this was the end of something really special. We were also glad we had started from San Pedro in Chile. Admittedly starting from Uyuni in Bolivia would have saved us around 40%, but to end the third day on the salt flats themselves, well, nothing could top that. And you only get the sunrise on the third morning coming from the Chilean side. If you start from Uyuni, everything is downhill from day one. Just my opinion but worth noting I feel.

TUESDAY 5 OCTOBER UYUNI – POTOSI, BOLIVIA

There are exceptions to every rule in life. I've been going on about how superb buses (coaches) are in South America. Well, today we encountered the exception. In a dusty main road in dusty Uyuni were a number of ramshackle outlets offering bus services on ramshackle buses. Hanging around this small authentic Bolivian town, away from the tourist and traveller haunts, we felt this was the South America of time gone by.

I really felt I was 6000 miles from home and the feeling was wonderful. We saw very little concession to modernity. Women wearing the famous bowler hats stopped or stared at us. This was their land, their town, on their terms. We were inconsequential. We weren't a cash cow, we were invisible. We meant nothing to them and inexplicably I felt an overwhelming feeling of joy that this was real and not for our benefit.

I've witnessed hundred's of years of history and tradition eradicated in a single generation as the tourist dollar arrives and transforms unique cultures into another stop on the trinket selling package tour merry-go-round. Not here, and it's altogether a better experience for everyone. If you want your hot and cold running tour guide, this is not the place for you. But if you want an experience that reeks (in all senses of the word) of authenticity, then rural "outback" Bolivia is the place to come. Rewarding in ways that's hard to quantify or articulate. It's certainly not sophisticated, but then you could argue that sophistication is just another layer away from reality.

Reality certainly reared its ugly head as our two hour late bucket of rust came round the corner. We, meaning I, had to lift our two heavy rucksacks up onto the roof of the bus. No mean feat for a skinny runt like me, and no holiday rep to commandeer local muscle. (You win some, you lose some)

This was a local bus for local people and we were the only non Bolivians going to get on it. I put my black Manchester manufactured Regatta rain-jacket on the overhead luggage rack and settled down for our six hour multi-stop marathon along roads that were often no more than dirt tracks. Our driver battled with a rapidly failing steering column and all the bumps and grinds began to take their toll. From time to time we could see evidence of a new road being constructed but we'd obviously arrived a few years too early and were confined to wild stretches formed before the invention of the wheel.

The entire journey was spent holding onto anything that gave us support as the ancient bus twisted and turned around mountain passes and hairpin bends. Numerous times the road seemed to just disintegrate and how we survived the sheer drops I'll never know. (I've read since that it is not uncommon for buses to plunge over the side, especially during periods of sustained rainfall. Nice.) The relief at the end of the journey was palpable as I could finally unclench my stomach muscles.

Just to let you know, in all Hélène and I spent 5 months in South

America, and by doing our homework based around the philosophy "If you fail to prepare, prepare to fail" we avoided all the horror stories that can befall the unwary traveller, with one exception. When I reached above my head to retrieve my rain jacket it was conspicuous by its absence. Someone had made off with it during one of numerous stops along the way.

Hélène had told me more than once not to let our possessions out of my sight, but after 6 weeks I had possibly become a little complacent, lulled into a false sense of security by journeys in luxury coaches populated by luxury passengers. For one of the locals between Uyuni and Potosi Christmas had come early and my Manchester made Regatta jacket now resides somewhere in Bolivia. If that's the worst that's going to happen… happy days.

However, one disturbing thread throughout our long distance bus journeys in South America was the proliferation of "they're so bad they're good" 60s Chinese/Japanese kung fu movies. OK, we can laugh at the amateurism but the over the top violence is there for all to see on the bus, including the many very young children on board with their parents. Not a good idea.

They say that every cloud has a silver lining. I don't know about that, but I do know that if it wasn't for silver, Potosi, one of the highest cities in the world at over 4000 metres above sea level, probably wouldn't exist today. The town was founded in 1545 as soon as this ore was discovered under the nearby Cerro de Potosi, or Cerro Rico (rich mountain). Pretty soon the silver extracted here was bankrolling the entire Spanish empire.

No one is certain how much silver has been extracted over its four centuries of production, but a popular boast was that the Spanish could have constructed a silver bridge all the way to Spain and still have silver left to carry it across.

We took a tour of the Royal Mint. It is considered one of the most important civil buildings of Latin America and from the outside this formidable building constructed of stone, brick, tiles and cedar wood looked like a virtual fortress. The tour itself though was flat and boring and the bastards didn't even give away any free samples at the end of our visit.

To say that Potosi is a city of contrasts is an understatement. The vast fortunes earned by those in high places, when the town was the wealthiest in the whole of the Americas, has led to the creation of, architecturally, one of the most beautiful and ostentatious cities in South America with its magnificent Baroque style cathedral and grand churches and plethora of ornate colonial buildings. However, this came at an extraordinarily high price, as millions, I repeat, millions of miners, both locals and imported African slaves, died in some of the most abysmal conditions imaginable.

Needless to say you can now take a tour of the mines, where even in the 21st century the sights you'll see will provoke disbelief at just how appalling the job still is. Except that I didn't see it. Hélène thought the sights would be just too horrendous, and we'd read that it was not uncommon for the odd tourist to be added to the growing list of dead statistics as the guided tours would never pass Health and Safety guidelines back in the UK.

My reaction was bittersweet. To come all this way and not discover for ourselves what had put Potosi on the map would be a huge disappointment, but I had to admit that overwhelming sense of claustrophobia I had experienced in the tunnels in Vietnam probably indicated I would have shit myself in the coal seams deep underground the Bolivian countryside.

In the end we spent two very pleasant days and nights here. The locals were friendly, the food superb and no United matches to distract me.

WEDNESDAY 6 OCTOBER - POTOSI TO SUCRE, BOLIVIA

After our experience of mixing with the locals on their death defying rust bucket from Uyuni to Potosi, we chose a more conventional bus from Potosi to Sucre. This time we secured the front sleeper seats upstairs and had a comparatively restful overnight trip to the country's former constitutional capital, competing for the title of most beautiful city in Bolivia.

At a mere 2750 metres above sea level the weather here was pleasant enough. Wandering round in the afternoon we came across a sign proclaiming Sucre was twinned with Cardiff! (Has anyone from Sucre ever been to Cardiff?) Beautiful city, bustling market, all traces of previous civilisations ruthlessly eradicated by the Spanish and replaced by wonderfully ornate churches as a monument to mammon. Another elegant main square that was almost a replica of the one in Potosi, which itself was a replica of... you get the picture. We could have been in any provincial town in Spain, which shouldn't come as a surprise as this had been part of the Spanish empire. It's what dominating invaders do, isn't it.

Lovely views from the hills overlooking the town. We met many travellers who decided to stop awhile in Sucre and take up one or two week intensive Spanish courses. Can't argue with the inspirational backdrop. Better than your adult education centre back home that's for sure.

In all we spent another few days slowing down and exploring at our own pace. For a country that doesn't get a lot of travel press, Bolivia has been surprisingly stunning in many different ways, and cheap too. Our next stop was to be the capital, La Paz, back up to 3,650 metres above sea level, making it the world's highest "de facto" capital city in the world.

We arrived late afternoon at the rather ornate La Paz Bus Station, built by French architect Gustave Eiffel (not a lot of people know that!) and took a taxi to our hostel. Like most hostels in major cities in South America, it was situated in the favelas, the poor steep hillside neighbourhoods surrounding the city centre. By the time we went down for our first evening stroll in the Bolivian capital it was already dark and the lights from the favelas on the hills opposite rose up majestically and touched the sky. What for most people living there was just a daily life of existence for me was a magical twinkling light show which dominated the skyline. Had a pizza then went to bed.

SUNDAY 10 OCTOBER LA PAZ, BOLIVIA

Today we just walked around the capital soaking up the atmosphere, the focus being the highest point some 12,000 feet above sea level, and attempting to get inside Estadio Hernando Siles, the national football stadium.

Now, we've all heard of ground sharing. The Italians have taken to it like ducks to wafer thin pizza, but in the UK it's never taken off. It makes sense to me to cut costs, but 100 + years of tribalism still hangs heavy over the British game. Not so in Bolivia. The Estadio Hernando Siles stadium, as well as hosting the national team, is also the home of some of the biggest football teams in Bolivia. Club Bolivar, founded in 1925 and named in honour of the liberator, Simon Bolivar, The Strongest, founded in 1908, although they also have their own stadium named Rafael Mendoza, and La Paz FC. It also plays host to several other teams that play in the first and second divisions such as Mariscal Braun, Always Ready, Municipal and Chaco Petrolero.

The taxi dropped us off in front of the main entrance of the stadium, a dated, non-descript dark beige concrete edifice that occupied one complete roundabout. I tried a lot of locked doors. Eventually I spied an entrance to a gym, went inside, but there was no exit into the stadium from there, just sweaty middle-aged men. Then I spotted an open door and beckoned Hélène inside. A dark corridor led to iron gates barring us from the pitch on the other side. We walked around until I found an unlocked gate and we were in!

Hélène and I walked around the running track circumventing

the pitch (always hate that) and saw a load of 7-8 year old school kids practising various sporting activities. One look at us and they burst into a fit of giggles so I went over to greet them, my non-existent Spanish at the ready.

Then I noticed that one kid had a United top on and another had a Liverpool top on. Cue finger sign language with 3 fingers on one hand and 2 fingers on the other indicating our recent victory at Old Trafford. This I accompanied with smiles and a thumbs up towards the United lad and a frown and a thumbs down towards the Liverpool lad.

I repeated this action a number of times to make sure both kids got the message.

Pleased with myself I walked back to Hélène, imagining what the kids would say to their parents later that day. The previous day Bolivia had lost 3-1 at home to Venezuela, so I didn't mention that. Well, you have to be diplomatic, don't you.

On the way out, with no security whatsoever inside the stadium, I was presented with an Eric given opportunity for LUHG sticker numbers 57 and 58 to take pride of place in the home and away dug outs, with LUHG sticker number 59 resplendent in the directors' seats. Just hope the main men see them before the cleaners do their rounds.

PERU

TUESDAY 12 OCTOBER PUNA, PERU - FULL DAY ON LAKE TITICACA. (DISNEYLAND)

Lake Titicaca is the highest navigable lake in the world. It also has a name that makes young kids giggle. The very mention of Lake Titicaca brings one out in awe that such a remote place actually exists and we were going to go on it. It's a long way to Tipperary, the road to Mandalay, Kathmandu, Timbuktu, these mystical paces at the end of the rainbow that mere mortals rarely visit. Well, knock Titicaca off the list, thank you very much.

The day started in pouring rain, but the manager of our hostel assured us it would stop by 8 o' clock. With hindsight he was right about the morning, but he conveniently omitted the fact that the rain, together with hail, thunder and lightning would return in the afternoon whilst we were in the middle of the lake. But more of that later.

A minibus took us down to the little harbour where the side of the lake was knee deep in small pleasure craft bobbing about in the water. We clambered over a number of boats, which was no mean feat as the rain had made everything so slippery. I admit I laughed when a couple of tourists slipped and fell, negating all their efforts to keep dry. But that's the sort 'o guy I am.

Once out onto the lake, our guide began his spiel, first in Spanish and then in English, which hardly mattered as the loudspeaker was shot and both languages sounded like static passing through a comb.

After about an hour we arrived at the famous floating villages, where indigenous tribes had lived the same way for hundreds of years. The islands themselves floated on reeds two metres deep packed tightly together. Many refused to let tourists land, fearing (correctly) we would infiltrate and dilute their way of life.

We were greeted by four women in brightly coloured costumes singing unenthusiastically and out of tune such authentic Bolivian island ditties as "Michael Rowed The Boat Ashore" and "Blowing In The Wind". It was obvious the women didn't understand a single word they were singing. The sheer unbridled commercialism stuck in the throat and it was embarrassing in the extreme.

The moment we alighted we felt the weird sensation that the world was moving, and it was. We bounced around and it was great fun. I looked sheepishly at the tribe, conscious that my actions might be interpreted as childish by the islanders, but then I reckoned they must have seen boatloads of tourists over the years all performing the same mini pogo dance.

I then ventured inside one of their reed huts, only to discover conventional city clothes hanging on the walls. It transpired they hadn't lived on these floating islands for years but on the mainland. They just made their way out here before the tourists arrived, and left once we had departed.

"This is worse than Disneyland." I thought. Then for a hefty (by Bolivian standards) fee a couple of young men offered to row us to another island. Of course we all said yes, only to witness a carbon copy of the first island. Oh well.

Then we piled back onto our motor launch and we were taken to a conventional island in the middle of the lake where a really steep climb up hundreds of steps lead to our lunch at the top. I'm not saying it was steep but I swear some of our elderly passengers never made it to the top. No-one had warned us about this and many pensioners could see their lives flash before my eyes.

The view from the top, however, was magnificent and the meal was surprisingly good. Lots of nice chat before descending down to our motor launch. The return journey was barely ten minutes old when dark clouds suddenly appeared out of nowhere and before we knew it the horizon had disappeared and we were in the midst of one almighty storm.

We weren't all that worried until we spied the crew with fear in theirs. Hélène noticed it first as one of the three man crew ventured outside in the wind and downpour and made his way gingerly round the outside of the boat until he got to the front and did an impersonation of human windscreen wipers. That was the moment we knew the captain steering the boat couldn't see a fucking thing and, of course, there was no electronic navigation equipment onboard this ancient vessel.

Oh dear.

We hoped the rest of the passengers hadn't picked up on this situation as mass hysteria is not a pretty sight. The captain kept motoring along but we knew he hadn't a clue in which direction we were headed. Eventually we caught sight of another boat and ours just followed it until we finally made our way into Puno harbour. (I've since read many boats with passengers onboard have sunk with all lives lost. This was one occasion when it was not good to be wise before the event).

WEDNESDAY 13 OCTOBER. PUNO – CUSCO, PERU

Today we plumped for the more expensive US$45 option of the Puno Cusco VIP Tourist Bus with commentary in English and various historical stops along the way. The price included tea, coffee and lunch. All we had to do was lie back and think of Peru.

The bus departed on time at 7.30 am and arrived in Cusco at 5.00pm.

On the way we stopped at, notably, Raqchi with the remains of its Temple of Wiraoocha and the Raya Pass with stunning mountain views 4310 metres above sea level. This point is the conjunctions of the cordillera and the origin of the Vilcanota knot. (No, I didn't know that either till I read it on someone's blog). We were able to breathe in the incredibly fresh air as well as the obligatory row of tourist stalls. I actually love South American ethnic patterns but resisted this overpriced arcade set up purely for tourists. I also annoyed Hélène by taking pictures of gaily coloured girls with llamas and alpacas in tow through the bus window, because if you step down they charge you an extortionate fee for their photo to be taken.

Our buffet lunch in Sicuani Village was excellent, with llamas and alpacas running around free in the grounds. And so friendly too. I could almost make one stand still for me while I knitted myself a pullover on the spot.

All in all a most pleasant excursion and we arrived fresh and raring to go for one of the highlights of the entire world tour – Machu Picchu. Say it loud and there's music playing. Say it soft and it's almost like praying

Just typing the name gets my keyboard all moist in anticipation. One of those 99 places you have to visit before you die, and here I was about to see Machu Picchu and live.

Arriving in Cusco, the former capital of the Inca empire, we took a taxi to our hostel just off the main square. However, the taxi had been diverted a couple of times by police and road blocks so he indicated that 'this' was the nearest he could get to our hostel. We thanked him and, armed with one of my trusty maps, I instructed Hélène to follow me as I was sure our hostel was just the other side of the main square.

Sweating and dragging our rucksacks along the heavily cobbled streets of the historical centre, finally arriving where our hostel should have been. It wasn't there.

I could have sworn…. Back we went from the direction we had just come, Hélène's caustic French coming to the fore. Bloody map.

We asked numerous people for directions, but just as in any city in any country in the world, replies varied from, "Don't know" "We're not from round here" "Down there" "No, over there" to "Back the way you've come."

Eventually we tracked it down to a different address to the one I had printed out from one of the hostel booking sites. Of course, the reception had to be on the second floor of a narrow building with no lift. We bumped and grinded our way up to the second floor, but as soon as I gave our names furtive looks were exchanged between the two people on reception and I knew something was up.

"I'm sorry sir. There's been a problem. We haven't got a room for you."

Eight months in and our first hostel bombshell.

"I'm sorry, but I have a printed confirmation from HostelBookers. com. Look."

"Yes, I know. It's our fault but there's been a mix up and we don't have any rooms available."

"Look, we've just been trawling up and down the streets here in Cusco as our taxi driver couldn't get near your hostel. Your address is different to that printed on this hostel website, and we've just dragged our luggage up two flights of stairs after coming all the way from Puno. And we've paid a deposit. I think you have a responsibility of finding us a room."

And so began some farcical frantic calls until they secured us a room across the square. On arrival the room turned out to be better than the one we had booked, and at no extra cost. Sorted but exhausted we calmed down, unpacked slowly then drifted onto the streets. Magical.

Yet another one of the most beautiful towns in the whole of South America, with not one but two massive (whoops, sorry, got a little carried away there) churches on two sides of the really awesome main square. With all the lights on and buildings lit up it looked like Christmas every night of the week in Cusco. With three days to go before our home game against West Brom, my two week football exclusion order was coming to an end. Macchu Pichu or Manchester United? What would occupy my thoughts more? Our faltering start to the season, blowing hot one moment and cold the next. A magnificent Berbatov hat-trick against Liverpool or last minute giveaway goals by our defence? Underwhelming performances in Europe but holding out for qualification and better times ahead… or Macchu Pichu?

I'll let you decide.

SATURDAY 16 OCTOBER CUSCO, PERU
MANCHESTER UNITED 2 WEST BROMWICH ALBION 2

Had a bad night. After three consecutive 05.00am alarm calls, I was looking forward to a decent night's sleep, before waking up just before 09.00am Peruvian time for the WBA match on Fox Sports. Unfortunately stomach cramps had set in the previous evening and I'd made the mistake of drinking a cup of coca tea before going to bed. Just like marijuana, it has medicinal properties. In the case of coca tea it helps alleviate altitude sickness, reduces hunger and keeps you going.

It was the third benefit that was my downfall. I just could not fall asleep. I must have done eventually, of course, but I certainly felt under the weather by the time dawn arrived. Then another quandary arose. With breakfast finishing at 09.30 am should I get up and have breakfast early then come back to bed, or just lay here and wait for the match then grab something to eat later? My life is full of conundrums such as these. I specialise in trivia.

Needless to say I took the lazy man's route and stayed in bed until the match started. What's annoying about channels such as Fox Sports is that they don't go over to the stadium until the match is just about to kick off, so I had no idea who was in our starting line-up. I picked out Chico, our Mexican, which pleased me, then noticed we kicked off with Chico and Berbatov up front. Fergie's traditional sergeant major attitude had once again relegated Rooney to the bench. I wasn't surprised, as I believe Rooney's personal problems were affecting his play, and no amount of money can compensate for affairs of the heart. Fill a bath full of water or fill a bath full of champagne, you can still drown.

Meanwhile we started quite brightly and it was extremely pleasing to see Chico follow up a Nani free kick and side foot the WBA goalie's rebound into the net. I was even more pleased to see Nani slot home our second after a great, slick move down the right.

The rest of the first half was fairly even and I contemplated, for the zillionth time, whether our failure to increase our lead may come back to haunt us once again. After all, WBA had won 3-2 at Arsenal in their previous game after going a goal down.

The second half saw us playing the same attacking football, but then again, so were WBA. Full marks to De Matteo for implementing an attacking philosophy even away from home. But then disaster struck. Anderson, who had somehow wormed his way back into Fergie's good books, was once again short of pace and positional sense as he tracked back and gave away a needless free kick at a tight, but horribly close to our goal.

What can I say? Confusion in our ranks and WBA got themselves back into the match. 2-1.

Right, let's see if we've learned anything from the dreadful capitulations at the end of the Fulham and Everton matches. No, we haven't. Berbatov missed a couple of chances and we still looked good going forward although the nervousness in the team was evident. Then came such an uncharacteristic unforced error from Van der Sar. A cross comes over and without being challenged he let the ball slip though his fingers into the path of two WBA players who gratefully accept an early Christmas present.

Full marks to the Baggies for not capitulating themselves, but once again we had committed football suicide. Even with Ferdinand and Vidic back in defence together I was never filled with complete confidence. Unlike the Liverpool game, Berbatov looked to have shrunk back into his shell and a winner never looked on the cards.

Something is fundamentally wrong with the team at the moment. With Chelsea drawing away at Villa there is still all to play for, but only totally blinkered United fans could realistically believe this team is capable of winning the Premiership. All I can hope is that our problems are sorted in time for a run in the Champions League and FA Cup. We are weighed down by the Gimps and their choking debt on the club's finances, and Fergie, despite him paying lip service to his employers, is restricted in the transfer market whilst our youngsters are not as good as we would like to believe.

I gathered my thoughts and posted the following onto my Facebook page.

"So, what has today's result taught us?

1) WBA are better than Liverpool.

2) We are light years away from winning the Premiership."

Within seconds I had generated over a dozen replies, the vast majority extremely angry at Fergie's selection policy and the detrimental affect the Glazers' spiralling debts were having on the club. There were some no holds barred comments, and I only wish Fergie could feel the groundswell of emotion the current situation is generating.

SUNDAY 17 OCTOBER CUSCO – MACHU PICCHU, PERU

There are various options of getting to the ancient Inca city from Cusco. The most well known and inexpensive for healthy boys and girls (was I just about to include myself in this category? Surely not!) is the 3, 4 or 5 day hikes up the Andes. We had contemplated this option, despite reading on various blogs that the trek was much harder than organisers let on, only to read that March's earthquake had rendered many of the passes impassable.

That was it. With no roads up the mountain we decided to let the train take the strain. But even that wasn't a simple option. The trains are run by PeruRail, a private company and take you to Aquas Calientes, a village 8000 feet up at the foot of Machu Picchu itself. There were four classes of carriage to choose from…least fucking expensive, fucking expensive, extremely fucking expensive and …how fucking much?

How fucking much is called 'Hiram Bingham' and named after the American archaeologist who discovered this hidden site in 1911, subsequently one of the few not to be destroyed by the Spanish in the quest for world domination centuries beforehand. It's decked out like the Orient Express and priced accordingly.

'Expedition' is the least fucking expensive but also comes at a price. It's the first to sell out (surprise), whilst the other carriages have windows in the roof as well at the sides. We bought 'Vistadome' (fucking expensive) on the way up and 'Expedition' (least fucking expensive) on the way down.

Needless to say, the higher we went the more spectacular the views. Arriving at Aquas Calientes, we dragged our rucksacks through the obligatory souvenir market to the outside world, over a bridge and up the narrow road (what other direction is there in the world of Blatt?) to our hostel.

An early night was called for as we wanted to get up early and miss the umbrella lead tour groups crossing Macchu Picchu off their lists.

MONDAY 18 OCTOBER MACHU PICCHU – CUSCO

Didn't need the alarm. The similarity between Machu Picchu and

Manchester United intensified, as neither require a mechanical awakening device. Mother nature and adrenalin combined to bring me to full consciousness in seconds. Waking Hélène we went down for breakfast at 04.30, in time to catch one of the first shuttle buses to the entrance of one of the world's 'must see' sites. (No, not Old Trafford)

Arrived at 05.30. Only a small queue. Paid for our tickets and began to climb up the steps in front of us. The sun wasn't up yet but the light was bright and clear and shone on the magnificent Andes peaks all around us. Up and up we went. Surely they're taking the piss, I thought, as we wound our way up well worn but uneven steps. Suddenly, without warning, they stopped and we found ourselves on a sort of plateau named Guardian's Hut, and there before us, below us and in front of us was the sight that had brought thousands of men and women to tears for almost one hundred years.

Machu fucking Picchu.

It was exactly like all the postcards and all the magazine photos, but in 3D. It was everything and more. No amount of clicking, snapping, camcording tourists could dispel the magic and mystery that lay before us.

No Health and Safety barriers to stand behind. This was it.

GGMP. Glory Glory Machu Picchu.

You've all seen photos so I'm not going to attempt to wax lyrically about one of the world's most awesome sites. I haven't got the vocabulary but, believe me, it's everything I ever dreamed it would be x 10.

At just gone 06.00 the sun came up behind us and the magic was complete. Time stood still as Hélène and I just took in the vista all around us. The ancient Inca site, the peaks of the Andes, the sense of history and wonder. Just how did they get builders to come up here with all their materials all those centuries ago?

Then came the obligatory photo session with every pose known to man, every angle explored, every social media accounted for. Hélène's sense of history kicked in as she reminded me that she wanted to explore the site itself before it came knee deep in bus loads of tourists, so we made our way down.

The first building we saw was the Sun Gate with more awesome views, then on to the Temple of the Sun with its incredibly intricate stonework that was the pinnacle of Inca technology and which proved they were so far in advance of the all conquering Spanish.

By now the tourist hoards were descending like locusts so we got in as much in as possible before returning to the exit and our bus back to Aquas Calientes. With still 45 minutes to wait we had a drink and stale pie from the one overpriced concession stall outside the railway station.

Boarding the Vistadome carriage, we really appreciated the glass windows in the roof as we could see the peaks of the Andes as we descended to civilisation below. The odd couple opposite were real old colonel types. The man had a book in front of him entitled, Birds of Peru (he must be the life and soul of the party) and got noticeably excited when he claimed to have spotted a condor high above us. It was true. We all had a condor moment as we witnessed these majestic birds circulating effortlessly above us. He pointed to a page in his book so were left in no doubt that we had indeed seen a condor.

As we were in a fucking expensive carriage we were served a complementary hot meal with drinks. It was all very civilized, by jove. All in all a most wonderful day. My only regret is that I didn't adhere a LUHG sticker, but it just didn't seem right.

Do you forgive me?

TUESDAY 19 OCTOBER CUSCO – LIMA. PERU

The 05.30am alarm worked a treat, and we had a full hour to get dressed, washed and have breakfast before the arrival of our taxi to take us to the airport. A flight of one hour for $76 seemed like the height of luxury after our many long bus rides, and twenty hours from Cusco to Lima by bus didn't seem worth the money saved.

As luck would have it, the timing couldn't have been better, as Hélène had spent the whole night alternating between the bed and the bathroom with a bottom like an open dam. She often claims my stomach is more delicate than hers, so as we had both eaten the same food during the day, she put the feeling of nausea and the reality of diarrhoea down to the new tablets she had started taking to stop her runny nose and clear her nasal passages.

Obviously the flow of mush from above had been transferred to the flow of sausages from below. The "bottom" line was that a smooth but more expensive one hour flight was preferable to a cheaper twenty hour bumpy on the rumpy bus.

We arrived at Cusco airport in good time and joined the only TACA queue.

Finally arriving at the check-in desk I handed in my e-ticket.

"Your booking has been cancelled." claimed the flustered young thing in front of us.

"Not by us it hasn't." I retorted, envisaging a nightmare scenario about to unfold. The check-in girl stared intently at her screen.

"Yes. Your booking has been cancelled."

"Look." I said, showing her my printouts. "Look at the booking confirmation. See, they've even included my VISA details proving we've paid."

Her monitor wasn't listening to me. It said my booking had been cancelled and there was nothing we could do.

"Can we buy another ticket here? Now?" enquired Hélène, resting weekly against the counter, mirroring my thoughts.

A flurry of fingertips on her keyboard produced the following response.

"US$132."

I quickly worked out that was almost $60 more than the ticket I thought I had bought over the internet. Yet, interestingly, around $30 less than travel agents in Cusco had quoted.

Hélène's bottom dominated my thoughts.

"We'll take two." I said, and prepared my VISA card for the oncoming onslaught. I moved along the counter where check-in girl's credit card machine was located.

She swiped it once, twice, three times a shady look of annoyance flickered over her face.

"Your card doesn't work." she said.

"It's not my card, it's your machine." I replied in a menacingly low voice. "Please try again."

Try she did. Work it didn't.

"Here." called out Hélène. "Try a different card", as she fumbled in her knickers for her money belt and handed me her warm, flexible friend.

That didn't work either.

We knew we had money in both accounts so this was getting ridiculous, as was the shortage of time now left to get on the flight. The check-in girl called over her supervisor who made the credit card machine respond favourably to my plastic friend at the first attempt.

I gave the girl one of my most superior, mocking smiles as she finished processing our two tickets in a flurry of fingertips and fading finesse, her face flushed with a faint film of fear and frustration.

You've guessed it. She could "F" off for all I cared.

Armed with our new tickets, we rushed to the departure lounge and through personal security where a young man was waiting to run us to the plane as we were the last ones to board.

"Sorry. We don't do "run". I thought. "My wife's not well. We'll do "brisk" if it's alright with you" as we followed his disappearing frame along the corridors. Round one last bend and the open door of the TACA flight beckoned. We scrambled inside, avoiding the eyes of fellow passengers as we made our way to two separate seats in opposing isles.

The short flight was uneventful, but fate was to play one last hand when we landed at Lima airport. The arrivals hall was a crowded and confusing place for a couple of tired gringos as we tried to get our bearings. We manoeuvred our luggage trolley into a corner together with assorted personal belongings. Once we had worked out where to catch the airport bus we loaded everything onto the trollies, our backs and our hands and made our way to the exit. It was only as we divested ourselves of our belongings on the bus did I realize I had left my sleeping bag on the floor in the corner of the airport.

Damn.

It had survived the Bolivian Salt Flats but soon we would be travelling down to Ushaia, the southernmost town in the Southern Hemisphere, just a short hop from Antarctica. I just hoped our hostels would be up to the task of keeping yours truly warm enough.

If Hélène's hairdryer treatment berating me for my stupidity was anything to go by I could always call on her services in my hours of need.

WEDNESDAY 20 OCTOBER. LIMA, PERU
MANCHESTER UNITED 1 BURSASPOR 0 CHAMPIONS LEAGUE

After a whole afternoon, evening and night in bed, the bug that was causing Hélène grief finally exited her body and she felt right as rain this morning, just a little slow. Which was no bad thing as I now had an equal to deal with.

As our bus to Tumbes on the Ecuadorian border didn't depart until 4.15pm we had a whole morning to fill in Lima, so the easiest thing to do was to take a half day city tour. We had two choices. 09.00am coach $50 (£10) or 10.15am start double decker bus $55 (£12). Everything pointed to a 10.15 start. Staying in bed longer, saving money...it was all there, BUT, taking the 09.00am tour meant that we would finish around noon and time enough to get back to the hostel in time for the 13.45 Champions League kick-off, the Bursaspor game and all the Rooney shit surrounding the match.

I wanted to hear the crowd's reaction to team selection and throughout the match. I wanted to know if they reflected the anger and betrayal I felt inside.

But this time I took a calculated gamble. I put Hélène first. (no comments, please). I reckoned if the 10.15 tour finished around 13.15, that would still give us enough time to get back to the hostel and watch most of the match before departing for the bus terminal, and, you never know, there may even be internet or wi-fi available. Think positive. Think positive.

We had a simple continental breakfast, then prepared ourselves for a pleasant thirty minute walk round the bay in the Miraflores district to the Turibus pick-up point for our three hour city tour of Lima. It was warm but the sky was grey and so was the sea. Not picture postcard stuff and the buildings were decidedly 1960s high rise so I wasn't expecting too much. Everything I'd read and everybody we'd met painted Lima as a poor man's Buenos Aries. Dusty, dirty, and an overabundance of dangerous bits where it would be unwise to walk at night. Half of the city's estimated 10 million inhabitants live in sprawling shanty towns that surround the historic centre and vacant desert sands.

However, we were pleasantly surprised. I know they only took us to the good bits but there was a lot more than I'd been led to believe. An earthquake in 1746 had destroyed all but 20 houses. Following this devastation the opportunity was taken to elaborately rebuild the city. Today's wide streets, huge plazas and old houses with ornately carved balconies are a legacy if this period.

The Main Square (Plaza Mayor. I'm getting good at this Spanish lark) was dominated by colonial buildings all painted yellow. Don't ask me why. Lots of historical buildings, which is all well and good, but I don't travel just for history lectures. But special mention should go to the San Francisco Convent and catacombs. If bones and skulls are your thing then this element will satisfy the Stephen King in you. The underground galleries and catacombs were only discovered in 1951 and are gloomy and impressive, containing the remains of some 70,000 people buried there when it was the town cemetery during the time of the Viceroys. In the beautiful chapter house there is a collection of paintings of the Apostles. (Never heard of 'em. Must be an old Peruvian pop group)

On the way back to Miraflores the traffic was getting ridiculous. All the roads seemed to be clogged up and any resemblance of common courtesy went out of the window. At each intersection, irrespective of whether the lights were red or green, every car fought for that extra inch in front and gridlock was the name of the day. Such ignorance. Such idiocy.

The end result was that we didn't get back to the end of the tour until 14.15, thirty minutes after kick-off. Hélène and I agreed to take a taxi back to the hostel to save time. I explained in broken Spanish and hand signals to the yellow cab driver waiting in line outside the Marriot hotel that we wanted him to take us to our hostel a few blocks away, wait two minutes, then drive us to the CIAL bus terminal where we were due to catch a bus to Tumbes on the Peru-Ecuador border. We showed him the address. He showed us a printed tariff.

"10 solas."

This was actually more than the local taxis charged but these yellow cabs outside the 5 star hotels by the sea were a law unto themselves. However, as Blondie once sang, time was tight.

"OK." we said.

Unfortunately Hélène ignored my pleas to check out the score on the hostel's computer, so we just collected our luggage and went back to the cab.

The driver showed us a chart.

"20 solas".

That's not what we'd agreed but we were in a hurry so I nodded. Arriving at the bus terminal he said.

"30 solas."

"What!" I exclaimed. First we agreed 10 solas, then 20 solas. How come it's 30 solas now?"

It transpired 10 solas was just for the short trip from the Turibus pick-up/drop-off point to the hostel and 20 solas was from the hostel to the CIAL bus terminal.

What's Peruvian for rip off?

I argued, but my lack of Spanish and the overwhelming desire to locate internet or Wi-Fi within the bus terminal dictated events. I paid the money like a reluctant schoolboy so that Hélène and I could drag our luggage into the terminal, process our ticket voucher, and catch the end of the match before grabbing a bite to eat.

What can I tell you? There was no internet or Wi-Fi in the bus terminal, not even in the VIP lounge.

And to make matters worse, the bus was almost an hour late, so I could easily have watched the end of the match back at the hostel.

Double bastards with knobs on.

So for the first time in over eight months of travelling I didn't get to see the match or even know the result before leaving for our next destination.

Bah! Humbug!

ECUADOR

THURSDAY 21 OCTOBER. LIMA – TUMBES, PERU – GUAYAQUIL, ECUADOR

Had a surprisingly comfortable night on the bus. Their semi-cama seats worked a treat. I didn't even get up to go to the loo during the night. That's two nights in a row. I must be growing up.

Still no result though. Breakfast was passed around by the hostess which meant we weren't going to stop. Bugger. Looking outside, the dry, flat, sandy landscape had turned into lush vegetation as we headed north, then back again. I was confused. The weather was getting warmer though, which was a good sign.

Finally, at around 5.00pm we pulled into the ramshackle Tumbes bus terminal on the Peruvian border. As we disembarked taxi drivers hovered around like flies.

"Where you from?"

"You crossing border?"

Hélène and I studiously ignored them, having read numerous blogs warning us of the scams these taxi drivers imposed on unwary foreign travellers, claiming the border was dangerous but with their help they could get us across for just a few dollars. Rubbish!

In fact, the safest and easiest way was simply to buy a bus ticket in Tumbes for any bus crossing the border. The town hadn't looked all that on the way through, so as we spied a CIFA bus parked in the same terminal we considered hi-tailing it out of town. It transpired the CIFA bus was just about to leave for the port of Guayaquil, the largest town in Ecuador, and we were assured it would be easy to get a bus from Guayaquil to Quito.

"OK. Let's do it." we agreed, so after twenty five hours on a bus, we were immediately on another bus and a further five hours beckoned.

As far as crossing the border was concerned the bus simply took us from the Peruvian customs control then over the border to the Ecuadorian customs control, and "Oley!" OK, the waiting in line was frustrating but that's only to be expected. No money changed hands and soon we were driving slowly through Ecuador on route to Guayaquil.

Darkness had fallen by the time we arrived in the large and impressively modern Guayaquil bus terminal. It looked more like the Trafford Centre with a bus terminal on the ground floor.

First stop was to find a phone and book ourselves into a hostel. My first choice within our price range, as recommended by Lonely Planet, was Hotel Versailles. However, the receptionist didn't speak one word of English and ignored every attempt I made to communicate in Spanish. He then put the phone down on me.

Cretin! (Him, not me, in case you're wondering.) I then tried my second choice, Hostel Suites Madrid, and our booking sailed along without a hitch. One taxi ride later and we were signing in and ready for a quick once round the block before turning in for the night.

FRIDAY 21 OCTOBER. QUITO, ECUADOR

Quito, like many South American cities, has a fascinating historical centre and boring suburbs. With one exception. There is an area downtown that is their equivalent of the Northern Quarter in Manchester, a neighbourhood full of trendy bars, cafes and nightlife. A gringos haven. Only many of the blogs we read suggested drunken or spaced out tourists and travellers were ripe for muggings by locals as they staggered out in the early hours.

So, after much research, I upped our budget and settled for a £40 a night private double room with en-suite facilities at the Jumbo Hostel in the old town. Nowhere was there a mention that this particular hostel was at the top of a steep hill. This was getting to be a regular feature of descriptions of South American hostels, whether on the net or in guides. "Don't mention the hills."

This is going to keep me fit, I thought, anticipating an upwardly mobile trek each time we returned to our base from excursions near and far. After over eight months travelling in heat and dust I was all skin and bones, which meant my body was fit but my clothes didn't. My belly had disappeared, which I was really pleased about, even if shorts and trousers tended to slip alarmingly below an acceptable level of builders crack. So much so in fact, that I had gone mad recently and spent a pittance on two or three new pairs of shorts and a couple of pairs of linen trousers. Wonder if Michael Palin ever had this problem?

The hostel itself was superb and deserves a special mention. For £40, not only did we get a large room with antique furniture but our own little corridor leading to our own bathroom and toilet. It felt like a suite, not just en-suite.

Then there was the breakfast. What's Ecuadorian for Wow!

By far the best breakfast of the whole trip so far. And the healthiest. The man about the house, his three daughters and housekeeper prepared mountains of the freshest fruit, fruit juices, eggs, breads, jams and cereals we had ever witnessed. He took a personal pride in everything he presented, happy to explain the origin of each element set before us.

He also told us a little of his life story. Originally from Ecuador, his family had emigrated to Spain in the 80s, only to return last year due to the recession in Europe, with Spain one of its more serious victims. Talking to him and his daughters they all missed the life and sophistication of Madrid, but needs must as they say.

Hélène and I had a good feeling about the place and looked forward to our time here before flying down to Patagonia and our first taste of cold and snow since we had left England in February.

Before we retired to the boudoir I had one last session on the hostel's internet.

I wish I hadn't. I picked up the whole sorry Rooney saga. When I first read about Rooney scoring a couple in the prostitute's net my mind drifted back to a Monty Python sketch.

"You've been a naughty, naughty boy."

What a plonker! Here was England's most high profile footballer. Even though he had cornered the ugly market, his wealth and notoriety meant he could buy many a beautiful starlet or wannabee. Not that for a moment do I condone his actions. Here was a man with everything. Clearly in love with his wife and totally obsessed with his baby. With more money than sense, he had it all. But a man's libido is an independent animal.

And when it all came out in the media, I'm sure he was hurting like hell and wishing he hadn't led from the front. I have no doubt he regretted what he did but the decimation of his home life has had a direct affect on his form which has dipped alarmingly.

Unlike most people I talked to, I have a spark of sympathy for Rooney's predicament. I always thought one of the golden rules of a "professional" prostitute was secrecy, so blabbing to the papers for money I consider the lowest of lows.

But now, prior to the Stoke game, I read that through his Hoover selling agent, Paul Stretford, he had refused a new contract and wanted to leave.

I couldn't believe it. And I had supported him when all around were calling for his head (well, meat and two veg actually). Reds on various United forums were furious. Spain was mentioned, but he can hardly speak proper English, what chance has he got to speak Spanish?

Sympathy was draining away. Then the following day a statement was released, in such elegant English that I knew Rooney couldn't have written it himself, claiming that he had become disillusioned with the lack of investment in world class players at United since the Glazers took over and the sale of Ronaldo.

He had a point there, of course. A lot of us had been saying the same thing so we could hardly have a go at him for that. But then figures of between £200,000 and £250,000 a week were mentioned and many thought pure selfish greed was at the heart of his transfer request.

I was numb with the sense of betrayal many of us felt. Fergie even went on MUTV to comment on the situation, something he rarely does but the level of media and supporter interest meant the story couldn't be brushed under the carpet.

Fergie looked tired and almost at the end of his tether as he re-iterated his and the club's position, but tellingly, stated the door was still open for Rooney. Whether he believed his own script is another matter. Most talk amongst supporters was to which club he would join. Only Chelsea, City and Real Madrid could afford him, yet Colleen had already stated she didn't want to move from the North West they knew.

The following day the media began to analyse the story and a number of interesting angles began to emerge. Mostly the papers were full of speculation of how he would fit in with City. You can imagine United fans' reaction to that! Hadn't he learnt anything from the Tevez debacle

The one option most of us hadn't considered was that he would stay. I mean, where would the Glazers find upwards of £200,000 a week whilst servicing the largest debt in world sport. Was Rooney really Baldric in disguise? Was this the most cunning of cunning plans?

Two days later it appeared that it was. The headlines screamed "Rooney Stays - for £250,000 a week!" How they knew the figure was pure speculation of course, but I was caught unawares (not unusual that) as was Lou Macari on MUTV.

"I never saw it coming," he said.

SUNDAY 23 OCTOBER. QUITO, ECUADOR
STOKE CITY 1 MANCHESTER UNITED 2

This morning I woke up 2 minutes before the alarm was due to go off. That's the power of United for you. Crept out of bed, switched off the alarm, got dressed and took my laptop out into the hostel corridor to get the Stoke match streaming going.

I still fucking hate streaming though, just in case you've forgotten. Is it just my laptop or does everyone have this problem? Jerky pictures that freeze just as an important bit is coming. The first half was spent criss-crossing between the two best feeds. Fortunately, unlike Fulham away, I didn't miss too much.

I had hoped to be able to pick up United fans' reaction to Rooney but the sound was poor and indistinct. Or quite simply it could have been down to my hearing. At my age... After a to-be-expected "bat out of hell" start by Stoke the match settled down with both sides even on points. Few chances were created by either side, but we wasted a superb 3 on 2 breakaway, only for Chico to mis-direct his back header to Berbatov and the chance went begging. But the Little Pea more than made up for that a few minutes later when a short cross came over in the Stoke box and he somehow managed to back head the ball into the net. Brilliant!

I stood up in the corridor and whispered, "GOOOAAALL!!!!"

The half ended with our Gary lucky not to be dismissed for a late tackle and I was not surprised to see Wes Brown come out for the second half. Only now I had a problem. My streaming had stopped streaming.

I couldn't wait. I rushed downstairs and asked one of the owner's three pretty daughters if I could possibly use their computer. It was a guest computer after all, but at $0.60 an hour I begrudged paying for something that would otherwise have been free. But needs must, and United needs above all.

I got logged on and, needless to say, the picture was far better and smoother than anything I could download onto my laptop. So now, back to the match...

As the second half wore on we asserted our superior technique and with ten minutes to go I prayed that today at last we would secure the three points we so desperately needed to close the gap on Chelsea.

Nobody told Stoke's Etherington. He cut in from the right and unleashed an unstoppable shot into our net. The drawing curse was about to strike again. How many more fucking times was this going to happen this season? United upped the intensity of their attacks and a wicked turn and shot from Evra was tapas home (sorry) with lightening reflexes by our little Mexican to put us 2-1 up with just four minutes of normal time remaining.

I celebrated sitting down this time because the hostel computer was in the lounge/dining room and everyone was watching. But I knew just how much that goal meant for us and sent out a warning to the rest of the Premiership that you write off United at your peril. The curse of Fulham, Everton and WBA had been broken. The United faithful behind the goal were raucous in their acclaim and the celebrations continued long after the final whistle.

I reluctantly switched off the streaming and went back upstairs to see if Hélène was awake and ready for breakfast. I certainly was. I could eat a llama!

"Did you win?" she croaked.

"Yup. 2-1 and our Little Pea was an inspiration."

That was too much information for her to decipher, so she turned over and closed her eyes again.

Great. Fanzine time.

TUESDAY 26 OCTOBER. QUITO - TENA, ECUADOR
MANCHESTER UNITED 3 WOLVERHAMPTON WANDERERS 2 LEAGUE CUP

For the first time in four days we weren't the only ones staying in the Jumbo Hostel. We came down for breakfast and there was a grey haired

American with his son and a pair of young Australians. Over another delicious meal we all exchanged stories, as you do, and time flew by.

In the end Hélène and I had to cut short the conversation as we wanted to catch a reasonably early bus to Tena for two nights and one full day in the Ecuadorian rainforest.

Three hours later we arrived in a small town which would be our base for an illuminating journey into the Ecuadorian rainforest, for the purpose of being introduced to the indigenous Kichwa people by the environmental agency, Ricancie. From the bus terminal we dragged our luggage the short distance to our hostel by the side of the river.

"Very picturesque," I thought, imagining the mosquitoes that would welcome us throughout the night. We set up our mosquito net as a precaution then went for a walk. I had read about a voluntary organisation that helped indigenous tribes adapt to the outside world, and they offered limited visits for travellers to witness their traditional way of life.

I switched on the laptop but the wi-fi signal was so weak I couldn't get the internet. Of course, my first priority was to find out the score of our League Cup home tie against Wolves. The littlest of the four tournaments United were involved in, yet an ideal opportunity for fringe players and youngsters to stake a claim for the first team. I was more interested in the line-up and how we played than the actual result, even though we hadn't been beaten for more than two seasons, having won the tournament the past two occasions.

But it was no good, so as a last resort I switched on the TV in our room and there was our match in all its glory! Eric be praised.

With the score delicately poised at 2-1 I used up every excuse in the book to prolong the time we'd have to go out for our obligatory walk round the block. No sooner had I focused on the play Wolves's Kevin Foley turned and his excellent low shot made it 2-2.

Oh, come on United. Send me on my way with a win. Please. Once more Chico came to our rescue. Coming on as a substitute eight minutes from time, he collected Darren Gibson's pass and fired in to win it in the dying stages. I'm falling in love with this man.

Hélène also fell in love. But for her it was the monkeys at an animal sanctuary deep in the rain forest. You should have seen her/them. She never looks at me like that.

SATURDAY 30 OCTOBER. QUITO, ECUADOR
MANCHESTER UNITED 2 TOTTENHAM HOTSPUR 0

Well, here we are. Tonight we take the 21.45 overnight flight to Santiago arriving 06.15 in the early hours of the morning. Then it's a five hour wait at the airport before boarding another flight to Punta Arenas and the wonders of Patagonia. The only question now is how to spend our final day in Ecuador?

Last Saturday we visited the famous ethnic market in Otavalo. One thing I have to say though. I love South American ethnic clothes, and Otavalo is a fantastic outlet BUT it seemed to me that every stall got their wares from the same wholesaler. Yesterday we visited the equator. Hélène in the northern hemisphere and me in the southern hemisphere. How cool was that! The gloss wore off slightly however when I read that the real equator was 300 metres away and out of bounds to tourists.

In reality the only thing left within easy travelling time of the capital were the hot springs and spa about a two hour bus ride away. I was game for that but Hélène wasn't keen on the schlep. Of course, what I didn't mention to her was the Tottenham game kicking off at 11.30am Ecuadorian time.

This was a tricky one. I'd been overdosing on United for the past few weeks and to say the other half was getting peeved would be putting it mildly! If I didn't want a second Jewish operation I would have to play this one very carefully. The best/worst part was kick-off local time split the day in two and put a mockers on anything substantial. I may have to make the ultimate sacrifice here but let's see how the morning pans out.

We went downstairs for the last of our brilliant breakfasts and rabbited for a while with the American father and son opposite. At the same time we checked our e-mails and attempted to chat to our girls, but it was the weekend and they had better things to do.

In the end we decided just to stroll around the historical centre of Quito and soak up the atmosphere. I kept a lookout for bars/cafes showing Premiership football but drew a blank as 11.30am approached.

11.30am passed. I sacrificed the love of my life for the love of my life.

So the day passed quietly in the old town, with a pleasant meal on the first floor of this quaint little courtyard. Then Hélène reminded me that we needed to print out our revised travel documents including the change of times for our flight this evening to Punta Arenas via Santiago, and our final flight from Caracas via Madrid to London scheduled for 8th February.

To do that we needed to visit an internet café as the printer in our hostel didn't work properly.

"Yes." I thought, "I may just be in time to catch the final few minutes."

With renewed enthusiasm we scoured the streets for an internet café. Bloody hell, they're all full of kids on a Saturday afternoon playing computer games. What's Ecuadorian for Bugger?

At last one terminal came free. I showed remarkable self discipline as I checked my e-mails first and located the response from Travel Nation with our up-to-date itinerary. I downloaded and printed it successfully. Hélène checked her e-mails then I was free to click onto BBC Sport.

"Nani scores in controversial United win."

YAHOO!!!!!

Controversial my arse. Tottenham have come second, AGAIN, and that's all that matters. Our second three points in a row and the start of something serious, I hope. Then my mind drifted to my mate, Rick, of Leading Tower of Tottenham fame. A staunch Yid, he spits blood every time United beat Tottenham, (that's a lot of blood) believing every single conspiracy theory known to man. If the truth be told, he occasionally has a point. Today's referee, Mark Clattenburg, was the same referee that disallowed a clear Tottenham goal at Old Trafford when Roy Carroll scooped the ball out of the net when we all knew it had crossed the line.

Then there was the "controversial" penalty awarded couple of seasons ago, again at OT, when a Tevez inspired second half comeback had seen United fight back from 0-2 down at half time to stroll out 5-2 winners. All Rick would talk about was the penalty, and conveniently erasing the memory of another Tottenham capitulation.

They say that over a full season decisions tend to balance themselves out, however I feel the pain of those that go against us, such as Drogba's offside winner at OT last season, hurt a hell of a lot more than the pleasure felt by today's decision to let Nani's exquisite piece of quick thinking go unpunished.

Either way I was able to put on a happy face before we quit Quito. (You knew I was going to get that one in somewhere, didn't you? Wouldn't want to let you down, now would I?)

ARGENTINA

MONDAY 1 NOVEMBER. PUNTA ARENAS, CHILE – USHUAIA, ARGENTINA

At last, Patagonia. While lots of Reds I know were preparing for a little Turkey trot in Europe, Hélène and I girded our loins for an eleven hour bus journey from Punta Arenas in Chile, where we had landed from Quito via Santiago, to Ushuaia in Argentina, with a short stop in Rio Grande (what an evocative name!) where we'll change buses.

As we left the distinctly unimpressive town of Punta Arenas behind us, with the exception of our hostel room key in my pocket which I'd forgotten to return, (Whoops!) the vastness of the southern Chilean countryside soon left an impression. Sky as far as the horizon, with three distinctively different shades of blue punctuated with an array of cloud formations that dominated the vista. Sheep were in the ascendancy here, with very few signs of human life, save the odd, isolated farm and petroleum plant.

The bleakness of the landscape was strangely rewarding. There was a purity in the 360 degree views that pervaded our coach windows. Nothing but nature on the outside and a bunch of young (mostly) German travellers inside, sleeping or succumbing to the call of their mp3 players.

After a couple of hours we arrived at Primera Angosmana, the entrance of the Straights of Magallanos, a channel of water that our coach had to cross by ferry. We jumped down off the coach to take advantage of superior views offered by the upper deck passenger platform on one side of the boat. The earth looked extremely barren from up here. Cold, dark, flat and uninviting yet strangely hypnotic. How do you explain that? I think it's because back in the UK you're never too far from towns and cities, but here at the tip of South America settlements are few and far between and you get this pervading sense of isolation.

The boat slowly pulled away and soon the small white ferry terminal building was the only break on the horizon. Within minutes a school of small black and white dolphins were swimming alongside, occasionally jumping out of the water to our utter delight.

Camera, camera, camcorder, camcorder, camera, camera.

That should do it.

Then we came to the Chilean/Argentinian border and a wonderful opportunity presented itself for me to paste pristine "Love United Hate Glazer" stickers number 60 and 61 on the windows of both the Chilean and Argentinean customs halls.

That should expedite their demise.

You can thank me later.

As we approached the outskirts of Ushaia, capital of the Tierra del Fuego Province, wall after wall was painted in light blue graffiti proclaiming sovereignty over the Malvinas (Falklands). Got the impression they were still a bit peeved. I made myself promise not to mention the war.

TUESDAY 2 NOVEMBER. USHUAIA, ARGENTINA
BURSASPOR 0 MANCHESTER UNITED 3

It looked like Fergie and me both approached this match from the same perspective. United are in a comfortable position in their Champions League group. At this stage of the season, Premiership points are more important if we want to catch Chelsea. Although we struggled at home to the Turks, two consecutive league wins and six points under our belts testified to a growing confidence in the team, even if we're not firing on all cylinders yet. I expected a better showing in Turkey, only this time the lads would have to do without my real-time support.

Fergie decided to rest Ferdinand and introduce some youngsters to our Euro away. I decided the one chance in my life to visit the Tierra del Fuego National Park and visit a real live penguin colony would actually take precedence over this qualifier. I must be getting old.

As the excursion was not until the afternoon, Hélène and I had a lazy morning just getting our act together. After a tasteless breakfast of two mini croissants and a cup of tea in our hostel we went for a stroll by the shore. The sun was shining, and even though we were only six hundred miles from Antarctica we could both have been wearing T-shirts.

Cool.

And with the sun shining on the majestic snow-capped mountains behind that made up the 360° backdrop, I felt a really lucky man. (The lucky man didn't feel the same way though, and ran a mile. Boom. Boom) At 3 o' clock we boarded a bus which took us round the bay to board the only boat that is allowed to drop passengers onto the exclusive penguin only island. The rest of the boats have to stay offshore and their passengers click away from a distance. Not us.

As we approached the island we could see hundreds of Happy Feet waddling, standing and swimming. Their movements were a delight. So comical yet so adorable. And such cheeky faces, although they hardly gave us a nod of recognition.

I suppose once you've seen one human, you've seen 'em all.

We disembarked, with instructions to look but not touch, so no chance to p-p-p-p-p-pick up a penguin. We followed well indicated paths amidst the hordes of black and white creatures that regarded us with indifference. Unknowingly they posed for hundreds of photos. I may be no David Bailey but these creatures were a delight to photograph. Such posers. One was lying under the wooden walkway incubating her eggs. I bent down to within inches of her face and she didn't bat an eyelid. Of course, I'm not sure whether penguins can bat their eyelids, but whatever they can do, this one didn't. Just stared at me though half closed eyes.

Being so close was a privilege. They were playing at home and we were the away fans, so we respected their turf. Reluctantly the guide indicated we should return to the boat and so we left this magical island to its incumbents. One for the long term memory bank.

We returned to the mainland where the boat company laid on

afternoon refreshments. I had a delightful slice of cake and a nice cup of tea. Even when you're on the other side of the planet, nothing hits the spot better than a nice cup of tea. I'm sure you'll agree.

"Water, water everywhere and not a drop to drink."

An updated version could read… "sheep sheep everywhere and not a bite to eat."

Patagonia is famous for its lamb. Patagonian lamb. We had seen thousands of sheep through the windows of our bus and now one of those cuddly woollen creatures would be languishing at the bottom of my stomach. Tonight we were going to treat ourselves to this expensive but delicious local signature dish. Back at our hostel we changed into warmer clothes and set out on our mission.

We walked up and down the entire main thoroughfare. Tourist restaurant after tourist restaurant enticing us with Patagonian lamb on the menu but once we stepped inside the said eatery not one was able to offer us any. It transpired that whoever produced these famous sheep could earn more money by exporting them than by selling them to local restaurants.

I was bitterly disappointed and looked around for someone to blame. Someone I could take it out on. But there was no-one. The restaurant owners were as bitter as I was that they couldn't fulfil tourists' expectations. So in the end we settled on sausages with all the trimmings. Not bad, but to come all this way….

CHILE

THURSDAY 4 NOVEMBER. USHAIA, ARGENTINA TO PUERTO NATELES, CHILE

Early start this morning. Set the alarm for 04.00 and actually got up at 04.00. This morning we began the sixteen hour return journey to Puerto Nateles in Chile. As we approached the Argentinean/Chilean border Hélène began to panic as she had hidden some fruit bread in our rucksacks and this was on a comprehensive list of unimportables into Chile.

No worries. Everything went smoothly. Even my "Love United Hate Glazer" stickers were still resplendent in their locations. Next to us were a young couple on their honeymoon. Aaahhh!

"Leave them alone." Hélène whispered non-seductively in my ear.

"C'mon Hélène. We've got another 15 ½ hours. I've counted enough sheep to last a lifetime. It's time to talk." so before she could come back with the obvious retort I turned round and introduced ourselves. Stretched handshakes all round. We exchanged experiences, both being knocked out by each other's story. How long could I last before the subject of football would raise its beautiful head. I put it at about half an hour.

"So, who do you support?"

"I support Liverpool and (I've forgotten her name) supports Barnet. I see you're a United fan." he said. Nothing wrong with his eyesight then, even if his judgement was seriously impaired.

He seemed a nice young lad, so while I formulated my attitude to his mental deficiency I engaged his girlfriend. Ladies first and all that.

"Barnet, eh? Were you at Old Trafford for the Carling Cup match?"

Turns out she was. Respect. It was their cup final after all. I commiserated with her over the unfortunate sending off of their keeper in the first half which put a mockers on the match as a contest. Then I turned my attention to the lad.

I won't bore you with the details. Suffice to say that after an hour both me and his partner had had enough. His girlfriend actually stormed off, which on a 52 seater bus is a pretty hard thing to do. Hélène had found a soul mate.

Finally arrived in Puerto Nateles, a small town of just over 19,000 inhabitants. It was dark. After settling into our hostel we were dying just to go to bed, but we hadn't eaten a proper meal all day so we strolled round the small town looking for somewhere to eat. Most places were closed by now, in fact the only place we could find was this casual Italian restaurant which had one long wooden table and a couple of smaller ones.

As soon as we entered we felt the positive vibe. A mishmash of travellers and ageing hippies were scattered like the cushions on the seats. Soft rock was playing and a chalked up menu advertised it wares. I chose home-made lasagne and apple crumble. The lasagne was good, really good but the apple crumble was...WONDERFUL! 8,472 miles from home and I discover the best apple crumble I have ever tasted. Who needs drugs when something so perfect filled my mouth on the way to my stomach. So sweet, so hot, and with a crumble that didn't crack my dentures into submission. An orgasm of heat, flavour, taste and texture that defied the lack of foreplay. The shock of the first mouthful and I was hooked. Culinary sensory overload.

More! More! More! More!

Yup, I had second helpings.

Sweet, sweet dreams.

SATURDAY 6 NOVEMBER. PUERTO NATALES, CHILE
MANCHESTER UNITED 2 WOLVERHAMPTON WANDERERS 1

I've always maintained that football, and not English, is the international language. This fact was re-enforced today as conversation broke out in our minivan on the way to the Tierra Del Paine national park. The middle-aged couple at the back lived in Santiago, but the guy, an engineer working in the mining industry, was from Glasgow and a Celtic fan whilst the guy on his own up front turned out to be a Scummer. Originally from Southampton and now retired from a career with Boeing, he lived with his wife in Reno, Nevada.

The English speaking driver cum tour guide didn't. Speak a word of English that is, so between explanations in Spanish we made our own conversation and, needless to say, football topped the agenda. First the Southampton fan brought out his ABU credentials by listing all the reasons he disliked United. To give him his due, the Scottish guy was more interested in Celtic than United and didn't slag us off. Both however revealed admiration for our ability to attract the best youngsters and we went on to discuss who the best young players in the Premiership were. With the Scummer we discussed various United v Southampton matches we had seen down the years, including the invisible grey shirts and the year we lost 6-3. He would remember those. I retorted by saying Eric had taken revenge on Bobby Stokoe's offside goal at Wembley in '76 by recalling the player early from planet Earth. An unnecessary low shot I now regret.

We both agreed Bestie had put on a wonder show with four goals in our 5-2 trouncing of the south coast club in the early 70s. Later George described this match as one of the reasons he became disillusioned with United and football in general, as he pre-Rooneyed Rooney by claiming the rest of the team were not in his class and he could only see us declining from the heights of the European Cup triumph at Wembley just a few short years before.

Interspersed between footy talk were numerous geographical delights such as the famous "W" mountain formation and the Green and Grey lakes. Traipsing through the woods we came to an opening, and there before us, across a beach of charcoal grey stones, was the bluest iceberg you ever saw.

Blue! A mysteriously pale blue iceberg that defied logic with its living breathing colour. I'd always thought icebergs were white, like crushed snow. Where did the blue come from?

Some bits had floated to the shore and I was able to pick up a heavy slab and hold it aloft like a trophy for the obligatory photo. Now the ice was totally transparent. How did that happen? (I really should have concentrated more in science classes). My first iceberg, and it tasted….icy, but pure and icy if you can imagine such a thing. On the return journey someone spotted condors circling above so we asked the driver to stop, and even if I say so myself, captured a wicked shot of the bird's elegant flight on my camcorder.

The Southampton fan tried to get the football results on his iPhone but there was no signal. However, after visiting the Mirodor caves on our final stop, getting back onboard the minibus the Scottish guy informed me via his Blackberry that United had beaten Wolves 2-1. Relief and joy fought with each other as to which would be the dominant emotion. I'll call that a score draw. He then passed the instrument to me and I was able to read the report.

Translated into English, United had played crap yet secured their third three points in a row with a Ji Sung Park double, including a wonder dribble and strike in the last minute.

"Park. Park. Wherever you may be, thanks for the goals from a Red in Chile."

Reading further, it transpired that half the United team had caught the Turkey Trots on the way back from their Champions League tie against Bursapor and we'd fielded a team dominated by youngsters and reserves that had never played together. No wonder we were crap, in both senses of the word.

On the other hand, individual players came in for scathing attacks in the report that suggested the next generation still have some way to go before they became true "United" players. I have my personal doubts if some ever will but there you go. Goodbye Ronaldo, hello Obertan, as performed by The Glazernomics.

Still, the sign of a great team is getting a win when a defeat would be more appropriate, so at least this made up for the draws we had snatched from the jaws of victory at the start of the season. Lady luck was beginning to smile on us, and at the end of the day, victory is all important. It keeps us within striking distance of Chelsea and that's the main thing. Just wait till we start playing football.

Meanwhile tomorrow Chelsea meet Liverpool. Let's see if Gerrard gives them an early Christmas present like he did last season, or whether Liverpool's mini revival continues at the Rent Boys' expense. I don't hold out much hope, but you never know. Meanwhile Arsenal are at home to Newcastle, who they recently beat 4-0 up at St James's Park in the Carling Cup fielding a team of youngsters. Foregone conclusion, that one.

Back in Puerto Nateles it was back to the pizzeria we ate at on our first night and I order another hot apple crumble with vanilla ice cream. Life is too short, and I knew I would regret not indulging in this edible orgasm for the second time in two days.

Je ne regret rien. I came again with each hot, sweet mouthful. My stomach revelled in the afterglow before coming back to earth.

We made our way back to our hostel. A quick session on the internet later, within which I discerned we really had played awful, really awful and Ji Sung Park was "really happy" to have scored the winner in the last minute. I missed the goals but caught the last minute celebrations. I don't know what JSP has done to his hair, but if he continues in this vein he can sport a mullet for all I care.

Success at last on the Patagonian lamb front. We found a restaurant in the square by the church that had a lamb on a revolving spit. There was only one other couple in there when we arrived, which was not a good sign, but I can tell you the lamb was excellent. Tender yet with an exquisite taste. Perfect. All in all we ended the evening on a high.

ARGENTINA

SUNDAY 7 NOVEMBER. PUERTO NATALES, CHILE - EL CALAFATE. ARGENTINA

As our bus neared El Calafate I asked the Southampton fan if he could get the Premiership results on his iPhone. He checked the BBC Sport web site, which only informed us that Arsenal v Newcastle, Liverpool v Chelsea and West Brom v City were playing today. Shit. I was too early.

I had hoped to check the results on my laptop when we arrived at our hostel, but after booking our onward bus tickets from El Calafate to Puerto Madryn and obtaining the tour options for visiting the Perito Moreno glacier the following day, the afternoon was passing and Hélène wanted to take a fading daylight stroll around town. She gave me a look which translated into, "United aren't playing today so it's my time now."

Hmmm. OK, for the sake of preventing World War III I relented and didn't even take my laptop with me in case we stopped at a Wi-Fi café. I gave Hélène my undivided attention. That is until we met the Scummer and his mate who were sitting in a street cafe, sipping beer and scoffing pies as though they were going out of fashion.

"Have you caught the results yet?" he called.

"No, not yet." nodding my head in the direction of you-know-who.

"Chelsea beat Liverpool 2-0 and Arsenal lost at home to Newcastle 1-0."

"You're joking." I replied.

"No, seriously."

I hadn't known him long enough for piss-taking to be on the agenda, so, fuck me, I hadn't expected that. I wonder what the odds for that little accumulator must have been?

Our nearest rivals had beaten our most hated rivals. How did I feel? Good question. Yeah. Good. OK, let's walk.

MONDAY 8 NOVEMBER. PATAGONIA, ARGENTINA

Another of my lifelong ambitions was realised today. A one-on-one with the world famous Perito Moreno glacier in Los Glaciares National Park in Patagonia, Argentina.

We had discussed the one day Perito Moreno glacier tour options the previous afternoon. Our first choice included a one hour boat trip and a promenade along the five kilometre walkway with viewing platforms at various intervals. Unfortunately, only fit people between 18 and 50 are allowed to take a trek on the ice itself. I thought with my George Clooney looks and new dentures I could lie about my age but Hélène wouldn't have it, so we resigned ourselves to just the boat and walkway.

The ride from our hostel to the glacier was a pleasure in itself, as we passed over a dam and along one side the bluest of man-made lakes. The vast open plains of southern Argentina lay either side of our windows, with snow-capped mountains in the distance. We skirted Bay Redonda of Lake Argentino as well as having the chance to glimpse Solitare Island before crossing the Mitre river. Milky blue lakes accompanied us for miles, small icebergs breaking the surface at irregular intervals.

At Curva de Los Suspiros we got a sneak preview of the world famous glacier. Unreal. Then arriving at the edge of Lago Argentino 50 miles from El Calafate we could see the full majesty of the Perito Moreno glacier in the distance. Even from our coach window its living breathing sky blue dominated the skyline. Among the 365 glaciers in this protected area, the Perito Moreno is by far the most outstanding.

The vast body of ice, at 257 sq kms/97 sq miles, larger than Buenos Aries itself, loomed before us. A solid jagged wall of ice, five kilometres wide and with an average height of 74 meters/240 feet, just seemed to have stopped dead in its tracks. It was difficult to grasp what our eyes could clearly see. The bus parked near the water's edge and we walked down to where a boat was to take us on a one hour trip, up close and personal, with the glacier itself. We immediately ascended onto the upper viewing deck. As the glacier came nearer I was aware of skid marks on the ice, clearly dirt of some sort. Somewhat disappointed after the brilliant perfection of the icebergs we had encountered, the size and scale of the solid wall of ice still took our breath away.

I had actually hoped the boat would get a little closer, but the never-ending melting process forbids this. We watched the detachment of ice blocks of various sizes from a short distance and heard the roaring as chunks fall in slow motion and new mini icebergs were created. Each time I heard a roar I pressed the 'play' button on my camcorder a split second too late to capture one of natures enduring phenomena.

Steven Spielberg is not going to lose any sleep any time soon I can tell you. Once back on dry land we climbed the gently sloping ingeniously man-made decking walkway that circumvented one side of the glacier. The higher we went the more awesome the views. We just had to stop and feast our eyes and ears at each vantage point. I continued my impersonation of a fading gunslinger, my camcorder missing by seconds to shoot the moment giant chunks of ice tore themselves away from the glacier and fell in slow motion into the lake.

The whole day passed like this. My eyes saw everything, and I suppose that's what counts the most, but I have no moving record. Hélène took the snaps and she caught a couple of beauties so I'll have to live with that.

On the way back to El Calafate I followed the lead set by the rest of the passengers and drifted off to sleep. Hélène nudged me a couple of times, reminding me that we may never pass this way again, but I had seen it all on the way out, and even allowing for the opposite angle on the way back, heavy eyelids dominated my reflexes.

As I drifted I allowed my mind to wander.

Now, let's see. Tomorrow we arrive in Puerto Madryn around midday, so we should have settled into our hostel around 13.00. (Of course, in dreams I don't use the 24 hour clock, so I worked with 1.00pm) If City v United kicks off at 8.00pm and we are three hours behind, I have to get to a TV set or set-up my laptop for streaming before 5.00pm. OK, sorted. Now the only thing is not to let Hélène suggest anything that spoils this master plan.

I had missed both the Bursospur and Wolves matches as they happened, so I thought it would not be too much to ask for the derby to take precedence. And if not… bollocks! I'm still watching it. Encouraged by this positive outcome I let my mind drift in its normal undisciplined manner for the rest of the journey back.

The first thing I did back at our hostel was open my laptop and go to BBC Sport to check the football results.

UNBER-FUCKING-LEAVABLE!

FA Cup 1st round proper. Rochdale 2 FC United of Manchester 3

They'd fucking done it again! Created history by beating a league side, away from hone and reaching the second round proper for the first time in their five year history. Then I started to read the report. They only did a fucking United and scored the winner in the last minute! United by name, United by nature. What a night that must have been.

I was still shaking as I clicked onto my Facebook page and went straight for my Home page to read all the comments of my Red brothers and sisters.

Quel emotion!

Finally I came across a YouTube link and watched in awe as first FC United raced into a 2-0 lead, were drawn back to 2-2, then in the last minute a United breakaway saw the Rochdale goalie make a howler and there was Michael Norton to slot the ball home from just a couple of yards.

Pandemonium!

Eric, how I wish I had been there.

TUESDAY 9 NOVEMBER. PUERTO NUTELES – PEURTO MADRYN, ARGENTINA

Not much to report today. With a two o' clock departure for the bus to Puerto Madryn, we just strolled around town in the morning, sent off Lilyella's birthday present from the post office and went for coffee and dunkers. The only disturbing aspect of the morning was reading a thread I had started on Facebook regarding the mouthwatering possibility of FC United being drawn against Manchester United in third round of the FA Cup.

I couldn't believe the level of animosity between sections of both sets of supporters. Many, like me, have sympathies in both camps, but for many hard core Reds, supporters of FC United are seen as traitors, deserting the ship and, let's put it this way, would not be welcomed with open arms at Old Trafford.

The level of intolerance perpetuated by these cowardly keyboard cowboys disgusted me. Some of the most loyal and vocal United fans over the years; men, women and children who had stood up to be counted in the fight against Murdoch, considered the debt laden Glazers takeover as the final straw that destroyed their principles of club and community. They had made the ultimate sacrifice, turning away from their greatest love, but for many Reds this simple but most painful act of principle has been seen as betrayal.

I am MUFC first, and all other life forms second, but I admire all that FC United stands for and have achieved against the odds and will continue to follow their progress. If I lived in Manchester I'm sure I'd go to watch both. My only "live" experience so far has been a pre-season friendly against AFC Wimbledon down at Kingstonian's ground, and even though FCUM lost 2-0 the atmosphere was superb. Singing and supporting for the whole of the 90 minutes, with a variety and wit lost at Old Trafford and most sanitised grounds these days.

This was how United support used to be in the 60s and 70s. I know, 'cos I was there. Old Trafford was a fortress as far as away supporters were concerned. We were louder and more venomous than the Kop. Centre, left side or right side. If you were Stretford you were somebody. The Scoreboard ran the Liverpool supporters out of the ground in a Ted MacDougal (yes, you did read that correctly) inspired 2-0 victory.

Outnumbered, the end of the Cantilever would taunt the away support in the Scoreboard End. United fans were the most vocal and passionate in the land, but a combination of all-seater stadiums and club stewards trained in Gestapo tactics have all but destroyed one major aspect of United's great heritage.

Instead of berating FCUM we should acknowledge what brought them to where we are now. We're all United at heart. We all bleed red, white and black as well as Green & Gold and that's a fact.

WEDNESDAY 10 NOVEMBER. PUERTO MADRYN, ARGENTINA
MANCHESTER CITY 0 MANCHESTER UNITED 0

Riding in the back of a taxi from the bus terminal in Puerto Madryn we were impressed by the quality of the individual houses along the sea front. Made of brick and many seemed like new builds. We were obviously heading for an up market area of town.

Arriving outside Hostel Hipocampo I made a mental note to ask for one of the three rooms upstairs with a sea view. However that was easier said than done as both the ancient owner and his wife didn't speak a word of English. In fact I'm sure the old guy was born before language had been invented. And he had a stare on him that would have out Draculared Christopher Lee himself! Finally we were installed and so attempted to open up the hostel's Wi-Fi connection.

Nothing. A pattern was emerging right across South America. Hostels advertising Wi-Fi but in reality only availability in the common areas such as the reception, lounge and kitchen.

We went downstairs but still nothing. The old guy obviously didn't know how the internet connection worked, but conveyed the information that a woman was coming to the hostel this evening who spoke a little English and would be able to help us.

We weren't convinced, so walking along the sea front we agreed that if we couldn't get Wi-Fi up and running we'd move to another hostel. We needed our free day, the day after tomorrow, to book our onward hostels, try to find cheap flights in Argentina and Brazil and other time consuming activities.

We chose the first sea front restaurant to have a lovely seafood meal, then continued into town. I suddenly came over all funny.

"Wait a minute. No Wi-Fi means no streaming means no football." NNNOOOOOOOO!!!"

Right, plan B.

"Hélène, we've got to find a bar stroke café that shows Premiership football." Her expression told me she didn't share my anxiety or even give a shit. I did.

Strolling along, we met a couple from the bus sitting in a sea front bar. During our conversation I noticed a Wi-Fi symbol on the window, so went inside to talk to the staff.

"Hablas Ingles?

"Un poco."

"Bien", I said. "Do you know of a bar or café in town which shows Premiership football?"

Much conflabbing later, they told me of two bars opposite each other two blocks away in the centre of town. Heartened by this news, we said "adios" to our new found friends and I led Hélène to the first of the two bars.

The woman inside was pretty helpful (in fact she was both pretty and helpful, but keep that to yourself) but unable to locate any of the promised sports channels on their TV. We told her we would be back but went immediately across the road to the other bar where the staff were much more on the ball.

An hour later we were back and the game was literally thirty three seconds old. Hélène's complaints merged into the background as I got involved in the game. Looking around I could see I was the only Brit and the only one interested in the game. So be it.

After a scrappy first ten minutes United began to play the sharper, more incisive football, so the memories of the dire performance against Wolves the previous weekend began to fade away. With one exception. We weren't creating any clear-cut chances.

Half time arrived and I was satisfied with our performance. Just lacking a cutting edge. Berbatov was working hard but Park wasn't sparkling as of late. Defence-wise we looked solid, yet for the second season in a row I couldn't believe City were the home team. A team assembled for millions seemed content to hold out for a draw. What sort of mentality is that?

The one incident of note was a head to head confrontation between Rafael and Tevez, right under the nose of the referee. They must have been swearing at each other in Spanuguese.

The second half continued in the same vein, with United taking the game to their pale blue opponents. Without going on too long, the game ended 0-0. No glorious last minute Scholes winner this time. We had been the better team with the greater desire to win, but it also illustrated where our shortcomings lay. It's my belief they won't be overcome in time for United to be crowned Champions this season. Already we are light years behind Chelsea on the goal difference stakes. Let's just say I hope my words are stuffed down my throat come next May.

Admiring my passion, the bar owner let me put up LUHG sticker number 62 on the mirror behind the bar. You could say a better result for me than United.

THURSDAY 11 NOVEMBER. PUERTO MADRYN, ARGENTINA

Today has to go down as one of my greatest non-United days ever. Hélène and I had a whale of a day, thanks to the Southern Right Whale putting on a show right in front of us. I think they enjoyed our company almost as much as we enjoyed theirs.

The day had a superb beginning. A minibus picked us up from our hostel and drove along the coast. To one side, the desolate scenery of the pure Patagonian steppe. To the other, the deep blue ocean. Mighty impressive. We headed for the Carlos Amenghino Isthmus, the piece of land that joins the peninsula to the continent. The minibus came to a halt at the mouth of a perfect bay, a semi circular beach of flat yellow sand and the sea flanked by two natural headlands. The sky was the bluest of blues, the sun was shining and the sea was calm, all contriving to create the ideal backdrop.

We put on our life jackets and waterproof capes, then together with around a dozen equally excited tourists we clambered onboard our vessel and set sail for the ocean. The leaflet had claimed, in black and white, that we were GUARANTEED to see whales between June and December, when they come close to the shores of the Nuevo Gulf to mate or bear their calves. Quite a bold claim, I thought. Most times there's some small print at the bottom or on the back disclaiming any guarantee, but there it was in a screaming headline. Latin American bravado or a fact of life? We'll see.

We saw all right. No sooner had we left the shelter of the bay when we all gasped in unison as a giant iconic tail rose out of the water not 100 metres from our boat. If Hélène and I had thought the distant sight of a whale way out at sea five months earlier off Byron Bay in Australia had been one of life's defining moments, that paled into insignificance at this earth shattering moment. Our very own whale. Wow!

A few minutes later a collective gasp as an adult whale leapt majestically out of the water on the other side of our boat. At times of high excitement, we do come out with some shit, don't we? We had all witnessed one of nature's truly great spectacles, yet we all turned to each other and exclaimed, "DID YOU SEE THAT!"

Of course we'd all just seen that, but you just couldn't help yourself screaming the obvious. However, the show had only just begun.

The skipper shouted something and the boat turned a full 90 degrees. Another tail. No, two tails, but one was larger than the other. As Paul Simon would have been inspired to write, this was a mother and child reunion. A mother and her calf were literally swimming towards us. Before we knew it they had passed under our boat and come up for air on the other side. Then I realized what was happening. They were watching us! Fuck me, if that's not a Kleenex moment then I don't know what is! It sure wasn't sea spray that caused my eyes to mist over as both mother and child lifted their heads out of the water and stared at us!

Close up we could see what looked like giant boils on their heads but were actually callosites which represent their identification marks. Behind the callosites we could see the blowholes, used by the animals to breathe and blow air from their lungs.

The calf was more inquisitive than the mother and seemed to pose just for us. There was no need to scramble for shots as it played with us for well over half an hour before our boat left them to their aquatic wonderland.

I was in love with one of the ugliest looking mammals on the planet, but looks mean nothing at moments like these. We had connected, I know we had.

Women's lib have nothing on these creatures. They had made the first move and I had truly, madly and deeply fallen in love with a creature from the deep. OK, you can call it cradle snatching if you want, but that baby whale had had a shattering effect on my senses and I'll never forget it. Unrequited love? I expect so.

I didn't have its address. I suspect it couldn't read and I'm equally sure it forgot about me the moment we sped away, but I will never forget him/her/it.

SATURDAY 13 NOVEMBER. PUERTO MADRYN, ARGENTINA
ASTON VILLA 2 MANCHESTER UNITED 2

Despite there being no need for an alarm clock I woke up early, and by the time I twisted Hélène's wrist in my direction, her watch read 07.40.

"OK. Still time to lie here and put off the decision." Now the rest of her body followed her wrist. She spoke.

"You making tea?"

Our daughters have now followed Hélène in this subtle combination of asking a polite question, but leaving no doubt an order is implied. As this was an opportunity to move things along I agreed and crawled out of bed.

I'm not good in confined spaces, and our kettle was sitting on the fridge in the small narrow corridor by the door, which also housed a microwave and various cupboards. In one of these cupboards the hostel owners had supplied the noisiest crockery on the planet. No matter how hard I concentrated, loud cracks resounded in our room as I removed two large plates from under a pile of smaller plates and saucers.

"Ssshhh!!" growled Hélène. "Have some consideration for other guests."

What about me? It's not my fault the crockery was so noisy. What else could I do? Meanwhile I unplugged my laptop from its overnight charger and attached the kettle to the adapter and plugged it in. As the kettle took its time to come to the boil I monitored Hélène's condition.

Slow. Very slow.

Somehow I didn't think getting washed and dressed with any sense of urgency was on the cards, so I resigned myself to watching the Villa match either on the hostel TV if by a miracle I could find ESPN or Fox Sports, or streaming on my laptop, the worst case scenario as I STILL FUCKING HATE STREAMING!!!

I allowed myself to drift back to sleep after orange juice, tea and pain raisin. I set my body clock to 09.30 as the match kicked off at 09.45 Argentina time. Hélène's steady breathing suggested she had fallen asleep again whilst I drifted between semi-consciousness and consciousness, my normal state if the truth be told.

No, this is not good. I have to get up. I untangled myself from Hélène's arms and legs (she kept all the good bits to herself), got up, dressed and crept downstairs with my laptop.

There was no-one in the hostel lounge so I tried all the channels but no Premiership football. I wasn't surprised, so I went to free-football.tv, logged in and chose the top channel. After the ever more annoying 30 second commercial the fractured picture appeared on the screen.

Shit, fifteen minutes gone already but the score was 0-0. Shouldn't think I missed anything then. As the first half wore on, two things became apparent.

1) We weren't at the races

2) I FUCKING HATE STREAMING!!!!

Half time arrived. A chance to catch-up on my e-mails. And Hélène's too.

The second half began where the first half ended, with Villa clearly on top. As the half wore on we began to achieve greater possession but with little penetration.

Then it all started to go wrong.

The streaming that is. First one channel froze altogether, then the second and third wouldn't let me back in. Oversubscribed came the message on the screen. Oversubscribed! What the fuck does that mean? Bastards!

Finally the first one came back, only for the referee to award Villa a penalty.

Bastards! Jesus, Ashley Young is taking a hell of a long time to take the penalty.

Oh no. It's frozen, AGAIN!

AAaaaahhh!!!

No. Nothing.

I went onto BBC Sport. Villa 1 United 0 Fucking Bastards!

Nobody was letting me back in. All the streaming channels, for one reason or another, were denying me access.

I FUCKING, FUCKING HATE HATE STREAMING!!!!!!

Back to BBC Sport.

Villa 2 United 0. M. Albrighton 76'.

What the +*!**"!+!!

Eric give me strength.

Ah! It's come back. What's this? Macheda...GOAL!!

2-1.

C'mon United!

The disjointed images on the screen showed United dominating proceedings at last. 2-1 down and with eight minutes to go they finally wake up. Another disjointed attack. Another frozen moment in time. Did I say "moment"? It should have read "minutes". Back to BBC Sport.

Villa 2 United 2 .....Vidic 85'.

"We'll never die, we'll never die, we'll never die, we'll never die. We'll keep the Red flag flying high, 'cos Man United will never die."

Vidic, I love you. You're turning into a star this season now you're back.

In the final ten minutes we saw the real United for the first time but it was too little too late and 2-2 was a fair result, all things considered. Of course, that meant another draw and a golden opportunity for Chelsea to extend their lead at the top to seven points.

I posted a cryptic comment on my Facebook page, closed the computer and went back upstairs. Hélène had her typical post match expression. In the two hours I had been downstairs she had packed both our cases and obviously the gloss of looking at whales from our hotel window had worn off.

Ho hum.

TUESDAY 16 NOVEMBER. BUENOS AIRES, ARGENTINA
RIVER PLATE 1 BOCA JUNIORS 0

For all of you out there who don't believe in the possibility that the world is flat, or ghosts, or God, or politicians, or global warming or fairies at the bottom of the garden, I've got news for you. The day I believed I'd never see came to fruition tonight.

Hélène actually ENJOYED a football match!

Even as I write the above sentence the significance of this remark sends reverberations through my entire being. However, we're not talking about any old match. Oh dear me no. We're talking THE "Super El Clasico": River Plate v Boca Juniors taking place in the very stadium in Buenos Aires used for the 1978 World Cup Final.

You see, this all came about when we arrived at our hostel in Buenos Aires on Sunday afternoon. Whilst waiting to register I looked round the reception area at all the notices and posters and....wallop! "Super El Clasico" THE "EL CLASICO" and it was happening this coming Tuesday evening.

I couldn't believe my luck. Hélène cursed hers. I explained how, apart from Eric's Disciples on Earth, this was the one match I would die to see. (And if Hélène had her way, I probably would) I tried to convince her this was no ordinary football match but one with an atmosphere like no other on the planet. I'm not sure she swallowed this argument, but she could see how much it meant to me so she agreed to come with.

I checked out the prices.

HOW MUCH?

I knew the average ticket prices to be between £5-£10 so £70 was a complete rip-off of gringo proportions but I bit the bullet and purchased two tickets without informing Hélène the price I paid. I'm nothing if not a coward.

The evening of the match arrived and we all gathered in the hostel reception. I couldn't make out any British football fans by their satirical inelegance so contented myself with the thought that I was "keeping it real". I'd plumped for my white United polo shirt with red trim, enough to make me inconspicuous amongst the red shirted home supporters of River Plate, but informative enough for the more "Red"ucated to acknowledge and respect my allegiance.

We were divided into four minivans and told in no uncertain terms to all keep together, follow our guide, never let him out of our sight and don't take out anything out of our pockets/bags that looked expensive. The words, "aggressive thieving Argie bastards" never actually passed his lips but we all knew what he was really saying.

I had butterflies in my stomach as the perfectly oval River Plate stadium came into view, set as it was in a park in the suburbs. There was red and white everywhere. Couldn't see any of the famous Boca blue and yellow. Couldn't see any aggro either which was mildly yet inexplicably disappointing. So much so in fact that I took my camcorder out and filmed the scene from the coach window.

Not only that, as we crossed over the dual carriageway by means of the pedestrian only bridge I got a reluctant Hélène to take a picture of me with the stadium and throngs of River Platians in the background. Not a hint of bother. Groups were singing all over the place. Couldn't understand a word but the sentiments were clear. Boca fans didn't have human parents, if they had parents at all.

We showed our tickets at the turnstiles, then we were in. Followed our guide up some stairs and there was the stadium and pitch before us. I'd never seen so many flags and flares. The air was thick with red and white smoke that almost obscured the pitch itself. What impressed me more than anything was the fact that all the River Plate crowd were singing the same songs at the same time. At Old Trafford I'm used to pockets of Reds trying to get nearby Neanderthals out of their comas at various points during a game.

Then as the two teams came out a giant (and I do mean GIANT) flag was unfolded at our end behind the goal which spread almost halfway round the stadium. Coupled with the smoke from the flares we couldn't see a thing, but the noise was deafening and I tingled all over from the atmosphere. Glazers. Gill. Gestapo stewards. Get your asses down here and see where you're going wrong.

With the whole crowd wrapped up in this frenzy of excitement I thought the coast was clear to take out my trusty camcorder and record the events for posterity. No-one even glanced at me as I filmed sweeping shots from one side of our goal to the other, capturing sights and sounds that would back up any exaggerated accounts in the future. To be on the safe side I delved into the substitutes bench of Hélène's handbag and drew out her digital camera and snapped away, just in case my camcorder and me parted company at some later stage. We'd already been together for nine months, and both Hélène and I were amazed I hadn't lost it yet. Only three more months of our world tour to go. Would we both make it back safely to Blighty? Only time would tell.

When the smoke and flag finally disappeared we could see the blue and yellow of the Boca fans bouncing up and down in the upper tier behind the opposite goal. The noise from both sets of supporters was a continual source of amazement. It didn't let up for a moment and more songs than chants meant that everyone joined in. I tried to make out the words and remember the melodies in case I could lead a vocal renaissance at Old Trafford but blessed with the memory of a goldfish this was beyond my limited powers of recall.

All around the stadium were draped flags with messages of love and affection directed towards the Boca fans, with words that no self-respecting Spanish dictionary would contain. I glanced at Hélène. Fuck me, her eyes were shining and there was a wondrous smile that lit up her whole face. It had got to her. The whole fucking nine yards. I'd never seen an expression like that on her face before. Had a younger Eric Clapton just sat down next to us? Had Johnny Depp asked her what she was doing after the match? No, she was actually getting turned on, in a football stadium, with me!

Now I've seen everything. Next I expected to see a pig flying above the stadium (and I'm not talking about the Pink Floyd inflatable from the Animals album cover) I'm going to have to milk this for all its worth.

As Hélène succumbed to the sensory overload I began to concentrate on the match and soon came to the conclusion that both sides were crap and, like Celtic and Rangers, wouldn't last long in the Premiership back home. Boca had a tricky left winger but that was about it. Neither side created many clear cut chances, and even when they did both sides' finishing was poor. No, I wouldn't be texting Sir Alex with a glowing report on an unknown Argie to replace Tevez in our line-up.

With the stands offering more entertainment than the pitch, I watched in awe as half time approached. Then as if by telepathy, with the score at a predictable 0-0, immediately the half time whistle blew our giant semi-circular flag appeared once more and fifteen minutes of white, smoke filled fun and frolics ensued.

Hélène and I sat down to recover and put the previous 45 minutes into some sort of perspective. Wow! If only Old Trafford could match this. We can all make lists of local derbies and each can make claims to being an El Clasico, but I can tell you boys and girls, nothing on this planet can beat River Plate v Boca Juniors, with the possible exception of Boca Juniors v River Plate at Boca's own stadium, Estadio Alberto J Armando, colloquially known as La Bombonera, set in the poor working class La Boca neighbourhood.

The second half had already kicked off when the flag was brought down and the smoke had cleared for the second time. Then, on the hour mark, the moment I had been waiting for arrived. One of the teams scored. In this instance it was River Plate, and the stadium which had been in a constant state of highly charged excitement simply erupted. It almost reminded me of Barca '84 and Barca '99. I scrambled to fetch my camcorder and record the scene for posterity, only to find my hands shaking so much, by the time I was able to press the record button correctly the initial ecstatic euphoria had receded into sustained mayhem. I alternated between camcorder and camera. Later on we'll see who has pride of place on my Facebook page.

The noise had now reached Spinal Tap "11" proportions. Meanwhile darkness had fallen and the Boca end was a mass of bright yellow flares. From our position they looked like real flame torches that you used to see in all those Robin Hood / Lancelot films on TV and in the cinema.

Even though they were now losing, the Boca fans never let up for a moment. Against the night sky their flaming end seemed to be on fire. Then the inevitable happened. They began to throw their naked flame flares down onto the River Plate supporters in the lower tier. Somehow the whole of the lower tier squashed itself under the overhang as the flares rained down.

I looked around. Nobody amongst our excited throng was batting an eyelid. This must be standard procedure around here. Meanwhile, on the pitch the one dimensional football continued with Boca never looking likely to equalize. A couple of River Plate breakaways would have brought goals in the Premiership but not here. The finishing was laughable.

For atmosphere, only United 3 Barcelona 0 in the Cup Winners' Cup quarter final at Old Trafford in 1984 has matched the atmosphere I experienced this evening. All 360 degrees of the stadium at full throttle for the entire 90 minutes. In the end the match finished 1-0 to River Plate. River Plate moved up to 4th in the table whilst Boca remained in 16th place.

As we scrambled down the stairs from the stands I was able to stick

LUHG decal number 63 on the inside of the large red double gates leading out onto the street. Up yours Glazer! The drive back into the centre of Buenos Aries was a procession of horn blaring cars, buses and motorbikes with red and white scarves flapping in the wind behind. This was a hell of a way to celebrate a simple league victory, reminding me of my approach to the ferry in Calais on May 27, 1999 as hundreds of United cars returning from Barcelona let it all hang out. The sound that night as our cars filled the hollow metal hull of the ship still sends thrills down my spine in moments of recall.

I was too excited to go straight to bed, so with Hélène back to normal in our room I spent an extremely pleasant couple of hours with fellow match devotees in the hostel bar until I put LUHG sticker number 64 up on the hostel notice board to muted applause from those around me who simply didn't get it. Disappointing. I tried to explain but it became apparent these were glory hunters for whom the experience of actually attending THE El Clasico was just another tick on their travelling box.

It transpired that by the end of the season River Plate were relegated and not Boca. How did that happen? Then one year later Boca are crowned champions while River Plate remain in the B league. This year River Plate are back in the top flight. It's all go there, isn't it!

URUGUAY

WEDNESDAY 17 NOVEMBER. BUENOS AIRES – MONTEVIDEO, URUGUAY

I hadn't realised how close and easy Uruguay was to get to from Buenos Aires. Here in BA we could take a ferry, the Colonia Express, and in little more than an hour we would be in the land of Diego Forlan. Certainly the cheapest and most practical way to travel between these two countries, and the price includes the connecting bus between Colonia and Montevideo.

First thing in the morning we took a taxi to the ferry terminal and bought our return tickets to Montevideo via Colonia. Colonia del Sacramento, to give it its full name, turned out to be this oh so pretty little town on the dirty brown river/estuary Rio de la Plata. What originated as the only Portuguese settlement along the Rio de la Plata in 1680, it is now a touristically restored Disneyland Uruguayan village. With Portuguese style houses and cobblestone streets, the historic portion of Colonia is reminiscent of old Lisbon. Winding streets and colourful houses are laid out in a pattern different from Spanish colonial cities. The historic quarter, Barrio Historico, on a small peninsular jutting out into the river, was named a UNESCO heritage site in 1995.

In fact it was so appealingly squeaky clean in order to appeal to the tourists that it lost its appeal for me soon after we had walked around a little. That's not to say it's not worth visiting, and I'm sure it entices many who enjoy the experience, but I could see through its one dimensional façade.

Then in the afternoon we caught the bus for a two hour ride into Montevideo. From the bus station we dragged our wheeled rucksacks along main streets that looked like the wrong end of Oxford Street in London, and were much longer than they appeared on the map, until fully one sweaty hour later we found the hostel I had booked for one night in the city centre.

A quaint little colonial town house in a backstreet with rooms with no windows or the advertised free wi-fi. Our room on the first floor was dark but adequate, with an abundant supply of fleas in the bed and in the carpet. This is one establishment in which yours truly will not be divesting of any clothing as the hour for nocturnal activities arrives.

We stepped outside for a late evening stroll in the teaming streets that could have been any large town in any country on the planet. Grimy worn-out skyscrapers, tacky high street shops, polluted air and honking taxis. Nothing to write home about. Maybe tomorrow will reveal a bit more Uruguayan character.

Goodnight folks. Goodnight fleas.

THURSDAY 18 NOVEMBER. MONTEVIDEO, URUGUAY – BUENOS AIRES, ARGENTINA.

We couldn't wait to get out of the hostel in the morning and divest ourselves of the fleas that had had a good night's sleep courtesy of Mr & Mrs Blatt. Almost immediately I came across this giant poster of Diego Forlan smiling down on me from across the road.

"Hélène. Take me and Diego please." I gave her precise directions for this ultimately defining Uruguay photo opportunity. She may not agree but me and Diego make a pretty good pair even if I say so myself. We even sported matching haircuts.

"That's one for my Facebook page." I thought to myself.

According to my map, down by the port the Mercado del Punto had been spruced up so we started to walk in that direction. We arrived at Plaza Independencia which didn't live up to its guide book recommendations. The port area however was more interesting with its older buildings and selection of up-market cafes and restaurants.

We had a lovely meal in a new restaurant opened by this enthusiastic young couple, then made our way back to the hostel, collected our luggage and opted for an alternative hour-long walk back to the bus station.

Trying not to look like a gringo tourist, we followed my route through a selection of boring and dodgy looking suburbs. At one stage heat and exhaustion demanded to be addressed, so we entered this local bar that felt like the Uruguay's answer to Royston Vasey. "Local Bar for Local People" couldn't have been more accurate.

It took ages to be served, even though it was almost empty. Hélène picked up the vibe that this wasn't a place to linger. I agreed with her. We drank up quickly made our way outside. Just at that moment a gaily dressed man was passing by on his horse and cart. So colourful and a welcome contrast to the drab grey surroundings. I whipped out my camcorder and began to film him. Almost instantly Hélène grabbed my camcorder, thrust it in her rucksack and marched us both briskly along the road.

As we huffed and puffed our way towards the bus station, she informed me in no uncertain terms that the moment I had taken out my camcorder, every sleepy local had been alerted as by an invisible bush telegraph and were eyeing this innocent Mr Bean gringo with dubious intent.

Needless to say, our fast-track out of the danger zone resulted in an early arrival at the bus station where Hélène could give full vent to her feelings, once she got her breath back. I honestly hadn't picked up the vibe. Another idiot abroad moment.

Overall we weren't impressed with Montevideo. Only a few months earlier Jose Mujica had become President and, conscious of the poverty that some of Uruguay's society suffers, began donating 87% of his monthly salary to social services. He refuses to live in the Presidential Palace and instead leads a humble life and exemplary lifestyle on his farm on the outskirts of the capital. He also drives an '80s Volkswagen.

Maybe it was too early but we didn't see signs of his honourable sacrifices. I'm possibly doing Montevideo a disservice. I've subsequently read about the exclusive residential suburb of Carrasco, the historic downtown business district and the art deco and neoclassical buildings, but we never saw them.

SATURDAY 20 NOVEMBER. BUENOS AIRES, ARGENTINA
MANCHESTER UNITED 2 WIGAN ATHLETIC 0

Today was Lilyella's birthday. It seemed only a year ago she was eleven. How time flies! Next year she'll be a teenager. Look out world...

So, the master plan was to wake up early and phone home, only Hélène had had a bad night. First with flea-bites left over from the cheap hostel in Montevideo, then by noise outside our main road hostel window back in Buenos Aires. BA is an all-night city, which is great, except when you want to sleep.

Therefore the world did not find Hélène in the best of moods this morning. We got dressed and rushed outside, only being Saturday no internet/telephone place would open till 10.00am. Hélène went a darker shade of black.

Meanwhile I was racking my brain to see if there was any way I could catch the Wigan game. I'd used up my nine lives a long time ago on this trip. Liverpool, City, Chelsea, Arsenal, vital Champions League games and even "Super El Clasico". I had ready made excuses why my world would stop turning if I didn't get to see these matches.

"This is our most important match of the season" had been used to excess and was wearing a bit thin. This was also our last day in Buenos Aires and we hadn't been to up-market Palermo yet. And what chance was there of our game being shown? I mean, no disrespect to Wigan, but....Wigan! I could imagine TV sports producers armed with Arsenal v Tottenham and Birmingham v Chelsea busting a gut to transmit our game ahead of the competition.

No, this was one day when I really would have to put the little lady first and relinquish any lingering possibility of getting football on the agenda. This is what modern men do, don't they?

I was mentally prepared as we trooped round the corner and, after an age of engaged signals, finally spoke to our granddaughter. Actually we started by singing "Happy Birthday". Embarrassing I know, but it's what grandparents do, isn't it?

Much gushing sentimentality later we exited our oven, I mean telephone booth and went to cool off with a refreshing glass of freshly squeezed orange juice. Nice.

Now to find out how to use the Buenos Aires underground system. We studied the map and got on the first train, only to exit at the wrong stop. Boarded the following train and this time we got it right. One change and ten stops later we were at Palermo station.

Hélène and I differed in how to interpret the local road map and, needless to say, I got it wrong. Backtracking for a quarter of a mile, we eventually found ourselves in what the guidebooks describe as BA's trendiest neighbourhood. That's as may be, but what was left of the elegant, colonial style buildings were in various states of disrepair.

You can also tell when an area is "trendy" – there's an extra "0" on the end of each price tag. Restaurants and boutiques abounded as we strolled around the streets leading from Place Serrano.

We passed an Irish pub. It was now just gone midday, the kick-off time for our match.

"I wonder if they've got our game on?" I thought to myself, forgetting that women can pick up on thought waves.

"Don't even think about it." came a retort out loud.

"I was just looking."

In fact they were showing a rugby match.

Boring.

We continued on our stroll. Christmas presents for our girls were high on the agenda. There were some nice shops but nothing we couldn't buy back in London... and the prices!!! Don't let anyone tell you South America is cheap. There are some mighty big exceptions.

By this time Hélène's stomach was demanding attention.

"Are you feeling peckish?" she enquired, which translated into English means, "I'm hungry – it's time to eat."

As luck would have it we were passing the Irish pub again. I looked at the menu. Not bad, considering the area. Still rugby on the telly though, but you never know.

"Why don't we eat here? It'll make a change."

"OK."

We sat down with me facing the TV screen. The waitress came over and we ordered.

I enquired as to whether I could order an additional side dish of Manchester United v Wigan Athletic. At first she pretended she didn't understand, as though language was a barrier. However I insisted she ask her boss sitting by the till.

He came over.

I enquired if it was at all possible to show Premiership matches on the TV.

It was. Good. We were over the first hurdle.

"Is it possible to show the Manchester United game, please?" I asked, in a nonchalant yet somehow desperate way I have perfected over the years.

I interpreted his reply as "Let me see."

A few flicks later and two middle aged gentlemen filled the screen, with the Barclays Premiership logo in the background.

Success.

I had killed two birds with one stone.

1) We were eating a reasonably priced meal in an expensive area.

2) I WAS GONNA WATCH UNITED!!

Sorted, as long as I would be able to make the meal last until full time.

They flashed the half time scores on the screen.

Arsenal 2 Tottenham 3 Full time.

YAHOO!!

Birmingham 1 Chelsea 0 Half Time

DOUBLE YAHOO!!!

Wow! What a wonderful pub! I couldn't believe it.

Surely Chelsea would turn their match around in the second half? Still, this was more than I could have hoped for, so I settled down to my plate of chips covered in melted cheddar cheese and bits of crispy bacon with a renewed appetite. Hélène and I have had some wonderful meals on out travels, each country wowing us with their local fayre, but occasionally only a plate of hot British stodge hits the spot. My spot was well and truly hit.

They showed highlights from our first half. Wigan had a couple of decent moves and half chances whilst Evra's headed goal, his first since April 2007, was to be enjoyed. I'd read that after Rooney's much heralded return from a week or more at Nike's headquarters in Oregon, he would be used as a substitute in today's match. I wanted to gauge the crowd's reaction to his tawdry tabloid revelations and public relations disaster of last month's wrangle over his future playing career both on and off the pitch, and if and when he would be brought on in the second half, but there was no sound in the pub save for the 80's American soft rock over the sound system. To be honest I was also more than a little concerned that last season he had scored 34 goals and up till now, for reasons well documented, he'd only scored one, and that a penalty against West Ham. Hardly Golden Boot material even if his wallet is now lined with gold.

I tried to recognise our players on the small screen. If I was right there was no Ferdinand or Vidic or Berbatov. I could make out Macheda, Ji Sung Park, Obertan...

Oh oh. Have we underestimated the opposition again, in a calculated risk management strategy designed to save our best players for the more important games, forgetting that the three points at stake against Wigan were worth as much as the three points to be gained at the expense of our nearest rivals at the top of the league? I wasn't holding out too much hope of a free flowing United tearing the opposition apart, and I was exactly right.

We dominated possession but laboured in all departments, Wigan matched us in midfield whilst we seemed to offer little of note up front. I imagined the first half must have been similar. Oh well, today was a day to win at all costs and hope we start to play "United" football soon.

Shit, the season was now three months old and United had yet to start playing "proper" football. I know this was a side in transition, what with the likes of Scholes, Giggs, Gary and Van Der Sar coming towards the end of their illustrious careers, but once again the quality of our youngsters was questionable to say the least and despite what Fergie and the board might say, we don't have the funds to compete for the best players in the world. And we are the so-called biggest club in the world!

Now, all things are equal in love and war. I didn't see the first half so I didn't know which Wigan players, if any, had got themselves yellow carded, but within a few mad minutes around the hour mark two Wigan players, captain Antolin Alcaraz a second yellow for felling Darren Fletcher then striker Hugo Rodallega was given a straight red for a two-footed lunge at Rafael, got themselves sent off. So within minutes they were down to nine men and a golden opportunity for United to make a dent in Chelsea's far superior goal difference.

Not tonight Josephine. Macheda and Ji Sung Park were substituted for Scholes and Rooney but still we laboured. Rooney must have been desperate to make an immediate impression but his first touch wasn't there. It will take a few games for his body and head to get themselves together, but just how long will United fans wait for a guy on a reported £250,000 a week?

However, with more room down the flanks Rafael supplied numerous crosses, one of which, thankfully, was headed in by Hernandez with 13 minutes remaining. The last minute was almost scripted. Another cross came over but Rooney scuffed his shot straight at the keeper. Not the last minute scenario United fans have been used to the last few years.

Three points is three points, but together with Wolves, our least convincing performance of the season. Chelsea score seven goals on the final day of last season against Wigan and we only score two against nine men. Says it all really doesn't it?

I eeked out the remaining few minutes in the pub, trying to keep Hélène on the leash until the final results come up. To say she was bored was an understatement. The novelty of actually enjoying a football match last Tuesday had well and truly worn off and it was the good (bad) old Hélène that was giving my ears a bashing.

Just a few more seconds…that's all I need…

Birmingham 1 Chelsea 0

"YEAHHH!!!" We play like shit and now we're equal top of the Premiership. How'd that happen? My bubbling enthusiasm impressed the bar owner, who had no hesitation in putting up LUHG sticker number 65. Good man.

Outside Palermo looked wonderful. A kaleidoscope of colour and vibrancy. With renewed strength I attacked the uneven pavements and boutiques. When United go top, the top go shopping. I wore an expression of absolute delight as Hélène went from boutique to boutique searching for that one "special" present for each of our offspring.

Now mid afternoon, we decided to go to the parks that Palermo was famous for, where we spent a pleasant couple of hours despite the best efforts of the Gestapo park attendants whistling at every opportunity to warn us and everybody else not to sit on the grass.

TUESDAY 22 NOVEMBER. IGUAÇU FALLS, ARGENTINA

Depending on what guidebook/blog you read, you can catch almost 80% of Iguaçu Falls from the Argentinian side and just over 20% from the Brazilian side. No matter, we were going to both, with a little Paraguay thrown in for good measure.

Standing outside our hostel, it soon became clear the tour company had forgotten all about us, so it took a flurry of phone calls for them to send a taxi to pick us up and join the minibus. It was only a short journey to the entrance however, although to maximize our encounter with the falls themselves we forwent the nature trail and elected to take the Rainforest Ecological Train, similar to the one found in Disney's Animal Kingdom. The train brought us to the entrance of the aptly named Devil's Throat. From there we walked the one kilometre trail and soon we were passing though lush gardens then on metal walkways above the forest. We could hear this gentle roaring in the distance and my heart began pounding as I anticipated my one on one with one of the world's greatest waterfalls.

Soon the air was filled with an ultra gentle light silver grey mist and the roar was getting louder, and deeper. We walked above a number of tributaries and islands of the Iguaçu River that were a sight in themselves. Then suddenly the trees parted and we were greeted by the full majesty of Iguaçu Falls.

WOW!

I'm sorry, there's no other word that can convey our immediate, jaw-dropping reaction to the world's most spectacular waterfall. In fact I'd more accurately describe them as a series of 275 separate raging torrents forming 360 degrees of visual sensory overload, as water tumbles over the 1.7 mile long edge of the Parana Plateau.

Taller than Niagara Falls and twice as wide, with double it's surface water flowing over the falls, Iguaçu Falls had just been announced as one of the seven winners of the New 7 Wonders of Nature, and it's not hard to see why. Although the Victoria Falls is the world's single widest curtain of water, Iguaçu is actually wider but is made up of more individual falls and has islands perched at the top.

My lifelong football supporter training came in useful here as I elbowed and jostled Hélène and I to the front of the viewing platform. I just stood there in awe and wonder at nature's immense contribution to my ever expanding memory bank of sounds and images that would come back to me for the rest of my days.

It's only when you get up close and personal with all things nature does that the true impact hit you. They say that size isn't important, but at a moment like this the sheer size and scale of the falls and cataracts was a very humbling experience. The power and the glory of nature at work certainly put me in my place, and for ages I dismissed the hordes of camera snapping tourists all around me just to stand there and stare into the abyss.

I didn't say anything. I didn't have to say anything. It was like a real life, out of body IMAX experience. All sound and vision orifices were full to capacity, pounded mercilessly by the deep throated roaring violence of up to 450,000 cubic feet of water per second relentlessly crashing down, my peripheral vision invaded by a series of permanently intense rainbows shimmering above the unrelenting cascading concave falls.

We stayed and stared whilst others snapped and departed. So you see, it's not only Old Trafford that has been invaded by superficial glory hunters. Something that bugged me throughout this incredible trip repeated itself here, just as it had done at the Taj Mahal, the World's Fair in Shanghai, Machu Picchu and numerous other jaw dropping destinations around the world. Namely hordes of ignoramuses in tour groups that crowd walkways, eating and smoking and moving along at a snail's pace. The slow progression here wouldn't have bothered me as much if they had been looking around at the beauty of the rainforest surrounding the falls but they generally only slowed down to quench their thirst from such strenuous activity or stuff another biscuit into their mouths in between puffs on a cigarette. More fool them I say. It's their loss not mine if they'd rather spend longer looking at a photo album than the real thing.

Meanwhile, back at the Falls, and saturated with sensation, we reluctantly disgorged ourselves from Devil's Throat and made our way along the walkways to the other viewpoints with overhangs to appreciate the beauty of it all. From these smaller, narrower outlets we could really take in all the flora and fauna, as well as multi-coloured butterflies so sadly disappearing from the British countryside. Each new angle brought another dimension until we went as far as it was possible to go. I looked at my watch.

"Is that the time?" I said to Hélène. That's what watches are for. Of course it was the time, which meant we'd better get a move on if we wanted to get up close and personal UNDER the waterfall as opposed to this privileged overview.

Everyone's heard of the boat, Maid of the Mist, that takes passengers up close and personal to the base of Niagara Falls. Well, Iguaçu Falls has a fleet of high speed inflatables that perform the same function. We took the Micky Mouse train round to where we could board the vessels and bought our tickets which included the temporary loan of waterproof clothing and rucksacks for our personal belongings, then joined the nervous queue waiting to board. Suppressing our giggles I made Hélène join me in the front row, my philosophy being, "If something's worth doing, it's worth overdoing". (Something that's carried me through more than 50 years following United, so why stop now?) I mean, there's only so much 'wet' you can become, right?

Ever so slightly disconcerting was the sight of both the driver and the cameraman dressed head to foot in single waterproof membranes resembling the giant condoms featured in Naked Gun 2 ½. They warned us that when they give the signal we were to put away all cameras and anything else we didn't want to drown.

We pulled away with a fierce acceleration and soon we were skimming along one side of the immense falls, which looked so much steeper from this angle. I camcorded and Hélène snapped (with her camera, not at me this time.) The faintly ridiculously overdressed cameraman recorded all of us on his own waterproof camcorder. From inflatable boat to inflated prices in the souvenir shop. (Sorry, couldn't resist that one)

Then, after a complete circuit of the falls, he went in. The now not so ridiculously overdressed cameraman recorded all our exaggerated screams and actions as the icy cold water hit us like a hammer. As someone commented afterwards, "I felt a little like being an ant in a washing machine."

It was breathtakingly brilliant and we were all soaked to the skin. But, what the hell! Stepping onto wet dry land at the end the faces of people still queuing up to go on were a picture. Little boys shouting and (I believe) screaming in Spanish or Portuguese the equivalent of "Fucking magic!" whilst most of their parents' faces belied the expression, "Shit, what have we let ourselves in for?"

We clambered up the slippery slope (literally) to the walkway above and slowly strolled and steamed back to the little train to take us back to the exit. What a fantastic day. Once again, Nature 1 Man 0.

BRAZIL

WEDNESDAY 24 NOVEMBER. IGUAÇU FALLS, BRAZIL
OVERNIGHT BUS FROM PUERTO IGUAÇU TO SAO PAULO, BRAZIL
GLASGOW RANGERS 0 MANCHESTER UNITED 1 CHAMPIONS LEAGUE

This morning we did it all over again, but this time from the Brazilian side. Another minibus, although this time we had to cross the border for our first taste of Brazil. The countryside looked the same (no shit, Sherlock) as we drove to the impressive, although quite frankly unnecessarily OTT entrance and information building.

More overpriced souvenirs and coffee were on offer which we politely declined before getting on an English speaking bus which took up the mantle of the little train on the Argentinean side. It stopped in front of the only 5 star hotel within the entire national park where we were given maps and routes. This time we took our time to follow the nature trails which were a delight. The highlight was an abundance of multi-coloured butterflies, the lowlight was an even more abundant swarm of mosquitoes.

We made our way out to the main viewing platform which juts out over the river and offers another IMAX view of Devil's Throat and the falls in all their glory. The experience was not as intense on the Argentinean side but a grander, more panoramic overview nonetheless. We stayed for ages just "soaking" up the atmosphere before making our way up the elevator to the rooftop viewing platform and another angle on proceedings. This time we could see the Upper Iguaçu River as it approached the falls themselves and fully appreciate the lush terrain as far as the eye could see.

We didn't want to leave but there was one more stop on this remarkable excursion to one of the world's greatest natural wonders. Well, two actually. First they insisted on taking us round the boring grey steel and concrete monstrosity of a dam which has caused the deaths of thousands of life forms and displaced thousands of indigenous tribes. Then they took us for one hour into Paraguay, not to look at the falls from another angle but to buy dodgy electronics. Brazilian tourists like to take advantage of the significantly lower prices on offer for cameras, hifi equipment, laptops, mobiles, etc… What they don't tell you is that much of the merchandise on offer is fake. If you ask to see and feel an item for yourself they get a well-worn box and take out the said item that's been man (and women) handled several times already. Then if you ask for a pristine model untouched by human hands, someone goes out the back and comes back with your fake. Hard to tell the difference until your thousands of miles away back home.

The border town itself turned out to be a right scruffy place and felt extremely dodgy, the locals looking on the (mostly) well heeled tourists as prime targets for whatever scams they had in mind. My advice – avoid at all costs.

Happy to get back on the bus one last time, it was back over the border and on to our hostel in Puerto Iguaçu. One quick change and brush up later we were soon in the old routine of dragging our luggage back up the road to the bus station for another overnight bus ride, this time to Sao Paulo and Brazil proper.

I couldn't make up my mind which was the more awesome natural phenomenon – the sheer size and power of the magnificent Iguaçu Falls, 2.7 kilometres wide and with a drop of 80 metres, or the fact that United were joint top of the Premiership playing their worst football in years.

But now my mind turned to the Champions League. Glasgow Rangers v United was another match I knew I had no chance of catching live as we would be four and a half hours into our 18 hour overnight bus journey from Puerto Iguaçu in Argentina to Sao Paulo in Brazil when the match began, so I mentally prepared myself accordingly.

I reasoned that as we only needed one point from our two remaining Champions League group stage matches, even a below par United performance was capable of obtaining at least a draw in Glasgow. And in case a passionate Rangers crowd pushed their team to an unlikely and undeserved victory, one point in the home tie against Valencia was surely an odds-on certainty.

On the other hand, this is Manchester United we are talking about. What's to say we couldn't grab a defeat along the way at some stage, especially the group stage of the Champions League? With the way we were(n't) playing this season, anything was possible. And with Fergie deciding to rest our defensive pair of Ferdinand and Vidic, was this to be another case of complacency costing us dearly? It wouldn't be the first time.

As I sat in the bus terminal in Peurto Iguaçu waiting for our bus which was late, I spied two lads a few metres away and one was wearing an Arsenal polo shirt. A chance for a little footy banter? You know, something along the lines of: "What happened to your lot last night?" (they had lost 2-0 to Braga in their Champions League qualifying match, letting in two goals in the last ten minutes) "Losing 2-3 to Tottenham at the weekend must have been a killer, especially as you were 2-0 up at one stage and playing Spurs off the park." "We did the double over you last season."

Nothing provocative you understand. I looked down. Damn! For some reason I had decided not to wear one of my United tops today so I had no common catalyst to open a conversation with.

I looked at his polo shirt again. I had to admit I liked the style. Maroon and navy blue horizontal stripes. Something you could wear on non-match days without looking like a complete plonker. That has always been my challenge, to wear something United not in brightly coloured shiny polyester to work and when fulfilling my social engagements. It's not easy you know.

I decided now was not yet the time to make contact. I mean, we had 18 hours ahead of us, surely an opportunity would arise at some stage. (not the group stage reference again! It was a poor joke the first time round). An hour later our bus turned up. We registered our luggage in the hold then went on board. The two lads were sitting behind us so I considered a nod was sufficient communication at this stage. A couple of hours into the journey and Hélène decided she had to go to the loo, so I stood up to let her pass.

That was the opportunity I had been waiting for.

"Hi." I said, looking down at the face above the Arsenal shirt. "What happened to your lot last night?"

"Do you know the score?"

"Yeah. You lost 2-0." He also knew the score. I think he was just testing me. And so began almost an hour's worth of footy talk. It turned out his mate was a United fan but not a regular match-going Red.

First I continued with the Gooner who seemed pretty peeved to say the least. Recent results and performances had dissolved the brittle confidence many Arsenal fans seem to possess in the face of adversity. Just like their team.

The United fan was rather shy, especially in the face of my rather assertive interrogation technique, contributing mono syllable responses to my open questions until he grew in confidence and we were able to discuss all things United from the Glazers, FC United, the kids coming through, etc...

Surprisingly the Arsenal fan interjected at this point, claiming his team were also producing quality youngsters but he quite openly suggested it was time for a complete change and the end of the Wenger era. I wondered how representative he was of current Arsenal fans' thinking. But not for long as I was back discussing United with my fellow Red.

Suddenly I could hear the sounds of country rock emanating from the bus's sound system. I looked round, only to discover the feature film had started. I forget the title but it starred Jeff Bridges. As it was in English with Spanish subtitles I would normally have jumped (or sat) at the chance to break the tedium of an overnight bus ride but by now I was in full footy flow and carried on regardless.

I looked down at Hélène and she was giving me another of her looks. I couldn't decipher the meaning or reason for her negativity, and frankly I didn't care.

Eventually I thought it time to close the discussion and settle down for the night, but not before Hélène had given me an ear bashing for talking so long and so loud when others on the bus had wanted to watch the film.

"No consideration." she called it.

"Bollocks." I called it.

The two lads were taking the bus all the way to Rio so they were still asleep when Hélène and I disembarked at 07.00am the following morning in Sao Paulo, the largest city in Brazil, the largest city in the southern hemisphere and South America and the world's seventh largest city by population. (Just thought you'd like to know).

Once inside the cavernous halls we looked for the banks of sales counters normally ever present in South American bus terminals, as we found this the most efficient use of our time when buying onward tickets.

Nothing.

We dragged our luggage this way and that.

Nothing.

Obviously we had missed the obvious because they just HAD to be here, but lack of sleep (and the desperate desire to find out the Rangers result) re-enforced the need to take a taxi to our hostel.

The Sao Paulo bus terminal, and I suspect airport as well, had reproduced the system we found throughout the Far East, where after years of ripping off foreigners, taxis have to be pre-paid and a slip handed to the driver, so that both sides know exactly how much the fare will be. Still overpriced but on a more reasonable scale.

Upon entering the early morning flow of polluting traffic responding to the needs of its nineteen million inhabitants, I immediately spied floodlights.

"Aha! A stadium!" I cried, with an involuntary mouth spasm, but something wasn't quite right. Either side of the main stands were more floodlights and long narrow stands for more spectators.

"This can't be a football pitch." I mused to myself, "unless the local team are wingless wonders out of the Ramsey era." But curiosity got the better of me, so I leaned forward towards the driver and pointed outside.

"Carnival," he explained, then continued in Portuguese too fast even for Hélène to pick up more than the odd word, but it transpired that this stadium was indeed used for carnivals, all groups passing along between two banks of spectators and the judges. Wow, these guys sure are serious about carnival.

We had chosen a hostel in a safe, upmarket neighbourhood within walking distance of the Sumere subway station. All in all our stay in this characterless but thriving metropolis would have been uneventful, save for rendezvous with two widely different characters.

First we met up with Alex Sabino, a lifelong Red and regular contributor on my Facebook page. As a native Sao Paolovian (is there such a thing?) he was our window onto Sao Paolo. We spent a very delightful day trekking around the city centre by public transport, discussing all things United, with me even having to tone down the Red conversation so that Hélène didn't totally disintegrate. We visited some of the remaining historical parts of the city. He also showed us where we could buy our onward bus tickets. He was also full of appreciation as I stuck not one, but two LUHG stickers, numbers 66 and 67 on appropriate walls. I also gave him a couple so he could spread the word. Good man. That's LUHG stickers 68 and 69 accounted for.

We also met up with Karim. younger brother of Ras Smaila, the afro/funky/rockin'/blues musician based in Paris that I have been championing for years, together with his wife and newly born daughter. We had been invited over for dinner in their apartment with stunning views over the Sao Paolo skyline, so it was only right and proper to buy something as a welcoming present. Then we saw the prices!

I never realized Brazil was so expensive. A lot higher than the UK. In the end we settled on a little dress for their baby daughter that was double the price compared to back home. That hurt. Karim's a film maker/director, both feature films and documentaries, whilst his wife is a hot-shot lawyer. Not much opportunity to talk football then, even in Brazil. Nevertheless we had an extremely pleasant evening before returning to our hostel.

SATURDAY 27 NOVEMBER. BUS FROM SAO PAULO TO PARATY, BRAZIL
MANCHESTER UNITED 7 BLACKBURN ROVERS 1

Today I set a new record, and one I wasn't particularly proud of. For the second time in three days I would miss a United match live and there was nothing I could do about it.

Kick-off time in Brazil for our home game against Blackburn was 13.00 and by this time we would be 45 minutes into our bus journey from Sao Paulo to the delightful coastal town of Paraty, halfway up the coast between Sao Paulo and Rio de Janeiro. At the same time FC United would be creating another piece of history by taking on Brighton & Hove Albion away in the second round of the FA Cup.

Today, Melanie, our eldest, was flying to Australia. She was terribly excited. (We knew, because we had been following her entries on her Facebook page all week), as she was going to be a guest contributor on "I'm a Celebrity, Get Me Out Of Here" on ITV2 from Monday. We sent her gushing good luck messages before settling down to breakfast. With Brazil only two hours behind the UK at this time, we hoped she'd catch our best wishes before she flew off.

Meanwhile I kept my football thoughts to myself as we packed our rucksacks for the 11.00 check-out deadline in our hostel. With the sun beating down and a perfect temperature of 28*C, we were under no pressure as we took a taxi to the bus terminal.

The bus ride began uneventfully. I used the time to write up my diary, then Hélène made me aware of a low droning sound coming from behind. It was in fact an old American lady who never stopped talking the whole time. Try as I might her low monotone voice penetrated my senses. I could never quite eradicate the noise, like a wasp forever bumping against a window trying to get out.

My thoughts turned to football in order to suppress the woman's voice. Having struggled to overcome a Rangers side away in the Champions League, I hoped the expected return of Ferdinand and Vidic might release our forwards from their shared responsibilities and attack with more conviction as we were at home.

Blackburn had beaten Aston Villa 2-0 in their last outing and I was sure Alex's close pal, Sam Alladyce, would make them hard to break down at Old Trafford. I wasn't expecting a great game, so I just prayed (who to?) we would obtain the crucial three points whilst little by little regain the form that had been sorely missing for much of this season.

The final couple of hours on the bus saw us driving north along the Brazilian coastline and it was pretty amazing. Little islands dotted the various bays, providing a wonderful ever-changing vista to occasionally keep my mind off all things United. It also enabled me to find some pertinent non-football comments to enliven my conversation with Hélène as we sped along.

Arriving in Paraty we took a taxi to our hostel. Immediately Hélène commented that our hostel can't be in the centre if the taxi driver's route was anything to go by. I reminded her that it wasn't in the centre but right on the beach but just a short walk into town. She wasn't convinced.

Getting Hélène to admit she was wrong, as we pulled up outside our beachfront hostel with spectacular views across the bay, was as likely as me allowing Malcolm Glazer to enter my house on Christmas Day dressed as Santa Claus. I contented myself with an internal smile as we unloaded our luggage.

As we registered I asked for the password for the hostel's wifi. Suitably armed we decamped to our windowless room, put down our luggage and took out our laptop. Normal procedure was to see if there had been any messages from our girls, but as Hélène went to the loo, I intended to get the Blackburn result up before resuming my duties as a parent. Damn. No connection. Not for the first time, connecting to a hostel's Wi-Fi was proving problematic. Often the signal is so weak, Wi-Fi only works in the reception area. After a fruitless ten minutes we trooped back to reception and asked the tall young man behind the counter to help us. He offered me to check our e-mails on the hostel's own computer whilst ours was being worked on.

Right. Straight to the BBC website. A few seconds later... 7-1!!!!!! Berbatov scores 5!!! I raised both my arms and let out a "WHOOP", which indicated to Hélène I couldn't possibly be looking at our e-mails as this was not a sound associated with Google mail. Sheepishly I put them down and quickly read the leading paragraph before indeed directing the mouse to our respective e-mail accounts.

Reading through them I thought, "What planet am I on? Jesus H Christ!!! I don't believe it! Brilliant! Totally brilliant." I then looked for the FC United result in the F A Cup. Brighton 1 FC United of Manchester 1. Last minute penalty save. Jesus H Christ, who writes these scripts? Hollywood would never believe it. Football, bloody hell! Well done lads. The dream continues. This is why Cheshire grins were invented, for nights like these.

SUNDAY 28 NOVEMBER. PARATY, BRAZIL

After an early morning stroll around this delightfully picturesque, cobblestoned little town, Hélène and I were lying on the beach in front of our hostel. I was happily dozing, re-running the football results over the weekend and analysing and pontificating to myself on all possible permutations when I heard this female voice cry: "David BLATT!"

Obviously the morning's aftershave was having its desired effect, so I opened my eyes and stared at two of the loveliest breasts you are ever likely to meet on a beach in Brazil (and that's saying something!) And they belonged to a woman!

I forced my gaze upwards and recognised the receptionist from our hostel in Sao Paulo we had left the previous day. A little light conversation followed, my eyes drifting downwards of their own accord. Her boyfriend was taller than me however so I kept my carnal thoughts to myself.

It transpired they were here for the weekend. They had come by both bus and boat, yet it couldn't have been any quicker than our six hour bus only journey. I suppose for a country as large as Brazil, a twelve hour round trip would be the norm. The same as me driving from London to Newcastle or Sunderland and back for a game. Yeah, I suppose it made sense after all.

TUESDAY 30 NOVEMBER. MARACANA STADIUM, RIO DE JANEIRO, BRAZIL.
WEST HAM UNITED 4 MANCHESTER UNITED 0. CARLING CUP

Despite the "Super El Clasico" between River Plate and Boca Juniors creating the earth shattering sensation of my wife actually enjoying a football match, lightning was never going to strike twice within the same month, so I put aside any thoughts of Hélène accompanying me to a match in Rio de Janeiro. Moreover, with the decaying Maracana Stadium undergoing extensive and much needed renovations in time for the opening ceremony of the 2014 World Cup, all teams were now fulfilling their fixtures in the Olympic Stadium.

On top of this, we had been following the ongoing story of the riots in the favelas as the police and military were now in all out war on the drugs gangs in the poorest favelas north of the city. Forty five dead in the last week alone. And the Maracana was in the north of the city. Hmmm.... I shall have to be careful.

Whilst enjoying a tango evening in the famous Cafe Torini in Buenos Aries a couple of weeks back, we had befriended this really nice young couple from Sao Paulo. It turned out the guy's brother-in-law was in a special crack police unit and a chat on Google the previous day had revealed that the authorities were going to send in special units to occupy the worst of the favelas which should make them safe.

I wasn't over confident, but enough to relay the news to Hélène that the fevalas would be safe by tomorrow and we could visit the Maracana without a care in the world.

She bought it! Yipee, we're off.

The Maracana subway station was on the same line as our hostel's nearest station so it was a simple twenty minute ride, made all the better by the fact that the train emerged from the tunnel just as the stadium came into view. What a welcome.

The day was warm but overcast as we walked along the overhead walkway above the dual carriageway. I spied a small stadium in front of the real thing. It turned out to be a running track with a training pitch inside. The newly painted light blue Maracana (light blue! Ych!) rising non majestically behind.

Like the Nou Camp in Barcelona, first impressions can be rather underwhelming. Recognised as the largest stadium in the world, the Maracana looked big, but not that big. No towering stands to gaze up at in awe. The naked eye gave way to imagination as I realised its history as an iconic centre for the beautiful game. Pele's 1000th goal. How I would have loved to have been in the crowd for that one.

Hélène was already bored as we did a circuit round the outside of the oval stadium, trying to find our way in. Then I spied a small group of Japanese descending from a minivan and I guessed they were doing an official tour so I suggested to Hélène we tag along, so as to see all the good bits.

"We can't do that. They'll notice."

Nonchalantly tagging along we found ourselves under an archway and in front of what seemed like the main entrance. Outside were foot impressions of many past and present Brazilian master footballers, similar to those famous hand prints outside Grauman's Chinese Theatre on Hollywood Boulevard in LA. I had Hélène take my picture in the very footsteps of Kaka, Didi, Dida, Garrincha, Jairzinho, Zico, Socrates, etc... I was in football heaven but for the life of me I couldn't find the greatest of them all. No, not George Best or even Duncan Edwards - Pele!

We then paid ten Brazilian real to gain entrance to the museum, the souvenir shop and, wait for it.... the stadium itself. I had been worried about this for quite a while, as I feared the renovations would have put paid to tours inside the stadium. I was in misty eyed reverie as I read the history on the walls, saw re-runs of famous goals on large screens and imagined where I was when these events were unfolding.

Then the moment I had been waiting for. Up to the sixth floor and, whoa!.... Look at that! What a load of rubbish! Literally, what a load of rubbish. There was broken concrete and crumbling walkways everywhere, together with groups of men in hard hats discussing the broken concrete and crumbling walkways. Still, there was work to be done as I handed Hélène the camcorder and directed her in where to film and what scenes I wanted to capture.

"Stay! Stay!" I barked, as I manoeuvred myself around the terraces for one shot after another. It would have been too much to ask for Hélène to do the moving, so if the mountain can't come to Mohammed...well, you know the rest.

Then it was time for a little sit and think. Me time, just to breathe in all the memories, the players and celebrations this stadium had witnessed. A giant characterless oval overflowing with larger than life moments that gave meaning to the phrase, The Beautiful Game.

Strangely we were the only non-workers inside the stadium. It was all mine.

"Can't we go now?"

"No, we can't. I've waited a lifetime to make it here, and here I'll stay a little longer, OK?"

I'm afraid I didn't make it to United's ill-fated, ill-advised trip to Brazil in January 2000. Bullied by the Football Association in its ill-fated, ill-advised attempt to win FIFA's members votes for hosting the World Cup in 2006, United had had to forego their defence of the FA Cup won amidst the glory of the greatest year in their history, the capturing of the treble for the first and still only time in English football history.

It had been a disaster all round. As we all know, England failed to host the World Cup in 2006, Germany claiming that they had arrived at an agreement with our FA that Germany would back England in their bid to host the European Championships in 1996 in exchange for England backing Germany for the 2006 World Cup. The English FA denied this but I know who I tend to believe.

Ah, yes. Just sitting in one of the yet to be renovated stands, reliving scenes I had witnessed on TV over the previous five decades. I reminisced until Hélène couldn't take it anymore, so reluctantly I stood up, turned round and slowly made my way up to the back of the stand and the lift which would take us back to the ground floor and a different kind of reality.

A last turn back to take in its giant oval majesty, then the lift doors closed, but not before I'd stuck LUHG sticker number 70 on the outer doors, and it was gone.

Back on the ground floor we made our way to the pitifully small souvenir shop, only to see Lawrence Dallaglio talking to one of the sales assistants, with two children in tow. Listening in to his conversation while pretending to browse the merchandise on offer, he was gushing how he was a Manchester United fan (I didn't know that), his son was a Manchester United fan (I didn't know that) and that it meant such a lot to him just to be here.

Now, if he had said that to someone in authority in the stadium it might have carried some weight, but these two bored sales assistants could hardly speak English, hadn't a clue who he was, and just wanted to get back to talking to each other. I groped for a way to wangle myself into the conversation. Hélène was no help, of course, and I admit I failed to find a route in before England's rugby captain and World Cup hero had left the building.

Damn.

I went back to the piss-poor selection of merchandise and in the end settled for a white T-shirt one size too small, with a reasonable set of three colourful drawings of the Maracana. If only I was in charge here. To re-work the Stephen Foster chant from the FA Cup Final replay against Brighton Wembley in 1983, "What a difference I would have made."

Lost opportunity is not the half of it. Still, I can still look anyone in the eye and say, "I was there!" In an attempt to bring me down to earth, a quick peruse of the internet back at our hostel revealed our youth team (plus Giggs) had finally lost its 2 year grip on the League Cup with a resounding 4-0 defeat away at snow encrusted West Ham. Shame, but when you consider that at the end of last month we were five points behind Chelsea in the Premiership and now we were two points ahead at the top, I wasn't going to lose any sleep over it.

Let the 'ammers enjoy their cup final. We had bigger fish to fry.

TUESDAY 7 DECEMBER. SALVADOR DEL BAHAI, BRAZIL
MANCHESTER UNITED 1 VALENCIA 1

Nowhere on earth have I experienced such energy and unadorned beauty as the coastal town of Salvador de Bahai, the largest black town outside of Africa. Often simply called Bahai by locals (and Hélène) it is Brazil's Afro-Brazilian jewel. Built from the proceeds of slavery, (six times as many Africans arrived here in Bahai than in the whole of North America) the historical centre is a living museum of 17th and 18th century architecture and gold laden churches, although the boring outskirts are decidedly dodgy. More importantly it is the home of Olodum, widely credited with developing the music style known as Samba Reggae. The narrow streets reverberate to the deafening sounds of dozens of drums played by kids of all ages.

Set up by percussionist Neguinho do Samba to combat racism, encourage self esteem and pride among Afro Brazilians, and to fight for civil rights for all marginalized groups, the pounding rhythms hit your heart, stomach and enter your very soul. Listen in the streets to drums set up at a Spinal Tap 11, the effects are sensational. And the looks on the kids' faces are a wonder to behold.

I implore anyone considering Brazil as a destination to make Bahai happen. You'll never be the same again. There is no other place in the world where descendants of African slaves have preserved their heritage as well as in Bahai, from music and religion to food, dance and martial arts.

Don't believe me? Just ask Paul Simon who used Olodum on his 1990 album "Rhythm of the Saints" or Michael Jackson, who featured them in his video for "They Don't care About Us". In 1996 Olodum also appeared in heavy metal band Sepultura's album "Roots".

One word of warning though. Don't go swimming alone on any of the beaches outside the city centre, 'cos when you come out of the water I guarantee your stuff will have been nicked. When I went for a dip Hélène stayed on the beach and vice versa. Reality check.

With the Valencia match happening later that afternoon I suggested we have a quick bite in one of the colourful restaurants around the main square. Having already qualified for the knockout stages of the Champions League, it may not have been the most important match of the season, but it was Manchester United after all so I had a duty to perform, in front of my laptop.

We sat down and ordered, then waited for our food. People came in, ordered, ate and left and we were still waiting for ours. This is a joke, I thought. They're doing it on purpose because Hélène must have tipped them off I want to get back to watch the footy. I was getting more and more agitated. Hélène tried to calm me but she acknowledged that something must have happened.

"I bet you they've forgotten our order." I cried. "Let me call the waitress over."

She assured us it was coming but I just know she had forgotten to place our order with the kitchen. Forty five minutes after entering I ordered Hélène to stand up.

"We're leaving. This is past a joke."

As I was pushing back my chair our red faced waitress came over with two plates of admittedly delicious looking food. I hesitated. That was enough for Hélène to sit down again. United is to me what food is to Hélène. Food won.

I took one mouthful of my lobster filled with rice, pineapple and a fusion of other assorted ingredients and I was in heaven. Only the best mother fucking lobster I'd ever tasted in my life! I had so wanted it to be shit so I could storm out, but now I was hooked. Salvador de Bahai, how could you do this to me. The match, chomp chomp, is about to start any minute, chomp chomp, and I'm stuck here with, chomp chomp, the best fucking lobster in the world.

What a cruel mistress my stomach can be. To make matters worse I'm a slow eater, so when I was finally sated I left the money with Hélène and raced back to our hostel and my laptop.

I turned it on just as the sides were coming out for the second half.

What! We're 1-0 down! Don't tell me Fergie has been complacent again with team selection. How many more times? We need to finish top of the group to make life easier for us in the next round. Checked the team sheet. No, it seemed a pretty strong line up. So what's gone wrong?

The second half kicks off and it's all United. Have they been given the hairdryer? Ah! At last, Rafael down the right, pass to Park and... wallop. Shit, straight at their keeper. No matter, there's Anderson to tap in the rebound. This wakes Valencia up but they seem to be implying eleven Ray Wilkins as pass after pass goes nowhere.

That'll do for me, Tom, but I wish United wouldn't take their collective foot off the gas. I've seen this so many times.

With both sides assured of qualification to the knock out stage, by the final whistle the ground is half empty, which says it all, although our hostel bedroom doubled in capacity with 10 minutes to go with Hélène and her Sudoku. Luckily for her there was nothing for me to shout about. We're through, we're top of our group, but was it worth the possibility of lobster indigestion?

MONDAY 13 DECEMBER. CARACAS-BOGOTA-SAN SALVADOR-CANCUN
MANCHESTER UNITED 1 ARSENAL 0

I looked at it every which way but loose. I tried to anticipate time changes in my favour as we flew east throughout the day, but the inescapable fact remained: I would be 36,000 feet up in the air when United kicked off at 8.00pm UK time and I would still be 36,000 feet up in the air when (hopefully) United would have kicked Arsenal off the top of the league and the Reds reinstated as the most unlikely leaders after a season of nondescript performances.

Today we were flying to Cancun in Mexico to meet up with our two daughters and granddaughter who we hadn't seen since our previous reunion in Thailand eight months ago. We were terribly excited, but this excitement was tempered by the fact that we had to take three flights with three different airlines in order to get there.

As our first flight was at 06.15 the following morning we decided the most time and cost efficient option was to spend the night on the floor of Caracas airport, which turned out to be the most naff major airport we encountered in twelve months of travelling. What can I tell you?

How long have you got? First of all there are no trolleys for your luggage when you arrive. The porters' mafia made sure you had to use, and pay for, their services. No chance. Fortunately our two major rucksacks had wheels so we took care of them ourselves, with our "normal size" rucksacks on our backs. But what was really ridiculous was the sight of passengers, especially families that had just landed, emerging from the baggage hall into the arrivals hall with their luggage piled high on trolleys. They were immediately forced to leave their trolleys behind and continue across the crowded arrivals concourse and out into the real world having no choice but to pay for the services of a porter.

From the vantage point of a table on the mezzanine, we could see perplexed and angry confrontations repeating themselves like a soap opera whilst we ate our criminally overpriced airport fayre. Meanwhile we had tried and failed to find Left Luggage. There wasn't one so we had to drag our luggage around with us all night. And there was no wi-fi anywhere within walking distance of the airport.

No seats anywhere in the departure lounge either, not even those metal ones designed to make sure haemorrhoids are more pleasurable than sitting, so we had no choice but to lay down under harsh white fluorescent lighting on the cold hard tiled floor and cuddle our luggage against the distinct possibility of theft.

The airport and airline staff we talked to either knew nothing or told us porkies. Useless. Needless to say we didn't get any sleep but the anticipation of seeing our offspring kept the demons at bay. The check-in finally opened at 03.30. Normally we don't rush at moments like these but we wanted to be sure of a good seat so we would have at least a chance of fourteen winks. Once in the queue we were badgered by money changers reminding us that we had to pay 180 Venezuelan pesos departure tax and the authorities only accepted cash or Venezuelan credit cards. How convenient. Of course, they offered the perfect solution. If we had US dollars or Euros, they would offer us preferential rates to change them into the local currency.

"OK, punk. Make my day." I thought as I prepared for the battle of wits to come. At least it would help me stay awake until Avianca Airlines opened their check-in desk.

"How much?" I exclaimed, as six pesos were offered against each of our Euros. "I got twelve pesos in our hotel in Macuto." (it was nine actually) There then followed the cat and mouse game as he rolled his eyes and walked away a couple of times. I kept smiling.

Eventually he settled at 8.5 pesos to each of our Euros, which I knew he wasn't happy with, but he still made a profit. And why should I lose any sleep over crooks not making their margins? Bow locks.

When it was our turn to check-in I showed the girl behind the counter that our following two flights, from Bogota in Colombia to San Salvador in El Salvador and then from San Salvador to Cancun, Mexico only had a 45 minute gap between them. Could she re-assure us we had time to make the Cancun flight. And as she was checking us in for all three flights, could she possibly give us two seats near to the front of the plane as possible. We would then be able to perform a very unBlatt-like manoeuvre and be the first off the plane and run to whatever gate was assigned our next flight.

With our eyes and stomach affecting our will to live, security and customs seemed to take an intolerably long time. When we at last escaped their clutches, we discovered there were no chairs air-side either, or anywhere for a coffee. Nothing. To paraphrase FCUM, "This is the worst fucking airport, we've ever been to."

The flight to Bogota was late taking off but uneventful. We now had four and a half hours to kill before our flight to San Salvador at 11.55. I worked out that was 3.00pm Colombian time so nothing to do here but to fret and anticipate. Much contributing to Facebook, Red News and Red Issue fans' forums later it was time to board our flight, but not before an excuse to go to the toilet resulted in LUHG sticker number 71 proudly displaying its message on the first mirror inside.

Now, you won't Adam & Eve this, but row 25 was right at the far end of the plane, right next to the toilets and as far away from the front exit as it was possible to be. Thank you Avianca check-in girl. I called over one of the stewardesses and explained our situation. She promised to see what she could do. She came back with.. wait for it... row 11, the emergency exit row!

Now I know some of you out there would give your right arm (or leg, to be more appropriate) for these seats but the down side, and it's a very big down, is that the seats don't recline. You sit bolt upright as though the possibility of Liverpool actually winning the Premiership had sent a shockwave through your body.

When you're dog tired this is the worst possible position. There was no way we could find comfortable positions on this two hour flight. Every bone seemed to ache. But we kept reminding ourselves of the bigger picture, arriving in Cancun before our girls.

The stewardess also assured us the following flight knew about our reservation and not to worry. They then gave us a reason to worry. We were delayed in taking off for fifty minutes. Why us? Why now?

However there was nothing we could do but curse to ourselves. The final straw came when over the communication system the pilot informed us that we would be landing in San Salvador at 3.20pm, a full 35 minutes after our connecting flight would have departed. A curse on your first born!

We slumped in our seats. Meanwhile my mind began to race. If we had time to wait at San Salvador airport it would be around 3.30pm, which meant our match would still be being played. I kept that thought to myself. Every cloud has a silver lining, or in this case, red. As long as Wi-Fi was on offer at the airport I could stream the match on my laptop. Things were looking up.

I couldn't concentrate on the plane's entertainment system so I just switched on the "follow your flight" screen and let the information wash over me. When the time zone screen came up for the umpteenth time something masquerading as my brain suddenly came to life.

San Salvador was one hour behind Bogota. Surely that meant we would land at 2.20pm not 3.20pm? The pilot must have got it wrong. Yes, I was sure I was right.

I clung onto this belief as we came into land. As soon as the plane came to a halt I got our two rucksacks down from the overhead compartments and unceremoniously pushed the first ten rows of people aside as, with Hélène in tow, we rushed out and into the arrivals section. The gate for our connecting flight was at the end of a very long corridor, so with my rucksack on my back I began to run like Woody from Toy Story, back bent almost double and my legs going like pistons.

I arrived at the gate with, literally, seconds to spare. Unfortunately they couldn't let me onto the flight as Hélène had our boarding passes and she was panting some way behind me.

Made it! Who dares wins! We were through and on the plane, against all the odds.

Oh well. It looks like I will now have to wait until we arrive at our all-inclusive US$60 a night hotel in Cancun before I'll be able to find out the Arsenal result. How frustrating!

Waiting outside Cancun arrivals hall for our shared taxi to arrive, we both commented on how cold it was. Not what we had come to Mexico for. I wondered for a moment if I might escape back inside the arrivals terminal under some pretext, with the obvious mission to find an internet cafe and the result.

I failed on both accounts, but at least I adhered LUHG sticker number 72 to the large clear sliding doors for the growing number of British holidaymakers to gaze at wonder. (Wonder how long it will remain there though?)

By the time we were on our way darkness had fallen so we weren't able to take in the Cancun coastline. Our hotel was on a narrow strip with the Caribbean Sea on one side and a lagoon on the other. With a choice of ocean or lagoon views and either balcony or terrace I had opted for ocean view with terrace.

We got a quarter view of both with neither terrace or balcony. So that's why it was down from US$192 to US$60 a night on the hotelbycity. com web site.... it was shite.

OK, that's being a little too harsh. It was just that everything was so dated, the all-inclusive food was really tasteless and they even served Tequila in plastic cups. All things considered I suppose US$60 a night was a good deal bearing in mind the price included dinner, breakfast and lunch but quality was definitely lacking.

But back to more important matters. The United result. Almost inevitably the Wi-Fi didn't work in our room so we went back to the lobby (see, I can speak American) "I'm first. I'm first" I thought as I switched on our laptop. With Hélène distracted I went first to the BBC Sport web site.

Manchester United 1 Arsenal 0

"YESSSSS!!!!!"

There it was in black and white, with a joyful Ji Sung Park in full colour after scoring with an improvised header and Nani screaming to the heavens behind him. United go two points clear with a hard fought 1-0 victory over the Arse. I read on.

"What's this? Rooney missed a second half penalty that could have put us 2-0 up?" Shit, literally. I imagined all Reds changing the colour of their underwear as Arsenal bossed the second half, though reading further they didn't create many clear cut chances as Ferdinand and Vidic re-established their impregnable partnership at the back.

So, it had all been worth it. The horrible night at Caracas airport, three flights including a Guinness Book of Records dash between planes, cold Cancun and naff hotel. When all's said and done one has to get one's priorities right and United certainly came through for me. Oh, yes. And we also arrived in Cancun in time to meet our girls the following day. All's right in the world tonight.

MEXICO

TUESDAY 14 DECEMBER. CANCUN, MEXICO.

If last night ended on a really high note I made sure the following morning would bring us back to earth with an almighty bump. I'd like to blame someone else for what happened next, so let's start with Hélène suggesting (forcing) me to change shorts. Instead of my cool yet practical mock army pair, I was persuaded to wear a pair of sophisticated, (me?) over-long white shorts with massive pockets either side.

I suppose those snotty skinny pouting young toffs that adorn all the male fashion adverts in glossy magazines these days might have been at home in them but I was self conscious, especially with those oversized pockets.

After a forgettable breakfast Hélène and I decided to go for a stroll along the beach. Cancun, lovely beach, lovely sand but Mexico's version of Benidorm. All concrete but no character and no soul. We started with a drink on the beach, sitting on the sand with our free drinks in plastic glasses, watching the waves crash against the shore.

I filmed Hélène and the sea with my camcorder, put the camcorder back in my oversized pocket then sat down again to finish my drink.

Suitably refreshed we strolled along by the sea shore for about an hour until we came upon a piece of wasteland between the terrace row of hotels. We climbed up, although half way there I sat down on a rock to put my sandals back on.

Aah. That's better. It wasn't long before we were back in our hotel via the main road. We'd checked out and vacated our room earlier so I went to the loo in the lobby.

Needs must and all that.

I lowered my shorts but something didn't feel right. In fact, I didn't feel anything. Anything against my left thigh, that is. I thrust my hand into my pockets.

Nothing.

NO CAMCORDER!!!

NOOOOOOOOOOooooooooo!!!!!!!!!!

After ten months, four days and twenty two countries I had bowed to the inevitable and lost our camcorder. I shit myself, literally. And I was in the perfect place to do so it has to be said. All the pleasant afterglow from the Arsenal result disappeared down the toilet along with this morning's breakfast.

My mind raced, hoping against hope there would be a simple explanation. Hélène had put it in her handbag. I had put it in her handbag. I had put it in its case. I knew all these wishes were fruitless. I retraced my steps in my mind, from the moment I had last used the camcorder. It had been on the beach in front of the hotel.

Well, there you go then. Father Christmas had come early for some lucky bastard passing by. It was gone, and so were all my films from Santiago onwards, as that was the last time I had transferred all my recordings to a CD-rom and sent them back home. That's virtually all of South America..... the Bolivian Salt Flats, Machu Picchu, Perito Moreno Glacier, Ushuaia, whale watching off Puerto Madryn, Super El Clasico –

River Plate v Boca Juniors, Ipanema Beach, the drummers in Salvador. You name it, I'd lost it.

Don't think Hélène will be best pleased.

Well, I'd better pull up my shorts and face the music. Hélène was lying on a sun lounger by the pool.

"Hi darling. Eerr... have you by any chance packed my camcorder away?"

"No. Why?"

Bollocks.

So I told her.

For someone who picked up English without much formal training, her command of genuine Anglo Saxon was impressive. I hadn't heard her come out with language like that for...... well, never, to be precise. She'd make an ideal football companion, if only she didn't hate football so much.

Of course I deserved the verbal onslaught. The pitiful excuse of massive pockets wouldn't stand up in a court of Denis, plus the fact remained I was more gutted than she was. Guilt and loss ate away at my insides.

Being ever the practical one in times of stress, she suggested we retrace our steps along the beach. A glimmer of hope hovered around the waste ground we had clambered up to make our way back. I had put my sandals back on, sitting on a stone. It may have fallen out there, and Hélène reckoned there would be no reason for anyone to walk up that bit.

Clutching at straws, I thought anything was worth a try. I rushed ahead of Hélène to the spot but nothing. Not surprised really. And that had been our only hope. All the way back I could feel the steely eyes bearing into my back, like daggers in my heart. The delicious anticipation of seeing our offspring became muted as a consequence. And it was all my fault.

That evening we drove the 120 kilometres back to Cancun airport in our rented people carrier to greet our girls in a whirl of hugs and kisses, topped off with LUHG sticker number 72 in the arrivals hall.

At least that took my mind off my camcorder catastrophe for a couple of minutes.

WEDNESDAY 15 DECEMBER. TULUM, MEXICO

For Christmas and New Year we had rented a beachfront villa in Tulum, Mexico, on the Caribbean coast. Hélène and I had originally been keen on Cuba, hence our choice of Caracas as the take-off point as it was the cheapest South American gateway to the island. However our girls thought differently so we left it to them. Being all together was our overriding desire. We gave them our budget and let them get on with it.

We were met by Gianni, the Italian owner, who explained in broken English the workings of the villa. With the potential 6 pointer against Chelsea coming up on Sunday I asked politely about the advertised wi-fi. He said the villa was not equipped for Wi-Fi but he would lend us an external modem which we could use during the day. This was not entirely satisfactory, as we would be out most of the day and so we needed it in the evening and at night. Not happy about that, especially at the price we were paying.

Once Gianni said his goodbyes and wished us a pleasant stay, one of the first things I did once we had installed ourselves in our various bedrooms was turn on the TV. Gianni had promised cable TV and this was the moment of truth. There were three remote controls which did my head in, but eventually I worked out which did what.

Yes, there was Sky TV. Not British Sky but a similar set up. I scrolled down the listing until I found the sports channels, then I went forward day by day until I came to Sunday 19 December.

There it was. 10.00 Chelsea v Manchester United. Panic over. Now I could look around the villa and relax. The villa was indeed right on the sea front, but the man-made beach could not disguise the lethal rocks at the seashore and into the sea. Crocs or other protection would be mandatory if we were to wade into the water here.

The villa's description had contained the fact that one hundred metres further along the beach lay a "proper" sandy beach. No it didn't. Another untruth. If that is what the brochure called a sandy beach then I'm the Archbishop of Canterbury.

Nevertheless the view was delightful. The sound of the waves crashing against the rocks drowning out any attempt at normal conversations. It immediately became apparent that we needed to rent a car if we wanted the true picture postcard sandy Caribbean experience.

SUNDAY 19 DECEMBER TULUM, MEXICO
CHELSEA v MANCHESTER UNITED (POSTPONED)

I didn't know whether to laugh or cry. Switching on my laptop, the first thing I did was to go to BBC Sport, only to find out that heavy snow in the UK had decimated the weekend's football programme, and our potential "6 pointer" against Chelsea had been postponed.

Shit! A winter weekend without United, what the hell was I going to do? Stuck in the luxury of a sunny Caribbean resort, I'm sure I'll think of something.

SUNDAY 26 DECEMBER. TULUM, MEXICO
MANCHESTER UNITED 2 SUNDERLAND 0

This promises to be a good day. Yesterday we met up with Kim and Shelly, two of Mel's best mates, who arrived to celebrate Christmas and New Year with us. Kim has offered to take us all to a large Dolphinarium where we can swim with the dolphins and mannequins. Personally I'm not comfortable with animals in man-made environments but I know Lilyella will get a thrill out of it. Jasmine, my youngest, and her friend Julie were due to take the final part of their PADI certificate exam in the morning, but with the promise of swimming with dolphins on the horizon (well, under the sea actually) they postponed it till the following day.

To make sure everything fitted in place like a jigsaw puzzle it was agreed we all meet up around 11.00am. This would give me the two hours I needed to watch the Sunderland game due to kick-off at 09.00am Mexican time. Sorted. For a change, everything went to plan.

Berbatov headed home a Rooney cross early on and we dominated the entire match. The only down side – this could and should have been another 7-1 but the festive spirit had affected the players. We were creating real chances this time, not pussyfooting outside the penalty box. Berbatov got a second in the second half but could easily have emulated his five against Blackburn.

Lovely moment just after Berbatov had been substituted for Hernandez in the 81st minute. Ferguson, all smiles, was seen to lean forward and whisper in Berbatov's ear, all the while beaming from ear to ear.

Yes, everyone's in the festive mood. Can't believe we're now 6 points ahead of Chelsea who are now down to fourth place AND we have a superior goal difference. If you had told me where we would be just 3 months ago I would have sent you to the funny farm. Pity City won though.

TUESDAY 28 DECEMBER. COZUMEL, MEXICO
BIRMINGHAM CITY 1 MANCHESTER UNITED 1

Today was Julie's last day with us. Jasmine's best friend was flying back from Cancun to Lucerne tonight via Madrid, Gatwick and Geneva. Oliver, another of Jasmine's best friends, was arriving tonight so we hoped to kill two best buddies with one stone. It was agreed we should visit the island of Cozumel, half an hour's ferry crossing from Playa Del Carmen on the mainland, then end the day by driving to Cancun airport as we would already be halfway there.

With United kicking off in Birmingham at 2.00pm local time I knew chances of watching the match live would be remote. And I have to admit I was taking more than a passing interest in the Ashes series down under, where for the first time in 24 years England had the chance of retaining the Ashes in Australia's back yard. I wanted to revel in the collective celebrations whilst watching the Aussies squirm, their own press sledging them to death. Yes, I am that sort of guy.

So come the evening we deposited Julie and picked up Oliver, but I couldn't leave before putting up LUHG sticker number 73 in a prominent place in the arrivals hall to replace LUHG sticker number 72 which had mysteriously disappeared. With Cancun the Benidorm of Mexico, I hoped a number of Brits would arrive and be duly impressed how far and wide the hatred of the Glazers had spread. We arrived at Kim and Shelly's villa and after a round of hugs and air kisses we settled down to a little polite chatty poos.

Shelly was lying in one of the two princess four poster beds behind us, gamely getting over whatever had prevented her from joining us the previous evening for a delicious, if overpriced meal in one of the beach clubs.

I stared at her in her revealing nightie and something in my stomach did a backflip. I sauntered over, sat by the side of the bed and put my arm round her shoulder. She was all lovely and warm. I looked deep into her eyes, then down at her lap.

"Shelly? I know it's a bit naughty, but can I ask you a personal question?

"Go on."

"Can you get the internet on your laptop?"

"Yes. Of course."

"Brilliant! Any chance I can have a go"

"Yeah. No problem."

And before you could say, "City are a massive club" she had escaped from my clutches and I was alone on the bed with her iMac.

I went straight to BBC Sport.

"England regain Ashes with innings victory" Brilliant! But more of that later. Needs must, and all that. I clicked on Football. "Ferguson fumes over last gasp equalizer." Shit. So, we woz robbed. Let's read on.

Now let's see. Bowyer's last gasp equaliser was definitely offside. We had more shots on goal. We dominated possession. OK, what else?

City 4 Villa 0.

Double shit. That now means they're level on points with us, although we retain the top spot owing to our superior goal difference, plus we have two games in hand.

I'm always wary of games in hand. I much rather have points on the board. My mind often goes back to the dark days of May 1992 when, in pole position to become champions for the first time in a quarter of a century, those lovable old rogues at the FA decided in their collective wisdom to make us play four games in seven days. And ABUs wonder why, for us, United > England. (To those unaware this means United are greater than England – Ed).

Still, I re-arranged my thoughts to put things into perspective, Chelsea's crippling malaise had continued, with a further two draws and a defeat in December. This meant that in the seven league games the Rent Boys had played leading up to Christmas Day, they had taken just seven points whilst in that same period we had picked up seventeen. Without ever hitting top gear we ended 2010 top of the league and unbeaten. That was beyond my wildest dreams, especially when I reflected back at the opening six weeks of the season.

Now I began to dream the impossible dream N-N-N-N-Nineteen! No, stop it! You're old enough and ugly enough to know better. I gave myself a mental bollocking. How long had I supported United? How many times had glory slipped through our fingers? Yes, but think how many last minute goals had had Glory written all over them?

Stop it! Stop it! Calm down! Calm down! I sat still for a moment. Luckily no-one had been arsed to look in my direction. I ordered my breathing to go back to normal.

Keep it under wraps, David. Keep it under wraps. I returned to the throng gathered in the open lounge. By this time darkness had fallen and we couldn't see, only hear the sea. I went for a stroll, by myself.

SATURDAY 1 JANUARY 2011. TULUM, MEXICO
WEST BROMWICH ALBION 1 MANCHESTER UNITED 2

Hélène and I had left the New Year celebrations at Kim's villa soon after midnight in order to take Lilyella back to ours, leaving the entourage and hangers-on to indulge in a lot of gay debauchery, and a little straight debauchery as well if I'm not mistaken.

Being the only teetotaller left on planet Earth, I had little trouble in waking up the following morning, giving me plenty of time to warm up the cable element of the TV.

The camera focused on the United players stepping off the bus and I spied Michael Owen back from another injury. Mmmm, how long will he last this time I wonder?

Right. Let's go. The ball soon found it's way to Gabrielle Obertan who overdid the trickery by the left corner flag but was able to pass the ball back to Evra who sent over a nice cross that Rooney, sandwiched between a couple of defenders, pinpointed his header past the Albion keeper into the net.

You should have seen his face. Rooney scoring from open play, the first time since the infamous match against Bayern Munich back in March 2010, was like a caged animal having just killed his prey. 1-0 up after only two minutes. By George, this tea tastes good. Why doesn't the referee blow for time? Three points now would be more than welcome.

Then after thirteen minutes a lucky/superb punt by Morrison of West Brom (depending on your allegiance) brought the score to 1-1. Shit, who made this tea? Rubbish.

It was now all end-to-end stuff. It was good to see Gary Neville back, but in the 23rd minute he could well have given away a penalty with a rash challenge inside the box. By this time West Brom were looking dangerous. In the 29th minute Obertan lingered a split second too long but a through ball to our Wayne allowed Rooney to slide a shot at a ridiculous angle across the goal go agonisingly close. That split second would have made all the difference.

What's wrong with the pitch near the right corner flag? First Fletcher, then twenty minutes later Obertan send over wild, over ambitious crosses that wasted the openings we created. Although a statistic flashed on the screen after 40 minutes showed West Brom enjoying 69% of the possession I felt we were more than holding our own. Only a couple of spectacular long range shots had spelt real danger, but fair play to West Brom, they were only one of a handful of teams that delight in attacking United at home and not just rely on intimidation and breakaways.

By now it was getting rather warm and I was dying to take off my LUHG T-shirt and take out my false teeth, but not knowing who, if anybody had made it back to our villa during the night I kept both firmly in place. Half time. 1-1.

The second half carried on like the first with United yet to exert a sustained period of pressure. Then WBA are awarded a penalty against Ferdinand. A much less obvious one this time but given nonetheless. Up comes Odemwingie and slices it across and to the left of our goal. What a plonker. What a lifeline. West Brom seemed shaken by this possible defining moment and United enjoyed a sustained period of pressure for the first time. Then in the 79th minute it all came to fruition as another Rooney corner came over and there was Hernandez to head his, and our second goal of the afternoon. Oh me of little faith.

COLOMBIA

TUESDAY 4 JANUARY. 36,000 FEET BETWEEN CANCUN AND BOGOTA
MANCHESTER UNITED 2 STOKE CITY 1

What can I say? Can't lie. Missed it. Had to rely on online newspaper reports when we finally got to our hostel.

Bogota. What can I say? Interesting historical centre. Boring suburbs a non local wouldn't want to walk around. It was cold... and it rained a lot. Nice coffee shops though. Bogota. The most uninteresting of all the South American capitals. End of.

SUNDAY 9 JANUARY. VILLA DE LEYVA, COLOMBIA
MANCHESTER UNITED 1 LIVERPOOL 0. FA CUP 3RD ROUND

Tension and vitriol had been building up all week. Facebook and various United fans forums had been full of it, and try as I might I couldn't help but allow a frisson of excitement enter my stomach at the thought that, after sixty one years on this planet, I may be in a position to witness United finally overtaking Liverpool as the most successful First Division/ Premiership team in the history of the world.

During the 70s and 80s, a number of false dawns had inspired Reds to chant "Champions" at various matches. I never did. Some sixth sense told me not to let go inside. And I was proved right on a number of bitter occasions. I've been there too many times, got too much white hair EVER to let my guard down. I know this was a cup game but it leads you down the road...

Meanwhile, with perfect timing, lovable Woy Hodgson had been dismissed by Liverpool one day before the match, "by mutual consent". Mutual consent, my arse. Now I like Roy Hodgson. In interviews on TV and especially on radio he comes over as a sensible, intelligent and caring man, so I was upset when he took over at Anfailed as I would have to join in all the piss taking. However, his reign was such a monumental failure I could only love the man more for putting Liverpool in their rightful place. Nowhere to be seen in the race for the title.

So, how to see the match? Hélène and I had arrived in the truly delightful town of Villa De Leyva, a hairy four hour bus ride presided over by a death wish driver into the Colombian hills north of Bogota. Built in 1572 and preserved in its entirety, Villa De Leyva nestles in the hills with a purity of simple one and two storey constructions, with white walls and dark green window frames that are a delight on the eye. The individual cobblestones were cut so deep that any young female upper middle class Bogotanos that decided to get away from the capital for the weekend wearing heels would come a cropper as she crossed the main Plaza and only increase the entertainment level for all of us sitting around the gargantuan, low lying main square partaking of liquid refreshment.

Our newly opened hostel was run by a young couple, he Colombian, she Londoner, who had packed their bags, sold their Islington pad and decamped to Villa De Leyva with their three kids. I could relate to all that, but my immediately priority was the hostel's wi-fi, but I found it impossible to get connected, so I spent an hour downstairs with the female co-owner who eventually got me going (!) However the connection was so slow I decided a major investment was in order, so I agreed to pay COP1400 (40p) an hour to watch the streaming of the game on the hostel computer. Is there no limit to my generosity?

I set my mobile phone alarm for a civilised 08.00am so I'd be fully functional by the time the match kicked-off at 08.30 local time. Needless to say I woke up long before the alarm, got out of bed without waking up the other half, put on my LUHG T-shirt hoping it would initiate a conversation with fellow guests and made my way downstairs.

The husband was speaking to his staff as I switched on the computer. He came over to find out what I was doing, and when he found out there would be football on offer he sat down behind me on the sofa. He turned out to be a luke warm Gooner (is there any other kind?) and I got the impression he was just in the market for a little footy talk.

I logged on to my streaming site and waited for the annoying thirty second commercial to finish. Perfect. The scene that greeted me was the two teams about to kick-off. As we mounted our first attack I turned round, only for the husband to point frantically at the screen.

Penalty! We had been awarded a penalty! How? Show the slow motion replay.

Bastard! That was a clear penalty. No question. Berbatov had got past and he'd been tripped. c'mon Giggsy. You can do it. GOOOAAALL!! Great penalty Ryan. Reina guessed right but perfect placing by our left wing legend put us 1-0 up in the very first minute.

Wow! Kenny, what a difference you have made! However, as the match progressed we didn't really press home our advantage and Liverpool were proving to be tough, if unimaginative opponents. Rafael was lucky to connect with the ball after attempting a two footed tackle on Mereilles who bottled it by jumping out of the way. A few minutes later, camera swallowing Steven Gerrard perpetrated the crime that Rafael a few minutes earlier had failed to commit. Carrick was the victim of Gerrard's two footed lunge.

Confusion reigned for a few moments as referee Howard Webb called Gerrard over. We held our breath. Would justice prevail?

BYEEEEEE!!!

So sad to see little Stevie walk off the pitch. I just had to wave at him through the computer monitor. It was the least I could do. I settled down, and so did United. A few attacking forays but not what could be called flowing football by any stretch of the imagination. To make matters worse, the curse of streaming was making its presence felt. Picture freezing, which only increased the lack of flowing football on my screen

At half time I tried to connect to other streaming sites but the hostel's computer hadn't installed the latest media playing software so most failed to produce any picture at all.

The second half saw both United and my streaming site stutter and splutter in an unconvincing display. But at the end of the day we'd beaten the scousers and nothing else mattered. The owner agreed to LUHG sticker number 75 on his hostel notice board. Good man.

SUNDAY 16 JANUARY. PLAYA BLANCA, ISLA DE BARU, COLOMBIA
TOTTENHAM HOTSPUR 0 MANCHESTER UNITED 0

With over a week until our next match, the away league fixture at White Hart Lane, I told myself I should fully immerse myself in my glorious surroundings, the impressive Spanish colonial town of Cartagena on the warm Colombian Caribbean coast, a far cry from the cold and damp capital, Bogota.

I'd chosen a hotel that the Lonely Planet web site showed was literally on the beach, so I was a little disconcerted when our taxi from the airport left the coast road and went three quarters round the block and came to a halt in front of a hotel with the same name as ours two blocks from the sea front. Not happy about this.

I refrained from saying anything as we checked in and were shown to our room on the first floor. I wanted to get my facts straight. I told Hélène not to unpack as I established my wi-fi connection and brought up the hotel's details on the Lonely Planet web site.

There it was as plain as could be. The red arrow sitting squarely on the yellow of the beach indicating its position. So either Lonely Planet had got it wrong, or the hotel had supplied wrong information to Lonely Planet.

I went downstairs and asked to see the manager, keeping a polite, if slightly false smile on my face. (I should be in politics) I explained, with the benefit of exhibit A on my laptop, that we had booked this hotel as it was on the beach (see exhibit A) yet here we were two blocks from the sea. What gives?

A reciprocated false smile from the manager failed to placate me. Obviously she wasn't going to admit liability for the photo, adhering to the strict business philosophy... blame somebody else, but I did manage to get an upgrade to a superior room on the second floor. Not ideal but if you don't ask...

By this time it was late afternoon so we decided to visit the much heralded historical centre within the ancient city walls the following day, and decided instead to walk down the aforementioned two blocks to the sea.

The sun was going down over the grey sea but the intensity of oranges, pink and purples were amazing. Amazing, but for altogether the wrong reasons, were the dozens of families that were now vacating the grey sandy beach and leaving behind mountains of rubbish. Absolutely filthy. They don't show you pictures like these in the holiday brochures.

We didn't linger as we had originally intended but made our way back to the main thoroughfare with its motley collection of garish bars and restaurants and had a nice Italian meal. Our conversation was dominated by what we had seen. Cartegena was meant to have been our final exotic fantasy beachside Caribbean destination of our incredible one year, round the world odyssey, but we couldn't leave it like this. We'd planned one week here, mainly relaxing in the sun before continuing through Colombia (the safe bits) and onwards to our final "ultimate" destination, the Galapagos Islands.

This was our last chance to do absolutely nothing, interspersed with a little culture in the old town, but the filthy beach (sorry to disappoint you, but I'm not doing that pun) had caused us to rethink our plans.

Back in our room I re-read the Cartegena entry in Lonely Planet and discovered that the best beach was actually 20 kilometres away. Playa Blanca. That's it then. We'll spend three days here and four days there. From the port there were boats offering day trips to Playa Blanca so we decided to book one of these to check out the area for ourselves. Sorted.

MONDAY 17 JANUARY CARTEGENA, COLOMBIA

The following morning we took a taxi to the old town, first stopping at the port which turned out to be but a short walk away from the main opening of the historical old city and bought 2 x one day return tickets to Playa Blanca.

That's tomorrow sorted then. But now it's Cartegena old town time. And what an old town it was. Superbly maintained, such a contrast to the beach just a few metres away. Beautiful narrow Colonial streets and squares. After a couple of hours of wandering round the hot streets we retired to the shade of a first floor bar overlooking the main square and witnessed street artistes, kids break dancing for money and snake lines of ageing American Tourists well into their second millennia, some of whom we were sure would never see another sunrise. They brought a new meaning to the word 'doddery'.

A second wind lured us to another square where, lo and behold, there was a Hard Rock Café. I hadn't been in one for five years at least so you'll never guess where we had lunch. The best burgers and an apple crumble to die for. That's two in one year. First Puerto Nateles in Patagonia in November and now less than three months later, Cartegena in Colombia. As 10CC might have sung, "Life is an Apple Crumble".

Well, maybe not.

One thing's for certain though, just like in Puerto Nateles, I'm coming back for second helpings. You can count on that. Left LUHG sticker number 76 in the men's loo. Rock on!

TUESDAY 18 JANUARY CARTEGENA - PLAYA BLANCA, COLOMBIA

This morning we took our pre-booked 2 hour boat ride to Playa Blanca, although the choppy sea made an effort to extract portions of my breakfast from me. Approaching the narrow strip of low lying land it reminded me of Formentera, the upmarket island just south of Ibiza with its immaculate turquoise sea, pristine sandy beaches and overpriced restaurants. Except Playa Blanca benefited from being decidedly down market in a laid back traveller/hippy sort o' way, with numerous hammocks, a cluster of bamboo constructed cabins and a ramshackle collection of open air bars and cafes.

This is going to be good. We trekked along the beach until we came to the cabins and duly booked ourselves in for four nights from tomorrow. Sorted. We spent the rest of the day just sunbathing, sea bathing and food bathing in a hedonistic display of over indulgence. Lovely jubbly.

WEDNESDAY 19 JANUARY. PLAYA BLANCA, COLOMBIA

Three days of slow motion sun, sea, sand and.... thousands of sand flies that attacked Hélène and me day and night. Some so tiny they waltzed freely through our mosquito net.

We didn't let this put us off though. Oh, deary me no. A lazy, hazy, non-crazy three days of "busy doing nothing, working the whole day through, trying not find lots of things not to do", and succeeding.

SATURDAY 22 JANUARY. MEDELLIN, COLOMBIA
MANCHESTER UNITED 5 BIRMINGHAM CITY 0

Having only recently been liberated from the twin threats of drug barons and left wing gorillas, Medellin was a town with the shackles removed. Confidence has returned with investment in projects such as the new cable cars connecting the town centre to the previously no-go favellas, which now boasted two magnificent black textured cubes of the giant Porque Espana Library at the very top.

With a lovely squeaky clean private room on the first floor of this newly opened hostel in a leafy Medellin suburb, I relaxed in the knowledge that for once everything worked, including the TV with its forthcoming Fox Sports broadcast of Manchester United v Birmingham City. LUHG sticker 77 had duly been strategically placed on the hostel notice board upon our arrival. All was right in the world.

So many times over the past eleven months I'd had to battle the forces of transmission terrorists, just for their pleasure in watching me suffer in my attempts to watch United in whichever of the four corners of the world I happened to be. Now with a 17.30 kick off in the UK equating to a civilized mid morning in Medillin, I settled down to a leisurely breakfast. What could possibly go wrong?

Hélène could go wrong. Back in our room she sat on the remote control and we lost the picture. No problem. Just press the button. Nothing, just black.

"Stop mucking about." I thought. She's extracting the urine. Hélène knows how remote controls work far better than me. She just wants me suffer for making her watch the match in our room.

"Give it to me." I called. Surely it's just this button here…

Nothing.

Shit.

Now I was on red alert (get it?). I rushed downstairs and appealed to the girl on reception. She seemed to shrivel up before my very eyes. She then disappeared without a word.

"This sketch is getting serious." I thought.

A few moments later a man came but in broken English admitted he knew nothing about TVs. Oh, great.

"Can I see the manager, please?" No response.

I don't know what the formalities are around here but I'm going to find him myself. Found his office and invited myself in. Explained the problem. His shrug was unacceptable. I asked if he could have a look at it, or if not, supply me with another TV.

He got up as though he had the weight of the world on his shoulders and gestured for me to follow him. We went into another room where he unplugged a TV and carried it upstairs to our room.

Plugged in it, it worked perfectly. Thank Eric for that. Or more precisely I thanked the unsmiling manager and settled back for the start of the match. The pre-match preamble uncovered a little gem. Despite not firing on all cylinders United had now gone on a 27 match unbeaten run.

How did that happen?

The question remained though. When were we going to see the real Manchester United?

Today!

We were brilliant from start to finish. Incensed by their last gasp equalizer a few days ago at St Andrews, United were sharp and incisive today, or "rampant" as the press like to describe performances. Dimitar Berbatov scored a hat-trick and actually managed to smile.

In fact I'd hardly stopped sitting at the end of the bed when after just 95 seconds Berbatov scored from a corner. That in itself was significant. How long has it been since United took advantage of corners? Must be Birmingham's fault.

Berbatov's second came on the half hour when oh so generous Birmingham defending allowed Anderson to pass to Rooney who in turn released Berbatov who cut inside and finished with a low drive. The killer goal arrived just before half time. A lovely build-up between Berbatov and Rooney, who swept a cross into the path of Giggs to score. Proper United football at last.

I'm enjoying this. 3-0 up. No tension. Secure in the knowledge 3 points are on the way. I wish we had a few more non underwear changing matches each season, I wouldn't have to invest so heavily in Grecian2000. United continued their total dominance in the second half. Peppering shots from all angles, something we haven't done for ages.

Eight minutes in and Berbatov's third hat-trick of the season arrived after Rooney had brilliantly controlled a punt from Edwin Van der Sar, released Giggs who crossed for the Bulgarian to score from 6 yards.

"AAhhh. Fucking brilliant!"

Cue much bouncing up and down on the bed, much to the annoyance of hers truly who dropped her Sudoku on the floor.

He He.

In the end, Rooney made way for Michael Owen. We should have overtaken the Blackburn score but in the end had to settle for 5, with Nani firing in with his umpteenth shot of the afternoon in the 76th minute. I relaxed in the afterglow, reflecting how refreshing it had been to watch Birmingham not treating a match against United as their Cup

Final but playing to their true potential as relegation candidates. More teams take note.

"Right Hélène. What shall we do today? I'm up for anything. Anything!"

TUESDAY 25 JANUARY. CALI, COLOMBIA
BLACKPOOL 2 MANCHESTER UNITED 3

First of all I have to apologise to all United fans everywhere for our first half performance. Or more accurately, my wife should. I didn't realise the attraction South America's largest shopping mall would have on her. I anticipated a couple of hours would be enough to see everything, which in turn should give me more than enough time to make it back for a 2.00pm kick off.

But I was so wrong. At 2.00pm we were still finishing off a dogburger in McDonald's, whose culinary delights I think you'll agree you don't wish to rush, as the chances of its contents entering one orifice and exiting another increases in direct correlation to the speed of digestion.

Thus it was almost 2.30pm when we exited the said establishment. I didn't want to appear too pre-occupied so we strolled back to our hostel, the sweat on my brow in no way due to the heat and humidity all around us. With our flight to Quito departing from Cali airport at 7.00pm, I'd booked a taxi for 4.30pm from our hostel, just after the final whistle. (Baldrick has nothing on me when it comes to cunning plans).

As we passed through reception I couldn't help pontificating on the paradox that life throws up. On the one hand, my heart warmed at the sight of my LUHG sticker number 78 taking pride of place on the hostel notice board, but not for the first time on our trip I was perplexed by the sight of mainly young Westerners just hanging around the bar. The same guys and gals we had left in the same pose hours earlier this morning. Why travel halfway round the world, just to stay and drink cheap beer when there is a big wide world out there to explore? Talkin' 'bout the next g-g-g-g-generation.

Still, no time to linger with these wasters. I arrived back during the half time advertisements, so it was a good (or as it turned out, bad) few minutes before "Blackpool 2 Manchester United 0" flashed up on the screen.

"What the f★★★!"

After visiting the loo, Hélène joined me and switched on our laptop. Whilst waiting for the second half to start she hit me with another hammer blow to the unmentionables. An e-mail from our Galapagos Island travel agency specialising in last minute deals informed us that our booking had been cancelled as the boat company in question had released the cabin to another couple who had sent their money in first.

I was furious. Not only were we losing 0-2 to Blackpool, Hélène's game of "let's wait and see if we can find a better deal in Quito" had backfired spectacularly. My "a bird in the hand is worth two in the bush" had a hollow ring in victory.

My look also had "I told you so" written in every crevice of my face. Twitching overtime, I sent her downstairs to try to salvage something from her self-induced catastrophe.

I returned to the screen seething with anger, indignation and frustration. How could we have let two goals in without reply in the first 45 minutes? Our rivals must be pissing themselves, waiting for our unbeaten bubble to burst. I checked on the team sheet as the players came out for the second half. Berbatov, Rooney, Nani... at least we seem to be at full strength.

I checked the other half time scores on the other channels. Arsenal 2 Ipswich Town 0 in the Carling Cup semi final second leg and Wigan Athletic 0 Aston Villa 0 in the other league game on the night. That must be a riveting watch. Just then a tall young man came into the TV lounge area.

"Hola."

"Hola. What game you watching?" Ah, an English accent.

"Blackpool versus Manchester United, but we're coming second at the moment."

"Ah, you're a United fan?"

Quick on the uptake, I thought.

"What about you? What team do you support?"

"The Villa."

"Ah, we play you next week, on the 1st of Feb."

It turned out he was a TEFL teacher like myself and was living in the hostel whilst teaching in Cali. We exchanged a few niceties, as you do, then he came out with a telling, and soon to be proved, providential statement, namely...

"I was at Villa when we were 2-0 up and you came back to win 3-2."

"Yes, I was at that game. FA Cup, Ruud was on fire that night. Brilliant atmosphere in our end. One of my all-time favourite United matches." I gushed.

We spoke a little more, but my mind was working on the possibility of history repeating itself. Was this prophetic or what?

I settled down for the second half. I was under no illusion as to the size of our task. Blackpool had recently completed the double over

Liverpool, which in itself was the cause of great merriment in my side of the Blatt household, and Ian Holloway was one of my favourite managers. He was literally living the dream. Having managed lower league teams throughout his career, he had won the manager's equivalent of the football pools and now he was pitting his wits against the top managers and sides in the Premiership.

Man for man we were clearly the better team, on paper, but unlike most newly promoted sides, Blackpool's gloss hadn't worn off after a few weeks. The players were still playing above themselves and the credit must go down to Ian Holloway's motivational skills. I'd met him a couple of years back in the Green Room before and after a TV sports programme on a now defunct satellite channel and he was genuine, witty, honest, insightful and a great piss taker.

Yes, you could say I liked him a lot. But not for the next 45 minutes. From the moment the second half kicked off we dominated possession and attacked with determination. I don't get it. What could possibly have happened in the first half if we were playing like this?

Then in the 73rd minute our pressure paid off as Fletcher sent over a low delivery and there was Berbatov to tap the ball into the net. "AAAhhhh!!!" as a hostel in deepest darkest Cali resounded to this particular Red jumping up and down in the first floor lounge.

"We can do this! We can do this!"

Hélène came bounding up the stairs. To join in my celebrations?

No, tell me to tone it down.

No chance.

"You're gonna win this." interjected the Villa fan.

"You better fucking believe it." responded the demented United fan (me)

She'd hardly disappeared from sight and sound when from United's next attack Giggs floated a ball into Hernandez's path and his shot swept past the Blackpool keeper.

"AAAAAAHHHHHHhhhhhh!!!!!!"

The floor of the hostel strained once more as every element of my anatomy reacted in deafening, uncontrolled movements.

Hélène came bounding up the stairs once more.

Hélène who?

I was totally riveted on the screen. My breath coming out in short, punctured spurts. This was United. This was it. This was us. Wave after wave of United attacks followed. Sitting was out of the question. I headed every ball, I kicked every pass.

Now you know United, and Ferguson in particular, have a reputation for influencing referees to allow us more injury time so we can fathom out a last gasp winner. Well, put my wife in the anti-Christ category.

With five minutes to go, she re-appeared once more to inform me our taxi had arrived to take us to the airport.

"He'll have to wait." I said breathlessly

"Don't be ridiculous." came the reply.

"I'll pay the waiting time. I'm not leaving. Five minutes."

Sensing there was no point in arguing Hélène disappeared from view once more. A godsend. With just 2 minutes to go Berbatov ran onto a Scholes pass and his left foot shot slammed into the net.

"AAAAAAAAHHHHHHHHHhhhhhhhhh!!!!!!!"

Cue screaming, piston like air punches into an imaginary punchbag, and other assorted and uncontrollable bodily and verbal movements as the enormity of the second half comeback registered within the fog of my brain. Five and a half thousand miles away I could hear the raucous United fans in the stadium.

It's games like this that define us. Define United. Define me. There goes the final whistle. "Hurrah!" and more standing ovations from yours truly. A pivotal moment in the campaign, in the season, in our quest for N-N-N-N- Nineteen. In fact in our history. THAT'S how important this result is.

"What's that Hélène? The taxi's waiting. Yeah. Coming."

That was said in autopilot. Every other element of my being was regurgitating the previous 45+ minutes.

"Sorry, where're we going to? Oh, yeah. The Galapagos Islands. That's nice."

GALAPAGOS ISLANDS

THURSDAY 27 JANUARY PLAYA MANN, GALAPAGOS ISLANDS

As a potential but now discarded publisher warned me recently, this is a meant to be a football not a travel book, so I have decided to condense the Galapagos Islands into one segment. Those of you who followed us on facebook will have seen the pictures, but one thing has to be said. For the sake of the animals and birds themselves, travellers are not allowed to get too close. So visions of us walking, talking, eating and singing with the animals a la Dr Doolittle were sadly misplaced. The satisfaction comes from knowing we are contributing to the welfare and preservation of unique species, but with a few exceptions, you get closer to living creatures in a zoo than here in the Galapagos Islands.

The main exception was wandering round the port on Playa Mann, our base for a couple of days prior to the cruise itself. We truly interacted with the sea lions as they waddled along the coast road and the beach, or simply snoozed anywhere they could. At night lots of giant turtles came ashore and slept on the beach.

That was cool. I stuck LUHG sticker number 79 on a lamppost. That was cool too. The following day we hired a taxi for a tour of the island and its main sights. Climbed to the top of a volcano and watched as frigates swooped down and washed their wings and feet in the lake created in the crater.

Visited the Galapagos National Park and met the one and only Lonesome George, believed to be the last of a dying breed of giant tortoise. Scientists estimated he was over 100 years old. With no offspring and no known individuals from his subspecies left, Lonesome George became known as the rarest creature in the world, a title Liverpool supporters who last remember their team winning the League will soon emulate. He survived our visit but finally met his maker in June 2012. Such a privilege for us.

In the afternoon we went swimming and sunbathing on a beach round the bay. Swam with giant turtles and sea iguanas and sunbathed with the sea lions. What a privilege. (For us, I should mention. Not them) Only one drawback, nobody mentioned the thousands of flies that descend the moment you make an appearance on dry land, and no manner of swatting and waving of arms would distract them from the goal. Attacking Mr & Mrs Blatt. Nobody mentioned them in the brochures. Mr Darwin, could I possibly have a word…

SATURDAY 29 JANUARY PLAYA MANN – EVOLUTION, CRUISE SHIP, GALAPAGOS ISLANDS SOUTHAMPTON 1 MANCHESTER UNITED 2 FA CUP 4TH ROUND

Went back to the airport to meet our cruise rep at 11.30. Hoping we'd be late to board the bus as I could follow our Southampton cup tie on Live Football on BBC Sport. Got to 12.45, score 0-0. Second string XI. Shit. Not again.

That's it. Who knows when I will find out the final score? We're off on an adventure to the nearest place on Earth to Jurassic Park. So, not all roads lead to Wembley then. Lunch on board was surprisingly delicious, though at these prices it shouldn't be surprising, just delicious. Still, credit where credit's due.

The cabin was rather small with bunk beds, but after we'd sailed round Isla Lobos and Leon Dormido we were upgraded to a cabin with a double bed, and a porthole! Yeah!

Our two guides gave us a presentation in the main salon. Seems we must get up at 06.30 every morning. No comment. Docked in Playa Ochoa and swam with the sea lions, as you do. Early night after delicious meal Bed early. Set alarm for 06.30.

SUNDAY 30 JANUARY GALAPAGOS ISLANDS

Walked on rocks on Isla Espanola for two kilometres. Landed in a bay with sea lions and colourful sea iguanas found only on this island, the oldest in the Galapagos. Small yellow breasted birds bounced all around us. We observed the breeding grounds of the brown & white boobies and saw our first blue boobies. And an albatross. Had been warned we'd arrived too late in the breeding season but this one was obviously waiting just for us.

Nice.

Back on board we ate a delicious cruise ship lunch, then changed ready for snorkelling. The tight wetsuit squashed all my bits into a reasonably attractive package. One 45 minute boat ride later Hélène and I were happily snorkling around and below the surface of the Pacific. We saw two giant rays and a giant turtle as well as a multitude of multicoloured fish.

I came back on board first though, my resistance to the cold water lowering as each minute passed. Once everyone was back on board they performed a roll call, and guess who was still in the water. You guessed correctly – 'er outdoors. The boat had to turn around just to pick Hélène up. Typical.

Late afternoon they served complimentary caprinia (a rum based cocktail) and hot nibbles in the bar on the upper deck. I could get used to this. And I did. They provided this little delight each afternoon.

MONDAY 31 JANUARY SANTA CRUZ, GALAPAGOS ISLAND

Aha! Forget the amazing wildlife. Santa Cruz has an internet café. Now we're talking. At last I can find out about what happened in Southampton. Left the Charles Darwin centre around 3.30pm and made our way slowly in the heat back to the Puerto Ayora, my eyes alert for the first sighting of the internet cafe.

Gotcha!

"Dos internet, por favor."

"3 and 4"

My stomach was quite calm as I waited for my machine to warm up, which is a good sign, as United catastrophes are normally preceded by knots in stomach. It's called mens' intuition. However, rigamortis was setting in as I waited for my machine to make contact with the intergalactic highway. Did I tell you the Galapagos Islands have the slowest internet connections in the world?

No? Well, here goes. The Galapagos Islands have the slowest internet connections in the world. There you are. So bad I wrote it twice.

Step one – log on to bbc.co.uk/sport

Step two – football

Step three - results

You can't imagine how long that took! I wanted to walk out but Hélène said it would probably be the same in all internet cafes on Santa Cruz. I'm sure she was right but it didn't make the situation any more bearable. Eventually the scores came up. First thing I noticed was Fulham 4 Tottenham 0. Whoops! Rick won't be pleased, I thought. Then I scrolled down to Saturday's results.

There it was. Southampton 1 Manchester United 2

Both arms raised in a silent salute (not silent according to Hélène, but that doesn't count.) Our second string had pulled us through. I could imagine what sort of game it must have been, so I clicked on "report" to have my suspicions confirmed. And they were.

Not only that, Southampton had deservedly scored first. Their fans must have wet themselves until Owen prodded home our equaliser, then with Nani and Giggs on for the ineffective Gibson and Anderson (so it read) Little Pea popped up, yet again, to grab our winner. With that team a win was the best I could have hoped for, and they duly obliged.

I felt sorry for all the Manchester based Reds who must have spent an arm and a leg getting down to the south coast, only to watch our second team perform. Yet looking at the bigger picture quickly dissolved my initial disappointment when I had read the team sheet before the match.

After the opening half a dozen matches of the season, I felt we had as much chance of winning the Premiership this season as the Glazers winning the BBC Sports Personalities of the Year award. Chelsea were unbeaten, scoring a bucket full of goals without conceding one, whilst we were struggling just to play football. Rooney's off field exploits were having a detrimental affect on his on field performances. We were giving away last minute goals instead of scoring them ourselves.

Everything pointed to a second year as also-rans as far as the Premiership was concerned. So to find ourselves five points clear at the end of January was nothing short of a miracle. But now we had to work to make sure the miracle didn't disappear. And if that meant placing the F A Cup behind the Premiership and the Champions League in the priority stakes, then I for one would go along with the decision.

I know the FA Cup has a special place in the hearts and minds of

United supporters. In my case I had to endure 8 losing semi finals in all competitions between West Ham in the mud at Hillsborough in 1964 through to Leeds United in the second replay at Burnden Park, Bolton before creaming myself amidst the ecstasy of Hillsborough in 1976, beating Derby County. I'd watched that game through a veil of tears as soon as Gordon Hill put us ahead in the 11th minute. I knew, I just knew, and all those years of frustration melted away in a haze of euphoria.

To have been a United fan that day was something special. Left the internet café with LUHG sticker number 80 taking pride of place on the front door.

TUESDAY 1 FEBRUARY SANTA CRUZ, GALAPAGOS ISLANDS
MANCHESTER UNITED 3 ASTON VILLA 1

This morning we walked on the black sand and rocks for 20 minutes barefoot, then along the rocks in sandals. Fur seals, Galapagos Flycatchers. Swimming and snorkeling. Hélène saw a hammer head shark and rays. Where was I? After lunch we took the inflatable to Gardner's Bay for more swimming and snorkelling. Turned out the panga would be returning to the boat giving people a chance to shower and change. Having woken up at 06.30 every morning since the cruise began, Hélène and I looked at each other, and without another word jumped straight back into bed. The rest, as they say, is biology.

16.30. We were given the choice of climbing up a mile for stunning views or walking along the beach to see penguins. Hello penguins.

In the evening one of the guides told me the captain can radio for the football results. I asked him. No such luck, we were too far from the mainland to get a signal. I would have to wait until we get back to San Cristobel on the 5th. Arrgh!!

Went to bed early in case we heard the 05.00am call informing us that whales or dolphins were outside. I cuddled Hélène as she went to sleep, with a silly grin on my face. What the hell was I doing here on a bijou luxury cruise ship in the middle of the Galapagos Islands? Surely this wasn't for the likes of someone like me? I couldn't believe my good fortune.

But I still didn't know the Villa result.

FRIDAY 4 FEBRUARY GALAPAGOS ISLANDS

When we returned to our cabin after lunch there was a four page questionnaire and three envelopes waiting for us. The envelopes were for the tips.

"These are fucking big envelopes!" I thought.

I checked in the ship's manual. It stated that although tipping was discretionary, you were left in no doubt that anything less than a king's ransom would condemn you to walking the plank, and to be eternally classified under the category of tight fisted bastard. At the bottom of all the warm words and drivel it suggested the following;

Each of the two naturalist guides should receive $60-80 each from every passenger. You have got to be joking. Doesn't the cruise company pay these guys? Fuck me, I'm in the wrong job!

A quick calculation followed (well, quick by my standards anyway). At an average of $70 each, our compliment of twenty four passengers would enable the two guides to pocket $1680 each for seven and a half days work! And when the ship is full, i.e. thirty two passengers, this rises to $2240 each!!! On top of this, the third envelope was for the rest of the crew. For them every passenger was "advised" to give between $140-160. So for Hélène and I, on top of the last minute cost of US$2300 per person for the cruise and return flights from Quito to San Cristobal, we were expected to outlay a further $370 each. No way, Jose.

"Excessive" doesn't begin to cover it. Sophisticated blackmail is more accurate. After a heated discussion Hélène and I decided that together we would award $60 to each guide and $100 to the crew, a total outlay of $220. This still hurt, especially as Lonely Planet, in their latest edition, recommended a tip of around $20 each.

Welcome to the real world guys. Not for the first time, both Lonely Planet and Rough Guide were way out on figures.

SATURDAY 5 FEBRUARY. GALAPAGOS ISLANDS TO QUITO TO GUAYAQUIL, ECUADOR
WOLVERHAMPTON WANDERERS 2 MANCHESTER UNITED 1

This was our last day aboard "Evolution". We were assured we could have a lie-in till 07.15am, as the only organised activity this morning would be a one hour visit to the Introduction Centre back on San Cristobal, where it had all began eight days ago.

Much hugging, handshakes and air kisses abounded as twenty four weary and significantly lighter of dollar passengers waited to be taken off the boat and deposited ashore by panga. In our case all but two of the addresses and e-mail addresses we collected were confined to our mental out-trays.

Inverted snobbery? Perhaps, but Hélène and I couldn't imagine many of these people comfortable in our world, and certainly not my Red world. A certain conversation stopper amongst the retired Republican right-wing Americans if ever there was one. To them, anyone left of Attila the Hun was a Communist.

The knots in my stomach were tightening as my reunion with the internet, and by definition, the Villa result drew closer. This is where it had all started almost a year ago to the day. A result against the Villa. At 08.15am we descended the stern steps of Evolution for the final time and took our places on the panga. As it drew away I filmed the boat receding into the distance. My first, and probably last proper cruise I'd ever take. It was certainly one up from Brittany Ferries but not a classic cruise as in QE2 or the like it has to be said.

From the quay we were herded onto a bus and taken straight to the airport. The two guides were waiting for us by the departure gate, wishing us a fond farewell. I wondered if they could tell who had given the biggest and smallest tips. I monitored their faces for any tell-tale signs but they gave nothing away. Had plenty of time to adhere LUHG sticker number 81 in the departure hall of the single hall airport.

Landing in Guayaquil Airport and waiting for our connecting flight to Quito, my first priority was the internet. What followed next was a classic case of good cop bad cop. Good news first. Brought up the Villa result. We won. 3-1. Yippee!!

Before I could revel in the details and check on the Premiership league table, one of my fellow cruise passengers past by and matter of factly informed me by means of his Blackberry that we had just lost 2-1 away to Wolverhampton Wanderers.

Fuck. That played havoc with my emotions. Laugh or cry?

Shit, no time to find out the details, our flight has been called. A quick LUHG sticker number 82 hastily placed near the boarding gate and we were off.

SUNDAY 6 FEBRUARY QUITO TO GUAYAQUIL, ECUADOR

Put out a request for a City ticket on Facebook. Thought I'd let the pain of the Wolves defeat ebb away a little before I made my move. Let a Saturday night drinking session put fellow Reds in a more receptive mood. I'd put out feelers a few weeks previously but no-one had taken the bait. Now the situation was getting serious.

Guayaquil was a bustling city, but the best part was the newly constructed riverfront walkway by the side of the brown murky River Guayas. Bought a Panama hat at a fraction of the price in the UK. Good quality, nice tight weave. It got me thinking though. Why call it a Panama hat? After all, all genuine Panama hats are made in Ecuador, so why not call them Ecuador hats? Let Panama design their own headwear I say.

Together with my long, white hair, I was the picture of an English eccentric. However I felt it was one size too big, and if and when Hélène cuts my hair when we get back, the bloody thing will drop down to just above my nose. I'll look like Smiffy out of the Bash Street Gang! Not cool. Panted up the 465 steps to the top of Santa Ana Hill, passing colourful restored Spanish style houses in the historical neighbourhood of Las Penas. Everyone outside, all ages listening to loud music, talking and drinking. A real community atmosphere. Nice. It was raining and grey by the time we got to the top, so just like Jack and Jill we made our way straight down again. Still raining so we went to the pictures for the first time in a year. Saw Natalie Portman in the original version of The Black Swan. On that performance, I would.

Back at the hostel and straight onto the internet. Hélène says I'm obsessed. So, I'm obsessed. Who cares? Paul Gray answered my prayers for City ticket. Stretty or North Stand? You choose you wonderful man.

Now, here's a problem, how to get up to Manchester from London early on Saturday morning. Normally I drive up and share petrol, CDs, beer and funny cigarettes with fellow Reds, but there was no way I could purchase a new, second hand set of wheels in time, so it was a matter of putting out requests on Facebook, Red Issue and Red News fans forums for Cockney based Reds with a spare seat to let me come up with them. Perhaps Ralph Mortimer will have a spare seat on the London Supporters Club coach. It's late in the day but you never know. Not easy to make arrangements from the middle of Ecuador.

We arrive back in the UK on Thursday morning. That's less than 2 days to make all the arrangements. I wonder how global executives cope.

MONDAY 7 FEBRUARY GUAYAQUIL, ECUADOR TO CARACAS, VENEZUELA

Our 10.30 flight from Guayaquil to Caracas was delayed. Plenty of time for dunking and internet, and LUHG sticker number 83 placed on a metal pillar near the boarding gate. Learned Chelsea had lost at home to Liverpool on Sunday, a result that, together with Arsenal's inexplicable gift of four second half goals to Newcastle and the loss of two away points, meant our defeat away to Wolves was not the disaster it had first appeared to be. Now, like most Reds I hate Liverpool more than any other team in the UK, but as a forward thinking, professional United fan, I had been hoping against hope for them to make amends for Gerrard's suicidal back pass last season which ultimately handed the Premiership to Chelsea.

And they did. King Kenny, I salute you. For now... I checked the Premiership table. So we were still four points ahead of Arsenal in second place and with a superior goal difference. City were third and Chelsea fourth. Liverpool, though, had inched up to fifth place. Don't like that. I was hoping to join in their relegation party at the end of the season. I'll have to put that on hold for now. I never seriously believed they were in real trouble, I just revelled in their anguish and the fact that Liverpool supporters had cricks in their necks looking all the way up the table to see Manchester United sitting way up there at the top.

N-N-N-N-N-N-Nineteen anyone? Stop it David. Stop it.

WEDNESDAY 9 FEBRUARY. CARACAS, VENEZUELA.

Our last departure. We started on a high and left on a low. Caracas Airport. For fear of repeating myself, the least said about this least airport the better. Left my mark though with LUHG sticker numbers 84 and 85 in the departure lounge and men's toilet.

Flew through the night and landed in the gleaming glass and steel of Madrid airport for our connecting flight to London. Our second last stop. Our second last airport. 364 days after leaving terminal 5 at Heathrow we were about to land once more in our green and pleasant land.

On some pretext I escaped Hélène's clutches, claiming I just wanted to go for a walk. She thought I needed time for a little quiet reflection. In fact I was looking for somewhere out of sight for LUHG sticker number 86. Success. And I've still got 14 left to continue my anti-Glazer guerilla campaign back in the UK!

After 35 years of marriage Hélène and I had finally had our honeymoon. I sat on the unforgiving metal seats awash with emotion. (No, not piles) I had been mentally planning this trip of a lifetime and now it was almost over, yet in just three days I would be sitting (shame) in Old Trafford about to watch United, top of the Premiership, at home to City. What a homecoming. After 62 years on this planet, was I really going to witness the greatest football club on the planet overtake the enemy up the East Lancs Road to become the greatest ever football club in England. In my lifetime!

Unber-fucking-leavable! Kleenex moment. I tried to keep a lid on it. A glance from Hélène and I would claim I was just anticipating meeting up with Melanie, Jasmine and Lilyella again. Which I was, of course. I'm not that inhuman. But I had been with Hélène since February 14, 1973. Melanie was 36 years old and Jasmine 25.

I have been supporting United since February 1958. Go figure.

THURSDAY 10 FEBRUARY LONDON, ENGLAND

Got home. Hugs, kisses, Kleenex, yelping dog, disinterested cat, tea and dunkers. At the first opportunity I open my e-mails. Scroll down in order to priorities and there's an e-mail from Oli Winton. Articulate Red. We don't correspond that often as he's gone all Twitter so I made him my first choice.

What a premonition that was. "Dave, blah blah blah.. Your mobile number doesn't work. I have a ticket for you, but I have to know NOW."

I look at the time the e-mail was sent. 2.20pm. What's the time now? 7.30pm. Shit! David, get your arse in gear. Quick, send him an e-mail. Sent. Shit, what if he doesn't read it until after he's given away the ticket?

I know I've got his number here somewhere. Look up my address book that I haven't accessed for over a year. Is he under "O" for Oli or or "W" for Winton? C'mon Dave, think! What difference does it make? How long does it take to go from one page to another? Shut up. I'm shaking. Ah. Here it is. Under "W". We're not interested. Just phone you tosser.

"Hi Oli, how are you? Did you get my e-mail?" Before he could answer, I chipped in. "Basically mate, of course I want the ticket. It's bloody brilliant. You're the man. The only thing is, thinking I'd missed the boat I contacted the various London based supporters clubs and told them I no longer needed a seat on their coach/train. Can you give me 5 minutes while I try to get it back?"

"Sure."

"You're the man."

Shit. Now I've got to find Ralph Mortimer's number. I'd found his address on Google but not his telephone number. Up till now all communication had been by e-mail.

C'mon Dave, think!

Google. Manchester United London Supporters Clubs. First on the list. Pride of Manchester. Scroll down. There it is. I'll never remember that, I've a memory of a goldfish. Quick. Pen. Pencil. ANYTHING!! 0208 *** **** Ring ring.

"Ah, Ralph?"

"Yes."

"Hi Ralph. It's Dave Blatt. How are you?"

"Fine."

"Ralph. Is that spare seat on your coach still available? A ticket has just come up."

"Well done, mate. Yes, it's still available."

"Brilliant. You're the man! (See how fickle I am). I'll take it. Where exactly do your coaches start from?"

"Well, tomorrow we depart Victoria coach station at 06.00am but you have to be there by ten to six at the latest."

"Victoria Coach Station is a big place, Ralph. Where exactly do you meet?"

"Smedley Place. It's at the back of the coach station. Our coach parks in the street, not in the coach station itself.

"Fine. Brilliant. I'll be there. Thanks once again, Ralph."

"No problem."

Right. Back to Oli.

Shit, where did I put his number? C'mon Dave. Think. You had it a moment ago. I know, I'm just having a senior moment. Don't push me. Ah. Here it is. Phew! Shit. Answer phone. Not now! I leave a message.

"Hello Oli, Yes, I want it. Phone me back on Mel's home number. 0207 *** ****"

An extraordinarily long fine minutes later the phone rings. It's Mel's phone but I pick it up. "Hello?"

"David? It's Oli."

"Ah. Did you get my message?"

"Yup. No problem. When are you coming up?"

"I have to be at Victoria Coach Station at ten to six, but you remember what happened last time? We made arrangements to meet outside Old Trafford, but we couldn't get a signal and almost missed each other. I'd rather pick it up tonight, if it's alright with you."

"Well, I haven't got the ticket on me myself, it's with my mate Gerald. He lives in Golders Green."

Two hours later I'm back in Mel's flat with his mate's mate's season ticket in my wallet, but not before I'd paid £7.60 for a return underground ticket to go two stops between Belsize Park and Golders Green on the Northern Line, and a £10 black cab wait and return taxi fare from Golders Green station to Gerald's house.

I'd forgotten about rip-off London Transport prices. Welcome home, David.

Right, I'd better get to bed and prepare myself for the great homecoming and great awakening. The great awakening being getting up at 04.30am.

I'm excited Tommy.

ENGLAND

SATURDAY 12 FEBRUARY LONDON – MANCHESTER – LONDON
MANCHESTER UNITED 2 MANCHESTER CITY 1

The first time I went to Old Trafford to see United I was eighteen years old. The Manchester United (London & District) Supporters Club coach used to leave from the Embankment by Charing Cross underground station at 08.00am, which meant I had to get up at 05.00am without waking up my younger brother, so no alarm clock.

No need. I was always so excited my internal body clock woke me up, because I WANTED to wake up. Now, forty four years have passed and nothing has changed. Today I woke up at 4.30am before the alarm went off. The only problem was that there was no underground train running at this time so last night I booked a mini cab for 05.00am. (You can't be too careful. What if he was late? What if the cab company lost my booking or couldn't be arsed?) Fortunately my fears were groundless and I arrived to a pitch black Victoria Coach Station at five thirty with not a Red in sight.

What now? Walk around as though I know what I'm doing. Ah. Closed shops. Yes, let's take a look. I feel like I'm acting that scene from When Harry Meets Sally. OK, that didn't take long. Let's get back. Ah, two United scarves with bodies underneath were walking towards me.

I nodded, nonchalantly, acknowledging their subtle, Mona Lisa smiles. Yes, Reds together. "We are family, all my fellow Reds and me." I let them pass, hoping they understood why I was walking in the opposite direction. Once they had turned the corner I raced back and struck my head round.

"Where are they going? I thought the coach picks up people here?" I hung around, straining to locate more Reds. Nothing. Hmmm. No. Not worried. I know this is the place. What's the time? Hmmm, quarter to six.

Surely I should have spotted a few more Reds by now? And where are the two Reds I had bonded with earlier? Smedley Place is only a small road. Let's see what's at the other end. As I walk up the road in the dark I spot three other shapes walking in the same direction. What's that? Is it a bird? Is it a plane? No, it's a coach rising phoenix like out of the gloom. And yes, there are groups of Reds waiting patiently on the corner. I've arrived! Thank Eric for that!

They look at me suspiciously and I give them a weak smile. Oh, and a nod, just to be sure. Moments later someone comes round with a clipboard and asks for our names. I give him mine and I'm ticked off the list.

Phew. I'm on. Next thing I know the coach door opens and we shuffle onboard. I take a seat by the window, with an unnecessarily wide window pillar obscuring half the view. What view? Yeah, right.

At Staples Corner more Cockney based Reds get on. Paula, a nice adoption social worker from Chadwell Heath sat next to me. Little did she know she drew the short straw as she took her place, only one year without any real United fans to talk to I re-enacted that scene from Airplane where everyone who sat next to the pilot who lost his nerve committed suicide as he went on and on and on.....

I went on and on and on, regaling anecdote after anecdote, till her eyes glazed over (what a horrible choice of vocabulary) and sleep offered a welcome relief. In the end we slept together, the effects of boring grey motorway and 04.30am wake-up call. (What were you thinking?)

Ralph only allowed a five minute stop on the way up, so only one orifice was taken care of. On the way back to the coach I couldn't help but notice the ever present, ear to ear smile of Mick Groom and his pal. We'd exchanged banter on Facebook the past year but we only had a few moments here to exchange greetings before being herded back on our respective coaches. Having said that, we did arrive in the coach park at 10.30am, so plenty of time to satisfy other areas of my anatomy.

The ground looked the same, no obvious changes to my naked eye. I gazed lovingly up at the bronze statues of Best, Law and Charlton. Surprisingly I saw people selling stuff in the forecourt in front of the Megastore, which in my previous incarnation had been out of bounds to traders not handing over extortionate amount of wedge to the club.

Even from a distance those ears stood out a mile.

"Barney! How are you mate?"

"David. When did you get back?" And so I re-acquainted myself with the fine, upstanding editor of Red News, as he bellowed out in an increasingly husky voice the benefits of purchasing his periodical. By now my stomach was making its presence felt. Was it the up and coming Manchester El Clasico or the wide empty spaces in my stomach?

11.30am. Brunch time. Normally I'm torn between the Caribbean stall in Chester Road opposite the Bishops Blaize or a meat and potato pie with chips and curry gravy as I walk towards the ground, but today I needed to sit down to eat. Lack of sleep and lack of mid morning dunking had taken its toll. As I walked along the Chester Road I heard a voice.

"David. You made it then!" It was Gary who ran the United supporters club in Glasgow.

"Hi Gary. Yup. Long story, but here I am. Can't wait."

With the latest copy of Red News in my pocket I opted for Harry Ramsdens. In the past I'd found the franchise to be overpriced for the size and quality of fish and chips on offer, but a revamp of the menu made it a much better proposition this morning. Although I was on my own I had something United to read, so enveloped myself in all things anti-Glazer as my excitement grew. Only an hour to go before my self-imposed exile came to an end.

I chose the senior's special, not due to my age but because it was the cheapest all-inclusive on the menu. (Yup, some things don't change). Cup of tea, cod or haddock with chips, two slices of bread and butter and bread and butter pudding, all for £6.99. (This is riveting stuff, don't you agree?) In the end I exchanged the bread and butter pudding for mushy peas. No, not as a desert but to compliment the fish and chips. Gotcha.

As I ate I listened to my stomach. Not for signs of hunger but as a barometer for the match to come. They go on about women's intuition but my stomach is a surprisingly reliable indicator on how a game will turn out. Really tight knots equate to a defeat, anything less and it's either a win, or at worst, a draw. My stomach was calm. Excited but calm. My prediction? A win but only just. Both teams had to make late changes, and we were without Rio Ferdinand (bad times) and also Johnny Evans (good times) Chris Smalling would accompany Vidic in the heart of our defense. Also Berbatov was on the bench. Hmmm...

Of course, you can claim it's easy to write this after the game, but anybody who knows me will vouch for "The Stomach". Just ask Jack and Steve who accompanied me to Rome for the Champions League final against Barcelona. Standing in front of the giant screen in Fergie Fields, I turned to them both and said: "We're going to lose this. Don't ask me how I know. I just know."

They both gave me dirty looks, and after ten minutes of the match when we could, and should have been 3-0 up I did question my internal organs, but they were not to be denied. After Eto'o's opener all our players got together and decided to have their worst games of the season, all at the same time.

Illogical. So un–United. So painful, but so true.

Today was different. I looked back over the past year and some of the places I had visited, people I'd met and sights that would remain with me forever. Where would I rather be at this moment? Go on, David. Be honest.

As Fat Boy Slim so emphatically put it: "Right here. Right Now. Right here. Right now."

Ridiculous, isn't it? I just hope Hélène doesn't read this. I'd waited 37 years for our honeymoon, but I'd waited my whole life to be in a position where my beloved United could overtake Liverpool and be crowned Champions for the 19th time, the greatest number in the history of the Football League. Just imagining the scouser's faces made me cream myself.

With a sterling effort I brought myself back to reality and the mantra... just one game at a time. I walked back down Sir Matt Busby Way, now a seething mass of one way traffic, and looked out for S20. I'd never sat along this side before, preferring the Stretty or Scoreboard, as close to the away supporters as possible. What would the atmosphere be like? Could the more expensive seats rouse themselves with so much at stake?

I'd soon find out. Once inside I made my way straight to my seat. I recognise those ears, and glasses, and beard, and that heavy metal bass player's type bald head.

"JD. What are you doing here?" It was JD Deitch, a fellow Red off Facebook.

"I got my ticket through Oli, just like you.

"So, you know Gerald then?" I said, shaking hands with the man I had only met the previous evening.

The board game "Six moves from Kevin Bacon" came to mind.

"No, we just met today."

We hugged, awkwardly, then I explained to Gerald how JD, an American now living just outside Paris, and me had communicated for years via our respective Facebook pages and this was the first time we had actually met in person.

Before we knew it the teams came out to an almighty roar and we were underway. As well as the widest pitch and tallest floodlights, City were now after the "tallest players in a first team squad" title as they towered over our lads. However, a number of them resembled Alan Gowling lookalikes (yes, even the black ones) as their arms and legs fired like pistons working independently of each other. (Yaya Toure, are you reading this?)

We started to play the more incisive attacking football, but City also attacked, a feature of their game so sadly lacking in recent encounters between the two sides, even at Eastlands. In fact, if only they had had a forward capable of shooting in a straight line, they could well have been leading at half time. (David Silva, are you reading this?)

A number of our players seemed off the pace. Ryan continually misplaced or under-hit his crosses as wave after wave of our attacks broke down around the box. Then just as I was about to question his parenthood, four minutes before the break Giggsy sent a delightful through ball with the outside of his boot into the path of Nani whose first touch took him into the penalty area, his second closer to Hart, the City goalkeeper, but it was his third, a cool left-footed finish that rolled into the net Nani that caused me to explode.

Queue three grown men going bananas in a group hug whilst trying to stay on their feet. I looked up at the heavens and let out a piercing scream that had been bottled up for thirteen months.

"AAAAAAAAaaaaaaahhhhhh!!!!!"

Boy. I needed that. It had been so long.

Then it was half time and a chance to analyse the first 45 minutes. It's what grown men do.

We all agreed we had edged the first half but our defense was still dodgy. Smalling had done well but an instinctive empathy with Vidic had yet to materialize, although as the game wore on his confidence had grown. Now all he had to do was improve his distribution and I believe we have a giant gem in the making. Rooney though was still not firing on all cylinders and I wondered how long it would take for him to start repaying his enormous wage packet.

City began brightly in the second half and there was a sense of inevitability when, after Shaun Wright-Phillips came on for the donkey Kolarov and initiated a number of dangerous looking attacks, City substitute Edin Dzeko shot into a crowd of players where it cannoned off Silva's back and deflected past Van Der Sar and into our net.

Lucky bastards.

Now, it's not often you'll find me writing anything positive about near neighbours but I have to admit to a quiet smile as the City fans in the corner turned their backs to the pitch and celebrated doing the Poznan by jumping up and down, arm round shoulder left and right. OK, that's enough.

Ah. At last! Wouldn't have said that last season, but like the majority of Reds inside Old Trafford I was more than a little relieved to see Berbatov come on for Anderson in the 67th minute and give us an extra attacking option.

We increased our assault on the City goal but added pressure didn't translate into attempts on goal. Rooney, like Giggs, was still not the complete article this afternoon and he was lucky to get a second chance to pass a ball out to Nani on the right wing. Nani's cross clipped Zabaleta and looped into high into the penalty area. The ball was falling behind Rooney but the ex-Toffee twisted and launched himself into the air before connecting with an acrobatic overhead kick that looped and screamed (yes, it can do both) into the top corner.

"AAAAAHHHHHHhhhhh!!!!!!!!!"

"AAAAAHHHHHHhhhhh!!!!!!!!!"

Take that the rest of the world. I'm here. I'm in Manchester and I've just seen one of the greatest goals I've ever seen in my life! Genius. Pure genius. Even in my dreams I've never had the audacity to attempt something like that..

"AAAAAHHHHHHhhhhh!!!!!!!!!"

Oh my Eric! Fuck me. Pandemonium all round. All the seats were up. Fuck the Gestapo stewards. Surely even they would make allowances? We sang the boys home. All parts of the ground rose as one to acclaim our victory. City were dumped and we were now four points clear. Who would have thought it just a few months previously?

I strolled and skipped out of the ground all smiles and chanted with the Stretty as they came under the concourse. I was halfway up Sir Matt Busby Way when I realised I was going the wrong way. So used to coming up by car, I had forgotten I had come up with the London Supporters Club so I turned round as though I knew what I was doing and made my way to the coach park against the onslaught of Reds coming my way

I resisted the attractions of the greasy dogburgers on display, my mind and stomach racing forward to our meal stop on the motorway on the way back.

In the coach park regulars were slapping each other on the back, revelling in the afterglow. I smiled to myself and nodded. Paula came over and we almost hugged, but didn't. I then noticed a non football looking couple waiting for the coach door to open. The girl looked oriental and the boy... didn't.

"Hi." I said. "Did you enjoy that?"

They nodded. A lot of people are good at nodding, I mused.

"Where are you from?" I asked the girl.

"We're from China." she replied.

Before I could help myself I said. "Ah. I was there in June. Really liked it." Their eyes opened wide. Not a comment they were expecting in a coach park near Old Trafford.

"Where you from?" I enquired.

She mentioned a town just outside Beijing. I then spoke to her boyfriend who turned out to be a TEFL teacher like me, and was currently working in Beijing. A pleasant ten minute conversation ensued. Admittedly I enjoyed 70% possession as I regaled them both with stories of our three weeks in China back in June. I think they were impressed. Either that or incredibly polite.

"Hssssst!"

What was that? Oh, the coach door had just opened, so we all clambered onboard and thus began our journey back home. As we passed along the coach asking people if they wanted to book for Crawley at home next Saturday or Wigan away the following Saturday, I asked Ralph what time we would be stopping to eat.

"We don't. We drive straight back to London." Oh, great. Thanks.

I looked around. Oh well. You live and learn, I thought, as nerve tingling moments from the match, coupled with visions from my trip competed with each other as I drifted in and out of sleep. Before I knew it we were approaching Staples Corner and it still was only 7.00pm.

I then asked the driver to let me off near Swiss Cottage and before you could say "City will never be a massive club" I was back home and eagerly anticipated Match of the Day.

WHAT A YEAR! WHAT A WORLD!

ALREADY PEOPLE have asked me what was the highlight of the trip. Impossible to answer, there were simply too many. I thought of compiling my own "seven wonders of the world" but getting it down to single figures is almost impossible. Most have been incredibly breathtaking, some have been horrific. Either way they've left an indelible mark on me and I implore everyone of you to visit each one at least once in your lifetime.

YANGSHOU, LI RIVER, CHINA
GREAT WALL OF CHINA, 90 KILOMETRES NORTH OF BEIJING, CHINA
HALONG BAY, 90 KILOMETRES EAST OF HANOI, VIETNAM
MOUNT FUJI, JAPAN
TAJ MAHAL, AGRA, INDIA
MACCHU PICCHU, PERU
WHALE WATCHING, PUERTO MADRYN, ARGENTINA
THE SLUMS OF MUMBAI, INDIA
THE KILLING FIELDS, PHNOM PENN, CAMBODIA
THE WHITSUNDAYS, GOLD COAST, AUSTRALIA
BYRON BAY, AUSTRALIA
MAUPITI, FRENCH POLYNESIA
EASTER ISLAND
THE SALT FLATS, BOLIVIA

One question I've asked myself, if I had the opportunity to re-visit only one of the above, which one would it be? With so many places left in the world and so little time (and money) my priority is to discover new and exciting places before mass tourism tames them forever. But if I had to chose one, without hesitation it would be Yangshuo along the Li River in China. We hardly scratched the surface of the 1,400 square kilometres of the most wondrous landscape on Earth. Truly magical.

It's certainly been a voyage of discovery. Trying to discover bars, pubs, clubs, restaurants and hotels around the world that broadcast Premiership football.

So what have I learnt?

That there's nothing in the world like being a Red. Absolutely nothing, nothing at all, nothing at all, nothing at all, nothing at all.